Critical Acclaim for Olivia St. Claire

'Steamy but oh so discreet, *203 Ways to Drive a Man Wild in Bed* is *the* sensual guide to the way around a man's body'
New Woman

'A mind-boggling array of tips on how to spice up your love life'
Daily Express

'This book really takes the biscuit . . . This indispensable manual by Olivia St. Claire covers every aspect of whacking up the intensity of your most intimate moments'
More

'Brighten up your love life . . . If you're short on ideas, buy Olivia St. Claire's
203 Ways to Drive a Man Wild in Bed'
Cosmopolitan

Also by Olivia St. Claire

**203 WAYS TO DRIVE
A MAN WILD IN BED**

227 WAYS
to UNLEASH
the SEX GODDESS in
EVERY WOMAN

OLIVIA ST. CLAIRE

BANTAM BOOKS
LONDON · NEW YORK · TORONTO · SYDNEY · AUCKLAND

227 WAYS TO UNLEASH THE SEX GODDESS IN
EVERY WOMAN
A BANTAM BOOK : 0 553 50485 1

Originally published in Great Britain by Doubleday,
a division of Transworld Publishers Ltd

PRINTING HISTORY
Doubleday edition published 1996
Bantam edition published 1997

Bantam Books are published by Transworld Publishers Ltd,
61–63 Uxbridge Road, London W5 5SA,
in Australia by Transworld Publishers (Australia) Pty Ltd,
15–25 Helles Avenue, Moorebank, NSW 2170,
and in New Zealand by Transworld Publishers (NZ) Ltd,
3 William Pickering Drive, Albany, Auckland.

Reproduced, printed and bound in Great Britain by
Mackays of Chatham PLC, Chatham, Kent

To the sensual goddesses of history and heaven—especially Aphrodite, Cleopatra, the Cloud Damsels, the Cosmic Yoni, the Djanggawo sisters, Hathor, Inanna, Lilith, Mother Earth, Nofretari, Oshun, Pele, Sekhmet, Shakti, the Snake Priestess, White Buffalo Woman, Wild Woman, Xochiquetzal, the Yoginis—and to the Sex Goddess in every woman

Acknowledgments

My deepest gratitude to all the women and men who so graciously shared their most intimate thoughts and feelings with me—we have all learned so much from you. Heartfelt thanks as well to the extraordinary women who so lavishly gave me their support, advice, assistance, and love during the writing of this book—Christine, Claudia, Deborah, Jane, Karen Marie, Marianne, Pamela, Paula, Sandy, and Tovi; to those who have so expertly guided me in birthing it into the world—Shaye, Paula, Shima, and Miko; and most especially to Henri, my wild inspiration, who has a magical knack for unearthing the most deeply hidden caves of my Inner Sex Goddess.

Contents

> *A woman learns to be a good lover from her own heart and from the heart of her being. She does not need to learn it from a man. She learns it from her inner goddess.*
> —Elaine Kittredge, *Masterpiece Sex*

1

awakening your inner sex goddess

every woman has an Inner Sex Goddess. She lives in your heart, your body, and your senses. She is the part of you that feels aroused by reading erotic literature or watching sexy movies. She is the part of you that skips a heartbeat when an attractive man in tight jeans walks by. She is the part of you that feels coy and flirtatious when you put on a clingy dress; after all, it was *her* idea to wear the dress in the first place. Your Inner Sex Goddess is the one who bought this book and who tingles with anticipation at the thought of becoming, at last, her most gloriously seductive self.

Whether you experience her as a feeling (like a buttery inner warmth), as one of the many roles you play in life (such as career woman, mother, friend, wife, party organizer), or as a distinct personality (like your inner child, inner critic, or inner male and female), your Inner Sex Goddess is a strong, important, and natural part of who you really are. And getting to know her is really getting to know your deepest self—your beliefs and values, your fears and dreams, and the very personal poetry of your body. The truly wonderful thing about your Inner Sex Goddess is that, without instruction from any person, book, workshop, or man, she already knows how to be fabulously sexy and alluring. In her bones, she knows how to *feel* sexy, even when you're tired and cranky, bored, or simply at a loss for inspiration. She knows exactly what to do with her hands when you are making love; she doesn't wonder if it's better to stroke his back or tickle his ear because, with unerring instinct, she automatically does the very thing that will most stimulate herself and her lover.

In fact, your Inner Sex Goddess is a boundless source of sexual energy, know-how, and charisma. Unashamed, self-confident, and regally proud of her sexuality, she understands that feeling and being sexy is a natural and beautiful way for a woman to nourish her spirit and learn to love the ecstasies of her sensation-rich body. Revealing herself to you with every swish of your hair or sway of your hip, your Inner Sex Goddess revels in the textures of life and the world of the senses—and the more you revel in those textures and senses, the better you will get to know her; the freer she will be to enjoy pleasuring herself and her lover; and the more lovely, bold, and exciting she will become.

It is she who lives in the vivid sensitivities of your body. She is there when you appreciate the look of candle-light on the curve of your breast, the smell of a gardenia in your hair, the taste of wine on your lips and tongue, the feel of sun or silk on your skin, the sound of sultry jazz or samba music, the luxury of a hot bubble bath or a full-body massage, the delicious flushes and tingles of self-pleasuring or lovemaking. These physical sensations are doorways to your rich inner world of lush romance and hot libido.

In fact, we women have a natural gift for combining romance, love, and sex into one magical art form. Even our enticingly soft and curvy bodies seem to be specially designed for exquisite pleasure. Did you know, for instance, that we females are unique in having a highly sensitive organ whose *only* purpose is sexual delight?

But even though we have all these natural erotic gifts, no one has schooled us in the art of being in tune with and expressing our inherent sexuality. So we have felt awkward, confused, and even cut off from one of the most precious and vital parts of ourselves. This is not the case in many indigenous cultures—for instance, Native American, tribal African, Tantric Indian, and some ancient Far Eastern societies, to name a few. Placing a high priority on developing sexual joy and proficiency in a sacred, loving way, these traditions often use specially trained sexual mentors to instruct and advise young people on how to appreciate the beauty and majesty of their bodies, as well as how to bring the highest sensual pleasure to their future partners—and to themselves. Naturally in touch with their Inner Sex Gods and Goddesses, people in these cultures believe sexuality is a divine gift and learn to treat their bodies with the utmost respect and reverence. We would be wise to learn from them.

the natural textures of life

Ancient indigenous cultures who were living closer to the earth and practicing rituals tied to the cycles of nature were more in tune with the senses and textures of life than our modern "civilized" society. Their uncomplicated existence and natural belief in the divine nature of plants, animals, elements, and life itself allowed them to be more intimately acquainted with the sensuality that dwelt within them—and left them with practically no inhibitions. To them, sexuality was a natural part of creation, and their sex organs were a chalice of the sacred energy of life. For example, one Stone Age cave painting shows a male figure holding a bow, his penis connected by an unbroken "power line" to the genitals of a female figure, suggesting that the female ritually empowered the man to go out for the hunt—archetypal roles that these early peoples acted out in daily life. In ancient India, men and women transformed themselves into gods and goddesses—meditating, anointing themselves, drinking sacred potions, muttering mantras over their bodies, and having ritualized sex—for the purpose of achieving enlightenment. Other prepatriarchal religions honored fertility, creation, and sexuality in their ceremonies as different aspects of the same divine force. The pagan rites of Beltane, for example, involved ritual or wildly abandoned sexual activity as the symbolic cause of the earth's fertility in spring, and the solstice celebrations of planting and reaping the crops as a gift from the sensual, abundant body of the earth as goddess.

The women of all these cultures innately understood that the power and divine sexuality of the feminine principle was inherent not only in the earth, the elements, the animals, and the goddesses their people worshiped but also in their own sex organs and instincts, in the smells and tastes of their fleshy bodies, and in the natural textures of their lives. They and their individual Inner Sex Goddesses lived interchangeably with each other on a daily basis, moving smoothly and powerfully from conjugal bed to cooking fire to sexual fertility rite to tribal council to wheat harvest to sacramental childbirth and back again. Though we have centuries of acculturation and stifling moral convention to conquer, we too can become the natural sex goddesses these women were born and raised to be. When we come to know, revere, and love our bodies and their pleasures, as they did, we will no longer see our sexuality as something separate from our everyday selves. For with knowledge, reverence, and love come power, respect, responsibility, control—and the natural manifestation of each woman's own brand of lusty and graceful sexual divinity.

Finding your particular version of vampiness means exploring the hitherto unknown territories of your body, your senses, and your hot-blooded imagination. Your Inner Sex Goddess waits there in the intoxicating realm of self-knowledge and self-pleasuring. In our quest to know her, then, we'll be investigating many of the different avenues of pleasure through which you may find and unleash her, including:

- Transforming reading, writing, breathing, walking to work, and wearing clothes into aphrodisiacs for your senses
- Reveling in creative autoeroticism and self-pleasuring
- Having revealing inner dialogues with your goddess self
- Exploring and eroticizing every square inch of your body
- Inventing and enjoying wanton fantasies, dreams, and visions
- Discovering new G-spots and lovemaking talents
- Having lots of earthshaking orgasms
- Playing with erotic toys, clothes, and props
- Making wild passionate love to your man

But before we venture onto the superhighway of rich physical sensation, let's start by exploring some simple but very fruitful *mental* pathways to your sensual kingdom. Your sexuality is contained not only in your five physical senses but also in the inner senses of your mind and heart, and the journey to your Inner Sex Goddess begins not with your lover or some esoteric technique but within the private realm of your fantasies, heartfelt desires, daydreams, and self-created images about who you are. Experiment with the following ideas and see which ones resonate for you.

daily dialog

Throughout the day make a habit of asking your Inner Sex Goddess how she would do things. Just pretend that there is some creature inside you who knows how to be appropriately and naturally sexy, and have a conversation with her. Ask her, "How would you dress this morning? walk down the street? talk to that man? move your hips? dance? put on your makeup? wear your hair? How would you make yourself *feel* sexy? In what ways would you pleasure yourself? What toys would you use? How would you respond? Which man would you choose? How would you make love to him? Where would you put your hand?" Maybe she would add a silk scarf to the conservative outfit you put on. Maybe she would walk to work through the sensation-stimulating park rather than taking the boring bus. Perhaps she would tango in the kitchen instead of going to the gym. Follow her advice and see where it takes you.

journal

Start keeping a journal for your Inner Sex Goddess. Slip into her mind and heart and jot down what you see through her eyes, hear through her ears, feel through her emotions, think through her thoughts, and do through her body. Let her write about what she'd like to do, how she'd like you to relate to her, how she feels about herself, and how she'd like to express herself. Ask her questions about your sexuality and let her write the answers for you.

When I did this one time, my Inner Sex Goddess wrote down that if you view any sensual act not as something you do but as something you receive, as she does, it takes on a whole new meaning. For instance, when you kiss your lover, don't think of what you are doing to him with your lips, but instead focus on receiving the softness of *his* lips, receiving the smooth texture of the skin on his neck, receiving the hard round energy of his fingers as you suck on them. She said to close your eyes and concentrate on drinking in your lover's very essence. As much as I have attuned myself to the many nuances of lovemaking, I never would have thought about kissing quite this way. But keeping a journal for my Inner Sex Goddess brought out a wonderful new perspective that I have since eagerly incorporated into my love life. Find out what unique insights await you when you visit with your inner sexual divinity.

bodyknowing

A particularly sensual woman I know says, "For me, being in touch with my sexuality means deliberately cultivating a sort of magnetic, earthy feeling. I focus on being fully in my body and using all of its instincts and sensations, really feeling the electromagnetic energy pulsing around me. I imagine that I am a wild creature of the earth, a wolf woman, and knower of the moon mysteries. At those times I feel like an untamed, exotic animal using my bodyknowing to move sensuously through the natural world. It is then that my Inner Sex Goddess seems most alive."

I recommend reading Clarissa Pinkola Estés's superb book *Women Who Run with the Wolves* to get an even deeper feel for the wildish woman inside you, so closely akin to your Inner Sex Goddess. Both these inner archetypes—sensual, electric, and instinctual—are characterized by their strong sense of bodyknowing.

inner movies

Use the screen of your imagination to conjure up your Inner Sex Goddess. You may be surprised at who or what appears. Get comfortable. Close your eyes, breathe deeply. Relax and go inside yourself. Imagine a movie screen in your mind's eye and ask your Inner Sex Goddess to reveal herself on it. She may appear full-blown right away or slowly with a foot first and then an ankle, a leg, and so on. What does she look like? How does she dress and move? Is she a robed ancient queen or a contemporary woman in business suit over leopard-print panties? Observe her activities. Does she do different things than you do? What kind of perfume does she dab on? How does she communicate with men, verbally and nonverbally? What does she do in your workplace? at home? at school? in the neighborhood? What does she call herself—maybe she prefers Angelique to your usual Anne. Ask her how you can be more in touch with her, in a safe, elegant, and appropriate way—and how you can do this quickly and easily when need be. Request that she come to you in your dreams and teach you. Ask her to be with you when you make love with your partner and when you pleasure yourself. Thank her for revealing herself to you and give her a gift of gratitude. Let her give you a symbolic present and take careful note of what it is, for she will surely be communicating something special to you with this inner gift.

Your Inner Sex Goddess may change her appearance from day to day, too. Sometimes mine appears as a beautiful naked Greek goddess and sometimes as the Great Cosmic Yoni (in the Tantric tradition, *yoni* means "vulva"), who is the source of ecstasy, sensuality, and womanness. She has given me all sorts of symbolic presents, including a gold key (the key to any sense or experience I might want to open), a marble sculpture of a breast (representing the female qualities of nurturing and sensual beauty), and a leopard-skin G-string to remind me to be raunchy and have fun. Pat, a business executive friend of mine, says that her Inner Sex Goddess looks like Catwoman and is always admonishing her to slink around more and lick all the flavors of life. Another friend tells me that her Inner Sex Goddess looks like Marilyn Monroe, calls herself Lolita, and often shows up when she's making love to point out hidden erogenous zones on her man's body by kissing them with her red, pouty lips. My friend Georgia says that her Inner Sex Goddess is more like a colored ball of energy—sometimes pink, sometimes turquoise—that floats around Georgia's body making tingly sensations and whispering sexual secrets in her dreams.

mythological journeys

As the brilliant modern-day philosopher Joseph Campbell asserted, myths are often the key to our innermost selves, and mythological characters are the archetypes of our inner personalities. Exploring the tales of some of the mythological goddesses of sensuality can lead you to new discoveries about your own sexual persona. Of the scores of magnificent erotic deities, here are just a few to consider. Read about them, contemplate their qualities, gaze at their images, copy their poses, bring their accoutrements into your everyday life, or have inner conversations with them. Call on them just before you make love. Let them seep into your consciousness and connect you to your innermost sexual self.

Aphrodite is the Greek goddess of love, sensuality, and passionate relationships. It is she who graces your life when you fall madly in love. As the only goddess portrayed nude in Greek art, Aphrodite is proud of her beautiful nakedness and potent sexuality. In fact, in one representation of her as Aphrodite Kallipygos (Aphrodite of the Lovely Backside), she coyly draws up her robe to admire her own round fanny. The rose and lily, symbolizing the vagina, are her beloved flowers. Try draping yourself in a Grecian-style robe, even if only mentally, and lean back to gaze at your own luscious derriere. Meditate on the ripe power of this fetchingly plump piece of human art, potent enough to drive some otherwise sane men to a state of crazed desire. In emulating Aphrodite, you become a regal feminine beauty with the magical transforming power of erotic love nestled in every angle, wiggle, and curve of your body.

In the Semitic tradition, Lilith was the first woman, created at the same time as Adam. But when Adam tried to have sex with her, she grew wings and flew out of paradise to live in the desert, later becoming the bringer of agriculture and the protector of children. God then created the more compliant Eve. Let Lilith's fierce drive for sexual equality, independence, and wildness teach you about yours. Imagine yourself taking wing to escape a brand of sexuality you no longer desire and creating a powerful new one fashioned after your personal tastes and talents.

Oshun is the African Yoruba goddess of the river, sensuality, and creativity. As her waters dance sinuously through the countryside, she adorns herself with bangly stone bracelets, the beautiful clothing of the landscape, and the perfumes of the wildflowers. Also presiding over the arts, gold, and love, she provides a sensual healing balm to all who dip into her liquid body. She is completely self-contained, self-aware, and lovingly self-conscious of her natural erotic beauty as she glows in the moon's silvery romantic light. Mentally immerse yourself in her fluid sensuality and surge, ripple, and murmur like the river. Adorn yourself with flowers, flowing fabrics, and gold bracelets that jingle. Revel in your self-contained, liquid eroticism.

In the Mayan tradition, Xochiquetzal (Precious Flower) is the female deity of flowers, beauty, pleasure, and sexuality. Always joyous and free in her sensuality, she is sometimes represented as a butterfly, and her ancient worshipers often dress as hummingbirds and butterflies to dance around her rose-covered image. Merlin Stone, author of *When God Was a Woman*, says that "when a woman felt the pleasures of her body, it brought special joy to Xochiquetzal." Imagine dancing amid rose petals, hummingbird feathers, and butterfly wings as a form of ritual adoration. Worship your divine femininity by pleasuring your own fleshy rosebuds.

Shakti is a form of the Hindu Great Goddess and symbolizes the energizing life force of the universe. She is often represented as a snake, uncoiling sinuously up the human spine, awakening the life-giving, sensual energies within. Through worship of this divine goddess—which included adoring a woman's body as the goddess's human form and having sacred sex with her—male Tantric practitioners hoped to reach enlightenment. Slither like a snake and feel how this undulating movement awakens your sexual instincts. Sense the creative power of the universe uncoiling in your womb, ready to give birth to new life, new ideas, and new inner enravishments. Worship your own body as the physical manifestation of all that is divinely female—

beautiful, powerful, innately enlightened, life-nurturing, and sensual. You are the embodiment of sacred union.

I also recommend that you read Hallie Iglehart Austen's inspired and gorgeously illustrated book *The Heart of the Goddess* for poetic and practical journeys with scores of other goddesses from many cultures and time periods.

sex initiatrix

Another friend of mine likes to fantasize that she, as the officially recognized Sexiest Woman in the World, is teaching an inexperienced lover the art of pleasing a woman. Or she is a tribal sex shaman who is initiating a young boy into manhood during a sacred puberty ceremony. Or she is Sharon Stone, reducing otherwise strong men to butter simply by crossing her legs or dancing provocatively with another woman. Whether she indulges in these fantasies while standing in line at the grocery or when she is pleasuring herself or her lover, she finds it a rapid and surefire way to make her sexiest inner self come alive. And it's no wonder, for initiating virginal or emotionally unawakened men into the intoxicating mysteries of the female body is a powerful ritual we women have been performing for countless centuries. Try it and see if it doesn't awaken magic in you.

the heart of beauty

The Hawaiian shamans have a lovely way of connecting with their inner graces. They suggest finding something beautiful, like a rose or a pretty stone or a piece of yellow silk. Focus on its beauty, singling out and appreciating all the various things that make it lovely. Find the qualities it shares with you. For instance, notice the way the open petals of the rose resemble your pretty vaginal lips. Observe that the stone has many different sides, facets, and colors, like your multifaceted personality. Revel in the cool smoothness of the silk, like your satiny skin. The more you focus on the textures and senses of beauty, the more your subconscious starts to bring it into your life, the more you see it everywhere, and the more your mind and body begin to mimic these innate qualities of your Inner Sex Goddess.

the temple of erotic love

One of the most potent pathways to your inner sexual sanctum leads directly through the Jade Gate, as the Chinese call it—your vaginal opening. Though Far Eastern and Indian Tantric cultures have bestowed upon the female sexual organs poetic names like the Grotto of the White Tiger, the Honey Pot, and the Valley of Joy, modern Western culture often views them as something unclean to be hidden and ashamed of. At best, "women see their sex organs as an absence rather than a presence," laments a well-known Western gynecologist. But ancient and indigenous societies have long honored the vulva in particular as the primary source of life, pleasure, and spiritual development. Identifying it with the lotus—flower of perfection and eternity, and the great void from which all existence arises—the people of south India rubbed carved wooden yonis (vulvae) as a form of worship. Statues and paintings from South America, Africa, ninth-century Europe, and twentieth-century Australia too show goddesses displaying their sacred vulvae with authority and pride as the source of fertility, inspiration, and protection. Many of these statues appear over doorways as a reminder that the vagina is the literal gateway to life. Numerous churches and castles in the British Isles of the ninth century were thought to be sanctified by sheela-na-gigs, stone carvings of playful, smiling women with their vulvae spread wide. These peoples wisely believed, as did the tribal wizards of New Guinea, that "All magic radiates from [the vagina] as fingers do from a hand."

That kind of reverence, respect, and love for this sacred part of a woman is an essential key to releasing the Inner Sex Goddess locked inside. So, like a female Indiana

Jones on a quest for your true sexuality, you must transform what for you may be a mysterious void into a sacred temple of erotic love.

There are several ways to undertake this quest. You could make a list of all the wonderful things you can think of about your vulva—for example, as the birth canal, it's the gateway to life; men go absolutely bananas over it; it provides the highest sexual ecstasy; its many amazing talents include vast expansion, tight contraction, and copious lubrication; it is cleverly hidden; its lips are provocative protrusions or delicate wings, whatever the case may be. Make a long, sensually detailed list. Or you could practice the following meditation.

First, honor the entrance to your temple of erotic love by rubbing oils or powder on it. Place your hands over your pubic bone and vulva, feel the powerful energy that emanates from this cave of creation. As you allow the muscles in your stomach, genitals, and anus to relax, imagine that the warmth and love in your hands is being pulled into your vagina, illuminating the dark spaces and making the walls glitter with a jewellike brilliance. See this inner space being transformed into a vaulted temple, an elaborately decorated mosque, a holy shrine, a vast cathedral, or a shaman's magical cave. This is the magnificent entrance to the mysterious worlds of sexual ecstasy, sacred union, and the beginnings of life. A male friend once told me, "When you give a woman oral love, your head is cradled at the source of woman, the source of life. It's a sacred place where you can worship, and the divinity you are worshiping gives you instant feedback and the most otherworldly sensations."

Allow yourself to luxuriate in your hallowed temple of erotic love. Explore its inner recesses, discovering the sacred sensual secrets hidden there. You may want to imagine that you are one of many priestesses studying your art together or that you are performing some sexual healing for a man who has petitioned the temple goddess for rejuvenation. Learn from these activities. Ask the deity of this temple, your Inner Sex Goddess, to cleanse you of any negative feelings you may have about this sacred space and to fill it instead with reverence and love. Inquire how you may come to know her better and help her be a larger presence in your life. Just for a moment imagine that the goddess magically embodies herself in you and that you have all her knowledge, majesty, charisma, and heavenly experience. Promise her that you will always honor her temple and request that she be instantly and fully available to you whenever you merely think of this part of you. Thank her for inviting you here and gently take leave of your temple of erotic love for now. Rest in the knowledge that it and your Inner Sex Goddess are always there to nourish, support, and eroticize you.

Because I am a goddess
I will come to your
heaven, and lie on your
cloud. . . .
Let my hovel be our
heaven, let my bed be
our cloud,
On which we are united
in perfect, heavenly bliss.
—Erotic poetry of
ancient Egypt,
from <u>Sacred Sex</u>,
Robert Bates

2

creating

your

sensual

garden

the essence of being a goddess is that you transform even the most mundane events and surroundings into a celestial garden of delights by your very existence. Cultivated and in full bloom, your inner garden grows to encompass the world around you, expanding your capacity for pleasure, luring divine consorts to your domain and elevating the quality of life and lovemaking, for you and for your lover, to sublime heights. It is your Inner Sex Goddess, who, by the simple act of viewing the entire world as a sensual paradise, creates this erotic garden, first in your own life and then by divine osmosis in the lives of those around you.

Now that you recognize your inherent, natural potential as a goddess, your first divine act must be to create the sensual garden that sustains and enriches your inner life and provides a perfumed playground for all who enter it. Start by tasting the ambrosia of life, reaching out and grabbing the sensuous feeling of wind in your hair or silk on your skin, savoring the magic of a striking piece of art, reveling in the mystery of a blossoming flower, sinking into the romance of a poetic phrase or a lover's sigh. These simple yet profound acts of transformation are your natural birthright as a woman.

While men have the gift of robust action, women have

the gift of powerful perception. Sensually, men tend to focus on their genitals, whereas women are more holistic, more interested in arousing their entire bodies and their feelings. A man often wants to get right to the physical pleasure, while a woman knows how to heighten sensitivity by first creating the mood of romance. She knows that stimulating your "romance hormones" will create the context for the magic that can come from stimulating your sex hormones. In fact, many women find that if they pleasure themselves and their lovers only in a physical way, they feel bored, dishonored, and cut off from their deep feelings and true Sex Goddess nature.

At the same time, though, women intuitively understand that the physical senses are the very doorways to inner eroticism—the openings through which magic passes from the outer to the inner world and back again, the alchemical tubing that transforms sunsets, cantatas, and freshly baked bread into the hot pheromones of love. To a woman's Inner Sex Goddess, the whole world is an aphrodisiac. It's simply a matter of noticing it. And a woman becomes a Sex Goddess not by virtue of a perfect body, a bag of exotic sexual tricks, or a Valentino-like lover but by virtue of her ability to abandon herself to the electrically sensual qualities of everything around and within her and to pamper herself with them.

So if you want to make your Inner Sex Goddess a larger part of your life, use all of your senses as doorways between the exterior world and the magical interior kingdom where she dwells. See, hear, taste, smell, and feel her in every fire flame, zesty orange peel, and cat's purr. Leave room for your efficient, taking-care-of-business self, yes; she's important too. But right now, it's your sultry inner seductress that we're showering with attention. Deliberately create occasions for her to come out and play. Pamper, treat, and romance her all the time. She will turn your everyday life into a garden of sensual delights, bring your spicy inner flavors to the surface, and galvanize your man to new erotic ecstasy.

sowing the seeds of sensuality in your garden

1. Send yourself flowers. Fresh, fragrant flowers not only make you feel beautiful and adored but also provide a pretty-to-look-at and heavenly-to-smell prop for your bedroom, or for your bathroom, kitchen, or living room — wherever you decide to take your self-love tryst. Get all of your senses involved with the flowers — arrange them in a pretty vase and place them in a different spot every day; inhale their fragrance deep inside you; caress your skin with their velvety petals; garnish your food with them. Let your Inner Sex Goddess select the bouquet for its sensual appeal—two blood-red roses, one lushly fragrant gardenia, several exotic and silky tiger lilies. Get luxurious!

2. Give yourself perfume. Your favorite kind. Something that smells wickedly sexy. Spray your sheets with it. Dab it behind your ears, between your beautiful breasts, along your soft inner thighs. Smell your luscious self. One hedonistic friend of mine likes to apply a musky scent between her toes and then massage them to bring out the aroma. She says it makes her feel pampered.

3. Have plenty of romance-making candles around—tapers for elegance, votives to create a soft glow, big fat ones to help you recall phallic encounters, aromatic ones to awaken your earthy nature. Light them in the bathroom when you luxuriate in the tub. Fill your bedroom with many flames of love. Look at your gorgeous body in the mirror in shimmering candlelight. Fantasize that you're performing a magic sex ritual by candle flame and the light of the moon. Become aware of the incandescent quality of your Inner Sex Goddess. Glow.

4. Prepare a candlelight dinner for one. Set a romantic table with flowers, special dinnerware, candles, a stunning centerpiece. Indulge in aphrodisiacal appetizers such as oysters, avocados, mangoes, figs, or other juicy fruits.

Savor an entrée that you can eat with your fingers, and lick them frequently. Indulge in a sinfully rich and gooey dessert. Relish your food. Inhale its aroma. Lick it. Tear it apart with your fingers. Taste it slowly. Fruits are lovely to rub on your body and gently, slowly lick off. Don't do the dishes. Go directly to bed with yourself.

5. Treat yourself to a bottle of good wine. Red wine makes me feel much more sensuous than white or pink, but follow your own sensual urges here. A wine with a good nose will add another texture. Pour it into a delicate wineglass. Savor it. Let it slide warmly over your tongue and down your throat. Pour it on yourself and lick it off. Allow yourself to slip into the relaxed, uninhibited playground of Dionysus, the god of wine. Become his goddess consort.

6. Humanistic psychologist Abraham Maslow stated that the two most common triggers for peak experiences are music and sex. How about music and sex together? Put on some evocative music and listen to it with your whole body. My Inner Sex Goddess loves cool, sultry jazz, but other women I know prefer hot, driving salsa, romantic Mathis or Vandross, lush and elegant Ravel or Chopin, dreamy Debussy, the fireworks of Tchaikovsky, earthy blues, electric, pulsing rock, or ethereal flute music. (See the "Inner Sex Goddess Scrolls" at the back of this book for lots more specific musical suggestions.) Play whatever

turns you on at the moment. Close your eyes and slip inside the sound. Let it loosen your pelvis and shake your shoulders. Slink around in it. Sing or hum. Feel your voice vibrate your chest, throat, and face. See the colors the music creates behind your eyes. Taste its brassy, peppery, or creamy essences. Exult in the emotions it provides. Melt into the harmony of the spheres.

7. Dance. Naked. When there's no one else around to criticize your technique, your Inner Sex Goddess is free to undulate, writhe, slither, rock 'n' roll, hula, fandango, samba, or even strip to her heart's content. Close your eyes and surrender to the mood of your movement. Or dance in front of a mirror and see how sexy you look with breasts jiggling and hips swaying. Dance *with* the mirror; press up against it and feel its cool slickness against your skin. Make a hot, moist patch on it with your breath and flatten your nipple against it. Perform the dance of the seven veils with a big filmy scarf or a fringed shawl. Be provocative. Not only is this fun, loosening, limbering, and hormone-stimulating, it's also great practice for the sexy striptease you're going to do for your man someday soon.

If you feel totally uncoordinated or sexless when you dance, then try almost any other form of physical movement—yoga, aerobics, stretching to music, walking, tai chi, swimming, running. I have a shy, pixielike friend who is actually embarrassed to go to the gym because she gets overly excited by the movements of her thighs while using the StairMaster!

8. Give yourself some sexy lingerie. I love to wear lacy camisoles under my sweaters, blouses, and blazers, letting enough show so that it looks very feminine and demure but at the same time revealing and sexy as hell. My Inner Sex Goddess simply adores peekaboo lace. My friend Jennifer, on the other hand, always wears satin panties and matching plunging bras under her accounting manager pinstripe suits. She says it helps her remember she's a shameless hussy. Let your Inner Sex Goddess investigate and supplement your wardrobe. Try sleeping in a silky teddy instead of your regular oversized T-shirt. Be aware of how these textures glide and flutter over your skin. Admire yourself in a mirror often. Pose like a Victoria's Secret model. *Feel* like one. Buy and wear—if only for yourself—something that makes you look and feel like an expensive call girl. My friend Lisa, a harried mother of twin three-year-olds, says the easiest way for her to feel sexy on command is to don her see-through merry widow with lacy garters and ribbons that untie in strategic places. When she wears it with lace-top stockings and five-inch heels, she says she looks and feels deadly. Sometimes she adds her G-string silk panties. Of course, she often sports these duds for her man, but just as often she wears them only for herself.

They make her feel expensively sexy. And they become exciting props for self- or partner-lovemaking.

9. Dress sensuously all the time. This does not mean you have to look overtly sexual; obviously that's not always appropriate. It means that you wear things that feel sensuous and soft; fabrics and shapes that heighten your awareness of your skin and movements. Even with your most severe business suit or your sportiest tennis togs, you can add at least one little thing, seen or unseen, that has a sensate quality to it. Silk, satin, cashmere, lace, Lycra, pearls, filmy scarves, fur, velvet, earrings that dangle against your neck, red lipstick, a push-up bra, see-through panties, a flowing skirt that billows against your bare skin, lots of bracelets, a snake armband worn on the upper arm, a wide choker, short tight skirts, silk or lace T-shirts, anything leather against your skin. Go braless. Go pantyless. Definitely go slipless, unless it's a sexy one.

It's amazing how sexy you will feel when you go without panties, particularly when you're wearing a long, flowing skirt that swishes when you walk; you're all covered up, but you feel so deliciously *exposed*. Whether your sensuous attire is demurely hidden from public view, proudly flaunted for your lover, or unabashedly admired in your own mirror, your Inner Sex Goddess will be softly vibrating and ready for further attention.

1 O. Soak in a hot, scented bubble bath. Spend hours at it. Read a steamy novel. Tease yourself with a soft skin brush. Bask in the glowing candlelight. Dream. Fantasize. Croon to yourself. Paint your toenails. Smooth the bubbles over your face, neck, arms, breasts, tummy, thighs, genitals. Arch your feet coquettishly and tickle your glistening toes. Massage your scalp as you wash your hair. Let the water drain while you're still in the tub. Or finish off with a cold shower. Pat yourself dry with the biggest, fluffiest towel you own. Or don't use a towel at all, and move directly into a thick terry-cloth robe. Or smooth perfumed body lotion over every inch of your skin. Float into your warm bedroom, and if there's a man in it, wake him up seductively. If not, sizzle to your own inner music.

1 1. Read something erotic. Curl up with a good story by Anaïs Nin and identify with the hot French coquettes she writes about. Transport yourself to another time and place where anything sexy, a little kinky, and very feminine goes. Like the women in the stories, allow yourself to be carried away by your passions until you feel that familiar warm glow begin to burn inside you. Then let your hands take it from there. There's lots of other good erotic literature out there too, something to fuel every fire, from the seductive S&M stories of A. N. Roquelaure to the taboo and poetic writing of Marco Vassi to anthologies like *Deep Down: The New Sensual Writing about Women* and *The*

Gates of Paradise. There's always Nancy Friday's *My Secret Garden* as well as many other collections of women's fantasies and even some of the letters and stories in magazines like *Playboy, Penthouse,* and *True Romance.* (See the "Inner Sex Goddess Scrolls" at the back of this book for a more complete list.) Or maybe a hot love scene from your favorite romance or trashy novel will light your inner fire. One highly organized friend of mine makes a copy of every good love scene she finds and puts it in a hot-pink file folder that she keeps locked in her nightstand drawer. Some of them are pretty dog-eared by now, but they never fail to arouse her passionate nature. Find your own favorites and keep them handy for reading to your Inner Sex Goddess or your real-life sex god.

12. Write your own erotica. Even the feel and sound of pen on paper as you write can be a sensual delight. Release your erotic feelings, hopes, and dreams onto the paper. Let your pen take flight, and follow its fanciful wanderings. Express how you felt when you last made love; recall the sensations that stirred you emotionally, sink into the feelings, and let them pour onto the paper. Invent a wildly romantic interlude in the forest, and write down exactly what you'd like to have happen. Describe a piece of music or a part of your body in sensual detail. Imagine your ideal lover and give him written instructions on how to drive you wild in bed. Tell the story of your bizarre sex-

ual experiences on another planet. Pen an imagined page from the journal of Fanny Hill, Cleopatra, or Oshun, the river goddess. Write intensely brief poetry, cool factual journalism, or hot turgid prose. Create a passionate romance novel or a porn comic book. Try on different writing styles to suit your mood or to create a new one. Since no one will be grading this paper, really let yourself go. Don't be afraid to dig down deep inside you and reveal your heart's secret erotic desires.

A single real estate broker I know told me she once spent a lone day at the beach feeling the blazing sun on her skin and fantasizing about a hot lover who would sneak up and inflame her body even further with steamy kisses. Later, feeling compelled to pour her sensual feelings onto paper, she wrote a rhymeless poem describing her fantasy love fest. She said that concentrating on finding the right words helped her relive and enhance the experience, and rereading it now and then recaptures all those sizzling skin sensations and simmering passions. Her poem turned out to be one of her most treasured personal turn-ons.

13. Ogle sexy pictures. Your Inner Sex Goddess is much more visually erotic than you might imagine, so give yourself permission to open the optic channels to your libido. She loves those bare-chested men in Calvin Klein ads, lovers in the ecstatic embraces and wild positions depicted so beautifully in Oriental woodcuts and Indian miniatures, pictures of luscious babes who look rather like you in men's magazines, beefcake postcards (one woman I know collects a few eye-poppers in every town she visits), hunky-man calendars (my calendar for this year happens to be "The Men of Hawaii," and are they hot!), nude photos you've taken of your lover, the sexually explicit drawings found in *The Joy of Sex* and other sex instruction books, museum postcard reproductions of beautifully sculpted nude Greek statues, the cover of a steamy novel, magazine photos of movie stars in action. Actually, some of the most erotic images I've ever seen are photographs or paintings of nature — Georgia O'Keeffe's paintings of flowers that look like women's vulvae; beautifully rendered still lifes where the soft fruit or flowers resemble swollen lips, rounded breasts, or plump behinds; photos of dense redwood forests exuding damp earthiness and phallic sensuality; drawings of curvy, openly inviting shells glistening with moisture.

Collect your personal preferences and keep them at the ready in your erotic file folder. Drool and fantasize to your libido's content. Imagine you are *in* the picture, and follow your bliss.

14. Watch X-rated videos. Yes, real women watch porn flicks. In fact, your Inner Sex Goddess can literally be transfigured by visual eroticism. One of the best descriptions I've ever heard of this phenomenon was reported by Sallie Tisdale in her fabulous book *Talk Dirty to*

Me: "Watching my first adult movie, watching for the first time a man penetrate another woman, was like leaving my body all at once. I was outside my body, watching, because she on the screen above me *was* me; and then I was back in my body very much indeed. My lust was aroused as surely and uncontrollably by the sight of sex as hunger can be roused by the smell of food."

Adult videos are much improved these days, and often you don't even have to fast-forward to get past all the boring or stupid stuff. For sleek erotic atmosphere with gorgeous men and women, try Andrew Blake's films. Candida Royale and her Femme Productions put out many sexy films that are more romantic and woman-centered. These and many other modern hard-, soft-, and medium-core porn videos (see "The Inner Sex Goddess Scrolls" for a more complete list) provide a great tool for expanding your sexual horizons and acting out vicariously what you might never do in real life. Whether you're into fantasizing about vampires, whips, bisexuality, group scenes, or just plain sizzling sex and plenty of it, there's a film made just for you. Your Inner Sex Goddess can also learn some interesting new tricks to try by yourself or with a partner. As my fiftyish friend Judy said when she loaned me one of her favorites, "I thought the film was trash, but it made me laugh, think, and swoon all at the same time. I couldn't wait to plug in my vibrator." I recommend that you (1) read the package carefully to get a feel for how kinky, outlandish, or romantic the film is; (2) trade videos and personal reviews of them with friends; (3) watch alone at first; and (4) watch with a vibrator in your lap.

15. Collect, admire, and play with erotic objects. Joanna, my plain but profoundly charismatic soul sister, likes to collect phallic objects, for instance. Her favorite is a two-inch-long crystal penis, every detail true to life. Obviously too small to do anything with, this toy is just for her Inner Sex Goddess to fantasize over. I have a stunning satinwood statue of a man arching over a woman's shoulder to kiss her breast; I love to gaze at it and stroke it. My pleasingly plump friend Marsha collects beautifully tasteful representations of women's pelvises and derrieres; they make her feel good about her own. Another friend likes lots of velvet pillows for looking, touching, and rubbing against sensitive body parts. Some women find that certain wild animals and the coiled power they represent arouse sexual thoughts—panthers, snakes, and stallions, for instance—and they enjoy having pictures, statuettes, or stuffed toys of these creatures around to inspire, admire, and pet. Pretty feathers, and even feathery plants, can be a sensual delight for the eyes and skin. Having a fetish for erotic collectibles not only results in some fabulous toys for your lovemaking lair but also keeps your sensual self alive and tantalized all the time, always on the lookout for a new addition to your secret sensitizing collection.

16. Aroma is another powerful stimulus for your Inner Sex Goddess. In fact, the ancient Egyptians, believing that fragrant oils were created by the gods, used scents to evoke in themselves the joyous sensuality of Hathor or the powerful regenerative qualities of Isis, for instance. Unleash your inner goddesses by inhaling deeply of *all* the "essential oils" of life—ocean air, baking bread, freshly washed hair, damp earth, baby skin, lemon peel, the musky aroma of sex, and especially flowers and their liquid essences. The lush smell of white ginger instantly unlocks all my voluptuous instincts, so I always return from Hawaii with ginger sachets to tuck in my drawers and pillows. Try placing a drop of your favorite essential oil on a bedside lightbulb or on melting wax as it drips down the side of a candle. Spray gardenia perfume in your linen closet and later unfold the fragrance onto your bed. Dip a cotton ball in jasmine oil and nestle it between the mounds of your breasts. Bathe in lavender-scented water. Saturate a lacy white handkerchief with ylang-ylang oil, wear it next to your skin for a while, and then carelessly leave it lying around in one of your man's favorite haunts.

17. Burn incense. A room filled with the heady aroma of musk, rose, jasmine, ylang-ylang, or amber, one of my favorites, somehow oozes sensuality. Like the ancient Tantricas, use the pungent smoke of your favorite incense to activate and eroticize your chakras (energy centers). Hold a stick of burning incense near your pubic bone and then move it slowly up the front of your body all the way to the top of your head, pausing for a few moments at your genitals, diaphragm, heart, and throat. Keep the incense about two inches away from your skin. Somehow this raises your sexual temperature and infuses your body and mind with heat, preparing you for an unusually sensual experience.

18. Develop an eye for the erotic qualities of nature. Women are especially talented at seeing and feeling the sensuous beauty in a vivid sunset, a purple craggy mountain at dawn, frothy ocean waves, emerald green rolling hills, tall grasses rippling in the wind, a certain iridescence of light and shade in the forest. Feel the thickness or sweetness of the air at the beach, in the mountains, in a forest glade, in the steamy jungle. Smell and taste it. Gardeners know that massaging wet dirt can be a sensuous experience. Caress the tender petals of a flower. Eat a blade of grass. Close your eyes and let the sound of crashing ocean waves wash over your body. Trickle hot sand over your feet and legs. Press your body against the rough bark of a tree. Walk barefoot in the grass. Feel with your eyes as you watch a horse run, a cat stretch, a bird soar, a snake slither, a butterfly float, a tiger spring, or a dragonfly mate.

If you live in the city and can't get away, take your Inner Sex Goddess to a museum or art gallery and let her drink in the sensual images of nature depicted in fine works of art. Luxuriate in Monet's sumptuous gardens or John Constable's overpowering, detailed landscapes. Absorb the subtleties of light or merge with the stillness in a photograph. Become intimate with Ansel Adams and his stunning black-and-white adorations of canyons and deserts. Imagine yourself into the setting of a van Gogh and let your animal senses run wild.

19. Mine your past for experiences and sensations that touch off interior sparks. Old love letters, postcards, snapshots, prom mementos, valentines, love songs, discarded clothing of his and yours, and even photos of a magnificent beach you went to by yourself are a living treasure chest of evocative sense triggers. Close your eyes and submerge yourself completely in the sights, sounds, and smells associated with that memory. Feel his arms around your waist as you danced to that old song; taste the souvlaki and baklava from that romantic trip to the Greek islands; drink in the smell of his skin when he wore that old flannel shirt. Vividly recall the rapid beating of your heart and the warm tingle under your skin that burned these moments into the very fibers of your body. Your Inner Sex Goddess lives in those vibrant sense memories.

20. As a little girl, you knew the power of your mother's lipstick and high heels to transform you into a sexy, grown-up chick; or a clown's hat to bring out your

silly oaf side; or a bandanna and a stick for a horse to turn you into a Wild West cowgirl. This stuff still works, even on your fuddy-duddy adult self, because Your Inner Sex Goddess adores the game of dress-up. Try on any persona that excites your erotic imagination and act the role to the hilt in front of your private mirror. Adorn yourself like a tart: net stockings, garter belt showing beneath short tight skirt, five-inch heels, brightly rouged cheeks, and teased hair. Wriggle your behind, whip your handbag around, expose your push-up bra and crotchless panties, and stand disdainfully arched against the doorway to attract imaginary customers. Dress up like a harem girl, with floating sheer scarves, beaded vest, lots of jangling jewelry, ankle bracelets, heavy Cleopatra eyeliner, and face veil. Pull the scarves provocatively across your breasts and through your legs; with head down, peek out from behind your veil with inviting eyes; let your scarves and ropes of jewelry fly out from your body as you twirl, dance, and undulate. Or be a demure geisha and don a kimono, wide silk sash, chopsticks in your piled-up hair, and the whitest makeup you can find. Geishas consider the nape of the neck very erotic, and they extend their white makeup around to the back of the neck, making a long, pointed pattern with it in the space where their kimono collar falls away. Step mincingly about the room, flutter your fan in strategic places, purse your lips, and enticingly caress your brazenly exposed neck and ankles. Or transform yourself into a hula dancer by baring your breasts, tying a sarong or big scarf low around your hips, and arranging flowers and leaves in your hair. Sway your hips, raise your arms gracefully to one side, and perform the sensuous *ami* movement by rotating your hips around in one big continuous circle. Slip into the memory of how you looked and felt, or take your harem scarf or your net stockings to bed with you, the next time you want to entice your Inner Sex Goddess or your consort lover.

21. Try the practice of vivification. The Native Americans believed that everything—rocks, trees, streams, animals, clouds—had a living spirit, and they addressed each one with the same respect, awe, and love they would give to any divine being. When you become conscious of every flower, shell, fig, painting, or piece of music as a living essence of sensuality, its vital spark will come alive for you, revealing all its rich colors, secret smells, and soul-tingling textures. And in getting to know this voluptuous being, you will be transformed. As Joseph Campbell said, "The [self] that sees a 'thou' is not the same [self] that sees an 'it.'"

your body: the temple within the garden

We don't need to attend a sex seminar, travel to an exotic locale, or search out the perfect lover to open wide the doors of our true sensuality. All we have to do is be fully present right here in the sacred temple of our own bodies. As the Boston Women's Health Collective has so brilliantly put it, "Our Bodies *Are* Ourselves" (emphasis mine). Through the senses of our bodies we know the world and ourselves. Through our bodies we *know*. We know what we want and need. We know what we feel. We know what to do. We know who we are. We know ourselves as women. In fact, the poet Adrienne Rich has written that women "think through the body."

By becoming more aware of our bodies, bringing our attention to each part as we observe or touch it, we tap into the deep wisdom contained in these our miraculous sensate morsels of flesh. We begin to learn the language of our instincts, which direct and guide us when we make love. All too often, though, we let our heads take the lead in bed and leave our wise bodily instincts behind. This separates us from our full sensuality and leaves us feeling unfulfilled, as though something were still lacking. It is! What's missing is the full experience of the senses we are trying so hard to stimulate, and the powerful sensate wisdom of our bodies. So often we criticize, ignore, or try to change our bodies. But without them, how could we have the wonder that is sex and sensuality?

Your Inner Sex Goddess knows that in order to be a great lover, with your man or with yourself, to enjoy lovemaking and discover new sexual delights every day, you have to be fully present in your body. You have to revere it as the sacred temple of your sensuality and consciously inhabit all of its rooms, hallways, and turrets. So when you want to tempt the voluptuousness out of your bones or turn your lover into hot mush, start by taking the time to consciously inhabit the temple of your body. Turn your mental switch from outer visual mode to inner sensate mode. Really *feel* the sensations of your skin. John Gray, author of *Men Are from Mars, Women Are from Venus*, says that women have more "cuddling hormones" than men and that the skin all over their bodies is ten times more sensitive than men's, as sensitive as the skin on a man's penis. So take advantage of those extra pleasure sensors. Concentrate on the tingles, the tickles, the heat rising and falling, the waves of pleasure. Luxuriate in your body. Here are some things you can do to increase your awareness and turn on your body senses.

$22.$ Rub your hands together rapidly for about ten seconds before you touch your body. This (1) brings your awareness to your hands and the physicalness of your body, (2) sensitizes your hands, (3) makes them nice and warm, (4) creates energy that you will definitely feel when you touch your hands to your body. Watch out for tingles!

$23.$ Close your eyes and take several slow, deep breaths. Feel the breath traveling to every corner of your body. Let it tingle. Imagine that you are breathing in through your breasts and nipples. Let them become filled with heat and energy. Focus intently on the subtle sensations and a new sense of presence in your breasts. Then imagine breathing in through your vagina. Again, really concentrate your attention there. Feel its fullness, warmth, and energy.

$24.$ Another sensitizing breath technique that comes from the Tantric tradition is called the Breath of Fire. Sit up straight and pant very fast and very hard. Make a hissing sound as you inhale and exhale. Continue this for about fifteen seconds (you can work up to two minutes, but take it slowly at first). Then inhale very deeply, hold your breath for a count of five, and exhale fully and slowly. As its name suggests, this technique will ignite your sexual fires; and if you want to direct them to a specific place in your body, you can do so simply by focusing your attention there as you perform your final slow exhalation. Feel the hot inner breath actually traveling to your favorite erotic hot spot.

25. During rhythmic activities like running, rowing, singing, and making love, people's breathing will often synchronize. If you consciously model your breathing pattern after the excited panting or deep moaning rhythms of peak sex, you will find your body and mind responding with the physical sensations of arousal, even releasing titillating pheromones.

26. Contract every muscle in your body as tightly as you can for five seconds. All at the same time, clench your fists, hunch your shoulders, curl your toes, pull in your stomach, tighten your leg and arm muscles, scrunch your eyelids shut. Contract everything. Then release your tension completely for five seconds. Do this five times. Finally, relax, relax, relax. Let go. See what happens.

27. Lick yourself all over. Start by sliding your tongue across the tips of your fingers. Then travel down to lap your palm, encircle your wrist with a wet tongue, lick the back of your hand and your knuckles, trace a tongue line down your forearm with occasional nibbles along the way, and flick your tongue in the hollow of your elbow. Continue languorously over the rest of your body. When

you are with your lover, ask him to join you by licking and biting your other arm.

28. Sensitize your head by massaging your scalp or by shampooing your hair while imagining that a lover is doing it, brushing your hair for a long time, pulling slowly on your earlobes, tracing circles on your scalp with your fingernails, pressing the hollows beside your eyes and behind your ears, tapping your head all over with your fingertips, rubbing your scalp with a rough towel. Close your eyes and let these physical tingles awaken the sensual you.

29. Bathe in the hot sun—nude, if possible. Sunlight actually increases the level of the hormone androgen, the female counterpart of testosterone, filling your body with delicious liquid desire and bringing your Inner Sex Goddess to life.

30. My friend Gloria has developed a simple but elegant way to be deeply in touch with the sensations of her body. She says that when her erotic feelings first start to blossom, the bottoms of her feet start to tingle. She then focuses on moving that tingle up to her vagina, or wherever she wants it, and she moves and breathes in ways that keep that prickle of excitement growing, no matter what else may follow. Whatever your body's calling cards of arousal are—tingling feet, melting chest muscles, burning palms,

soft tongue—focus on those sensations and visualize them expanding into your fingers, breasts, pelvis, toes, head, wherever. Feel them actually traveling along your nerve pathways, glowing, heating, and thrilling your entire body.

31. Rub your skin with fur, velvet, chamois, felt, honey, olive oil, cold cream, rough facial cleansing cream, suede, cold cans of soda, fresh porcini (wild mushrooms whose firm silkiness feels like the skin on the tip of your man's penis). Stand in the rain, run through the wind, dip your hands in snow, submerge yourself in a cool, bubbling brook. Lie naked on a rug, a wooden floor, the sand, a bed of leaves. Ask your Inner Sex Goddess what her favorite skin treat is and indulge yourself with it.

32. Sensuously apply perfumed lotion to your entire body. Don't forget the backs of your knees, your underarms, the nape of your neck. Really focus on the physical sensations as you do this—the place where you are rubbing, your hands as they caress your skin, the heady aroma. Be aware of every one of the millions of nerve endings all over your skin.

33. Give yourself a massage. It's a good idea to trim your nails first so you can use your fingertips without getting stabbed. Take your time and be very sensuous about it. Slather yourself with oil, scented or unscented. As you move your hands over your body, focus your attention on the delicious sensations that are exchanged between fingers and skin, each experiencing its own distinct pleasures. Start at your feet and slowly work your way up your legs and torso, leaving your genitals for last. Or begin with your face and scalp and work your way down. Spend lots of time on your fingers and hands because they are extremely sensitive to touch and because they take quite a beating during your busy day. Use long, sensuous strokes that go deep into the skin, or work in soothing circular motions. Large, two-handed circles over the tummy are especially nice. Let your hands discover all those little knots of tension, and knead them out. Cup your hands over your eyes, breasts, and pubic bone. Caress, hold, and cradle your body the way a lover would.

34. As you are performing number 32 or 33, do the following body awareness exercise. If you have started with your foot, for instance, close your eyes and "listen" to the sensate messages your foot is sending you. How does it feel? Does it want stronger or gentler pressure? Lift your hands for a moment and be aware that the foot you have stroked probably feels lighter and more vibrant than your other foot. As you massage your foot, tell it how beautiful and strong it is, and thank it for supporting you so well. Let your foot drink in all this pleasure. Continue in the same manner with every part of your body.

We human beings are
able to make love more
frequently and sensuously
than perhaps any other
animal. Yet we are often
disappointed after
lovemaking. Why?
Because most of us are
like owners of a precious
Stradivarius violin that
we have never learned to
play.

—Jolan Chang, *The
Tao of the Loving Couple*

3
—

self-
pleasuring—
the key
to the
kingdom

As a sacred temple, your body is the divine instrument of pleasures fit for the gods. And before you can use it to make beautiful music with your partner, you have to become a virtuoso on your own Stradivarius. In order to seduce others with your heavenly melodies, you must first seduce yourself by drawing out your deep, wild sexuality, turning on the magnetic firelight of your body, and inflaming your own delicious passion. Even the gods and goddesses of ancient Egypt obeyed this basic rule, for among them it is said that the sun brought the world into existence by first pleasuring itself. After that, it was the female sky who, by lowering her beautiful potent body over the male earth, created the union that produced life.

Autoeroticism has long been practiced as a natural and elegant way of honoring the glorious gift of a body and communing with one's inner divinity—from primitive cave drawings of masturbation to the erotic dildos found in ancient Egyptian tombs, to a Buddhist temple in Orissa that boasts beautiful bas-reliefs of men and women stroking themselves. Even today's sex therapists extol the benefits of autoeroticism as a vital tool for self-knowledge and relationship-enhancement, professing that sexual virtuosity with a lover is attained by first becoming a sexual virtuoso with yourself. Many ordinary women bear this out; they have told me that, despite the fact that their first experience with lovemaking was merely okay or even disappointing, they later learned to reach sexual heights and become extraordinary lovers by focusing on sensualizing their own bodies. Such was the case with me.

my story

I had a very strict and sheltered upbringing that did not include getting information about sex, although I always suspected that something mysterious, powerful, and potentially dangerous or enjoyable (both equally discouraged) lurked beneath the currents of everyday life. During high school I necked and petted with my boyfriends, but genital contact was so out of the question that I didn't even think about it. Then, finally, at age nineteen, I had intercourse for the first time—a somewhat boring encounter with a steady boyfriend that produced the required bloody sheet, but not much in the way of passion, excitement, or romance. Subsequent boyfriends helped me see that sex could be sexier than had been apparent in the first encounter, but my eyes weren't truly opened to the sensuality and power I owned for myself (and with which I could light all sorts of flashing sparks in men) until several years later when I bought a vibrator.

A trusted friend had raved about the fun she was having with her mechanical instrument of pleasure, and I wanted to explore too. Suddenly I could concentrate fully on my own body and the delicious inner and outer feelings I was having without having a man's wants and needs to worry about. And because the vibrator was so intense and indefatigable, and because it would stay exactly where I wanted it to, I found myself making a discovery: "Oh, *that's* what an orgasm is!" Over the next several months I explored every inch of my body and learned to love my hips, little toes, breasts, inner elbows, genitals, and earlobes for the voluptuous and powerful way they could make me feel. I gave up feeling embarrassed or ashamed about any of my body's shortcomings, and even about the fact that it could give me such pleasure. In fact, learning about my own personal poetry gave me greater self-esteem, zest, and natural charm. And the more I enjoyed my own body, the hotter and sexier I felt, the better lover I became, and the more men seemed to be attracted to me. That's why, when women say to me,

> "I have a really great lover. Why would I want to play with myself?"
> "If I masturbate, it means I can't get a lover and have to settle for second best."
> "I already know how to massage my hot button. Who needs anything else?"

"My man feels too threatened by my vibrator."

"I masturbate every once in a while, but it's kinda boring."

"I'm afraid I'll get so aroused by women's bodies I'll become a lesbian."

"Isn't that really more for men?"

"I could never do *that!*"

"I don't really know how."

"I'm not oversexed!" . . .

I say that you can settle for good sex or even pretty great sex if you want to, but I believe that self-loving is one of the most vital keys to your inner kingdom of abandoned, expert, and rapturous sexuality. It's certainly one of the easiest, fastest, and most reliable ways to unleash your Inner Sex Goddess. And if you want some sensible, virtuous reasons to spend precious time and energy on what may seem like frivolous, threatening, or wickedly self-indulgent pleasures, here they are.

Reason # 1

Self-Pleasuring Is the Single Most Important Thing You Can Do to Become a Truly Great Lover.

By focusing on your own total fulfillment, you gain access to the complete you—the savage you, the loving you, the lusty trampy you, the giving you, the unbridled you, the inventive and adventurous you, the magnetic you, the Aphrodite you, the instinctive wild you, the Sex Goddess you. You discover a whole new way of being a woman.

You have the keys to your body, your physical and emotional sensations, and your most lascivious libido. Self-pleasuring allows you to find out firsthand:

- What most turns you on—or off
- What makes you feel less inhibited
- What feels good real slow and gentle or very hard and fast
- How long you like to be stimulated
- How sensitive your nipples and clitoris are
- Where your G-spot is and how it likes to be rubbed
- The best way for you to reach orgasm
- How to extend your sexual capacity into multiple orgasmic bliss

By becoming familiar with your sexual organs and the pleasure they can provide, you discover just how beautiful and powerful they really are; your genitals may even become your favorite feature. I know a woman who feels that her pink flowerlike inner vaginal lips are one of her strongest assets. She says men are fascinated with her large fleshy petals and want to stroke and kiss them endlessly!

When you discover and awaken all of your personal hot spots and habits, when you find out for yourself what the tight contractions of your vagina feel like to a man, when you see how sexy you look with hips undulating, nipples erect, and in the full throes of orgasm, you have a visceral experience of the high-wattage sexual power that is yours to command, enjoy, and give. You *know* you are a deliciously dangerous weapon of love.

And when you're in firm control of all your rich sexual assets and weapons, needing nothing outside yourself, yet wanting and commanding the whole world of sensuality, you are prepared to fully inflame your man's body, his mind, and that most powerful erogenous zone of all—his imagination.

Reason #2

Self-Pleasuring Makes You *Feel* Sexy.

In *203 Ways to Drive a Man Wild in Bed*, I explained that the first secret of great sex is *"Feel* sexy, and you will *be* sexy." One of the fastest, surest, and most enjoyable ways to summon up that sense of power and sensuality is to titillate your body and mind with some self-loving.

That's because thinking about sex makes you feel sexy; preparing to have sex makes you feel sexy; knowing and appreciating your body makes you feel sexy; loving your genitals makes you feel sexy; seeing how beautiful you look when you are flushed with excitement makes you feel sexy; orgasm makes you feel sexy. And stimulating your sex hormones makes you feel sexy; that is, after all, their physiological function — to engorge your womb with blood, to start your vaginal juices flowing, to activate the sensation-rich nerve endings in your genitals and breasts, to stiffen your nipples, to flush your skin with extra blood and energy. In fact, the electromagnetic energy field surrounding your body begins to overflow with sexual energy and potency.

In fact, self-pleasuring actually expands your capacity for pleasure. The more pleasure you get, the more you want. The more you learn to enjoy, the more you can handle. It's like when you finally try the Flying Teacup ride at the carnival: you get off feeling giddy and exhilarated. *Now* you are ready to take on the Giant Killer Roller Coaster! Building the pleasure of sex and sensuality is similar. All of your senses come alive, expand, and reach enthusiastically for more.

And most important, being in touch with your Inner Sex Goddess makes you feel sexy. She is the repository of all your sensual drives, feelings, and knowledge. When you respect and love her and give her free rein to express herself, she will reward you with the riches of your own natural sexual power and artistry. Your Inner Sex Goddess *knows* how to feel and be sexy. She *is* sex.

Reason #3

Self-Pleasuring Puts You in Touch with Your Body.

We ignore our bodies most of the time. We're too busy organizing complex work and social schedules, we're devising five-year plans and household budgets, we're weighing the pros and cons of buying a new refrigerator or a new dress, we're making decisions and formulating opinions, we're determining if a new man is safe, mature, and stable enough to go to bed with. We even make physical exercise a rigorous mental obsession, calculating our heart rates and personal best scores. We tend to view the input and sensations of our bodies as less important, less reliable, and less real than those of our minds. But this separation of mind and body can be terribly self-destructive.

I find that when I neglect the pleasures of self-loving I become more critical of my body. I see it as a separate entity with cottage cheese thighs and wrinkles around the eyes. I lose a nurturing awareness of the rhythms and cycles of my body and of nature. I don't know and love myself as well. I start feeling powerless and depressed.

But a luxurious session of self-play can quickly restore my feelings of oneness with body and soul. It can do the same for you. By focusing your attention on the sensations of your skin, muscles, and seemingly countless erogenous zones and by feeling your womanness intensely, you come to know your body again and love all of its pleasures. You may find you actually like your fleshy thighs and crinkly eyes; they too are full of sweet sensations. Your body, mind, and soul begin resonating together once again. You feel healthier, earthier, more in tune with yourself, more human. Your body lets you in on its inherent playfulness and love of dancing, exercising, and making love. You reclaim the joy of being alive, and you feel glad to have your sensuous female body, which was made for pleasure.

Reason #4

Self-Pleasuring Strengthens and Increases the Flexibility of Your Love Muscle.

In case you don't already know it, the pubococcygeus (PC) is your primary love muscle. It's the one you use to stop the flow of urine, and if it's well trained, you can use it to massage a man's penis to ecstasy. It is also the muscle in which you experience most of the contractions of orgasm, and if you keep it well toned, it helps you have bigger, better, and more frequent orgasms. Just flexing it can make you feel sexy and hot. That's why having a strong and flexible PC muscle is crucial to great sex, whether you're flying in tandem or solo.

The increased blood supply and toning contractions of orgasm vitalize your PC muscle. It feels good if it's exercised and strengthened, and then it pays you back by giving you better climaxes and more control of your partner's pleasure too. And of course the easiest way to give yourself plenty of lovely toning orgasms—unless your man is available for hot sex twenty-four hours a day—is by self-pleasuring.

Reason #5

Self-Pleasuring Teaches You How to Have Orgasms—Lots of Them—Easily and Quickly.

Many women have never had an orgasm with or without a partner. Many are not sure if they have or not. Many women fake it just to keep the peace or to avoid hurting his feelings. According to recent surveys, only about 30 percent of women have orgasms through intercourse alone, but 80 to 99 percent achieve climax with masturbation. This is astonishing. It's completely normal and very common *not* to have an orgasm through intercourse all by itself. Most women need additional stimulation to experience their full sexual potential and enjoyment, but all the while they think they're supposed to be climaxing all over the place just from their lover's penis. While some women do, most do not. The truth is that once you learn how and where your body needs to be stimulated in order to have an orgasm, you can start having them any time you want to, easily and quickly—during intercourse, while masturbating with your partner, and through self-pleasuring on your own.

A woman's body is an amazing pleasure machine, capable of trillions of orgasms, big ones and small ones. In fact, according to Dr. Andrew Stanway in *The Art of Sensual Loving*, "any one woman's total sexual output through her life (intercourse plus self-produced orgasms) is probably more than a man's." It seems that a woman's capacity for sexual gratification is nearly limitless. And the more orgasms you have, the more your body learns to respond to all types of stimulation so that it is easier to have more and more wonderful climaxes.

The best way to teach your body to have easy orgasms is through self-pleasuring. You can try out all kinds of fun things in complete privacy, without having to worry if you're taking too much time, looking silly, or doing something incredibly weird. If you find it takes twenty minutes of constant clitoral massage to make you come, then you've discovered a great secret. If you learn that pulling on your nipples or massaging your anus while you thrust your finger in and out of your love tunnel throws you over the edge, then you've found the key to unlocking your orgasmic bliss. Chances are, you are not going to discover these things while having sex with your man. You'll be too embarrassed to explore yourself or too busy worrying about his pleasure, or you won't have enough time because he's already had his orgasm and gone to sleep. Stop denying yourself! Use your hands to teach your body how to have its ultimate pleasure.

Reason #6

Self-Pleasuring Puts You in Control of Your Own Pleasure.

When you know your body and its sexual responses really well, *you* can control whether, when, and how to have your orgasm. You know just what it takes to create warm liquid feelings throughout your entire body and to bring on those delicious orgasmic contractions. Then you can guide your man to help you have *multiple* orgasms, if that's your desire. The point is that you know exactly what you want and need, and you know precisely how to achieve it. You are your own mistress.

And then there are times when you don't have a man in your life. Fortunately that doesn't mean you have to give up being your Sex Goddess self, because while you are self-pleasuring you can fantasize the most outrageous encounters, imagining every single touch, kiss, and stroke being done exactly the way you want it, for as long as you want it, as tenderly or roughly as you want it, by whomever you desire. Your imaginary sex partner anticipates your every sexual wish and never tires of titillating you all the way to the outside edge of your pleasure envelope. I've had several lovely liaisons with a fantasy Mel Gibson, for instance, where he licked me all over for three hours, massaged and kissed my breasts just the way I like it for about an hour and a half, and then made hard and fast love to me for forty-five minutes without stopping till we both collapsed in luscious exhaustion.

And even when you do have a man in your life, he will sometimes be away, ill, or just not into it. Again, your own loving hands are always there to do your bidding. Sometimes your man may be just plain tired out from having given you ten star-burst orgasms in a row, but you want eleven that night. On those occasions you always have the ability to continue riding the waves on your own. In other words, you are not at the mercy of a partner's sexual whims, skill, or presence to enjoy your own ecstasies.

Reason #7

Self-Pleasuring Leads to Self-Confidence in All Areas of Life.

When you know how to turn yourself on and realize that you can do so anytime without depending on anyone else, you will gain a tremendous sense of self-control and self-confidence. You feel surer of yourself, more deserving, and more powerful.

This exhilarating sense of potency naturally spreads to other areas of your life. Learning to take responsibility for your own sensual enjoyment gives you the confidence to take the same initiative elsewhere. The aliveness and power you feel as a self-created Sex Goddess help you know that you are a fascinating and limitlessly capable creature, regardless of the role you are playing at the moment. My banker friend Charlotte says, "Now that I'm in touch with my full range of feelings and experiences, I am more complete, more integrated. I know the amazing things I'm capable of in all areas of my life. And I like myself for it."

According to research cited by Lonnie Barbach in *For Yourself*, "consistently orgasmic women tend to describe themselves as contented, good-natured, insightful, self-confident, independent, realistic, strong, capable, and understanding while non-orgasmic women tend to describe themselves as bitter, despondent, dissatisfied, distrustful, fussy, immature, inhibited, prejudiced, and sulky." Gee, I'd rather be around a frequently orgasmic woman. Wouldn't you? And so would your husband or lover, your children, your co-workers, and your friends. You become an asset to the rest of the world when you are happy, strong, and fulfilled. And you know it.

Reason #8

Self-Pleasuring Is the Key to Overcoming Sexual Guilt and Self-Repression.

The more time you spend getting to know your body—feeling comfortable with it and all the wonderful things it can do for you and seeing how beautiful it is at rest and during all stages of excitement—the more you come to understand that sexual pleasure is a natural and especially wonderful benefit of living in a body. Our bodies love to be stroked and caressed; they thrive on it. In fact, if deprived of physical affection they can become ill.

Finding out that self-pleasuring is a natural and beautiful function, something that makes you feel great about yourself and more loving to those around you, frees you from all that guilt you may have been carrying around. It breaks down the walls of inhibition and helps you let go of the fears and musty old taboos that have been keeping you from fully enjoying your natural Sex Goddesshood. And once you do release whatever sexual guilt is lurking in all those dark inner corners, you will be able to express your sexuality and your true self more freely—*with* your lucky lover. You can start enjoying sex more and regretting it less.

Reason #9

Self-Pleasuring Promotes Health, Well-Being, and Energy.

Your sex muscles are not isolated. To paraphrase an old song, "The sex bone's connected to the thigh bone; the thigh bone's connected to the back bone," and so forth. Healthy, well-toned pelvic and vaginal muscles lead to healthy, well-toned stomach muscles, leg muscles, and on and on. To say nothing of the increased flow of blood and energy that permeates your entire body when you indulge in a vigorous self-pleasuring workout. Exercise makes for healthy, happy muscles. It also boosts your energy production and releases endorphins that create a sense of well-being. In fact, according to Dr. Deepak Chopra, a chemical called Interleukin-2 floods the body during any positive exhilarating activity—and I think most of us will agree that sizzling self-play qualifies as such an activity. Interleukin-2 is a powerful anticancer neuropeptide, the body's chemical equivalent to a feeling of joy. So for a quick mental and physical pick-me-up that will also build long-term health—some women say it even makes them feel younger—indulge in your favorite form of self-play.

Reason #10

Self-Pleasuring Reduces Stress and Tension.

The intense muscular and emotional release of self-induced orgasm provides quite a tonic for anxiety, tense muscles, job stress, traffic jam tension, or the frustration of a bad hair day. Stress and tension restrict the flow of blood and energy through your body and cause blocks to creativity, good health, and joyful living. Like a good massage, self-pleasuring can soothe and release these tensions with the simple touch of a finger. My friend Diane, who has a very stressful job, says, "I sometimes masturbate every day if it's a tough work week. I don't know how I'd manage the stress caused by intense days filled with frantic meetings and impossible deadlines without it!"

Reason #11

Self-Pleasuring Helps You Sleep.

On those nights when your mind is racing, or you're all keyed up from some intense conversation or event, or worry is keeping your eyes glued to the ceiling, you can invite the Sandman into your bed by indulging in some stress-releasing self-massage. It has been scientifically proven that giving yourself a lovely orgasm relaxes your muscles and tunes your brain waves to alpha (the brain waves of dreaming sleep and creativity) or even theta (deep sleep). And it's a "sleeping pill" that has no side effects and will leave you energized, not stupefied, in the morning.

Reason # 1 2

You Don't Have to Stop Feeling Good When You or Your Sex Organs Are in a Delicate Condition.

Suppose that you have an infection, you've recently had non-womb-related surgery, you are in the last stages of pregnancy, you just gave birth, or you are having your period. These are times when it might not be comfortable, desirable, or safe to indulge in love play with a partner. But during such times, you usually need *more* loving, not less. During those times, you could really use the recuperative magic of sensual bliss. Fortunately, you can always give yourself just the right gentle caresses and love strokes to soothe your soul and keep you in life-affirming touch with your Inner Sex Goddess.

Reason # 1 3

For Older Women, Self-Pleasuring Increases Vaginal Lubrication and Lessens the Discomfort of Dryness.

This is true not just when you are pleasuring yourself, but all the time. By keeping your vaginal glands active, before, during, and after the menopausal years, you are encouraging them to produce more lubrication regularly. So you'll be juicier for your man too. When you keep your vaginal muscles contracting and those hormones secreting, you'll stay sexually active and in touch with your Inner Sex Goddess.

Reason # 14

Self-Pleasuring Provides Relief from Menstrual Cramps.

One of the benefits of having nicely toned and frequently orgasmic vaginal muscles is that they are stronger, more elastic, and much better able to handle the inner movements associated with your menstrual period. The spasms that release no-longer-needed blood from your uterus are therefore less intense, jarring, and painful. And these contractions don't have to enlist the support of surrounding stomach and back muscles to do their job. Most women who make self-pleasuring a favorite habit find that they experience much less pelvic cramping and greatly diminished or no menstrual backaches. A nice side effect, no?

Reason # 15

Self-Pleasuring Enhances Lovemaking with Your Partner.

If you are hot, you can't help but light his fire.

If you have a strong PC muscle to flutter on your lucky man's love organ, and if your body is willing and eager to have lots of deep orgasms, you are going to bring new vigor to his body and sexual imagination.

If you know all your secret erogenous zones and personal turn-ons, you can be much more confident and creative as a lover. You can gently guide him to massage your inner lips counterclockwise, if that's what makes you hot, and let him feel the power of bringing you to a teeth-chattering climax. You can teach him all sorts of sizzling new sex tricks. And if you think your man doesn't really want you to be so brazenly aggressive, think again. According to a book of sex surveys published in 1991, *Do You Do It with the Lights On?*, 91 percent of men—and a whopping 98 percent of men age thirty to fifty-four—not only wanted their partners to take a more active role in sexual play, they wished them to choose the position, place, and procedure.

If you are sexually self-sufficient, you are freer to express this wanton sexuality with your man. That way he doesn't feel so pressured to perform or to puzzle out how to make you fly higher than anybody else has. He doesn't have to spend sleepless nights wondering if he's man enough to make you have the multiple orgasms he's read women secretly expect. You can seductively show him how. Your relaxed self-confidence and euphoria gently rub off on him and magically bring out his natural savage aptitudes and talents.

If you learn how to be deeply intimate with yourself, you can be more intimate with your partner. Likewise, your increased openness encourages him to be more intimate with you. And so that elusive soul sharing that we call intimacy blossoms and grows in your most treasured relationship. A lover once told me, "When you are open with me about your feelings and show me your vulnerable, out-of-control side, I feel I can be open and vulnerable with you. And that makes me feel good."

If you pleasure yourself regularly, you will feel sexier. You will *be* sexier. You will want to make love to your man more often, and you will do so with more gusto and expertise. He will think he has died and gone to heaven.

And last but certainly not least, once you get comfortable with and good at pleasuring yourself, you can put on a really hot, provocative show for your lover. Men *love* to watch women give themselves pleasure. Whether you tie him down and make him watch you for hours or simply wet your finger and slip it quickly inside yourself while staring into his eyes during foreplay, he'll be bewitched.

Every true Sex Goddess has this mouth-watering act in her sexual repertoire. (More details on self-pleasuring for and with your partner in Chapter 10.)

Reason # 16

In the Age of HIV, Self-Pleasuring Is the Ultimate in Safe Sex.

Obviously, when you have sex only with yourself, you are in no danger of catching sexually transmitted diseases from someone else. No small concern these days.

But even in partner sex, masturbating with and for each other can be a delightful way to stay safe. Using your hands, vibrators, dildos, and a variety of other sex toys allows you to exchange a lot of loving and fun sexual energy without exchanging any body fluids. And even without body fluids, you can have the sensual moistness of hot sex if you add playful fruit—cucumbers, zucchini, peaches, mushed-up bananas, and so forth—to your repertoire as well. (More details in Chapter 9.)

Reason # 17

The Joy of Self-Pleasuring Is Always Available.

Morning, evening, and in-between times, at the office, while traveling, at the beach, on an airplane, when you're bored, when you look or feel too grungy to be seen by another human being, when he's sleeping or watching a football game, between the time he forgets the anniversary of your first kiss and the time when you forgive him, between lovers, after a divorce, when you have the jitters, when you're feeling lonely, when you're feeling sexy and there's no one else around, when you find yourself alone with an X-rated movie or a picture of a man with muscles to die for, whenever wild and crazy thoughts come bouncing unbidden into your head—you can always pleasure yourself and be your own Inner Sex Goddess anytime.

One friend recalls that when she was on her way to see her lover after a three-month separation, she became so excited thinking about his waiting erection that she slipped into an airport bathroom during a stopover, hid herself in a tiny stall, and hastily created her own urgent and explosive, if necessarily silent, orgasm. Thank Goddess, your hands always travel with you!

Reason # 18

Self-Pleasuring Is One of the Very Best Ways to Unleash Your Inner Sex Goddess.

Going all the way back to the ancient Sumerian goddess Inanna, divine and human women have innately understood that self-loving is the magical open sesame to the inner realms of power. In fact, Inanna is thought of as the patron goddess of self-pleasuring because she was in a constant state of ecstatic union with herself, and that inner union gave birth to the fertility of all living things. As a matter of fact, self-love *is* the creative state, because when you *know* that you are new each day and that you are a beautiful and perfect temple of pleasure, your benevolent, loving power gives life to all those around you.

Although there are many roads — mental, emotional, and spiritual — to the kingdom of your Inner Sex Goddess, the physical path of sensual awareness and self-pleasuring is usually the most direct route simply because it is so tangible, it is easily accessible, and it fairly bursts with the power of all the five senses. And you will find that if you perform any of what you might consider the mechanical or physically impersonal acts of self-pleasuring with self-*love*, you will evoke the very mental, emotional, and even spiritual feelings of love and affection you usually have only with an intimate mate. Not only is this more fun, stimulating, and satisfying, but it also expands your self-esteem and enhances your ability to communicate love to yourself and your partner — and to receive it from him. And this is what being a true Sex Goddess is all about.

Round her delicate throat
and her silvery breasts
they fastened necklaces of
gold which they,
the gold-filleted Hours,
wear themselves when
they go
to the lovely dances of the
gods in their father's
house.
—First Homeric
"Hymn to Aphrodite,"
translated by Jules
Cashford

4
—
awakening
aphrodite's
body

ℭven Helen of Troy, a woman so gorgeous and enticing that a war was fought over her, bowed to the awesome beauty and sensual power of Aphrodite, Queen of Heaven and Goddess of the Dawn. Despite one of Aphrodite's temporary disguises as an old woman, Helen recognized the Golden One by the "sweet throat of the goddess and her desirable breasts and her eyes that were full of shining." Most often portrayed nude, the goddess of love was completely unself-conscious about her body and its sexuality, often flaunting it by decorating herself only with golden ornaments. In fact, her unembarrassed naked sensuality and her skill at pleasuring drew countless lovesick men to her like a magnet. Aphrodite was a woman who knew her own erogenous zones and how to activate them to excite herself and her lovers. She truly understood that Woman embodies all the senses in their exalted form and that pleasuring her beautiful body is a natural way for a woman to nourish her erotic soul.

Awakening to the Aphrodite within you, then, means learning how to delight in the pleasures of your own flesh and opening your body to the rich sensations and wanton feelings locked inside. And your own hands, mythically adorned with Aphrodite's brazenly worn gold rings and bracelets, are the keys. So use your golden goddess fingers to love and awaken your body, exploring all its curvy contours, discovering and intensifying its unique pleasure points, and transform it, like Aphrodite's own body, into a sumptuous temple of erotic delights in which you and your man can worship regularly.

It's natural at first to feel some inhibitions about manually pleasing yourself in every wild way you can possibly think of, but try to let those impediments go. Be as bold and as reverent as Aphrodite. If you do feel shy about jumping right in to try *all* of the following suggestions, that's okay. Just start out with what feels comfortable and fun to you. All you may want to do just now is read about them. Don't be surprised, though, if you soon find yourself feeling tempted to try a thing or two, getting more and more adventurous, and even making up your own kinky list of self-pleasuring scenarios. Try to give yourself and your body the benefit of the doubt by crossing over your embarrassment threshold just a little bit. After all, there's no one around to judge you or find out just how much fun you're having. Sip some wine. Relax. Let go. Let your hair down. Brush it out. Like Aphrodite, throw caution, inhibition, and self-consciousness to the wind.

aphrodite's boudoir

It will be much more tempting for your Inner Sex Goddess to come out and play if you create a loving and sensual nest in which she can feel comfortable, safe, and uninhibited. So before you begin your self-play sessions, take the time to create a bedroom Aphrodite would have been proud of. Take the phone off the hook or use the answering machine. Lock the door, post a sign, or do whatever you have to do to ensure privacy. Make sure the room is warm and that you have something to drink. Gather together all the things you might want or need—oils, a towel, a large mirror, a handheld mirror, perfume, wine, sensual foods, music, lingerie, costumes, scarves, sensual fabrics, pillows, erotic literature, sexy pictures, X-rated videos, special erotic objects, vibrators, dildos, and other sex toys of your choice. (More on vibrators and other toys in Chapter 9.) You won't use all of these things every time, but have them handy and gather whichever items you want for that particular session *before* you start. Dress the bed in pretty, fresh linens. Artfully arrange flowers, candles, incense, and evocative paintings or photos. Really focus on creating a special, sensual, and freeing environment for your self-loving ritual. Doing so will make you feel special, sensual, and free.

You can even use your lingerie to add a touch of sass to the interior design of your Aphrodite-like bower. Hang a see-through negligee over the bedpost. Dangle a lacy garter belt from the knob of your dresser. Let several long strings of pearls cascade from one corner of a mirror, and float a silky teddy from the other. Drape lace-topped stockings over a chair. Adorn your pillow with a feather boa and your bedside lamp with a filmy scarf. Display your long satin gloves on the nightstand. Dressing your boudoir in lingerie and jewels will transform it into a sensual palace that beckons your Inner Sex Goddess to appear in its midst—*and* will be a real turn on to your lover.

the breasts beautiful

Aphrodite, like any clever Sex Goddess, certainly knew how to make the most of her feminine assets. So she is depicted, in many statues and paintings, winsomely exposing two of a woman's most naturally glorious and seductive attributes, her breasts. Wildly arousing to most red-blooded men and exquisitely sensitive to your own or a lover's touch, your golden orbs provide a softly feminine place to begin your erotic self-arousal, especially since there is a direct nerve connection between the nipples and the clitoris. Although the intensity of breast and nipple sensation is different for each individual Sex Goddess, Masters and Johnson, the definitive scientific sex researchers, found that about 1 percent of the women they studied were actually capable of going all the way to orgasm simply by caressing their own breasts. But even for the rest of us, breast and nipple massage can provide some highly erotic sensations, and it will usually start your libido sizzling and your divine vaginal nectars flowing.

35. Begin by using the feathery touch of your nails or fingertips to stroke the delicate skin on the side of your torso and under your arms. Slide your fingers down across your stomach and make circles all over your belly and midsection as you raise your hands, and your temperature, up to your swelling breasts. Repeat several times and let yourself float on the hypnotically languorous sensations.

36. Slide your palm in circular motions around the whole area of your breast. Press firmly. Do one breast at a time or use both hands for the two together. Keep this up even after your nipple has become erect. Go faster, slower, harder. Cup as much of each creamy globe in your hand as possible and move them both around. Pull them out. Press them in. Jiggle them. Squeeze them. Imagine that your lover is caressing them. Continue until your breasts feel very warm and tingly.

$37.$ One day, as I leaned over the side of the bed to retrieve the bottle of massage oil I had dropped, I discovered that my breasts felt more sensitive when they were hanging down. I later learned that this is because of increased blood supply to the nipples. So by all means try this leaning-over position. Besides feeling lushly full and tender, your breasts are freer to move as well. Shake them. Give them love taps. Push them together. Massage as in number 36.

$38.$ Massage your nipples. Press on them. Roll them gently between your fingers. Use firmer and firmer pressure. Pinch them. Pull them and hold, or pull and release completely in very rapid strokes. My friend Carrie, a computer specialist with no current lover but plenty of libido, says she likes to hold on to her nipples and shake her breasts with them. Try this for the intensity of the feelings and the visually exciting stimulation.

$39.$ Use one hand to encircle your breast and push it up and out, as a push-up bra would do. This pulls the nipple taut. With your other hand, roll, pinch, and pull the nipple. Wet your fingers and play with it. Rub your fingers back and forth rapidly. Use the pad of your index finger to rotate your nipple in small circles. Flick your fingers or fingernails across each bright berry. Know that your man would be fascinated to watch these maneuvers. Keep all of this up way past the point at which you feel the urge to move to your pubic area.

40. In one very elegant sex movie, I watched with fascination as a woman licked her own nipples. Even though she was rather small-breasted, she was able to accomplish this delightful trick by bringing her breast close to her mouth with her hand, bending her neck down, and using the *bottom* of her tongue to reach the nipple. Close your eyes and feel the lapping of your lover's tongue.

41. Rub your breasts and nipples with silk, velvet, fur, feathers, and even rougher textures like wool, terry cloth, or a very soft brush.

42. Write your partner's name or some sizzling words of love across your chest with your fingertips, spray-on perfume, or hot red lipstick. Use your nipples to dot the *i*'s or make lovely curlicues on appropriate letters.

43. Pull on long, tight leather gloves and play with your breasts and nipples.

44. One friend of mine suggests circling the nipples with an ice cube. She says, "It makes my nipples stand up immediately and feel all wet and fiery." Her husband often requests the pleasure of watching her do this, and he usu-

ally jumps right in to lick the watery drips from her up-
turned buds. Apparently it makes him "feel all wet and
fiery" too.

45. Dab whipped cream or honey on your nipples, or
dip them in wine. Lick it off—or let *him* lick it off.

46. Massage your nipples with Vicks VapoRub, Ben-
Gay, or some other cream that makes your body heat rise.

47. One day I got the idea from an old photograph of
a French courtesan to apply rouge to my nipples. While
this is a makeup trick you'll want to secretly expose to your
lover, try it on your own, too, and see how ripe and enticing your nipples will look. Let the color come off as you
massage your pretty rosebuds. Reapply as desired.

48. One bawdy corporate comptroller I know told
me that she likes to put her accounting pencils to better use
in the privacy of her own boudoir. Pinching her nipples
taut, she rubs the rounded pencil erasers, softened from
use on her daytime ledgers, against her sensitized areolae.

49. Put on a pretty bra or swimsuit top, but pull the
material away so that your nipples and most of your
breasts are exposed. Fondle your velvet tips. Now pull the
supporting bottom part of the bra up over your breasts so

that it rests above the breasts and pushes them down. Again, this puts more pressure into the nipple and sensitizes it. Massage, pull, and pinch your nipples. You can, of course, dress up in any sexy lingerie—camisole, teddy, merry widow, bra with the nipples cut out—and do the same thing. There's no reason you shouldn't look just as gorgeous for yourself as you do for your lover, and besides, your breasts will be sensitized by the extra exquisite pressure. As one young nursing student I know says, "The cool silk and low-cut lace bodice of my favorite camisole do wonderful things with my nipples, especially when I wear it under my uniform."

50. Adorn your fingers with rings before you begin your breast play. Depending on the rings, you may want to turn them around so the showy parts are on the insides of your fingers. They look great, and you can tease your nipples with their different textures as you massage.

51. Use a vibrator on your nipples. Put on one of the ridged or pronged attachments and hold it steady or move it back and forth across the areolae. Circular motions are good, too. My friend Brigitta, a pale Nordic beauty in a still-lusty twenty-year marriage, says she prefers to use a Swedish massager that fits on the back of her hand. She straps it on and lets her vibrating hand and fingers loose on her sensitive breast skin. Sometimes she shares the deli-

cious vibes with her man. (More on vibrators in Chapters 9 and 10.)

52. Get in the bathtub and use your shower massager to wash your nipples with sensation. This is a favorite with several friends of mine, who say it reminds them of being nubile young girls in the shower after gym class, giggling over all the exciting new sensations they were just discovering then. It makes me feel like a Polynesian beauty, standing naked in a steamy tropical waterfall. Discover your own liquid fantasy.

53. Watch yourself in a mirror as you do any or all of the above. Marvel at the hypnotic beauty of your golden orbs, radiating like the Aphrodite within you—to please your own aesthetic senses or titillate your favorite man.

aphrodite's private foreplay

As the Goddess of Love, Aphrodite knew instinctively that the flower of her desire lay resting lightly in her clitoral rosebud and that it had to be treated with the utmost delicacy in order to blossom to its full beauty. While no two buds of love are exactly the same, we modern-day Aphrodites know from all-too-frequent experience that most don't like to be attacked by a too-eager hand. They like to be slowly warmed up first. Hence, your Inner Sex Goddess has gifted you with the instinctive skill of your own brand of private foreplay for the clitoris. Use it for solo as well as partner sex.

While your breast play will already have begun to unfold the petals of your clitoral sensitivity, it's still a good idea to go gently and slowly when approaching direct stimulation of this sensitive area. In fact, some women never touch the glans of their clitoris directly when self-pleasuring; it's just too tender. Instead, they concentrate on the pubic mound. And even though most women do require at least some direct stimulation of the clitoris to have an orgasm, it's still best to start by stimulating the surrounding areas.

54. You might want to begin by stroking your inner thighs and buttocks. Remember to be present in your body, as we learned to do in the body-consciousness exercises in Chapter 2. Really feel all of the luscious sensations you are creating. As you reach the genital area, use a finger or two to gently massage around your anus. (Make sure you are freshly bathed.) Softly rub the perineum (between anus and vulva) with back-and-forth or circular motions.

Give it a few gentle love taps. Concentrate on building a fire in this lower portion of your genitals.

55. Most women enjoy the comforting feeling of cupping their entire pubic mound in one hand. Press and massage gently in circles, from side to side, or back and forth. Knead it like bread. Shake it gently. Recall the feeling of your man's pelvis pumping against this fleshy mound.

56. Still holding your pubis tenderly like a ripe fruit, press your outer vaginal lips together. Then caress them gently up and down so that they begin to open up and expose the moist inner lips. Continue this up-and-down motion, occasionally reaching farther down to include your perineum in one long sensuous stroke over it and your inner lips.

57. You may find it intoxicating to pay some special attention to your delicate perineum. Try sitting with feet flat, knees bent, and legs spread. Rotate your pelvis forward so you can reach it easily. With the touch of a butterfly's wings, caress your inner thighs and allow your fingers to cross over your perineum. Tease this dainty area with your fingernails and inscribe wings, flowers, and stars there. Brush it lightly with a feather or cosmetic brush. Wet your finger and make maddeningly delicious circles. Imagine how provocative this would look to a Peeping Tom.

58. My friend Jenny, a shy librarian with a hot lover who is cleverly disguised as an ordinary mailman, says that when self-pleasuring she loves to vibrate her pubic mound with her whole hand. She suggests laying one finger on each vaginal lip and vibrating them, too. You can use your other hand to vibrate your perineum and/or anus simultaneously if you choose. Jenny admits that she has taught this trick to her favorite mail carrier too.

59. According to Oriental erotic texts, a woman's upper lip is directly connected to her clitoris. While massaging your pubis or vaginal lips, try biting your upper lip, or run the fingernails of your other hand over it, to send tingly signals to the rosebud you're about to touch.

60. If the upper lip connection is not a powerful one for you, try moistening your lips with Vaseline or a lovely supermoist lip gel. Lightly rub your fingers over your glistening lips. Slip a finger between them.

61. Recline languorously on a pillow and let your legs fall open. Rest the palm of your hand on your pubic area but without touching your clitoris. Exerting a firm but light pressure, use your hand to move the skin of your pubis around in slow circles over the underlying tissue and bone. Occasionally release your hand and lightly pat your beautiful mound of pleasure. Alternate light patting with

deep circling until moans escape your lips. After observing their women get all hot and bothered by doing this, men seem to feel especially clever when they "invent" this foreplay technique to use on you themselves. So be sure to let your lover catch you at it.

62. While holding your vaginal area, move your hips around in circles. Undulate like a snake. Or do some pelvic thrusts à la Elvis. Keep your hand loose enough so that your pelvic motions cause it to slide lightly around your moving mound. I have a very modest friend who claims that pretending she's a rock star and flagrantly thrusting her hips around frees her wilder, lustier self to come out of hiding. So, with her hand suggestively placed over her naked sex, this is how she begins every self-pleasuring session. When you try this, you may want to imagine that you are getting private lessons in hip swiveling from the King himself.

the ripe rosebud

The lovely little organ whose only function is to give pleasure originally got its name from Aphrodite's compatriots, the ancient Greeks. Wise in the ways of both loving and philosophy, they understood that this tiny knob was the key to a woman's orgasmic pleasure. So from their word for "key," *kleis*, they coined the term *kleitoris*. Just as every door key is different from all others, every woman's clitoris looks and behaves differently and has highly individual preferences for stimulation. These preferences can range from no direct touch at all to indirect pressure with only the palm of the hand to intense and deep finger massage directly on the glans. So there is no "right" way to pleasure your ripe rosebud. There is only the way that feels good, comfortable, and sensuous to you. And that may change from day to day or from month to month, depending on your emotional state, your physical condition, and your monthly cycle. So consult your Inner Sex Goddess and be adventurous yet sensitive to the responses of your own body. Here are some suggestions to try out as you take the time to deepen the sensual bond between you and your own pleasure organ.

63. Lubrication is not only the key to a good relationship with your clitoris, but it also extends the sensations over larger parts of your vaginal area. So before you caress this delicate bud directly, make sure your fingers are moistened with your own saliva, the juices from your vagina, K-Y jelly, or oil. You can use baby oil, coconut oil, vegetable oil, or a good massage oil. Olive oil is probably a little too thick, but sunflower, safflower, and grapeseed are good choices. Scented massage oils add another dimension

of sensuality; the flower essences, musk, and ylang-ylang are particularly potent for sexual play. Just make sure the oil you use contains no alcohol, which can irritate the delicate mucous membranes. And avoid Vaseline too; because it's not water soluble it can be uncomfortable and unhealthy if it gets in your vagina or urethra.

Experiment with different lubes for different occasions. Your own juices are always available, completely natural, and very earthy and sexy. Oils, which are slipperier, are good for intense friction and hand gliding. Scented oils add luscious aromatic vapors and can catalyze some exotic fantasies. The choice is deliciously yours.

64. You may want to begin by using your entire hand—heel, palm, and fingers closed together. Cup your hand over your pubic mound, touching your clitoris lightly, and inscribe circles around and over it. Press with the palm or heel of your hand. Then try using your overhanging fingers. Keep the circular motions going as you explore the sensations arising from varying pressures and parts of the hand. Most women find that sustained repetitive movements are the most satisfying. Also lovely is imagining that your lover's hand or penis is caressing you tenderly there.

65. Karol, a sexy secretary I know, says she likes to rub her clitoris indirectly through its shaft. You can stroke

on the right side if you are right-handed and on the left if you are left-handed. Switch sides when you feel the urge; this technique can provide an entirely different sensation, and it can renew sensitivity when one side gets "tired."

66. Experiment with various kinds of touch and rhythms—light feathery pats, gentle massage, firm steady pressure, intense rubbing, playful love slaps, fast circles, slow back-and-forth movements, languid strokes alternating with quick taps, rolling motions, pinches, vibrating with your hands or fingers. When you find a touch that really lights your fire that day, stay with it for a while. As you explore your own key rhythms and touches, sense the wetness seeping into your loins.

67. If you can stand it, try massaging your rosebud firmly with just one finger. Play around with circling, side-to-side, and rolling motions. Create a vibrating motion with your finger as you press down hard. Rock your pelvis up to meet your trembling digit as you would to reach for a lover's touch. Add another finger and probe some more. If the pleasure gets too agonizingly intense, stop momentarily and massage your thighs or belly instead.

68. Like my friend Bess, a forty-something banker, you might like to try taking hold of the shaft of your clitoris with thumb and forefinger. Roll it between the fingers.

Pull on it. Move it up and down. Squeeze. Release. Roll it again. Try using two different fingers, or the fingers of your two hands. Bess says, "I need a lot of stimulation, and somehow this direct, forceful handling really gets my body humming."

69. Contract your PC muscles rhythmically while caressing your clitoris. Squeeze and release the muscles around your anus. These tightening movements heighten the sensitivity of your clitoral nerves. Let your contractions roll back and forth between the two areas as you continue rubbing your love button. Test varying rhythms. Do it to rock music.

70. I always wondered why the women in X-rated movies frequently use both hands to stretch their outer lips wide before provocatively stroking themselves. Often we think that their immodest actions are meant only to provide better sight lines or are done purely for the benefit of some debauched man. But I've found that, as usual, women are much smarter than that. After all, men don't invent these unusual and creative moves. Women do. Because, yes, they drive men crazy, but more important, they feel great. Through personal experimentation, I've learned that spreading your love lips open the way these women do makes the sensitive skin of your clitoris feel deliciously exposed and taut. Try it yourself, and then stimulate your

lovely pleasure organ any way you choose. Imagine that *you* are a raunchy porn star — and your man is salivating over every frame of the movie.

71. A luscious thing to do while gloriously outspread is to thump your clitoris lightly and quickly with your middle finger or the side of your hand. (Wouldn't a slap from your lover's penis be lovely too!) Alternate with hard circular massaging.

72. Sara, a dietitian with six kids, says that whenever she can steal a moment to herself, one of her favorite techniques is to stroke down toward her clit from the top of her pubic mound, not quite touching its surface or sometimes gliding lightly over the top of it. Adapting a technique she learned from her deliciously randy husband, she occasionally slides her fingers down farther to gather some juice from her vagina and then circles her wet fingertips around her sensitized bud. Try it. You'll like it too.

73. You can learn a lot from watching a man play with himself. Because the clitoris is closely akin to the penis, you can adapt almost any male masturbation method to the caressing of your love bud. For instance, try holding and stroking your clitoris up and down as he would his penis. Or slide from bottom to tip with the fingers of one hand, and then switch to the other hand. Do

this quickly and with upstrokes only. Improvise with anything that works for him.

74. While caressing your clitoris, squeeze or rub your vaginal lips. Using only one hand will keep the rhythms and movements in concert, but you could also try using two hands to circle clockwise with one while the other moves counterclockwise. Or one hand could administer gentle blows while the other presses and massages deeply.

75. Pull gently on your pubic hair while teasing your clitoris. For me, this always brings back arousing memories of a wonderful man who loved to reach around in front of me and hold my pubic hair while he rubbed his penis against my clitoris from behind.

76. Tug on a nipple in rhythm with your clitoral strokes. Roll both between your fingers. Massage in tandem circles as your legs fall invitingly open for an imaginary lover.

77. In one sex class I attended, the instructor asserted that "any good clitoral massage should include the urethra which is actually part of the G-spot and is therefore highly sensitive to erotic pleasuring." At the next class most of the women, including me, excitedly attested to the

truth of this theory. In the name of scientific research, test it out for yourself.

78. Tickle the underside of your love bud with one finger while stroking, patting, rubbing, or flicking the side or top of the clitoral hood with another. This intensely erotic trick can make you climb the walls, so apply it judiciously.

79. As you lovingly stroke your clitoris, be aware of how the sensations change. At the beginning it will be tender and want a light touch. But as your excitement grows and you get closer to orgasm, your rosebud will swell and become harder and stiffer, much as a man's penis does. At this point, press harder, circle or stroke faster, vibrate more intensely. Thrust your pelvis against your hand. Arch your back and pant, moan, or scream.

80. My friend Rosie reminds me of a plum—small, round, and sweet, but tart at the same time. Very frank about the fact that she's been self-pleasuring regularly since the age of five, she says, "I love to massage my soft spot [the perineum, between the vagina and anus] with the fingertips of both hands. Then I smooth my fingers up between my vaginal lips, collecting some wetness so my fingers can slide more easily, then I let them slide over my clit, down outside the outer lips, and back to my soft spot. Each

time I reach my clit, I give it a little extra push, squeeze, or roll. After about three minutes of this, I'm really shaking. But then I circle my clit and soft spot with both hands at the same time, which makes me feel unbearably sexy, until I have an orgasm that vibrates my whole body."

81. While you rub your pleasure organ, try bearing down as you do when you have a bowel movement. This pushes the entire pelvic floor down and brings more pressure into the clitoris, making it exquisitely sensitive and trembly. Many women report that this action alone can bring on an orgasm very quickly.

82. Don some of your laciest, sexiest panties and massage your clitoris through them. Pull the two sides together at the crotch so that you have a thin, taut ribbon of fabric to pull against your pulsing love bud. Since this is as exciting to feel as it is to watch in the mirror, keep it in mind for a visual turn-on when you're in bed with your man.

83. A technique I modified from an Oriental love text is really meant for pleasuring a man's "Jade Stalk." But there's no reason your "Rosy Stem" shouldn't enjoy it too. Hold your little stem between your fingers and stroke it in rhythm to the throbbing of your heart. Then give it one fast up-and-down stroke, and return to the slow, sensuous

stroking for about ten seconds. Then two rapid up-and-down strokes and back to the slow stuff for another ten seconds. Increase to three fast, and back to slow, and so on.

84. After your love button has become engorged with excitement, try holding it between your fingers while you use the palm of your other hand, or your flattened fingers, to massage lightly in circles over the tip. Fantasize, if you wish, that it's really the pulsing head of your man's penis that's rubbing you there.

the voluptuous vagina

Aphrodite wasn't the only one who was hip to the benefits of loving her own body. Since ancient times, Taoist medical practitioners and Tantric initiates have taught that to have a whole and healthy body and mind, you must fully love your genitals and the sexual energy harbored there. When you come to know and love your vagina as the mysterious cavelike home of the sacred life force, you will find yourself developing a new, more charismatic relationship with your femininity, your sexuality, and your man.

While some women prefer to explore the voluptuousness of their vaginas first before moving on to the clitoris —

feeling that the dainty bud is just too sensitive in the beginning—others feel that starting with clitoral massage warms
up the vagina's fewer nerve endings so that it becomes
more eager for erotic touch. But whatever your personal
preference, it's delicious to pleasure both erogenous zones
at the same time. You can practice the following techniques while you are massaging your pearly bud or try
them all by themselves. Mix and match to your libido's
content.

85. Stroke and massage all around your vaginal
opening. Run your finger up and down over the juicy slit,
gently opening it wider and wider. Pull the lips apart and
caress the moist skin just inside the opening. Many women
find that the wider their vaginal opening is stretched, the
more acute the sensations. Relish this feeling of vulnerable
exposure.

86. Dip one or two fingers into your voluptuously
wet furrow. In addition to keeping your fingers lubricated
for clitoral stroking, this adds another level of sensation.
(Short fingernails are a prerequisite.) Press upward to feel
the back of your clitoral membrane and explore its moist
sensitivities from this other side. If you curl your hand, you
can keep the knuckles of your free fingers pressed against
the outside of your clitoris at the same time.

87. Slide one or more fingers in and out of your vagina just as you like your lover's penis to do. Slant your hand and sweep your fingers around to feel the luscious friction from all angles and against all surfaces of your vaginal canal. Stretch your lips wide. Go fast. Go slow. Tease yourself unmercifully.

88. A very sultry woman I know says she likes to insert just one finger about two inches deep. Then she crooks her finger and tickles first the upper and then the lower walls of her vaginal barrel. It's "exquisite torture," says she.

89. While performing 87 and 88, use the thumb of the same hand to rub your clitoris or pull on your inner lips. This is much like the tug of your lover's penis as it dips in and out between all those sensitive tissues.

90. Adapting a cooking technique for stuffing chickens, I discovered that it feels heavenly to slip your thumb inside your vagina and then glide it in circular motions against your other fingers, massaging the thin, wet membrane of your vaginal wall between them. Try out your own inner recipe.

91. When your vaginal tissues are engorged with sexual juices and excitement, their sensitivity to touch and

pressure is magnified. One inch of thumb can feel like nine inches of a man. So if you simply anchor your thumb tip inside and press it down toward your spine, you can mobilize your fingers to simultaneously tease your clitoris with circular massage or up-and-down sweeps.

92. Plunge into the depths of your coral abyss with two or three fingers and rotate them as if you were stirring up a scrumptious batter. Or spread your fingers out like a scissors, as far apart as you can. Open and release several times.

93. Adorn your index finger with a big flashy ring and thrust it in and out of your steamy vagina. The X-rated movie stars who love to perform this act for the camera know that it adds elegant beauty to the scene and feels fantastic, too. Show this one to your lover.

94. Experiment with different body positions. Kneel, lie on your stomach, stand in front of a mirror. Or try lying on your back with feet braced against the headboard or wall. This, and kneeling with your legs spread, tenses the pelvic muscles and pulls your vagina taut to heighten sensation.

95. When her husband is away, my friend Karen says she uses one of those standing pillows with arm rests

as a substitute. She snuggles into its "embrace" or props herself against her stand-in hubby's open "legs" while she diddles herself just the way he would.

96. With the flat of your hand, try stretching the soft skin of your pubic mound upward toward your belly. Hold it taut while you slide the fingers of your other hand quickly in and out of your tightened opening. Conjure up your favorite fantasy.

97. Spread open your outer lips and use your thumb to gently strum the inner ones. Play this tune for your man and his drum major's baton.

98. My friend Gail, a brilliant graphic artist with fiery red hair and tons of freckles and boyfriends, graciously offered to share one of her favorite maneuvers. She says she loves to insert two fingers into her vagina and press her clitoris with two fingers of the other hand. Then she rubs the two sets of fingers together through all the sensitive skin between. I've found you can also do this with only one hand by inserting your middle finger and using your thumb for the clitoris. What a divine massage!

99. Hold open your vaginal lips with the fingertips of both hands. Knead the flower-petal skin in circular motions, down toward the anus, around toward the inner

thighs, and up toward the clitoris. Keep going around and around till you can't stand it anymore.

100. When a Hawaiian friend of mine mentioned that she likes to go "swimming with the dolphins" when she pleasures herself, I couldn't wait to hear the details. She says she lays her hand flat against the entire vaginal area. Then she lets the tip of her middle finger tease her vaginal opening and occasionally slide in and out. She alternates pressing hard against the top and undersides of her pubic mound with the heel and ball of her palm. Then she rolls and undulates her whole hand in wavelike movements, the way dolphins swim. Or you can let your middle finger lie against your clitoris with the fingertip just inside your vagina; then circle, roll, and undulate your hand like a sinuous creature of the deep.

101. While thrusting your fingers in and out like a lover's hard shaft, massage your inner thighs, belly, derriere, or nipples with your other hand. All of these sensitive tissues are erotically connected and will respond quite intensely to tender caresses at any location. You rarely get to experience these delightful combinations with a partner because it's just too awkward; so take the opportunity to treat yourself to this extra loving.

the love muscle

The PC muscle, the one you squeeze to stop the flow of urine, is one of the greatest love secrets in Aphrodite's body. Just by twitching it, any ordinary goddess can give and receive ambrosial delights worthy of the heights of Mount Olympus. A well-toned PC muscle will greatly enhance your pleasure during self-loving as well as while making love with a partner, and it will drive most men wild when flexed against their penis. When strong and healthy, this muscle is highly sensitive to vaginal stimulation and is actually able to bring his thrusting penis closer to your G-spot. It makes for increased lubrication, stronger clitoral sensations, more intense and more frequent climaxes, and even multiple orgasms. How does all this magic take place?

Lying about one inch below the surface of the skin, the PC muscle runs from the pubic bone to the tailbone, firmly supporting the anus and internal sex organs. It may be as thin as half an inch or as thick as two inches. In addition to cradling your organs of pleasure, the love muscle is also home to the pudendal nerve, which detects feeling around the clitoris, the vaginal lips and opening, and the anus. This nerve sends signals to the brain that say "This feels good; send blood and energy here," and it later receives brain signals that start the pleasurable contractions of orgasm. After every contraction of your PC muscle, whether you flex it deliberately or an orgasm does it for you, blood rushes into the vagina, making the tissue swell and darken and increasing lubrication. Some women describe this sensation as a melting or "I love you" feeling. In fact, besides the actual nerve connections between the PC muscle and the brain, there seems to be some extrasensory bond between the love muscle and the heart that, when activated, makes you feel soft, fuzzy, and warm inside.

The miraculous abilities and pleasures of a well-trained PC muscle are extolled in the ancient love texts of the Oriental and Tantric traditions, too. They describe women with such a high degree of PC control that they were able to pick up small objects and thrust them out with great force, using only their vaginal muscles. Imagine what they could have done with a man's penis! But the real beauty of such dexterity is that they were able to provide their own intense vaginal and clitoral stimulation — without a penis, dildo, vibrator, pillow, hand, or finger. Their agile vaginas were completely self-contained pleasure units. We too can share in this special female magic simply by exercising our PC muscles regularly. And you will find that these sexual calisthenics are a major turn-on in and of themselves.

102. The fastest and easiest way to get started enjoying your PC muscle is to simply flex it quickly about twenty-five times—anytime, anywhere; no one will know. The sensation will be more intense if you put your attention on your clitoris or vaginal opening while you are squeezing. This will strongly focus your awareness, energy, and excitement. In fact, some women say they can reach a climax from this exercise alone. At the very least, it will bring your Inner Sex Goddess immediately to attention.

103. When your muscles have something to resist their squeezing pressure, they can develop even faster, and you can get a better idea of just how strongly you are flexing. Insert a finger, a clean carrot, or a dildo into your vagina, squeeze and hold it for five seconds. Release and squeeze again. After several of these, do some quick clenches. Swoosh the inserted object around to provide differing levels of pressure and to excite your PC muscle into more intense flexing. See what it feels like to push the muscles *out* as well; you can accomplish this by pressing down as you do when you have a bowel movement. If you close your eyes and focus on your moist vaginal walls sliding against the object, you will find a warm, pleasurable sensation building up inside you. Let your libido and your Inner Sex Goddess take it from there.

104. Here's a Tantric PC exercise that always makes me feel like a volcano boiling, oozing, and erupting. You may want to perform this one to music, as I do. Stand with your feet apart at shoulder width and begin slowly squeezing your PC muscle. Breathe in deeply with each squeeze, and exhale with each release. Feel the volcanic heat coming up the insides of your thighs and into your womb. Keeping your feet firmly planted, rock your hips back and forth sensuously—rock forward as you inhale and squeeze, rock back as you exhale and release. Feel the heat building in your loins. After a bit, move your hips around in circles as you continue flexing and releasing. Imagine that you are a hula dancer or a belly dancer; sway your pelvis provocatively and perform expertly sexual internal dances. Feel the volcanic heat radiating from your pelvis as you release a low "ahhh" with each exhalation and PC relaxation. As you continue undulating your hips and flexing your love muscle, imagine that the hot energy you are generating rises up through your belly, breast, throat, and face to the top of your head, where it showers you with tingly liquid ecstasy. Slowly return to earth whenever you're ready.

105. The ancient Chinese Taoists developed a complex set of stone egg exercises designed to strengthen and tone the vaginal muscles. For a time, these exercises were taught only to the Empress and the Emperor's concubines in the royal palace, supposedly so they could better please the Emperor. And I'm sure they did. But these wise women knew that they were secretly enjoying themselves, enhancing their health, and even prolonging their youth. If, like these multitalented royal ladies, you'd like to increase your sexual energy and expertise, here's a simplified version of the egg techniques.

Select a stone or a wooden egg about one inch in diameter from a gem store or a New Age shop. Keep it scrupulously clean with soap and water. Always perform the egg exercises while standing, feet apart at shoulder width, and warm yourself up first with some self-massage. Insert the egg into your vagina, large end first, using your own juices or some oil to lubricate it. Hold the egg inside you by clenching the muscles at the opening of your vagina. When you first start practicing, simply feel your internal muscles contracting against the smooth egg. Get used to holding it inside you and feeling how it moves.

As you become more expert, you can move on to more advanced techniques such as the following. Inhale as you squeeze the muscles at the other end of your vagina, deep inside. Then begin to move the egg up and down, and from side to side, with the muscles in the middle section of your vagina. This takes practice and dexterity, but the sense of passionate control you will experience is worth the effort. Even if you just learn to keep the egg snug inside, you can't help but revel in its smooth sensuality and the delicious feeling of fullness it provides. Try different size eggs, too—bigger egg, more fullness; smaller egg, more exercise and control. Eventually you can train your vaginal muscles to draw the egg in all by themselves and expel it forcefully. Your vaginal expertise, whether applied to an egg, a finger, or a penis, is limited only by your imagination.

the bewitching behind

Aphrodite Kallipygos (Aphrodite of the Lovely Backside) captivated scores of lovers simply by undraping her fleshy fanny. She truly understood that a woman's behind has the power to ignite her own inner fires as well as to bewitch almost any man. You'll begin to understand the fanny's electric power if you use your erotic imagination to recall how delicious it feels when you rub yours up against your man's body while lying in the spoon position, or when he cups your luscious cheeks in his hands as you make love. I didn't really catch on to this myself until about the twentieth time my lover, plunging into me from behind, moaned in the throes of ecstasy, "Your ass looks so fine when it quivers, and it feels so good bouncing up against me." Meanwhile I actually *was* quivering, with even more intense pleasure than he! So complete the awakening of your Aphrodite's body by discovering, with your own gentle hands and fingers, the unexpected pleasures of derriere and anal massage, a sensual treat fit for a goddess.

106. While you are pleasuring your vagina or your clitoris, smooth your hands over the silky curves of your behind. Use feathery fingertips or firm palm pressure; squeeze gently or hard; scrape your nails across the delicate skin; it's especially sensitive because it is rarely exposed to sun and air. Rub the rough lace or cool silk of a camisole against your fanny. Don your elbow-length gloves or furry mittens and massage your rounded curves and the deep valley between them. Experiment with wet hands, ringed fingers, naked knuckles, and rolling forearms. Have fun with feathers.

107. Diane, an otherwise very buttoned-down attorney friend of mine, says she likes to rub her behind against the cool sheets of her bed the whole time she is pleasuring herself in other ways. Sometimes she places a pillow between derriere and bed to add a new sensation and a higher elevation. Or she lays her backside against the rough wool of the blanket and undulates with the motions of her vaginal self-play. Occasionally she even stands with her back against the wall—she has textured wallpaper, but even smooth paint will do—and slides up and down while she uses her hands to caress the front of her body. She loves to find different textures to stimulate her bottom during self-play and often sits in various locations to produce interesting new effects—smooth, hard wooden chairs; rocking chairs; plump velvet couches; canvas deck chairs; rope hammocks; fabric-covered office chairs that roll around; desks; kitchen countertops; toilet seats; bathtubs, dry or with a thin layer of water; rugs and carpets; stairs; grass; sand; the rough bark of a tree limb; a swing; a large basket—the possibilities are truly limitless.

108. The anus is one of the most erotically sensitive spots on your body, and if you are freshly bathed, it's just as clean as the rest of you. So don't be squeamish about discovering its pleasures. Just remember that the secret to enjoying anal play is lubrication—either your own saliva or a good massage oil. Start out by simply wetting your index finger and pressing or massaging all around and over the outside of the opening. Keep your mind and body focused on the erotic by simultaneously massaging your nipples, clitoris, or vagina. As you enjoy these luscious sensations, let yourself relax and feel good about this often outcast part of your body. Indulge in ecstatic sense memories of your lover's tickling caresses to your behind. Breathe deeply and consciously relax your sphincter muscles. Then gently and slowly work your finger inside your anus and keep massaging. Circular or come-hither motions are best at first; save the in-and-out movements for later when you're more accustomed to the feeling and more

relaxed. Discover your personal internal hot spots by trying different pressures, motions, and locations. Many
women find an especially delicious place to rub is on the
vagina side of the anal canal, which is really the other side
of the magical G-spot. In fact, this is how many otherwise
nonorgasmic women finally achieve a shuddering climax.
But even as a simple accompaniment to the main melody of
clitoral or vaginal self-pleasuring, anal massage is a delight
you won't want to miss.

109. An especially deep and earthy feeling of ecstasy can be achieved by massaging—from both sides—
that thin, silken spot that lies inside between the vaginal
and anal canals. You can do this by inserting the finger of
one hand in the vulva and the finger of the other hand into
the anus, then rubbing them together. It's probably easiest
to accomplish this while lying on your back with legs
drawn up to your chest. One inventive friend of mine says
she likes to leave a hand free for breast or clitoral massage
at the same time. So she simply uses her thumb inside the
vagina and slides the pinky of the same hand into her anal
opening, bringing thumb and pinky together around the
delicate internal tissues. Considering the possibilities for
variation here, discovering your own style of anal play—
and later revealing them to your panting lover—can be at
least half the fun.

Woman is the creator of the universe, the universe is her form. . . . Whatever form she takes, whether the form of a man or a woman, is the superior form. In woman is the form of all things, of all that lives and moves in the world. There is no jewel rarer than woman, no condition superior to that of a woman.

—Saktisangama Tantra

5

the mirror of sensual transfor-mation

Priestesses of the Tantric tradition, sometimes called yoginis, took great pride in the firepower of their bodies and sexuality to burn up obsolete ideas and beliefs, transforming them into jewels of expanded sensual perception and wisdom. Intimately familiar with the physical and esoteric function of every part of their bodies, they deliberately adopted certain postures and palpated special body points that enhanced their sensual energy flow. They had the ability to see the true nature of their resplendent physical forms reflected in a quiet pool, a looking glass, or a lover's eyes.

By looking into the yogini's Mirror of Sensual Transformation and seeing yourself as a magnificent creature made for love, you too will be able to shed worn-out ideas about puffy tummies and sagging chins, throw radiant light on heretofore hidden and mysterious places, and come to truly understand that "in woman is the form of all things." If you approach this anatomical exploration as an exhilarating journey of rediscovery, you will no doubt have provocative revelations about yourself and your sexuality—revelations that will make you an unusually creative bed partner. In fact, sensuality experts as diverse as ancient Tantrics and modern-day sex therapists *require* expertise in this kind of self-pleasuring investigation before moving on to any other kind of sexual teachings. It's an eye-opening fount of knowledge and an autoerotic turn-on. So grab your Inner Sex Goddess, light a few candles, and make a special ritual out of discovering the divine firepower of your own sumptuous body.

110. Set up a full-length mirror and a good-sized hand mirror in a private, quiet room. Lock the door and make sure you will have at least an hour and a half completely to yourself. Then start out by creating a soft sensual mood—after all, you are about to seduce the sacred inner you. Take a scented bath. Light some candles and incense. Put on sultry music. Fix your hair in a pretty style and dab on some musky perfume or body lotion. Don your sexiest lingerie and pose before the mirror, proudly erect with hands on hips, as the yoginis do, or reclining provocatively like the centerfold models in *Playboy* magazine. Then seductively strip down to complete nakedness, or perhaps leave on a string of pearls or a thin chain around your waist, or a flower in your hair. Think of all this as preparation for your lover. Just as Cleopatra's attendants would have readied her for romance with scented milk baths and opulent adornments, so should you carefully prepare for a loving session with yourself. Crawl into the translucent, hot skin of your Inner Sex Goddess and enjoy.

Then sit or stand about ten inches away from the full-length mirror and stare gently into your eyes. Relax, breathe deeply, and imagine your eyes becoming like soft jelly. Look into your soul. The Tantrics recommend eye-gazing like this for about five to ten minutes, longer if you can. Really let yourself trespass on the inner you—sultry, deeply sensual, romantic, tender, and loving.

Begin to explore your body with your hands. Look at yourself from all angles—front, back, side, standing, kneeling, sitting with legs apart and together. Do not criti-cize. If you have to, imagine that you are from another planet where lumpy thighs are considered exquisitely sex-ual. Examine every nook and cranny with the handheld mirror, praising and patting each delicious body part. Many women find that looking at their own bodies this way turns them on. Admire and caress your entire body, except the genitals, for at least forty-five minutes.

Now lovingly examine your pubic area in both the full-length and handheld mirrors. If you have a makeup mirror with a magnifying side, use that, too. Observe the different colors, shapes, and textures. Label each part by touching it gently. Notice first the contour of your upper pubis. Does it slope invitingly down to your vulva, or is it a high, provocative mound? Is your pubic hair a dark, thick bush or more like wispy blond grass? Does it form a trian-gle? a bold band? a small circlet peeping over the edge? How would someone who was mesmerized by it, like an adoring lover, describe this part of you?

As you slide your fingers farther down and along the hair-covered outer lips of your vulva (labia majora), be aware of their spongy or pillowy texture. See if yours are puffy, flat, long, or curved. Would you describe their color as burnt sienna? dusky rose? amorous amber? Regarded by some as the female equivalent of a man's scrotum, these lips contain glands that, when aroused, release a film of sweat that chemically stimulates and attracts the opposite sex. Did you know they were so enticing?

When you stroke your hairless inner lips (labia minora), notice their smooth, moist slickness. They too contain glands that produce lubricating juices. Feel, smell, and even taste these fluids when they arrive. Try to characterize the size, shape, and texture of your inner lips, which vary greatly from woman to woman. Some women have described theirs as having "the feel of satin sheets," "caviar coloring," "edges like a doily," or "the clean lines of a Jaguar racing car." Do yours remind you of a flower? the inside of a peach? folded velvet? a sea creature? a fleshy heart? a yin-yang symbol? Is the left lip bigger or smaller than the right one? Do the inner lips stay tucked demurely inside the outer ones, or do they protrude or droop temptingly? Notice how the texture, moisture, and warmth of both your inner and outer lips change as you excite them, engorging with blood, thickening, and darkening.

Then slide on up to the clitoris, or the Jewel Terrace, as it's lovingly known in the Orient. Slip back the hood of skin that covers it and run your finger along the shaft. Although it is much like a man's penis, the clever little clitoris is unique—no organ whose *sole* function is to stimulate and elevate erotic pleasure exists on a man's body. The most sensitive of your sexual organs, it is often the *key* (remember that's the literal translation of "clitoris" in Greek) to sensual ecstasy. That's because it is crammed full of tender nerve endings, more than any other part of the vulva. Here too are intensely sensitive microscopic fibers called Pacinian corpuscles, jammed even closer together in the tip of the clitoris, making this apex a keenly acute receptor of sharp pleasure—or pain, if too roughly handled. Gently experiment with differing strokes and amounts of pressure on your clitoris, touching it directly—with a wet finger is usually best—and indirectly through the surrounding tissues, up and down the shaft, across the tip, circling the whole area. How does it look and feel as it receives these different types of loving attention?

Usually about 3/4 inch to 1 1/4 inches long, each woman's clitoris will have a size, shape, and character all its own. Some women have described theirs as a "tiny dewdrop," a "tight, pulsing rosebud," or a "big flashy cultured pearl." How would you describe your "love diamond"? In an Aboriginal creation myth, the two Djanggawo sisters had clitorises so long that they formed grooves on the earth as they walked, and the well-endowed sisters had to rest their clitorises on their thighs in order to have access to their vaginas. What is the relationship of your clitoris to the vaginal opening? Is it a mere finger's width away, or more like a wrist's width distant? It may be that women whose clitorises are very near to their vaginas are the ones able to have orgasms through intercourse alone.

As you press and massage your love bud, notice the tiny ridge of tissue that runs underneath. Not just the little pebble you see on the outside, the clitoris is actually a much larger organ that lies partially buried beneath the surface. In actuality, the clitoral system is at least 30 percent larger inside your body than it is on the outside, so you can experience flashes of burning pleasure when it is stimulated from inside your vagina too. The clitoral shaft is composed of two rods of spongy tissue that fill with blood during sexual arousal. (It should be enlarging and becoming more sensitive and "erect" right now as you touch it.) These two rods bend backward and connect with the pelvic bones on either side of the vagina, while another muscular rod extends from the inner part of the shaft, splits in two, and surrounds the vaginal opening. During arousal, these muscles contract and keep blood from leaving the clitoris, helping to keep it enlarged and tugging gently on it as well. Try stroking your vaginal lips as you watch in the mirror what happens when the pressure on these connected tissues sends thrilling messages to your clitoral bud. Imagine that your lover's penis, rubbing anywhere in the vicinity, will do the same.

As you massage your inner lips, notice how your vagina naturally opens to your finger. Approach this portal in a sacred way, as do the people of the Sepik River in New Guinea. They enter and exit their ceremonial houses by crawling between the outspread legs of carved figures of the sacred feminine form. Slip through the entrance of your inner cave to feel the creamy warmth within, and the differences in texture and sensation between all the sides of its elastic walls. Some sexologists assert that the first third of the vagina is more sensitive to touch than the remainder because more nerve endings are located there, and that the deeper two-thirds is more responsive to pressure and stretching. Many women feel differently. Slide your fingers deep inside and see what's true for you.

Feel the power of your PC muscles as you alternately squeeze and push them against your fingers. Watch your muscles contract in the mirror. Imagine how this milking action would feel to a penis. Explore the thick folds of your vaginal walls, some running horizontally and some vertically, and the milky secretions they produce. Feel, smell, and taste this love juice.

Delight in your vagina's miraculous ability to compress or expand to accommodate the smallest tampon, the largest erect penis, and even the birth of a baby. See if you can get your fingers far enough inside to feel the way the upper two-thirds of your vagina opens up like a sultan's tent, and the lower third swells to create a warm, spongy, soft area of tissue that will eventually grip a penis tightly. Experience the particular way your magical inner cave lifts and opens wide as you become more aroused, pulling your vaginal lips apart, sensitizing and flooding them, too, with blood and moisture.

In the Quodoushka tradition, a Cherokee equivalent of Tantra, the depth of the vagina and its characteristics are thought to be important clues to a woman's entire sexual temperament. In Harley Swiftdeer's *Quodoushka Manual*, five female genital anatomy types are described, including Dancing Woman and Sheep Woman. With a vagina of average depth, small inner lips, and a high, small clitoris that springs up from beneath its hood like a dancer, Dancing Woman prefers a lover with a short, thin penis (*tipili*, or "sacred snake"). Sheep Woman, on the other hand, has a deeper vagina, larger, thicker vulval lips, and a lower, more hidden clitoris. She produces copious lubrication and can climax only if she feels a heart connection to her partner. What is the nature of your "feathered flying serpent" (*tupuli*), as the Cherokees call it?

Look in the mirror now to see how gorgeous your vulva appears when excited with love, and how much it has changed since you started this scintillating adventure. Reconsider your vagina not as an unattractive and unknown void but as a divine portal to the most secret parts of the inner you, a doorway to your Inner Sex Goddess, a Vermilion Gate, as the Orientals call it, through which to receive your lover in the most royal fashion. Praise and perfume this wondrous, sacred part of yourself.

Since there are few things more beautiful than a woman aroused, gaze in the mirror now and see how gorgeous your whole body is—how pink your luscious lips have become, how your eyes have dilated and your skin flushed. Admire the way your breasts have swollen and your nipples have become harder and darker, erect with desire. Your clitoris, too, is erect and pulsating. Your vaginal lips may have swollen up to three times their normal size, and they may have darkened to a deep wine or a bright red. Your toes, feet, or stomach muscles may be fluttering or quivering in a high state of turbulent excitation. Notice how your body not only *looks* different but also *smells* and *moves* differently. Take in the whole image of you in full bloom—glorious, sensual, and powerful. Tell your reflection how radiant, delicate, sexy, graceful, glowing, shapely, and devastating you look. Bask in your beauty and thank yourself, your body, and your Inner Sex Goddess for revealing their wonderful secrets to you.

| | |. Finish off this mirrored self-play by continuing to arouse and ravish yourself almost to the point of orgasm—at least three times and maybe up to fifteen times. With each buildup to and retreat from the point of no return, your excitement will reach higher and higher levels. Then finally let yourself climax, watching your orgasm

in the mirror, and float in the dreamy sensations for an eternity.

112. A very saucy friend of mine, who actually appeared in a *Playboy* video of over-forty-and-still-fabulous women, suggests the following alternative way to discover your own body: perform all of the activities in this chapter not in front of a mirror but before a video camera. If you don't own one, you may be surprised to find out how inexpensive they are to rent. Watching your own sexy, self-loving video at a later time can be not only immensely informative but also a titillating turn-on—for you and maybe for a fortunate partner!

> Woman has sex organs
> just about everywhere.
> She experiences pleasure
> almost everywhere.
> —Luce Irigaray, _This
> Sex Which Is Not One_

6

g(oddess)-
spots and
love
nectars

Is there really such a thing as a G-spot? Does every woman have one? Will I be able to pinpoint mine? Can it give me a different type of orgasm? Yes, yes, yes, and *yes!* In fact, the G-spot is one of your Inner Sex Goddess's favorite treasures. She knows where yours is, and she's been eagerly waiting to initiate you and your lover into the hidden ecstasies of its potent orgasms and love nectars.

Although the ancient Romans, Japanese, Chinese, Tantric Indians, and indigenous cultures throughout history were intimately familiar with this special sweet spot inside a woman, modern society seemed to lose touch with its existence until 1950, when a German gynecologist named Ernst Grafenberg researched and wrote about it. His findings caused quite a stir among the medical and scientific crowd, but not too many other people knew about them. Then thirty years later a trio of psychologists and sex therapists expanded Grafenberg's work into a book and decided to name this ancient and utterly female body part after him — the *man* who supposedly discovered it! So it became known as the G-spot, although it does go by other, more accurate and interesting names. One woman I know affectionately calls it her love button. The Federation of Feminist Women's Health Centers refers to it, very clinically, as the urethral sponge. In Panama they speak of this savory spot as *la bella loca*, which literally means "the beautiful crazy." I like to think of it as a woman's goddess spot. Whatever it's called, this lovely hidden site is a pleasuring bonanza.

In fact, many sex researchers believe that learning to have a G-spot climax is an important key to achieving multiple orgasms. That's because after you've had one vaginal or clitoral orgasm, the extreme sensitivity of those areas will make you want to stimulate other less overwrought areas of your genital pleasure zone. Meanwhile, some doctors and psychologists are still haggling over whether women have vaginal orgasms, clitoral orgasms, or some combination of the two, or whether there even *is* a vaginal orgasm. We should do them a favor and clue them in to the fact that women have *all kinds* of orgasms, including clitoral, vaginal, G-spot, and breast! The beauty of the female body is that it's sensitive to orgasmic stimulation all over — and, yes, the G-spot is *especially* sensitive to the erotic touch, and can give you an entirely different type of orgasm than you've ever had before. It may be more subtle and somehow deeper than the ones you're used to, but maybe not; maybe your G-spot orgasms will be more electrifying or tinglier or more wavelike. Your own goddess spot mystery waits there for you to discover.

what and where is the g-spot?

Everyone has a pet theory. According to Grafenberg, the G-spot is an area in the vagina composed of the paraurethral glands and ducts, a complex network of blood vessels, nerve endings, and the tissue surrounding the neck of the bladder. The apparent function of this network is to act as a buffer between your lover's penis and your urethra by swelling and filling with blood during sexual excitement. But many doctors say the G-spot is merely a small cluster of nerve endings and blood vessels, like a little bean deep inside the vagina. And some feminist sex researchers claim it covers a lot more territory—that, in fact, it encompasses the entire complex of tissues around the urethral opening, all the way up the long bladder tube, and all around the vaginal canal.

The somewhat esoteric quality and imprecise location of any given G-spot may account for the fact that some women and their mates believe they don't have one; having been told it has to be located in one specific area, they conclude that a lack of special sensitivity there means the G-spot doesn't exist for them. How unfortunate, especially since, as we've seen, doctors and sex researchers can't even agree on where this one specific spot is! Some say it's about two inches inside the vagina, others say it's above and in back of the pubic bone, and still others say it's much deeper than that, almost at the end of the vaginal canal.

My Inner Sex Goddess and I have our own personal theory. Apparently there are very tender nerve endings associated with the urethra, at the opening and all along the bladder neck, probably designed to protect the very important function of waste removal. Since the bladder neck runs parallel to the vaginal canal, on the side toward your stomach, you can feel this tender bladder tissue through your vaginal walls. These urethral nerve endings are supersensitive in various spots along the way; and the exact location of these spots is *different for every woman.* In other words, every woman has her own personal G-spot— or even two or three G-spots!—that will look, feel, and locate itself in a manner completely unique to her. Just like everything else about a woman's sexuality, your G-spot is a highly individualized treat.

But most doctors and sexologists do seem to agree that the main function of the G-spot is to help you achieve a high degree of sexual intoxication! When you are drunk with rapture, just imagine what an uninhibited and wanton hussy you become, how much more intensely you feel even the barest touch, how much easier and more delicious it is to abandon everything to your feeling of pleasure and that of your lover. This is the special bounty of your G-spot.

How, then, do you find your special sweet spot or spots? Call on your Inner Sex Goddess to help you; she will raise your level of attunement to the subtler sensations of this area. The other helpful trick is to keep in mind the G-spot's second main function—to swell during sexual excitement for protection of the urethra and bladder. When you are aroused, the G-spot will rapidly become engorged, get harder, and may even develop well-defined edges, making it much easier to locate.

You can take the following steps to find your goddess spot:

Step 1. Get yourself into a state of arousal.

Step 2. Assume a seated or squatting position, like sitting on the toilet, for instance. It's almost impossible to find your sweet spots while lying on your back because gravity tends to pull your internal organs down and away from the vaginal entrance. (Remember this when you are trying to feel your G-spot during intercourse!)

Step 3. Lubricate your finger and first massage gently around the urethral opening, sometimes called the meatus, not around the vaginal opening. See if and how sensitive this external area is for you. A whole new experience opened up for me when I discovered this as one of my personal goddess spots, and I couldn't understand why I'd never thought of it before. But it may not be yours, so explore carefully and with an open mind.

Step 4. Still making sure your finger is lubricated, insert it gently into your vagina. Letting yourself be guided by your instincts, use firm upward pressure to slowly investigate along the front of your internal vaginal wall. (Some women find that pressing down at the same time on the outside of the abdomen with the other hand helps pinpoint areas of special sensitivity.) Because the bladder tube runs on the other side of the front vaginal wall, you'll find your own G-spot somewhere along this path. One woman I know said she found her special spot when she felt that she was touching "an inverted clitoris, one that was inside my vagina, and much more pleasurable for me than my clitoris." But anywhere you feel a slight jolt, a momentary urge to urinate, a small, rather hard lump, or a warm, deep sensual feeling is *it.* If you don't find a G-spot right away, or even after you do, don't stop searching. You may have more than one!

Step 5. A commonly found G-spot lies about half an inch inside the vagina at about eight o'clock or four o'clock (if the top of your vagina is twelve o'clock). One woman I know found her special spot "in front and a little to right of center. When I touch it, or when my lover's penis does, it feels pleasurable and kind of liquidy."

Step 6. Be sure to try the area just above your pubic bone. As you probe inside the vagina, you first encounter the lumpy Skene's gland just inside the opening. Then there's the hard area of the pubic bone itself. Beyond it lies a smoother area leading back to the cervix. From there, come back toward the pubic bone a little and hook your finger in back of it where there's a small hollow. Wag your finger right and left. Many women find their G-spot in this area; and it is the place to which most scientists refer. But if, like me, you aren't especially sensitive right there, don't stop searching yet!

Step 7. Keep tracing your finger along the front vaginal wall, as far as you can reach. Stroke and circle with your finger. Deep inside the vagina, almost to the end, is another very common sweet spot. I especially notice mine here when my lover's penis is thrusting deep into me from behind, but it's difficult to reach with my own finger. So don't give up too soon in trying to find a possible deep sweet spot. You may want to insert a wet finger or dildo and duplicate the angle of rear-entry intercourse to fully explore the path of your goddess spot.

Step 8. Notice and remember where your sensitive spots are and how they felt when stimulated. As I've mentioned, you may have one or more G-spots; some of them may be larger than others; you may be hotly sensitive to G-spot stimulation or just mildly warmed by it; upon contact with your G-spot you may or may not have an immediate orgasm, and it may feel sharper or softer than those that are clitorally stimulated. One friend of mine describes her G-spot climaxes as "sudden, sharp, and explosive," while another says, "It feels like a warm, deep wave spreading throughout my whole body." I don't always have an orgasm when I rub my deeper G-spot, but when I do have one, it's like a slow, pulsing release. On the other hand, massaging the sweet spot at my outer urethral opening can make me feel as if I've been shot out of a cannon. Your experience will be different still.

Here's what Diane, my buttoned-down attorney friend, says about her G-spot explorations: "At first I had trouble finding my G-spot because I had this set idea about where it was supposed to be. And it just wasn't there. Then one time when Tom was making love to me from behind and we were lying on our sides, he angled into some corner of me that felt really good. The next day I pressed around inside by myself and found it again—a sort of mushy, earthy place that made me feel as if I were melting down. When I told Tom about it, he probed around with his penis until I started shuddering. This made him really hot, and he just kept thrusting into that place. Somehow this spot seemed connected to a wild animal inside me, and once it got loose, I started bucking and screaming for Tom to 'fuck me hard!' That night we made love for hours with a ferocity and urgency I'd forgotten existed in our relationship."

love nectar

When you massage your goddess spot, you may find yourself ejaculating a small amount of clear fluid from your urethra. Despite appearances, this is not urine. It is not the color of urine, it does not smell or taste like urine, nor does it stain like urine. Furthermore, it has now been scientifically tested to prove it is not urine. This sweet juice is your love nectar, and it falls under the special province of Xochiquetzal, Mayan goddess of beauty, sexuality, and flowers. Sometimes represented as a butterfly, Xochiquetzal symbolizes the sacrament of sipping transformational ambrosia—as the butterfly sucks the nectar of the flower, so the lover drinks the honeyed liquid of his woman's vulva. Never be embarrassed by it; it is a lovely female ejaculation that announces the presence of your very enjoyable orgasms.

Grafenberg observed that with women, as well as with men, the ejaculation that occurs at orgasm involves fluid being ejected in gushes through the urethra and that this happens most often when the G-spot is being stimulated. Since we know that sweet spots are really urethral nerve endings and tissues this really makes sense. It also makes sense that G-spot ejaculation is intimately related to the strength of the PC muscle, the one that controls the flow of urine. The stronger your PC muscle is, the more likely you are to emit love nectar. Some women claim they ejaculate every time they make love; others say it happens only occasionally. Some detect a cyclical pattern, possibly related to the phases of the moon. And many women never ejaculate at all and have just as good a time. So whatever your orgasmic flow experience, don't think it strange.

In fact, the female production of love nectar has been recognized and even reverently cultivated for centuries. Aristotle observed that women expelled fluid during orgasm. So did the famous second-century Greek physician Galen. And in the seventeenth century, Dutch anatomist Regnier de Graaf described the "female prostate" and "female semen" in detail. The Bataro tribe of Uganda was known to have a custom called *kachapati*, or "spray the wall," in which older women taught younger ones how to ejaculate. And in some ancient and modern Tantric teachings, sexual intercourse is said to have the specific esoteric function of stimulating the flow of female fluid, which they call *rajas*. The men of this Tantric school even make a ritual out of collecting the precious juice on a leaf, adding it to a bowl of water, offering it to the deity presiding over the ritual, and then drinking it themselves.

The taste of this orgasmic fluid has been variously described as very sweet, tangy, bitter, or tart. Not only is every woman's flavor different from that of others, but the taste of any given woman's *rajas* may change depending on her mood and the time of month. I was once lucky enough to have a lover who delighted in what he called the "sweet 'n' spicy" flavor of orgasmic juice. He loved to stimulate me to produce this nectar so that he could drink it directly from my body.

So never try to inhibit the natural flow of your precious love fluids. Remember, the Tantrics worshiped them. Try seeing yourself as they did—as the embodiment of the divine female principle, fountain of life and pleasure, source of the magical elixirs of physical and spiritual transformation—at the very least, a Sex Goddess who's so hot she overflows with the sweet nectar of love.

the goddess spot pleasure dance

Now that you've located your particular sweet spot and learned that it's perfectly okay to secrete special love juices, let's explore the best ways to incorporate the G-spot into your self-pleasuring adventures. You may find a direct shortcut to the temple of your Inner Sex Goddess.

113. It's usually best to save the G-spot for later in your pleasuring session, maybe even after you've had your initial orgasm, so that it's swollen, sensitized, and easier to find and excite. Massage, stroke, tickle, and fondle your sweet spot as you would your vaginal lips or clitoris. You will probably want to use heavier pressure on your goddess spot than you would on your clitoris, and you will probably feel the sensation deeper inside your body. Abandon yourself to its earthier tones of pleasure. You can perform this erotic dance all by itself, or you can add clitoral, nipple, or navel and tummy massage to your private party. Or simply stroke yourself all over and dream about Antonio Banderas. With the G-spot, prolonged stimulation is usually the best way to rouse your Inner Sex Goddess from her sensual slumbers.

114. The *Kama Sutra* suggests rubbing your G-spot with the middle or third finger. The ancient erotic text considers the index finger too heavy and aggressive for this delicate pleasure. Of course the middle finger is often the longest one, too—making it easier to reach your G-spot. You may also want to experiment gently with dildos, vibrators, and peeled carrots to provide a longer reach.

115. Positioning is important. Remembering that lying on your back is not the best way to find your sweet spot, you will probably correctly surmise that it's also not the best way to stimulate it. Try kneeling, squatting, or sitting on your heels with your knees apart. The positions you get into for rear-entry sex are good, too. Sandy, a friend who has created the most sumptuous bathroom I've ever seen, likes to sit on the edge of her bathtub, knees spread wide, and feet in the tub. She says this position provides a great angle for finding and rubbing the somewhat elusive love button, and she can keep her fingers wet at the tap.

116. Get on your hands and knees and use your fingers to imitate a thrusting penis bumping up against your G-spot from behind. Make sure your fingers are well lubricated and the nails trimmed. You can achieve the best angle by sliding your fingers around behind your leg and fanny, instead of approaching from the front. The rear entry and the downward motion, along with maybe a lusty "being taken" fantasy, add up to an unusually exhilarating experience.

117. If you want to learn to make love nectar, or to do so more at will, here's how. First increase your PC muscle strength and control by conscientiously doing about one hundred quick squeezes a day for at least a month. Then, in one of your self-loving sessions, get really hot and ready by giving yourself several regular orgasms with your

favorite method of clitoral and vaginal stimulation. You should feel as if you're on an orgasmic plateau. Now stimulate your goddess spot with your fingers or a vibrator; if you have a sweet spot on the outside at your urethral opening, this is usually the best one to start with. Here's the key: push out and down with your vaginal muscles, rather like the way you would push with a bowel movement or when giving birth. Keep pushing as you rub, and do whatever it is that makes you so excited you feel like shaking or exploding.

David, a middle-aged accountant friend of mine, told me about the first time his wife favored him with her love juice: "First I got her incredibly hot by licking her lovely pussy until she came three times. Then I slid my two fingers just inside her opening and circled around the rough area there. She began to moan and cry 'Don't stop!' which really turned me on too. Pretty soon her vagina was pumping my fingers, almost shoving them out. And then she squirted the most delicious warm liquid all over my hand. I loved it!" The important things to take note of here are her high level of arousal, the sweet-spot massage, and the shoving that she did. These are the keys to making a successful and exciting brew of goddess love nectar, either by yourself or with your man. Happy trails!

> People walk down the street and see someone they are attracted to and they can undress that person right in their minds and perform all kinds of sexual acts on them in their fantasies. They go to bed at night and generate fantastic pornographic images in their sleep. This is just something that happens. It seems to be a natural activity.
>
> —James Hillman, former director, Zurich Jung Institute

7

fantasies from the cloud damsels

fantasizing is as natural as walking, sleeping, and breathing. In fact, we can't seem to stop doing it. And why would we want to? The exciting sensory images that come unbidden from our subconscious, from the heart of our most intimate erotic reservoirs, are as necessary to our lives as the bread we eat, yet as naughtily delicious as chocolate candy. They make our skin tingle, our hearts flutter, and our deep inner caves moisten. And like magic carpets, they transport us to enchanted realms of raging desire, perfect love, and unashamed carnality.

The goings-on in our heads—our attitudes, beliefs, personal rules and regulations, wishes and dreams—are at the very source of who we really are. They keep us posted on who we think we are now, who we'd like to be, who we'd like to "try on" for five minutes, and who we'd like our partners to be. And they determine who we *will* be, if we so desire. Erotic, irrational, and completely carefree, this private world is ours alone—unassailable by anyone else's opinions or needs, undemanding of anyone else's presence or good graces, unfathomable to anyone else's linear everyday thinking. Our personally fabricated mythology constitutes an intimate inner fortress and playground that gives us strength, joy, and freedom. For even if we can't quite manage to let ourselves go stark raving wild in our jobs, relationships, and bedchambers, our fantasies give us the opportunity to visit a land where letting it all hang out is deliciously de rigueur.

These exotic passports to otherwise forbidden erotic territory are issued by the ethereal Cloud Damsels who float through our imagination. Erotic nature spirits who live in a lofty dimension parallel to human reality, the Cloud Damsels, known as Apsaras in Hindu and Buddhist mythology, are sacred beings of both earth and sky. Originally human women but now goddesses (like you!), their special gift is the ability to combine sensuous flesh with divinity, sexuality with spirituality, fantasy with reality. With their fluid, sweet-smelling bodies, they may take one human lover or hundreds of godlike consorts, effortlessly combining the earthy sensuality of one with the impossibly wild and divine imaginings of the other, and vice versa. Tall, ornate headdresses sprout from their temples like the abundant fruitfulness of their erotic imagination. They delight in spicing up any and all sexual encounters with a tidbit of juicy fantasy, elevating the mundane to the glorious, human sweat to divine ambrosia, and solo sex to a magnificent garden richly populated with amorous Greek Adonises, dashing and swarthy sheikhs, and insatiable young sexpots of the male, female, animal, and extraterrestrial persuasion.

The Cloud Damsels, as close companions to your

Inner Sex Goddess, live in the most uninhibited and un-censored part of your mind. There they are free to reflect the vivid images of your raciest thoughts, your most inti-mate desires, and your most deeply hidden pleasure stimulators without having to bother with the complica-tions of real life, real people, or real consequences. They give you the freedom to indulge in any outrageous scenario you care to—being penetrated by a huge black stallion, making oral love to another woman, having wild sex with Björn Borg on Wimbledon's center court as thousands of horny onlookers applaud—while still keeping your mar-riage, your self-esteem, your emotions, and your pocket-book intact. What a divine luxury!

While the five physical senses are potent conveyances to the realm of your Inner Sex Goddess, fantasizing can be thought of as the sixth, vitalizing sense. Under the purview of the otherworldly Cloud Damsels, it's the sense that en-hances all the others, opening up even more diverse ave-nues for your unfettered sexuality, and, as Nancy Friday says in *My Secret Garden*, "taking one further, faster in the direction in which the unashamed unconscious already knows it wants to go." Your creative and erotic imagina-tion is the sense that can intuit, interpret, and invent intan-gibles—like romance, atmosphere, mystery, intoxicating danger, forbidden delights, and irrational, all-consuming lust—all the things that stimulate our particularly female hormones. For we women are creatures of rhapsody and enigma, more stimulated by emotion than by action, more aroused by the romance of sex than by the mechanics of sex, and more unloosed by imagination than by facts, formulas, and graphic realities. We come fully alive in our fantastical imaginings.

That's why your Inner Sex Goddess recommends investing *every* sensual activity with erotic imagery—exploratory sessions with your body, sybaritic warm-ups for sex, partner lovemaking, and especially self-pleasuring, where it's just you and your unbridled imagination. As the Cloud Damsels in you know, all of these fleshly pleasures can be even further glorified by healthy dollops of divinely inspired phantasm. And in this rarefied atmosphere of magical reality, *anything* goes. There is nothing to be ashamed of, for your daydreams, reveries, and mental inventions simply reflect your unique, and completely normal, sexual personality—uncensored, rare, courageous, and exquisitely precious. You don't have to act them out, tell them to anyone, or even figure them out. On the other hand, you can do all of those things if it would please and excite you to do so. Your flights of fancy are your private possessions to invent, modify, reveal, conceal, discard, repeat, and indulge in as you will.

having a pleasant flight

When you allow yourself to travel to the vast open spaces of fantasyland, you will find your sensual life taking on a new radiance. Women who give free rein to their Cloud Damsel visions report that their experience of sex is more intense, more ecstatic, and more full-bodied than they ever thought possible. In fact, many women say they can achieve orgasm by fantasy alone, with no physical stimulation at all. The key is to surrender completely to the irrational brilliance of your own erotic mind and to let your fantasies lead you, not the other way around. Here are some tips for making the most of your fantasy flights:

- Impose no limits. While few of us would actually have sex in the middle of Times Square, fantasizing about it can be delicious, healthy fun. So don't label yourself a pervert or nymphomaniac just because you like to dream about being trussed up, blindfolded, and ravaged by twenty-seven Mongol warriors. On the contrary, be as outrageous and outlandish as you possibly can. Enjoy the rare opportunity to explore the impossible and to step into someone else's skin—whether it be Venus de Milo, Irma la Douce, a nymphomaniac mermaid, a tightly laced Victorian damsel aching to have her bodice ripped, a primitive cave-woman, a creature from *Star Wars*, or even a male truck driver with "horns." Whatever your weirdest fantasy, there are at least a thousand completely normal women out there whose kinky castle-building is even more over-the-top than yours. So let your unfettered hallucinations bring out all of your muskiest natural perfumes, your most salacious proclivities, and your wildest primal instincts. Make no judgments. Take no prisoners or guilt trips. These private tours are safe within the boundaries of your head and heart.

• I think it's best *not* to share your fantasies with your mate. He might feel threatened, intimidated, outraged, or even betrayed, especially if his delicate male ego is called into question. Worse yet, he might criticize or belittle your fanciful efforts, puncturing a gigantic hole in your fantasy balloon. But most important, if you know someone else will be privy to your secret exotic dreams, you will not feel free to indulge in the really juicy, borderline ones—the most liberating and fun visions of all!

The exceptions to this are those fantasies that you specifically want to turn into reality and that you feel are safe, nonthreatening, and practical enough to do so. I once conjured up a vision of taking my lover to the opera, both of us dressed to the nines, and slipping off for a stand-up quickie in some dark corner while the onstage drama raged on. The elegance, furtiveness, and danger of this make-believe scenario really appealed to my naughty Inner Sex Goddess—and to my man, when I shared it with him. For months it was a joint fantasy that we used to titillate each other. Then one night at the theater, he got up in the middle of the first act and led me to a vestibule, where, behind a swinging door, we pounded into each other until we heard the audience applaud and begin to leave the theater proper. Just in the nick of time, we refastened our clothes and nonchalantly emerged from behind the door to join the exiting audience for intermission. It was fantastic, but then I had to think up a new outrageous daydream!

• Fantasize at every opportunity—while commuting on the train, lying in the sun, ironing tablecloths, enduring a meeting, fixing dinner, observing a flower, drifting off to sleep, showering, flying on a plane, walking to work, and especially when looking at and touching your body or that of your lover. Fantasize while you are preparing for a sensual encounter, making love to your man, or indulging in your favorite self-pleasuring activities. The more you flex your fantasy muscles, the more alive you will feel, the more abandoned and creative a lover you will be, and the better you will know your Inner Sex Goddess, for it is in the realm of your vivid imagination that she lives, breathes, and grows.

• Use props. Make your fantasies as real as possible by adding a dash of tactile reality—a filmy scarf for your harem sojourn (while in Egypt I bought scads of sheer belly-dancing scarves with dangling beadwork just for that purpose); a furry tail for your Catwoman reverie; a length of rope or a blindfold for your "rape" fantasies; mesh stockings and a brief, frilly apron for the French maid in you; sandalwood or musk incense for imaginary Tantric rituals; juicy fruits for fantasy love with Tom Jones. And of course always have your favorite toys readily available—vibrators, videos, scented massage oil, ben wa balls, and so forth. Your castles in the air become much more erotically solid when draped with the stuff of reality.

• Let your erotic visions speak a different language. In fantasies, men don't have "penises"; they flaunt swollen "cocks." You no longer own a "bosom" and "genitals"; now you've got creamy "tits" and a "juicy pussy." And horny hunks don't swarm around to have "intercourse" with you; they are panting to "fuck" you silly. For many of us, the brazen language of sex can instantly trigger your most wanton instincts and transform your fantasies from bland into sizzling. Foreign words, too, can add just the right touch of exotic romance when you are daydreaming about sexy Italian counts or rough-hewn blond Vikings. Phrases such as *"Baise-moi, chéri!"* *"Bums Mich Schneller, Liebling!"* and *"Chiavami, tesoro!"* are just the ticket to exciting foreign fantasylands. Learn to savor these powerfully evocative words. Whisper them to yourself in the dark of night. Chant them to yourself. Use them to catapult otherwise casual musings into the realm of hot, depraved fantasy masterpieces.

going to the source

I am in the African bush with an untamed lover. We roll in the leaves and wallow in the mud like languorous primitive beasts, and then he washes me off in a cool green river. We glide through the water on the back of an alligator, and when the creature tries to reach around and devour me, my wild lover saves me from its cruel jaws with the power of his muscled arms. He proudly parades me through the village, naked on the back of a giant wrinkled elephant. In his hut he leaves me bare but wraps himself up in white robes so that I can see only his dark smoldering eyes as they travel hotly over my quivering nakedness. Then he parts his robes for me so I can touch his hot, hard body, and I kneel down to take his swollen member in my mouth. Caressing my head as I suck him, he brings me under his robes, where it's even hotter than under the African sun. He pours his honeyed come down the front of my body and rubs it into my breasts so that I'll bear his scent. Slowly we sink down onto the rough mat, and he enters me from behind, biting my neck and growling softly like a wild animal. His huge shaft plunges hard against the very deepest part of my woman's well, and soon I am panting in uncontrolled ecstasy. Hours pass as he keeps me teetering on the brink of breathless release. Finally, possessing me completely by reaching around to put one hand on my throbbing bud and the other on a burning hot nipple, he thrusts even more powerfully into me, snarling like a great tiger—and I scream in the ecstatic agony of my body's surrender. Later he bathes me under a cascading waterfall and lies with me on the banks of the river, while we listen to the hyenas laugh.

■

One night, while out dancing in a tight red dress, I am suddenly grabbed by three men who blindfold me and throw me into the back of a van. Days later, awaking from the drugs they've given me, I find myself standing on the auction block of a white slave market. I am covered from head to toe with robes; only my eyes are visible. The auctioneer says, "The bidding will start at one million rupees for this exceptionally fine specimen!" Suddenly he rips away my robes, exposing my entire naked body; the audience gasps in excited approval. Several customers, men dressed in long robes and turbans, come up and bounce my breasts between their hands, pinch my nipples, and grab my bottom. One man in a blue sash even rubs my clit and thrusts an incredibly long finger deep inside me, pumping it in and out to observe my reaction. Though I should feel humiliated and angry, I find myself feeling haughty and sexy instead, because I can see that every one of these men has a huge erection jutting out under his robe. I start gyrating my hips, squeezing my own tits, and massaging my pussy. I look right into the eyes of the man with the blue sash and lick my lips suggestively. I take my fingers out of my wet sex and stick them in his mouth. He starts sucking them hungrily and whips out his iron rod to get at it with his hands. All the other men do the same, so that all I see are these gorgeous shafts aching and throbbing for me. I am turned on tremendously, and I keep undulating and fucking myself with my fingers until all of those men spurt their come all over my body—all except the man in the blue sash: he sticks his stone-hard member straight up my pussy and fucks me hard, fast, and deep, right there in front of everybody, and I explode in uncontrollable spasms. I select him as my lucky owner and lead him off to demand more fucking.

Though some women quite easily and prolifically conjure up elaborate visions like the ones above to accompany their self-pleasuring interludes, many of us are just as happy dreaming up much simpler scenarios—like "What would my next-door neighbor look like without his clothes? I'll bet his stomach muscles ripple, all the way down to his . . ." or "I'd love to rub my oiled-up breasts all over my husband's body." That's okay. Fantasies can run the gamut from simple musings about real men and situations to complicated visions of exotic lands, strangely sexed people, and bizarre or impossible copulations. Almost anything you see, read, hear about, remember, or experience can become a rich source of voluptuous inner visions for you. The world, and especially the sensualized domain that your Inner Sex Goddess perceives, is full of juicy ideas. So never feel stumped as to where and how to come up with really tasty fantasy material. Simply tune your otherwise rational brain in to the outlandishly opulent wavelength of your personal Cloud Damsels and view the world through their erotic-tinted glasses. Allow yourself to recognize a sensual image when you see one, relish it, take a mental picture of it, write about it in your journal, free-associate it with any people, places, or things that float across your mind. Let your imagination range freely over completely new territory. Then, when next you want to embody your Inner Sex Goddess—whether you are self-pleasuring, making love to your man, or standing in line at the bank—flip through your mental catalog of self-produced fantasy flicks and plug in the hottest one.

118. Recall a man, situation, or previous lovemaking session that made your love button shiver. In your mind, savor the sounds, smells, and textures that went with it. Embellish them. In your imagination let them evolve to an extreme pleasure point. Here's an example: "I had a lover once who had the most beautiful smooth brown skin. Just the smell of it drove me insane with lust. Whenever I want to get hot, I remember that musky scent and the feel of his skin against my chest. Sometimes I get to swimming in that smell and imagine that it's pouring in through my nose, mouth, and vagina to fill every corner of my body. It turns my insides to warm honey." And another: "My boyfriend and I used to jump on his motorcycle and go for wild moonlight rides. Remembering the feel of that vibrating hunk of metal and my boyfriend's ass between my legs makes me tremble even now. It works especially well in tandem with my vibrator."

119. Read steamy novels. Become one of the characters and immerse yourself in the hottest scenes—clothes, food, toys, locales, the whole megillah. Some of those anonymous Victorian porn books can be delightfully kinky—with wide-eyed, pantalooned maidens turning into sex-crazed, riding crop–wielding mistresses who love to

watch their brothers impale every servant in the house. Or become a different sex. "Henry Miller's books really get my juices flowing," a friend told me. "I love to put on my husband's clothes—when he's not around, of course—and pretend I'm one of Miller's cocky male heroes, throwing around words like 'prick' and 'pussy' and whipping out my huge member to fuck every woman who crosses my path. It's fun to wear the shoe on the other foot for a change."

120. Peruse adult magazines. The photos, especially in *Penthouse,* are often meant to be realistic fantasies. A ten-page layout of two women playing with ice dildos supplied me with raw fantasy material for months. Don't forget to read the stories and the letters from other readers too. "A man wrote in about secretly watching his wife shed all her inhibitions and have pornographic sex with two hunky gardeners, and for some reason that lit all my fuses," my friend Mary told me. "Improvising my own version, I have great fun imagining my husband spying on me as I have my way with the virile young guys who clean our pool. My favorite part is when I sit on the lap of one, his love-stick buried deep inside me and my back to him, while the other guy slurps on my clit. This is just too much for my husband, and he has to come out of hiding and join in by sucking my tits. Of course I would never do this in real life, but that's what makes it even more fun to fantasize about!"

121. Walk in nature. When you see a waterfall, fancy that you are standing under it with a long-haired Polynesian lover, feeling the water and his hands on your breasts. Let the intense mossy green of a forest return home with you as a mental talisman that evokes vivid color, moist earthy feelings, and romantic medieval imagery. See mountains as breasts to suckle, trees and skyscrapers as mighty shafts to penetrate you, rock clefts as mouths to kiss and be kissed by. Let a mud puddle conjure up visions of rolling in the mud with a crocodile, a wolf, or a primitive tribal lover. Use these natural spices to flavor your solo or partner lovemaking. One nature lover I know told me this fantasy. "All of a sudden this log became a platform on which I could display myself to hundreds of men. In my mind, I lay back on it, nude, the log between my legs so that I was spread-eagled, my sex open wide. I could imagine the bark prickling my bare back and ass as I massaged my juicy opening, and all these men with huge naked erections stared at me hungrily. But no one was allowed to touch me because I was the sacred white goddess of the forest, and they had to worship me from afar."

122. Become another woman—someone you've read about, seen in a movie, or heard of in a song. "I have different fantasy personalities depending on the activity," a woman told me. "For pleasuring myself, I mentally play the role of Salome, whom I see as someone unashamed of touching her body and with lots of marvelous veils and things to play with. With my husband, I imagine that I am Xaviera Hollander, the Happy Hooker, flaunting my bold sexuality and giving him everything a man could possibly dream of. And when I just want to relieve the boredom of ironing, I invent a scene where I'm 'Brown Sugar' from that Rolling Stones song. She's a saucy little tart who drives all kinds of rock stars wild."

123. When you see an attractive man, imagine what he looks and feels like naked. What outrageous things would he do to you? What naughty acts would you perform for him? How would his penis be shaped? What color is his pubic hair? Does he have a tattoo on his right inner thigh? Would he like to shave your mound? How does the inside of his mouth taste? Would he prefer you in white cotton, red lace, or black leather? Does he cry out when he comes? Are his nipples sensitive? his earlobes? his eyelids? Would he have a penchant for licking your cleavage? Would you like to lick his? The next time you play with your vibrator, imagine it's his hands that are giving you those sudden shocks of pleasure.

124. Read sex manuals. Pick out some of the kinkier suggestions that you might never have the nerve to do in real life—like having your man whip you lovingly, wrapping his penis with pearls, or inviting a third person into your love-play—and fantasize about them. Devise your own variations. Pretend that you are being photographed or drawn for the book's illustrations. As you fill your mind with these vivid images, let them stir you into self-pleasuring action. "I've always read about watching yourself have sex in an overhead mirror, but I'd be too embarrassed to do this with my husband. So sometimes when we make love, or especially when I'm by myself, I imagine that I can see the reflection of his tidy little rear bouncing up and down on top of me. It gives me the most amazing tingles," a friend told me.

125. Be alert for accidental triggers to your erotic imagination. Wrong numbers, incorrectly addressed mail, switched luggage or tickets, accidental grocery cart collisions, misinterpreted words or names, and unusually striking newspaper articles can all carry the seeds of a great fantasy garden. I used to get occasional wrong-number phone calls from people asking for Natasha. Eventually, one deeply disappointed caller told me that Natasha was a dominatrix who had always had this phone number, and maybe I'd like to get paid for "punishing" him instead of just insisting that this "bad boy" had reached the wrong number! I hung up on him and got my phone number changed, but in the meantime I had great fun fantasizing about rudely making appointments with these men—how they would love the verbal abuse!—putting on hip boots and chains, and satisfying their every desire for erotic leather punishment.

126. Let music shape your feelings into images. Brazilian music or reggae can take you to hot tropical climes where small bikinis, dark sultry men, and devil-may-care attitudes have free rein. The heavy drumbeat of hard rock may stir your primitive instincts. Baroque sonatas may turn you into a bird flying free of all society's limitations or a guitar being plucked by a man's strong fingers. "I don't fantasize about people or events but more about feelings," Carol told me. "I can put on a piece of music, concentrate on a particular instrument or melody line, and use that to focus my sensations and feelings into one electric-blue chord that flows throughout my body as I want it to. This chord feels hot, cold, and throbbing all at the same time, and it kind of beams into my hands, breasts, and genitals as the music trips along. It intensifies everything that I'm doing to myself, and if I focus it in my clitoris, it always gives me an orgasm."

127. Advertisements are a great source of fantasy these days. How about those Calvin Klein ads showing the naked torso of a perfectly sculpted man on the sand? Imagine rolling in the waves with him or feeling the bulge in his jeans. The ads for Guess jeans often depict a hot western scenario or a coffee-shop tête-à-tête with gorgeous men

and women lolling about. You could walk right into one of those scenes and get branded by your favorite cowboy. TV commercials for perfume are usually designed specifically to evoke romantic fantasies: Liz Taylor seductively bringing luck to some classy dude in a casino; a pouty-lipped woman challenging you that "not every woman can wear Red," apparently because it's so hot and bold; some Fabio look-alike galloping up on a horse to scoop you up and away to cloudland. And then there's the next-door neighbor who comes to borrow coffee. My friend Teresa fantasizes, "That sexy hunk rings my chimes all right. When he comes to ask for coffee, I invite him in, and while I'm reaching up to get the tin off the shelf, he comes up behind me, pins me against the cupboard, raises my skirt, and screws the living daylights out of me. Then I undo his shirt, put honey on his nipples, and lick it off, and somehow we forget all about the coffee."

_128._ Delve into your dreams for fantasy scenarios. As messages from the subconscious, dreams can give us clues to the "forbidden" desires and fears we otherwise keep hidden from ourselves, and in fantasy it's safe to explore them. I once had a powerfully erotic dream about the very ordinary man who was my boss at the time. Although in real life I liked and respected him, there had been no particular sexual chemistry between us—and it would have been a career disaster to get romantically involved with him. But in my nocturnal imagining, I let myself see the suave and sexy Don Juan personality that he probably never revealed even to himself and that lit a huge bonfire in my libido. Intentionally refraining from any real-life dalliance with him, I undressed him with my eyes and made dangerously abandoned imaginary love to him in the hallway for months. It made going to work such a treat!

You can also program your dreams to work things out for you. A friend told me she'd been having mental flashes of two of her female colleagues licking and biting her all over. She did not want to explore the idea of making love to a woman in real life, but these images were so persistent that she decided to tackle the idea in her dreams. After about five nights of falling to sleep deliberately thinking about these women, she finally had a dream in which the three of them made an intensely erotic porn movie together, stroking, sucking, tweaking, and kissing each other in every possible entangled combination. She enjoyed the dream so much, and it felt so natural to her, that she treasured it as a favorite fantasy for years. Even though she still had no desire for same-sex love in her daily life, she allowed herself to relish the beauty of woman in her dreams and fantasies.

129. Assign yourself a role—any role—and see where it takes you.

- You're a librarian who just can't help sneaking hunky young college students in between the shelves for some real education.

- You're a sports reporter, and when you find yourself in the football players' locker room, you tear off all your clothes and massage yourself to orgasm while the entire team cheers.

- You're a teenager on your first date, making out for hours, then finally letting him feel your breast, his hot, desperate panting loud in your ear.

- You're stranded on a desert isle with only the wild animals for loving company.

- You're a harem girl, pampered, perfumed, bathed, and licked by hundreds of beautiful lusty women every day and chosen to suck the sultan's golden dagger every night.

- You're a porn film star and have to watch hugely endowed men and beautifully molded women having sex constantly; then you let three men and two women suck, fuck, and bite you for ninety-seven camera takes.

- You're a nineteenth-century French maid whose master often finds it necessary to spank you for dereliction of duty.

- You're a Tantrica in an ancient Oriental garden pungent with the smell of orange blossoms and jasmine, and an Indian god with twelve arms smooths every inch of your body with his twelve hands while making transcendental love to you.

• You're an executive at a meeting, and one of your colleagues has slipped under the conference table to lick you between the legs.

• You're a hostage who is tied down, forced to perform cunnilingus on six women, spanked with the thick penises of ten huge men, and then taken from behind by each one in turn.

• You're Lady Godiva, riding bareback and bare-assed through town with only your long tresses to cover your voluptuous charms.

• You have a blind date, and you're getting dressed to go meet a new man for the first time, dreaming up all his sensational qualities and odd quirks, anticipating the flirtatious eye signals and dinner conversation, imagining all the salacious things he might try to (and you might let him) do to you.

• You're a despotic ruler whose male subjects must pay tribute to you by sucking your nipples and then rubbing their come all over your body.

• You're a glamorous gambler at a casino in Monaco, and a visiting Italian prince follows you around the casino all night and finally whisks you off to his yacht for a moonlight tryst.

• You're a waitress at an elegant restaurant who occasionally slips into the men's room and has sex with whoever is in there, no matter how many or how few.

- You're a bee who has ecstatic orgasms by flying deep into the well of fragrant, brilliantly colored flowers and rolling gleefully around in their soft golden pollen.

cloud damsel visions

While most fantasies are purely for lustful fun, a certain kind of imagining is meant for more serious business—the business of designing reality the way you want it to be. Whether that means making changes in the way your partner feels and behaves, making changes in the way you feel and behave, or calling a new lover to you, these visions are fantasies with a powerful purpose. Indulge in them often enough, and you will find your real life starting to take the shape of your utopian dreams. It's as if you and your Cloud Damsels sit around a white witches' magic cauldron: you throw in mental pictures of what you want, together you brew it up with imagination, and the resulting steam carries your desires to their intended destination in reality, infusing the person or thing with the smoky essence of your erotic vision. More potent than ordinary visualizations, these magnetic mirages carry all the power of your fervid physical desire, hotly charged emotion, and most unbridled imagination. Your inner voices will prompt you when it's appropriate to use them.

130. Imagine summoning a lover to you. When my friend Vivian wants to bring a new man into her life or make a long-distance connection with a current one, she merely thinks intensely of that person while she pleasures her body. She feels herself calling to him energetically and sees the man consciously receiving the connection. Vivian says this seems to work even better for her when done in the shower because her pleasure is more intense and because she envisions the steam from her very hot, wet body floating off with the powerful erotic magic of her dream. When I tried this once, I not only had a deliciously entertaining shower, but the lover I'd been thinking of phoned me from three thousand miles away immediately after I left the bathroom!

131. Design beautiful new feelings about your own body that will translate into bewitching behavior. Because I believe it's so important for women to learn to love and admire their genitals, I often recommend they try auto-erotic play enhanced with the following fantasy: Envisage your mate or imaginary lover ardently licking the lips of your sex and moaning, "I love your gorgeous pussy. It tastes sooooo good and makes me so hard." As your passion mounts, he kisses you even more intensely and groans, "Give me more of your delicious nectar. I love to lap it up." Embroider on this basic scenario as you wish and allow your hands or vibrator to act it out. In addition to being delectable self-pleasuring fun, this vision helps you (1) to know in your bones what a magical, sexy jewel your vulva is; (2) to radiate physical heat from your sex organs to those of your lover; and (3) to invent elegantly lewd pelvic moves.

132. Fantasize your mate into the Valentino-like lover you desire. Suppose your man, though he means well, just doesn't spend enough time on foreplay. You've tried retraining him with erotic massage, seductive self-pleasuring shows, and tender talk, but you've had only moderate success. Time for voluptuous visions. In a private pleasuring session, imagine that your once-reluctant lover is now slowly teasing you in all the sweetly agonizing ways you crave. In vivid detail, see him lovingly massage your toes; feel his slow, sensuous caress on your inner thigh; smell the scent of his fevered skin as he bites your nipple; hear the passionate endearments he whispers in your ear; taste his tangy tongue on the corners of your mouth. Simultaneously, inflame all these hot spots with your own loving hands, building your excitement to a feverish heat. The combination of the powerful creative juices of sex, your steaming emotions, and your fierce intention will drive this blazing message straight into your lover's heart.

And then it happened like
a miracle, this pulsation
of pleasure unequalled by
the most exalted
musicians, the summits of
perfection in art or science
or wars, unequalled by
the most regal beauties of
nature, this pleasure
which transformed the
body into a high tower of
fireworks gradually
exploding into fountains
of delight through the
senses.

—Anaïs Nin

8

the secrets
of divine
orgasm

We women know that orgasm is not a *goal* to be achieved at all costs, like a touchdown or a home run. In fact, sometimes we don't even care if we have an orgasm because we enjoy the sweet ecstasy of the *process* of lovemaking so much. Yet that pleasure "unequalled by the most regal beauties of nature" is a divine gift to which we are most definitely entitled, and which your Inner Sex Goddess most dearly wishes to bestow upon you. In fact, the blissful waves of orgasm are vital food for the goddesses within your body, strengthening all your subtle energy centers and nourishing your physical and mental capabilities as well. The ecstatic pulsations of your orgasm also constitute one of the most deeply satisfying gifts you can give your lover. Few things turn a man on more than knowing he has solved the eternal mystery, found the elusive Grail, and sent your body into uncontrolled spasms of rapture — which then cascade all over *his* body.

We Sex Goddesses have this divine frenzy well within our power — to receive and to give. The research of Masters and Johnson indicates that women's capacity for orgasm far exceeds that of men. And the more we exercise this ability, the more sensitive and responsive to orgasmic stimuli we become, achieving even greater heights of climactic ecstasy, capacity, and skill. In fact, Mary Jane Sherfey in *The Nature and Evolution of Female Sexuality* speculates that without the restraints of societal and internal taboos, women might be freed to behave more naturally, in a similar fashion to our close relatives the higher primates who copulate, and probably reach orgasm, up to fifty times a day when in heat. How happy and healthy they and their mates must be!

Not too far removed from this state of natural, sexually vibrant well-being are the islanders of Mangaia in central Polynesia. Believed to be the most orgasmically advanced society in the world, they consider female orgasm not an indulgence but a necessity. At puberty, Mangaian males are taught how to stimulate women to maximum sexual pleasure, and the man who fails to give his woman at least two orgasms every time they make love loses his status in the island's society. Sadly, our culture is not so advanced.

But actually it's much better to retain control of your own body and its pleasures anyway, to realize that nobody *gives* you orgasms. You create them yourself by knowing how your body reaches its peak and then directing your feelings and activities in a way that *allows* an orgasm to occur. This command of simultaneous control and abandon is the special talent and gift of your Inner Sex Goddess and of the many sex goddesses, ancient and modern, who have discovered the secrets of first-time, dependably regular, teeth-chattering, and multiple orgasm and have honed their skills into a fine art. Let's listen in on one of their powwows.

Once upon a time a group of ancient priestesses and modern-day sex goddesses sat around the campfire trying to figure out how to induce the Goddess Who Makes You Shudder Inside to visit them. They knew she could be elusive and that she required praise and petting that met certain very high standards. But these women had clues and secrets that they whispered to each other over the fire. "Try rubbing very fast." "Let yourself go." "Maybe worshiping a cucumber will make her come," they said. And lo, the mysterious seeds of their shared female wisdom eventually bore fruit, the Goddess Who Makes You Shudder Inside appeared full bloom in their midst, and they and their lucky mates lived ecstatically ever after. Each in her turn had revealed a secret. . . .

Secret # 1

Know and Love Your Sexual Self — Regularly.

This, of course, is what you've been doing throughout this book — exploring your body and finding not its faults but all of its sexy hollows and curves; discovering your personal hot spots, desires, and sexual style; becoming intimate with your Inner Sex Goddess; loving your sensuality, your wild erotic thoughts, and your genitals; learning how to pleasure yourself, and thereby your lover. As one woman said, "I never had an orgasm until I gathered up the courage to look at my vagina, decided it was beautiful and lovable, and finally got comfortable touching myself and feeling a little bit out of control. That's when all heaven broke loose."

A woman who loves her sexuality and regularly pleasures herself to orgasm has a high degree of sexual self-confidence. She wants to express herself sexually more than the usual woman and possesses a higher-than-average sensual thermostat. She likes her body and thinks of herself as lovable and valuable. She expects to delight herself and her lover more than the ordinary woman would; and she most often does. Her self-pleasure is its own reward. Yet it's because she's so hot that she gets the best lovers and the best loving. "When I realized that *I* am the one, not a man, who brings sexuality into my life, I felt as if I had been reborn. My body, now truly my own, seemed very precious and powerful. It showed me how to have *real* orgasms."

Secret #2

Surrender.

Wilhelm Reich, the psychoanalyst who wrote *The Function of the Orgasm,* described climax as "the ability to surrender to the flow of sexual energy without any inhibition." Abandoning yourself to your hot-blooded feelings is essential if you want to be carried over the orgasmic edge, for the very essence of orgasm is letting go, relinquishing control, being lost in the moment, submitting to your body's imperative. You must ask your critical, control-freak self to step aside and let your voluptuous feelings show the way. One very wise woman said, "You can't *force* yourself to orgasm; you have to relax, get in the flow, and let your body do its own thing." And yet another has said, "I get myself as excited as possible and then just let go. I kind of surrender to my sensations."

Secret #3

Focus.

Every orgasmic woman I know says she intoxicates herself to orgasm by throwing everything else out of her mind and concentrating only on her body and its heady feelings of pleasure. At that moment nothing else exists. "I empty my mind and merge with my feelings," one woman told me. "When I touch my breasts, I concentrate fiercely on the tips of my nipples. When I stroke my vagina, I am so focused there that I *become* my vagina, pulsing and contracting." This ability to loose yourself from the bonds of normal reality and focus totally on the altered reality of voluptuous sensation is what allows many women to achieve extraordinary or multiple orgasmic peaks. "In my private world, only the tip of my clitoris exists. But at that moment it feels bigger than my whole body, as if I'm one giant clitoris rippling on waves of vibration."

Secret #4

Get the Right Kind of Clitoral Stimulation —
and Plenty of It.

Whether you like it direct or indirect, fast or slow, hard or easy, with water or your hand or a vibrator, find out what drives your clitoris crazy—and stick with it until your body can't stand the agonizing pleasure anymore and has to climax to relieve the tension. One friend says, "My best orgasms happen when I spread my vaginal lips apart and let the faucet in the tub run full blast right on my clit. The faucet is fabulous and can last a lot longer than I can." Another self-educated woman chimes in, "I like to move a vibrator up and down over my clitoris for about ten minutes nonstop. Then I just hold it steady and push it in until I explode." Still another says, "I can accelerate my orgasm by holding the sides of my clitoral hood between my finger and thumb and gently massaging it while I slide a wet finger over the tip of the clitoris itself. Fireworks!"

Secret #5

Try Your Goddess Spot.

Wherever it is, your G-spot is *your* area of special sensitivity, so capitalize on it. Three different sex goddesses say: "I arch my back so my fingers can reach a real deep sexy place inside me. Then just a couple of strokes and I go off like a cannon." "I can come several times if I put a dildo just inside my vagina and rub it up and down quickly over that rough spot I love." "My G-spot is outside over my urethra. If I massage it in circles, orgasmic waves start right away."

Secret #6

Flex Your PC Muscle.

Contracting the PC muscle greatly increases sensation and adds enough additional stimulation to bring many women to the threshold of orgasm. One wild maiden confides, "Tightening makes the feelings stronger. When I get close to climaxing, I squeeze hard and hold my vaginal walls to-gether till the contractions stop." And another says, "After I have an orgasm, I use my PC to mimic the contractions until I come again."

Secret #7

Watch Yourself in the Mirror.

Many women are tantalized into orgasm by seeing what their own buildup of sexual tension looks like and watch-ing how their body moves with mild or intense orgasms. One says, "When I see my vaginal lips swelling, opening up like a hothouse flower and undulating real sexy-like, I start quivering inside and sort of roll into an internal shud-der." Another autoerotic voyeur declares, "My nipples get very dark and big, as if someone's been kissing and biting them for hours. And then my whole body seems to get pink and light up. Watching this sends me right over the edge."

Secret #8

Use a Vibrator.

This secret is especially helpful if you've never had an or-gasm. But even if you have, new sensual peaks await you, as the following story illustrates. "A friend told me about the fun she was having with her vibrator, and I wanted to explore too. It was great because I could direct the intense pulsing movements exactly where I wanted them and keep them going for a really long time. I felt that I was building up to some sort of explosion or precipice, and I remember thinking, Could this be dangerous? Soon I felt as if I'd reached the top of some mountain and then fallen off into a blissful state of delicious inner pulsing and uncontrollable contractions that I had never dreamed my body was capable of." (See Chapter 9 for details on using vibrators.)

Secret #9

Fantasize.

The most erotic organ in the body is your brain. It is the epicenter of your sexual earthquakes. And as you know from the previous chapter, your personal Cloud Damsels are intimately familiar with the wilds of your interior erotic terrain. In the blink of an eye, they can create at least ten hot fantasies that will expertly touch off any number of private landslides. So do as more than 80 percent of orgasmic women do: fire up your imagination to bring on a shuddering orgasm. Here's what just one of them said, "I like to get on all fours with a vibrator beneath me on a pillow and imagine that I am being taken doggie-style. This wonderful little fantasy brings on multiple orgasms and makes me really hot for more loving from my real-life man." Another creative vamp shares this fantasy: "I lie flat on my back, insert three wet fingers, and fantasize that an Arab prince has whisked me off to his tent and laid me down on a long table covered with luscious exotic foods. The women of his harem start licking me all over like a piece of fruit, and the prince himself slips his tongue deep inside me. That always makes me come right away!"

Secret #10

Play a Role.

Sometimes playing the part of a sex kitten, a dominatrix, or an innocent young girl can free the wildly orgasmic you from the bonds that restrain her. Dress the part and really act it out. Three playful Sarah Bernhardts confide: "When I wear my red lace bra and see-through panties, I start slinging my hips around and getting naughty. I feel like a high-class call girl capable of firing off a hundred orgasms." "I like to dress up like Lolita, with red pouty lips and little schoolgirl dresses. Then I do that 'shy Di' look. Sexy and sweet at the same time, I feel it's okay to do anything, including innocently losing control of my body and, 'Oh my! I've just had an orgasm!' " "I *pretend* that I'm having an incredibly intense orgasm. I shout and fling myself around in a frenzy. My body doesn't seem to know the difference and actually comes to a climax."

Secret #11

Vividly Picture a Body Part.

I used to think I was the only oddball who did this, but it turns out that many other women find visualizing body parts extra stimulating too. I usually imagine a close-up view of my breasts, nipples extended and quivering. Somehow this heightens their sensitivity and sends intense orgasm signals to my vagina. Other sensual visualizers share their secrets: "I get an image of what my clitoris must look like to a man, from a straight-on view. It seems huge, red, and wet. Then if I just touch it with my fingertip, I have an orgasm immediately." "I see my vaginal walls swelling and filling with blood, and the back of my vagina opening up to accommodate this huge dildo I have. I see the dildo in there, too, thrusting against the walls and forcing them to open even more. The power of this image really gets me, for some reason, and I then imagine I'm actually watching the spasms of these swollen walls as they release all the energy they've been holding."

Secret #12

Keep Your Rhythm and Pressure Steady.

This is a biggie. Almost every woman I know says the trouble with trying to have an orgasm with a man is that he's likely to change the exquisite thing he's doing to you just when you've reached a level of unbearable sexual tension. At that point, it's crucial to *not change a thing*. "Yes!" a friend of mine agreed. "It must be exactly the same rhythm, motion, pressure, speed, everything for the last twenty or thirty seconds. If not, the whole thing is ruined!" Another smart lady capitalizes on this essential element: "After I come, I just keep up the same steady, hard stimulation even though at first it feels like I can't stand to be touched. Pretty soon that intensity goes away and I just keep on riding the waves of pleasure into multiple-orgasmic bliss."

Secret # 13

Tease Yourself.

You can intensify and prolong your orgasm by building tension to a peak but stopping before you go over the edge. Lighten your touch or move to a different area while the level of arousal drops, then rises again. The more times you do this, the greater will be your release in the end. "I love to tease myself into a powerful orgasm by moving my vibrator down from my clit to my vaginal opening when I'm almost ready to come. I hold it there for a while and hang suspended until all pulse stops racing and then move it back to my clit," my friend Joan said. "I do this about ten times before I finally let myself come; then I just explode." Another shameless self-tease confesses, "If I take my time, build up slowly, then let myself come down again, maybe just rubbing my breasts between peaks, I get this almost unbearable feeling of wanting to jump out of my skin after about five times."

Secret # 14

Experiment with Breathing Patterns.

Every woman seems to have a different way of using her breath to enhance her orgasmic capabilities. Explore your breathing repertoire until you find just the right lung action for you. "I make sure that I have an orgasm every day, because it helps relieve the stress of my high-power job," a colleague told me. "I find that breathing deeply is very important for me, no matter what I'm doing, but especially when I'm pleasuring myself. I just breathe very deeply and imagine that the air is being breathed in and out of my vagina. It seems to make my insides tingle just enough to bring me off beautifully."

Other heavy breathers say: "I've found that if I hold my breath, it helps me over the plateau." "Panting in short, rhythmic gasps really increases the sensation in my whole vulval area and makes me come faster. In fact, if I keep up these pants after my first orgasm and rub myself more gently, the hypersensitivity in my clit disappears and I can go into another sexual buildup and another orgasm—even five or six more."

Secret #15

Make Sounds.

Withholding noises can stifle your orgasmic feelings, while letting them out frees you to express what you feel inside. Here's what several vocal women have to say: "If I don't scream like a banshee, I can't come." "When I moan, I get more into my feelings. I don't know if I could have an orgasm without letting these sexual urges out." "I actually talk to myself about how sexy I look and how good it feels. I say things I would tell a man, like, 'Ooooo, it feels so good when you suck my tits.' It makes me really hot, and then I just can't keep from coming."

Secret #16

Change or Combine Types of Stimulation.

Once you have an orgasm, try changing your type or place of stimulation to encourage another one. Or combine several styles at once. One voracious lady says, "My first orgasm comes from fingering my clitoris. But my second one usually arrives only if I plunge a dildo real deep into my vagina and pump it hard."

Many women say that if they simply change positions, with their fingers or vibrator approaching from a different angle, they can induce more orgasms. Another woman gluttonous for pleasure says, "After I come once, I just add on another erogenous zone. I keep my fingers in my vagina, but also rub my bottom or twirl my nipples to make more climaxes."

Secret #17

Push.

Bearing down or pushing seems to trigger orgasm for many women. Sara says, "When I want to have an orgasm, I just push down, as I did when I had my baby. The extra pressure sends me flying." Another multiply orgasmic lady says, "After my first climax, my clitoris is less responsive to touch, so I create more sensation by pushing hard against my fingers to bring on another one." And another affirms, "Bearing down on the dildo makes all my inner skin feel exposed and extra-sensitive. I come right away like that, several times."

Secret #18

Learn to Distinguish Between Clitoral and Vaginal Orgasms.

Vaginal orgasms are quite different from clitoral ones, and you may not realize you're having one because your contractions are not the intense muscular spasms of clitoral climax but the deeper, more oceanlike waves of vaginal orgasm, and this may set you on an orgasmic plateau that leads to other things.

"When I have a vaginal orgasm, my whole pelvis, and sometimes my entire body, bounces and shakes," Rachel explained. "It happens when I use my dildo to rub the very back of my uterus, deep inside. After one of these, I'm satisfied, but then I crave lots more sex, mainly with a real live cock. So my husband loves it when I please myself this way." One vibrating vixen says, "I love to make my clit come first with Jerry the Vibrator. Then I set him aside and use my fingers to caress just inside my vulva until it starts undulating inside. Then if I touch my G-spot, this delicious liquid starts flowing that feels like it comes from the middle of my being."

Secret #19

Ride Your State of Mind Beyond *Orgasm.*

One cosmic seductress shared these provocative thoughts on going beyond orgasm: "To me, orgasm is like the electric charge of putting your finger in a socket—an exciting feeling but a little crude. I find that if I get my head out of the way, feel completely safe, and let go of all my inhibitions and fears, I can go beyond that violent charge into a delicious hum, a state of bliss that can go on for quite a long time. When I'm completely in touch with my Inner Sex Goddess, she knows what to do with my body and leads the way. But you have to be willing to unite completely—not with a partner but with yourself."

The Taoist masters, too, have always regarded the feeling of oneness achieved during and following orgasmic ecstasy as the most easily accessible mystical experience. So if you approach pleasuring and orgasm not just as a physical release but as a spiritual adventure, you too may find that a mystical place even beyond orgasm lies deliciously within your self-loving grasp.

9

cleopatra's pleasure toys— electric, plastic, furry, and human

although it is said that, on many nights, Cleopatra would summon hundreds of her soldiers to take their individual turn satisfying and being satisfied by her seemingly endless capacity for sexual pleasuring, once she met Mark Antony she became a one-man woman. And while he was off fighting wars and acquiring new territory for their kingdom, she would slake her robust sexual appetite with a wide assortment of inventive and luxurious toys, from dildos fashioned of smooth wood or stone to gold-chain pleasure halters, papyrus reed ticklers, and carefully selected clusters of grapes. Aside from quenching a queen's lusty thirst, Cleopatra's pleasure toys also kept the jewel of her libido sparkling, piqued and developed her prodigious imagination, and enhanced her magnetically irresistible sex appeal. Her eyes literally smoldered with passionate invitation when Antony returned from campaigning, and she wantonly initiated him into whatever new and secret seductions she had invented during their long separation. She was a woman profoundly in touch with her Inner Sex Goddess.

As a queen, Cleopatra knew that gold and land were her most necessary allies. But as a woman, she believed that a finely carved dildo was truly a girl's best friend.

Much more charming and fun companions on a solitary evening, they're much more affordable and easier to procure too. Today's vibrating dildos and modern pulsing massagers provide a reliable source of high orgasmic pleasure that can't be beat—in fact, using a vibrator is how I discovered what an orgasm was in the first place. My friend Sally says she used to need an hour and a half of hand stimulation before she could have an orgasm, but with her trusty electric toy she can reach a shuddering climax in ten minutes or less if she wants to. Joan, a very focused and intense woman in her frisky sixties, reports that she needs up to two hours of rapid pulsation directly on her clitoris to reach her peak. For her, a vibrator provides the consistent, long-lasting stimulation her body wants and needs but that neither she nor her husband has the stamina to maintain by hand. Well-known sex therapist Pauline Abrams says, "It takes longer for me to come with a vibrator, because I can't control the feedback system as well as with my own hand," but most women find that the concentrated, unflagging stimulation provided by an electric pleasure toy makes for easier, faster, and often more intense orgasms than they can count on with any other method.

A vibrator works by quivering and shaking the millions of nerve endings in the skin of your genitals. It can trigger at least a million more sensors than the most skillful hand or penis, meaning that an intensely high level of arousal, if not ecstatic orgasm, is inevitable. But don't worry that you'll become addicted. In fact, quite the opposite is usually the case. Most women find that when they learn the full extent of their erotic capacity by self-pleasuring with vibrators and other sex toys, they are at last able to transfer these satiating talents and sensations to other styles of lovemaking, whether on their own or with their partners.

Just like sex goddesses, vibrators come in many styles, shapes, and sizes. Like me, you may choose to acquire an entire inventory of vibrating toys to suit your different sensual moods. Or, like Joan, you may prefer the simplicity of one perfect pleasure wand, always impeccably attuned to your particular cravings. Whichever your predilection, you can buy most types of vibrators in an ordinary drugstore because they are basically massagers for the whole body. For other types, such as dildo vibrators, you may need to visit your local sex store or browse through the many tasteful sex toy catalogs currently available. Once acquired, you can prolong your vibrator's life and the quality of service it gives you by storing it in a cool, dry place—I keep mine in a cloth bag, snuggled in a drawer—and wiping it clean after every use with a cloth moistened with warm water or alcohol. Never immerse your vibrator-massager in water.

swedish-style scalp massagers

Held on by straps around the palm, these massagers are small vibrating boxes that sit on the back of your hand. They make your whole hand vibrate gently. Although the pulsations they produce are not as intense as wand or coil-operated vibrators, the advantage of Swedish-style massagers is the skin-to-skin contact they permit and the versatility of being able to transport vibrations to any body area that your eager hand and fingers can reach. So for a lovely silky sort of vibratory experience, strap on your Swedish massager and make your hand flow sensually over your body like that of one of Cleopatra's handmaidens in the milk bath.

133. Glide over your entire body with your electrified hand, delving into every crevice and cranny with this quivering sensation. When you vibrate your skin, you stimulate the flow of blood to that area, a marvelous health and beauty treatment for the entire body. And you will discover that areas previously not so erotically sensitive will awaken to new sensual thrills at your vibrating touch — your scalp, lower back, fingers, and toes, for example. So skate lightly over the skin, hold firmly in one spot, or massage as you go. Tingle your soft lips, earlobes, and nipples. Massage your tummy and inner thighs. Tickle the bottoms of your feet, your inner elbows, and the curve of your fanny. Try performing the Mirror of Sensual Transformation ritual with a vibrating hand and see how marvelously different it feels.

134. Vibrate your vulva. Cup your entire pubic mound in your pulsating palm; slowly press in and feel the deep waves ripple throughout your entire body. Let your fingers rest lightly on your clitoris and vaginal lips. Massage your rosebud and moist vaginal opening with your softly buzzing hand. Squeeze them gently. Insert one vibrating fingertip inside your vagina. Just hold it there while you tingle; then rotate it and slide it in and out. Sneak up on your G-spot and make it throb. With your new quivering touch, you can add a fresh dimension to what you did in numbers 35 through 132.

135. If you didn't become an immediate fan of anal self-play in Chapter 4, try it with your *electrified* fingers. You may discover, as did my friend Sharon, that the delicate tissues there, richly endowed with sensual nerve endings, literally invite vibrations. She says, "I love to strap on my Swedish massager and lay the tip of my middle finger against the opening in my behind. The vibrations feel

sooooo good, and somehow primal. At the same time I rub my clit and labia with the other hand. It's kind of like being rocked in an unbelievably sexy cradle."

electric wand and coil-operated vibrators

As used by most modern sex goddesses, these vibrators are great for super stimulation of the genital area, especially the clitoris, thereby quickly propelling you into the blissful throes of first-time orgasms, nectar-producing orgasms, and even multiple orgasms. As such, they are highly recommended by Aphrodite, the Cloud Damsels, the sensual descendants of Cleopatra, and 99.7 percent of all Inner Sex Goddesses as an especially fine way to develop deep communion with them. And the more you express your Inner Sex Goddess self, the deeper and more electric is your communion with your lover. So pick out the vibrator type best suited to you, and aim for the stars.

A wand vibrator is composed of a tennis-ball-sized vibrating head attached to a foot-long phallic handle. One of the oldest and most popular types, this magic wand generates a strong penetrating vibration, diffused over the rounded rubber head, and it's very easy to maneuver. It can be easily stationed between you and your lover, providing both of you with powerful vibes and free hands.

Coil-operated vibrators have smaller handles, usually about seven inches long, and a vibrating metal plug on the side to which you can fasten a fun assortment of vinyl attachments—rounded, pronged, and cuplike. They generate more focused, super-fast vibrations, are relatively lightweight and quiet, and have the advantage of variety over the vibrating head. Both wand and coil-operated vibrators usually have two speeds of operation, which basically translate to "intense" and *really* intense." So handle these toys with care, but do handle them.

136. Since wand and coil-operated vibrators were really made to be body massagers, you can and should use them to voluptuously tingle the skin all over your body. Employ the longer wand vibrators to pleasure places you can't normally reach with your hands. Massage the middle of your back, for instance, while you twirl your nipples with your free hand, or extend the wand down to tickle the bottoms of both feet while you rub your clitoris with your free hand. Play with the attachments of a coil-operated model on different parts of your body—perhaps the suction cup over a toe, the pronged number to scratch your back, or the small rounded one to slip into your navel. Or simply give yourself an all-over vibrating massage before you move on to more sexual endeavors.

137. Although the possible combinations of body parts and vibrator attachments are tantalizingly endless, here are some suggestions for each tingling attachment that Cleopatra would have loved to have in her collection. The dome of the suction cup is perfect for crowning your clitoris with euphoric pulsations; it fits over and around your little Jewel of the Nile without touching it directly. Try using the pronged attachment to simulate the grazing of Mark Antony's teeth on your milk-wet nipples. The small rounded tip is excellent for penetrating *in* to sensitive places, like a smoothed Nile pebble having an earthquake inside your moist interior caves. And the ringed diffuser spreads the tantalizing tingles over the fleshy mounds of your honeyed breast or your jasmine-perfumed pubis; and, if pressed down firmly, it sends caressing pulsations deep into your very bones.

138. Nipples and vibrators go well together. The round ball of a wand vibrator can impart a wonderful tingly feeling when smoothed over or pressed deep into a rosy areola. Cupping a nipple with the domed attachment of a coil-operated model might remind you of a small, sucking mouth. For a sharper, more intense sensation, pass either the pronged or the spot massager lightly over your nipples; this can send darts of excitement to your lower regions, warming them up for further self-play.

139. When you feel ready to move the vibrator to your genitals, you may want to soften the intensity of its pulsations at first. Too strong a pressure or movement can kill your building passion. Try placing a folded towel, a pillow, or a piece of clothing, like maybe your sexy panties or teddy, between your delicate vaginal or clitoral tissues and the head of the vibrator. Or encase the whole vibrator in a thick cotton sock. This will help diffuse the vibrations, and the different texture against your skin will add a thrill all its own.

140. Massage your outer and inner love lips with the vibrator. Long, slow strokes bring out the best and hottest levels of sensation. At some point stop and hold the head maddeningly steady against your urethral opening or your vaginal opening. Let the constant, steady pulsations melt into you and spread a throbbing glow throughout your whole body.

141. You know how maddeningly exciting it is when your lover teases you by completely removing his penis from your vulva, pausing, and then resuming his amorous assault. Do the same with your vibrator by continually raising it away from your body and bringing it back again.

142. Try inserting your stone egg (from the PC muscle exercises) or some ben wa balls into your vagina and then holding the vibrator against your vaginal opening. The egg or balls will rattle around deliciously.

143. One sexy editor I know says she likes to rest a finger on her clitoris and then vibrate her finger with the rim of the suction cup attachment. Of course, this finger arrangement can also travel farther down across your inner lips to create a throbbing vulval massage.

144. Though this is a delicate undertaking, most women use their vibrators to bestow otherwise impossible raptures upon their yearning clits. Techniques for doing this are as varied as the women who invent and relish them. Some stir their wands over and around the clitoral tip in slow, lazy circles. Others rub up and down or back and forth. They may alternate these movements with simply holding the vibrator lightly in place or rhythmically pulsing it in and out like a slow, gentle love tap. One young and blissfully married swim instructor I know says she prefers to plant her vibrator firmly over her clitoris and then very slowly increase the urgency by pressing it in closer and closer until the vibrator is mushing her clitoris into her pubic mound and the entire area is throbbing wildly. Then she switches the vibrator control to high!

145. While vibrating your clitoris in the manner of your choice, trail your moistened fingers over the soft fur-

row between your labia, circle around your vaginal opening, and slip inside. Rotate, tickle, or thrust appropriately.

146. A favored method of my friend Beverly, a bookish professor of philosophy, is to vibrate her clitoris while manually massaging her nipples, and then alternate with the opposite procedure—vibrating her trembling tips while manually massaging her love bud. For Beverly, as for many women, there is a direct and powerful connection between these two hot spots that is electrified by the simultaneous pulsing and pulling actions. She says it's a great turn-on for her to watch this in the mirror too—as it would be for any lucky lover, by the way.

147. You can simulate the skin-to-skin pulsations of a Swedish scalp massager by resting your wand or coil-operated vibrator on the back of your hand as you stroke, knead, and slap with your fingers or palm. With a little imagination, these strokes could feel like the delicious ministrations of your man's mouth, hand, or "sacred snake."

148. Insert a fingertip to pinpoint your G-spot and then vibrate it by placing your magic wand on the part of your finger, knuckle, or hand that remains outside.

149. My next-door neighbor, an avid sensualist, suggests laying your vibrator, head up, on a pillow, kneeling or squatting over it, and touching your genitals to its pulsing head as lightly or firmly, as fast or slow, as you desire. Pump your hips, à la Elvis, over the humming surface.

150. Free your hands for erotic self-exploration by creatively engineering a harness to hold your vibrator in place against your labia or clitoris. Tie a long scarf under your pelvis and vibrator, and over your shoulder. Two scarves crisscrossed around your hips can work even better. Or don the bottom half of your bikini swimsuit and insert the vibrator head between cloth and skin.

151. I've found that if you hold the vibrator lightly against your love bud and use the middle finger of your other hand to tickle and caress the outside of your vaginal opening and the area just inside it, the voluptuous sensations and images of a lover's penis rubbing against your moist vulva are magically and meltingly evoked.

152. One day over crullers and coffee my friend Marion confessed to me, "I love to rent steamy sex videos and watch them with a vibrator in my lap. I copy everything they do in the movie, whether it involves somebody's hand or tongue or even a man's penis, except that I'm doing it with my vibrator. I rub it all over my face, breasts, genitals, and derriere. Whatever they do, I get turned on by watching it and feeling my own vibrations at the same time." A great way to double your pleasure!

153. Using either a wand vibrator or one of the smooth attachments on a coil-operated vibrator, slip the oscillating head around to your anal opening and massage gently. Don't try to insert it. With your free hand, rub your swollen labia and/or clitoris. Close your eyes and float on a dreamy, cradling cloud, or imagine your lover's tongue there.

154. Even though your vibrator is a wonderfully powerful love machine, don't make it do all the work. Move your body against it, gyrate your hips, swivel your fanny into it, undulate over and around its pulsing head. From a prone position with knees bent, thrust your pelvis up off the bed, tighten your tummy and PC muscle, and grind against the massager. Kneel or stand with legs outstretched and do the lambada or the limbo with your mechanical partner. Bend over and slip the vibrator between your legs to massage your tender thighs and labial mound; grip it with your thighs and squeeze, as if it's another phallus you know and love.

155. Get personal. Plenty of women have told me they have pet names for their vibrators—Sam, Vic the Vibrator, Thor (the god of thunder!), Valentino, Reginald Rutabaga III, and so on. The woman who dubbed her vibrator Valentino often plays flamenco music and wears one of those black gaucho hats with a chin strap when she has a rendezvous with her electrically powered lover.

156. Many sex toy shops and mail-order catalogs carry a variety of vibrator attachments specifically designed for sexual use—including "cliticklers" (perfect for focusing vibrations on one spot) and G-spotters (curved to tuck against your labia or to insert for vaginal vibration). There's even one shaped like a two-pronged twig that tingles your clitoris and your inner vaginal walls simultaneously or pulsates deliciously inside your anus. Sometimes half the fun of these attachments is shopping for them in the first place and imagining the dazzling variety of uses to which you can put them. So don't be too shy to indulge in this harmlessly pleasurable pursuit—or to actually cavort with these naughty little toys either!

157. Okay, say your vibrator has brought you to a thrilling orgasmic peak, and say your love bud is now supersensitive and shy of further vibratory touch, so you think the fun is over. Only your Inner Sex Goddess knows for sure, but you could probably go on to several more orgasms and reach places in your deep, hot sexuality you never knew existed. If you simply relax, take a few deep belly breaths, and let your hand rest between the vibe and you while you gently rotate against it, you can sustain the lovely orgasmic plateau and allow your clitoris to rejuvenate itself for further, heightened responses. This is when your Inner Sex Goddess *really* comes alive.

dildos and battery vibrators

Derived from the Italian word *diletto*, which means "delight," dildos are penislike objects used for delightful sensual pleasuring. Battery-operated vibrators are simply dildos that vibrate. Since you do basically the same things with both devices, I've lumped them together here for convenience — after all, it's their penislike quality that matters.

And that's of course what mattered to Cleopatra when she had her wood and stone dildos especially carved to order. We don't know for sure, but since clay dildos were found in Egyptian tombs around that same time, we can only imagine what elaborate pleasure wands the Queen of the Nile might have had prepared for her eternal resting place. We do know that Cleopatra treasured her phallic possessions as practical magic for keeping her ripe, vitalizing sensuality within easy reach. The Egyptian temptress intuitively understood that sense memories are stored all over the body, and the touch of phallus to vulva can spark off internal nerve messages that evoke lust and love.

Throughout the ages, people of all cultures have unabashedly used carved phalluses as delightful keys to unlock deep sexual feelings. The people of ancient times actually considered dildos sacred. Originally worshiped as fertility gods, they were believed to house the magical potency of life itself. In India, holy lingams made of stone, metal, or ivory, representing the god Siva, were used to deflower virgins as a sacred rite of passage before marriage. And in ancient Rome, it was a statue of the phallus god Mutunus Tutunus who presented his staggering equipment for affianced young girls to ceremonially straddle.

In ancient Japan and China, a wife would often have a replica of her husband's penis made of tortoiseshell, horn, or wood, with his name beautifully inscribed on it. Greatly cared for and kept in a specially made box, it was a much-venerated likeness of his actual form that could be doted upon and used for self-satisfaction during the prolonged absence of a loved and loving mate.

In the harems of Arabia and the social and sacred events of Greece, dildos continued to develop new and more interesting forms, and around A.D. 500 a nice touch was added: dildos began to be made from sealing wax so they would absorb body heat. By the 1100s, the clever French had invented long red rubber instruments called *consolateurs* that held milk or other liquids that could be pumped out to simulate ejaculation.

Today both vibrating and nonvibrating dildos come in an astonishing variety of shapes, sizes, and colors, perfect for each libidinous lady and her every sensual mood. Vibrating dildos made from plastic, vinyl, or rubber are relatively inexpensive and portable, and they produce vibrations gentler than the wand or coil-operated vibrators. Some are plain hard cylinders while others approximate the softer feel and luscious look of a real penis. Take your pick. I have a delightfully mischievous friend who loves to give the plain cylindrical kind—not very lifelike, but effective—as first-time vibrator gifts. Wearing a catlike grin, she told me, "They're nonthreatening, affordable, and always appreciated."

Regular dildos are equally insertable, portable, and affordable—they just don't vibrate. What they do is provide a delicious feeling of fullness in the vagina (or rectum); the movement is up to you. They too are made from rubber or plastic, but some are fashioned from a very lifelike silicone, and some even sport little protrusions that look and feel like testicles.

Because they come in a wide variety of shapes, sizes, and colors, buying a regular or a vibrating dildo can be a mind-boggling experience. I've seen them as small as 4 1/4 inches long and an inch in diameter, and as big as 10 inches long by 2 1/4 inches. They come in every color, from flesh to black to turquoise, and in shapes ranging from plain cylinders to ducks, whales, and dolphins to lifelike models of a famous porn star's equipment. Relying on your own personal tastes, you shouldn't have too much trouble selecting a color and shape to suit you, but size can be deceiving. Some women choose a dildo too small because they underestimate the expanded scope of an aroused vagina, while others find that their eyes are much bigger than their sexual appetites. I recommend experimenting with vegetables first—zucchini, cucumbers, and carrots—to determine the perfect fit for you. Then let your Inner Sex Goddess be your guide.

158. First things first. Always lubricate your dildo before use because, far from being innately slippery, rubber and plastic can be somewhat sticky and can even pinch or abrade your sensitive tissues. But the oiling-up process can be a scintillating project in itself. Like Cleopatra, you might want to wet your dildo with your mouth by sucking on it lustily, as you would your man's penis. When I attended a class in the art of fellatio, I was delighted to discover that the instructor actually got turned on by using a lifelike rubber dildo to demonstrate oral technique. This practice is not at all weird or perverted; it's sensual as all get-out. In fact, I often have hot oral sex with my dildo while I pleasure myself in other ways at the same time. Try it. The other lubing option is to rub your dildo with oil in the same sensuous way you would massage your lover's equipment. Again, with a little imagination, this procedure can be an entrancing turn-on for you.

159. Asking what women like to do with dildos is like asking "What do women want?" Basically, everything. Your repertoire should be limited only by your imagination. With your vibrating dildo, try everything you like to do with your regular vibrator. Use your nonvibrating dildo to perform some version of whatever you enjoy doing with your hands and fingers. Make either kind do all the lovely things to you that your man's love tool does, and all the things you *wish* it could do. It's your dream penis to do with—and be done unto with—as you please. Look at it. Fondle it. Lick it. Screw it. Make it last for hours. Experiment with wild new ways of making love that you can shock your lucky man with later.

160. Here's what my friend Charlene, a freckled, fresh-faced mom, likes to do: "First I smooth the oiled head of my dildo up and down my vaginal lips. Then I press it in a little deeper so it snuggles in between them. Still moving it forward and back, I bring the dildo up to massage my clitoris, then down to nuzzle it barely inside my opening—just enough so that the lip of the dildo head catches on the rim of my vagina. After I pull it in and out a few times, I start the whole routine over again, keeping myself from pushing the entire length deep inside as long as I can—because as soon as I do, I have the most fantastic orgasm."

161. Create a welcoming space for your dildo by fingering your clitoris long enough to get your juices flowing. Still massaging your delicate rosebud, dip the dildo into your musky lubricating fluids and slip it slowly inside you. Then slide it in and out, matching the cadence of your thrusts with your clitoral strokes and firing off all those lovely inner sex neurons. Keeping the two motions going, quicken your pace until you are thrusting and rubbing at lightning speed. See how far out into the galaxy you can take yourself.

162. As you are thrusting, you might want to get your PC muscle into the rhythm too, squeezing it around the plunging dildo so that you can feel its texture against your sensitive vaginal walls. Remember that contracting your inner muscles also pulls on your clitoris, so you'll get a double whammy effect with these sensations. And it's great practice for milking your man's hot member.

163. Try inserting your dildo as deep as possible and just holding it there. If it's a vibrator, flick on the switch after it's in place and let the vibrations radiate throughout your entire vaginal cavity. With a nonvibrating dildo, just focus on the luscious feeling of fullness. Let your other hand caress your body erotically as you fashion daydreams of cradling the love-swollen penis of the sexiest man alive.

164. I know a woman who prefers to insert her dildo at oblique angles so that it stretches and pulls at her vaginal opening yet penetrates very little. She says, "This way, it hits all those special spots, inside and out, that drive me crazy, and I feel always on the edge, craving more."

165. Many women like to alternate deep, powerful plunges that pound into the inner recesses of their love cave with shallow, almost playful thrusts that excite the tighter entryway section. You can even let the dildo slip out completely sometimes, experiencing a lovely tug against your inner lips and vaginal rim each time you reinsert it. Show your lover how to do this with his flesh-and-blood phallus.

166. Experiment with varying leg positions to achieve different effects: knees together or spread wide; sitting, reclining, or kneeling; standing in front of a full-length mirror; on your side with legs drawn up; on all fours; in a chair with your legs draped over the arms; face down while imagining being taken by a Mongol warrior. My manicurist says she likes to half recline with one knee up and the other flat on the bed. Then she brings her dildo in from behind, leaving plenty of room for the other hand to massage her clitoris or outer lips. This also brings the tip of the dildo in contact with the front wall of her vagina, where she undoubtedly has a goddess spot or two.

167. A great position, if you can manage it, is lying on your back, knees spread wide, feet together and drawn up close to your bottom. Hold the dildo inside you and maneuver it with your feet. All the muscles around your vagina and its lips are being stimulated by the stretch of your legs as well as the exertions of your feet. And this lightly athletic marvel leaves both hands free for erotic exploration to your nipples and clitoris or other erotic venues. If there were a Sexual Olympics, this would surely be a hotly contested event!

168. If you have a dildo with a suction cup base, try sticking it to the floor; then squat over it with legs spread wide and bounce up and down wildly. You can create very deep penetration and play with your breasts at the same time. Do your man the biggest favor of his life and let him watch you next time.

169. Mary Ann, whose husband is often away scouting locations, has become quite chummy with her vibrating dildo. She says it makes her even hotter for Bill when she stretches her love lips wide open with the fingers of one hand and plunges her dildo in and out with the other. She comments, "Not only does this feel great and remind me of my lover, but it's incredible to watch in the mirror too."

170. As you tease, thrust, and rub with your dildo, letting yourself get more and more rapidly out of control, you may find it amusing to deliberately slow the pace by plunging your dildo in as deep as possible and just letting it rest there. Massage your clitoris very languidly and gently until your breathing is back to normal. Then speed up again, bringing yourself to a peak three or four times before you finally let the overpowering spasms carry you over the edge.

171. Sex therapist Pauline Abrams says, "I have my best orgasms if I put a dildo inside me so that it touches my cervix and then use the vibrator. That makes my orgasms much stronger." You can use the vibrator to steam up your clitoris and, while doing slow, sensuous penetration, gyrate on the dildo and vibrator at the same time. Or occasionally move the vibrator to the base of the dildo to send fiery pulsations rocketing up inside you. Another idea is to hold the dildo inside you by squeezing your legs together so that one hand is free for the vibrator and the other is available to tease your nipples or to perform some other delight.

172. Insert your dildo about halfway and revolve it around and around the neck of your womb as if you were stirring up a delicious batter of passion cookies. This is especially intoxicating when done with a vibrating dildo turned up to full speed.

173. Adorn your dildo with a ribbed or contoured condom to create a subtle but stimulating variation on the sensations it produces. It's a great way to practice safe fantasy sex with your favorite outrageously endowed porn star.

174. Accessorize. Don a hat, scarf, gloves, shirt pulled open to expose your breasts, garter belt, and stockings under a tight dress, earrings in your pubic hair, temporary tattoos—anything you might not feel brazen enough to wear for your lover. The sight of yourself in the mirror, coquettishly attired, with a lovely plump phallus sliding in and out of you, may give you the salacious ideas you've always wished you had.

175. For a delightful tease, skim a vibrating dildo back and forth over your perineum for five to ten minutes

before allowing yourself to push it into the deep well of your vagina.

176. In some sex toy stores and catalogs, you can purchase hollow dildos containing a rubber or latex tube that's open at one end. You fill the tube with warm water or cream, or take a tip from the Italians and use egg whites or even fish eggs. Then you thrust the dildo in and out in your favorite manner and eject your fantasy lover's "vital essence" at the moment of your climax.

177. Though this may be not to everyone's taste, I just have to pass along what seems like an exotically stimulating idea from a very adventurous friend of mine. Says she, "I like that vibrating feeling in my behind; it seems to go all the way up through my vagina and stomach. That's why I often slide my vibrator dildo gently into my rear and smooth my fingers around the stretched opening there. Usually I just lie back and let the feeling build, but sometimes I play with my clitoris or the inside of my vagina. If I slip my fingers inside, I can feel the vibrations through the skin of my vagina, especially if I twirl the vibrator dildo around in that direction. It's a real deep, earthy sensation that makes me shudder and shake like a volcano."

178. And here's one more from yet another lusty adventuress: "I think two dildos are better than one, and I

like to come up with creative ways to use both my small penislike vibrator and my big lifelike dildo. First I make the little one slippery by sliding it into my cozy slit. Then I slip it into the hole in my bottom and switch it on. Next I glide my Superman-size dildo ever so slowly into my vagina, push it in and out, and churn it around in circles. I imagine that some burly, sweaty construction worker is having his way with me and being real rough. This somehow blasts all my inhibitions right out of the water, and I pound against him like a wild woman. And once I've got all that going, I still have one hand free to stroke my clit. I haven't yet tried using another vibrator for my clitoris, but that's next on my list!"

cleo's grab bag

With the power, ingenuity, and resources to have any sensual toy imaginable created for her, the precocious Queen of the Nile collected quite a cache of inventive pleasuring instruments. But her favorites were always her dildos and the simple little things like ibis feathers, lion fur, and of course milk baths. These pleasures she indulged in for both solo and partner lovemaking. While vibrators and dildos are at the top of almost every modern Sex Goddess's toy list, there is a veritable cornucopia of other scintillating playthings you too can use to coax delectable pleasures from your silky, sexy body—and that of your lover. Though some of the suggestions that follow may bend the boundaries of your self-pleasuring comfort zone, put on your sultry Cleopatra crown and let her try them out for you. You may be surprised at your exotically expanded capacity for pleasure.

179. Ancient Indian texts suggest that natural substances make the best penetration toys; they recommend radishes, mangoes, and gourds as well as the usual bananas, carrots, cucumbers, and zucchini. (One zany advertising writer says, "Thank God for zucchini—it has ridges! But I always practice safe vegetable sex and use condoms to avoid contact with pesticides.") Fascinatingly, the ancients also suggested a "reed made soft with oil" and the stalk of a plant which, when soaked in hot water, swells up and takes on an "agreeable warmth and texture." Mmm, sounds yummy. Of course, if they were around today they might also advocate using pickles (with their titillating knobs and crevices), Popsicles (deliciously icy, and fun to eat afterward), corn on the cob (lube it well first!), or even hot dogs (wet, slippery, flexible, cold, and sort of lifelike in color). Consult your Inner Sex Goddess on any richly inventive ideas she may have.

180. An artist friend of mine suggests sculpting your vegetable of choice to size, or to an interesting shape, with a potato parer, leaving enough skin at the bottom so it won't slip out of your fervid grasp. She says she goes into another world when she puts on her headphones, inserts her artistically molded eggplant, and lets her regular vibrator tickle her clitoris unmercifully. When designing your vegetable penis, don't trim too close to the center or it will go limp.

181. Almost any smooth object shaped like a cylinder can be used as a dildo—like candles, for instance. Just remember that your internal tissues are delicate; so don't use anything that's glass or metal or that has rough edges or sharp corners. Be as discriminating about your stand-in lovers as you are about your flesh-and-blood men.

182. Ben wa balls can provide an exhilarating internal massage, especially if you activate them with a vibrator (as suggested in 142) or by walking, dancing, or exercising while they jiggle around. These are especially handy for an ultimately unattainable fantasy—having a man's penis massaging your vaginal walls all day. You could also insert a vibrating dildo in your bottom and point it toward the ben wa balls just on the other side of the sensitive dividing tissues.

183. The Japanese have a slightly different version of their own ben wa balls—called rin-no-tama balls. One of these small brass spheres is hollow and the other contains a tiny heavy metal ball or quicksilver, so that the balls constantly roll against each other. You insert them in your vagina—put the empty ball in first—and secure them with a tampon. Any pelvic movement causes them to shimmy around and tickle your insides mercilessly.

184. Most sex toy stores or catalogs carry a little gem of an item called a Kegelcisor. Made of heavy brass, it's a small barbell for exercising your PC muscle (doing Kegel exercises), based on the concept that it's easier to build up strength and tone if you have to work against a resistive device. It's about 6 and 3/4 inches long and has three small spheres, one at either end and one in the middle, that are 1/4 inch to 1 and 1/8 inches in diameter. This fancy fitness tool builds love muscles to grasp your man with, and it can be a uniquely gratifying dildo as well.

185. Ice is a fabulous toy. Rub a frosty ice cube across your nipples, over your vaginal lips and clitoris, and inside the walls of your womb. You may prefer "warm" ice that has been sitting out for some time or the cold shock of ice cubes fresh from the freezer. Place an ice cube inside your vagina and let it melt as you massage your vulva, or use a vibrator on your labia to blend an internal "cherry" daiquiri. You can make a chilling dildo by freezing a cucumber or by very carefully filling an extra-sturdy and/or large condom with water and popping it in the freezer. A few hours later cut away the condom and *voilà!* — an ice penis to play with.

186. A truly marvelous toy for sale at most sex stores is a Venus Butterfly massager. This tiny vibrating pad, which lies over your clitoris and straps on around your thighs, allows you to enjoy continuous titillation on your love bud while your hands are completely free to roam over the rest of your hot bod.

187. Of course, it's good to have some playthings for the rest of your body too. Taking an inventory of the self-pleasuring treasure troves of several sensuous friends (nightstand drawers, shoe boxes under the bed, even safe-deposit boxes), I discovered the following collection of simple little toys kept handy to make the skin tingle all over the body: a small piece of rabbit fur, ostrich and peacock feathers, a feather duster, silk scarves, the satin from a discarded camisole, a lace doily, black leather gloves, a small rubber ball, wool mittens, the ratty pronged attachment from a long-abandoned vibrator, a satin-smooth wooden egg, a collection of thimbles for each fingertip, cloth flowers, a soft cuddly teddy bear, an old woven place mat, elbow-length cotton gloves, part of a beaded car-seat cover, felt squares, a terry washcloth, a large fluffy makeup brush, the ruffle from a taffeta petticoat, pieces of Velcro, and the long Cleopatra wig from an old Halloween costume. Whether you employ these skin-sational toys by your own private self or invite your lover to join in, they provide easy and fun inducements to coax your Inner Sex Goddess out of hiding.

188. Nobody talks about it, but millions of ordinary, virtuous, and sane women find that a little loving bondage provides a hot, intense, and daring addition to their self-pleasuring repertoire. If you've wondered about it but are a little squeamish, self-play can be a wonderfully private, fun, and safe outlet for your budding bondage fantasies—and a special delight for your sizzling Cleopatra-esque personality. While sex toy stores have all kinds of fancy handcuffs, whips, clamps, blindfolds, and chains, there are perfectly wonderful substitutes for all of these wicked toys right in the sanctity of your own palace. Scarves, stockings, bras, and panties make fabulous handcuffs and blindfolds; choker necklaces, ribbons, or long strands of pearls can become decorative slave collars; belts, towels, dustpans, and Ping-Pong paddles can be used for sensuous self-spankings. One friend of mine, who is particularly partial to nipple stimulation, says that clamping her nipples with padded clothespins creates a delicious teasing pinch while leaving her hands free for other

delightfully depraved activities. (If you don't have the padded variety, use cotton balls or scarves as a cushion.) Reading a book like *The Story of O* can give you plenty more inventive ideas for playing at submission while providing an erotic state of mind perfect for exploring the sweet tortures of passion.

189. Another unexpected pleasure can come from playing with toys especially made to fit into your bottom. Depending on your personal preferences, you can insert small dildos, carrots, or cucumbers to provide an exquisite feeling of fullness, or larger specially made anal plugs that stretch, and thereby titillate, your tight opening. Anything you insert into your nether regions should be completely smooth and seamless with a flared base to keep it from slipping all the way inside. And always use lots of lubrication. Once your fanny toy is comfortably and safely in place, you have both hands free to roam over other erotic territories. One woman who enjoys euphoric anal sex with her partner told me that, when alone, she likes to circle her fingers around the rim where her rear sex toy emerges while she massages her clitoris with the other hand. Another lusty lady says, "When I really want to come fast, I slide this special rubber plug inside my bottom and then stroke the inside of my vagina with my left hand. This turns my vaginal walls to warm pudding, and the plug makes me feel so wide and extended that my body just opens and comes."

190. Water as a toy offers a fount of sensuous possibilities. Sit in front of the hot, powerful jet stream in a whirlpool bath. Use a bidet, or simply pour warm water over your genitals. Lie in the tub with your vulva directly under the faucet and turn the water on hard, perhaps switching from hot to cold to hot. Remove the head from your shower and let the extra weight of the water falling from a height feel like a thousand tiny fingers rapidly running over your genitals. Marilyn Chambers, star of the classic porn video *Behind the Green Door*, says, "What's really good is a hose in your bathtub. You just die, I swear. Just hook a hose to the faucet and take the spray attachment off. You put it on your clit, then you turn the water up and down—hot or cold—and you go through the ceiling. It's the most wrenching orgasm you will ever have in your life."

191. Then there's a shower massager. The kind you can move around by hand is the only kind to have, of course. Dial the setting to any and every type of spray that takes your fancy—diffuse, pulsing, hard, soft. Wash your inner thighs and navel with hot, tingling liquid. Rub the hard spray directly on your nipples. Spurt pulsing water against your clitoris. Open your labia lips and let the warm liquid pour like cream all over your sensitive membranes. Focus the stream with your hand, and finger yourself within the gushing current. Let hot pulses cascade down

the cleavage of your bottom. Spray your entire genital area at different angles and from varying distances, in circles, in long sensuous strokes. Shake it over your throbbing bud and thrust the massager rapidly closer and farther away from your body. Let your Inner Sex Goddess splash around like a wild creature of the deep.

192. I'll bet you've never thought of your douching equipment as a toy, but many women have told me they find it extra-stimulating to pleasure themselves while douching. They say the warm water spraying inside and then dripping over their fingers as they rub their clitoris drenches them in ecstasy—and makes them think of penises bursting with love juice. Even if you don't wish to partake of this watery rapture, you can always use the dry attachments as delightfully different dildos.

193. Brightly colored ribbons, small soft flowers, and decorative hair combs can be used to adorn your pubic hair as a playful masterpiece of sensual art. If you want to go a little further, try shaving your genitalia (an erotic sensation in itself), admiring your innocently exposed elegance, and then applying a pretty, feminine temporary tattoo. Follow up these aesthetics with master strokes of pleasuring massage to your decorated pubis. Reveal your artwork to your man, if you dare.

> *You must perceive what you are through knowing yourself and your pleasures; for only then can you give the pleasure you seek and accept the pleasure given to you.*
> —Ashley Thirlby,
> Tantra

10

the goddess with her consort

now that you've awakened all the erotic centers of your body and mind and learned to bring yourself via a thousand different paths to the highest peaks of sexual ecstasy, it's time to invite your consort into the game. Of course you've been making love to your man all along, and he's been reaping the benefits of your rapidly developing Sex Goddesshood, but have you shared your hottest autoerotic expertise and passion with him? Have you, for instance, thought about tying up your partner and making him watch while you undulate, shiver, and throb to your own inner rhythms? Well, if not, now's the time to knock his socks off.

Goddess vamp that you are, however, even you may at first feel a little shy about revealing your intimate moves and feelings so boldly. But there are several good reasons for overcoming any lingering bashfulness.

Reason # 1. According to recent research, many couples have their best sex when they engage in self-pleasuring or mutual self-pleasuring prior to or during intercourse. It adds variety (a crucial element in any long-term relationship), spice, mutual trust, and vulnerability, and it deepens intimacy immeasurably. In *The Art of Sensual Loving*, Dr.

Andrew Stanway says, "The value of masturbation cannot be overestimated in any loving relationship."

Reason #2. You can turn your lover's flame up to extra hot with a simple twist of your nipple or stroke of your sexual triangle. Why do you think there's so much female masturbation seen in X-rated videos? Because men are intensely visual and begin to drool helplessly at the sight of a woman in the throes of her own passion. The fact that you are lusty and confident enough to allow him this intimate and thrilling sight of *you* is extra frosting on his erotic cake. A man once told me, "When a woman takes on the full power of her sexuality by loving her own body, and *lets me see it,* she empowers me to be my sexiest self and takes us to places neither one of us has been before."

Reason #3. It takes the passivity out of being the receiving partner. Even in partner sex, you must still be responsible for your own passion, arousal, and orgasmic pleasure. So it's fortifying to know that instead of simply having to respond and follow where your man leads, you can add some flashy steps of your own. And through some magical process of sexual osmosis, it turns out that taking the turns *you* like makes the dance much more exciting for both of you.

Reason #4. It's the best way for your man to learn your sexual needs and desires. You can show him, for example, that when you are touched lightly your body reaches out for more sensation, and that it contracts away if pressed too hard. You can let him see that when your nipples are twirled at just the right angle, your vulva opens up for him like a sweet, honey-dripping flower. Men want to know that their tremendous sexual prowess is propelling their partners to the heights of ecstasy. But never forget that, most of the time, they are completely mystified about what *really* turns women on. How provocatively refreshing it is, then, to be shown in such a nonthreatening and salaciously seductive way *exactly* how to drive you wild in bed!

Reason #5. You can learn hot new tricks from your man too. Not long after I vibrated my way to sexual self-rediscovery, I met Michael, a dedicated and natural sensualist. Sometimes I brought my vibrator to bed with us, but what Michael really wanted to see was me stroking myself between the legs, swelling, undulating, and oozing delicious, slippery moisture. He used to love watching me give myself an orgasm with my fingers and often said it was the most erotic thing he'd ever seen. I loved to watch him, too. In fact, that's how I learned most of what I know about exciting a man's penis. By watching him pleasure his own, I found out, for example, about that "one slow, five fast strokes" routine that drives most men insane.

Clearly, self-pleasuring with a partner can provide an electrifying boost to any couple's love life. But whether you discuss its lusty virtues with your mate beforehand—to feel him out, prepare, and excite him—or make it a sizzling surprise, it's probably best to start with a small, unintimidating sample of your self-pleasuring power. Over the next several days or lovemaking sessions, take your cues from each other, slowly getting used to your new erotic freedom, before you gradually crescendo to a stirring display of autoerotic fireworks. You'll probably both feel more comfortable that way.

194. Sometime during foreplay look him straight in the eye as you suck the tip of your forefinger and slide it seductively over your lips. Then use your wet fingertip to tease his lips and mouth or to give your nipples a slippery pinch, or insert it smoothly into your vagina. Although his eyes will be riveted to your actions, keep him physically involved too by using your other hand to massage his body somewhere.

195. As a variation on number 194, start by brazenly wetting your finger in *his* mouth before trailing it over, under, and into your body.

196. Cup your breasts in your hands and present them to him. Bring your nipples to his mouth, lift his hand

to them, or play provocatively with them yourself. Deliberately twirl, tweak, pull, and pinch in the ways that make you hot, so he'll learn something while he's getting an erection.

197. Provocatively slather oil on your breasts and then take your pleasure on his body, rubbing your slick, tingly nipples roughly or gently all over his face, neck, chest, nipples, stomach, legs, buns, testicles, and penis. Slide his toes, knees, flattened hand, and finally his hardened penis between your pearly globes. Let your deeply satisfied moans inflame him even further.

198. As a variation on the previous suggestion, do the same with your oiled pubic hair and vulva or (a personal favorite of my lover's) with your well-lubricated bottom.

199. Give your man a tactile and sensual thrill by asking him to lick your fingers while you massage your hottest erogenous zones.

200. Take photos of yourself massaging your body and send them to him, insert them in the folds of his newspaper, or leave them propped up on his pillow.

201. Some women prefer to blindfold themselves when first self-pleasuring for their lovers. Says my shy

friend Milly, "I can be in my own private world and feel free to do all sorts of naughty things I'd be too embarrassed to do otherwise. Sometimes I even keep the blindfold on after we start making love because the feeling of not knowing what's coming next and the heightened sense of touch are so exciting." In fact, not being under the scrutiny of your gaze can be freeing for your partner too.

202. You might try supplementing what your man is doing to you with *his* hands. A sensuous publishing exec I know says, "When my husband has his fingers in my vagina, it feels more intimate if I stroke his hand with mine. Sometimes I rub my clitoris or massage my outer lips against his fingers. We have fun getting our fingers all tangled up together."

203. Another opportunity for partial privacy is when your lips are locked together in a passionate kiss and your eyes are closed or busy staring into each other's orbs. This is a good time to stroke his back with one hand and massage your breasts or vulva with the other. He just makes you so *hot!*

204. Incorporate any of the sense-awakening activities from Chapter 2 into your partner self-pleasuring. Take a bath with him and run the water and your soapy

hands over your genitals and his. Dance for him while seductively undulating your hands over your private places. Use flowers, feathers, or fur to stroke yourself, and him, provocatively. Pour wine over your breasts or genitals, rub it in, lick your fingers, and press your wine-soaked parts against him. Smooth ice over your nipples and into the narrow glove of your sex, then let him lick off the cold drippings.

205. One closet vamp I know likes to use her lover's body as a self-stimulating tool. She says, "I rub my vulva against his knee, foot, or fanny cheeks. Or I tickle my breast with his chest hairs or pinch a nipple between his toes. Sometimes I insert his big toe in my vagina and use it like a dildo. Of course I'm fingering my clit the whole time, too, and looking him straight in the eye."

206. Actually, one of the best self-pleasuring toys you'll ever have is your man's very own love rod. Use it, slippery with your lubrication but firmly ensconced in your caressing hand, to trace circles around your clitoris; to tease your inner lips and coral opening; to tickle your nipples; to massage your facial muscles; and, keeping it decidedly under the control of your maddening grasp, to inflame the inner walls of your vagina.

207. Several sex toys have been specifically designed to transform your lover's penis into an even more exciting self-pleasuring tool for you. The fact that you show up with one of them in the bedroom will ignite his lustful imagination even before you start. Latex or rubber rings with beads in them or soft prongs all around can be slipped down to the base of your man's organ. The snug fit increases his erection, and the beads or prongs rub deliciously against your vaginal lips and clitoris as he thrusts in and out of you. The beaded ones can also be made smaller to fit around the base of his penis head, thus providing you with an outrageous internal massage. French ticklers, or rubber sleeves that fit over the penis and sport nubs all over or feathery plumes on the end, also tease your insides and may quickly stimulate you into a frenzied vaginal orgasm. How potent he'll feel then!

208. My friend Liana's husband loves to watch her do the vacuuming while she's dressed in her leather corset or lace teddy. To further relieve the boredom of this mundane task, Liana occasionally reaches down to massage her exposed love nest. And of course it just so happens that she has to bend over then to examine a speck of dust on the carpet, giving her husband a spectacular view. Apparently she sometimes rubs the humming vacuum cleaner wand between her thighs, too. I always wondered how she got her husband to help with the housework!

209. Men love to see a woman spread her sex lips wide while she plays with herself, but women often feel hesitant to do this because they think it must look grotesque. On the contrary, men find the sight intensely erotic and beautiful. One lover of mine watched fascinated as he moaned over and over, "You're so pretty, so pretty. Yes, open that flower for me." Soon he simply had to join in.

210. My friend Teresa, who's been ecstatically married to the same man for thirty years, says she likes to cup, lift, and massage her fanny while her man is on top during intercourse. In addition to providing a deeper angle of entry, this adds rear stimulation that excites her immensely. And when she wants to come, she can easily slip her finger into her anus and start the spasms rolling.

211. When he is taking you from behind, massage your breasts or reach down to rub your love bud. Again, you may want to include him in the massage by occasionally stroking his thrusting penis while you're in the neighborhood.

212. You can, of course, pleasure yourself from any lovemaking position, but spoon fashion is a particularly good one because your hands and the front of your body are completely free and, as you don't face each other, any embarrassment can easily be hidden. Even the mys-

tery of what your man can't see you doing but can feel in your undulating response is a veiled enticement for him. Anyway, most men are very aroused when a woman gets so excited, presumably by him, that she just has to touch herself erotically. So if you have any doubts, you may want to try the spoon position as a seductive starter.

213. Speaking of lovemaking positions, when you are lying on your stomach and he's taking you from behind, use the friction of the sheet or pillow to graze against your nipples and clitoris. Your deepened undulations will turn up the heat in his body as well as yours.

214. Sometimes it's easier to abandon your inhibitions when you dress up like a tart. As a birthday present for my man, I once donned a red lace merry widow with garters and stockings (no panties!) and let him ogle me as I stood up on the bed to dance, wriggle, and seductively stroke all my exposed parts. Later he raved that it was the best birthday present he ever received.

215. Tie him up and make him watch you give yourself an orgasm. Concentrate on your arousal, letting him see just what kind of stroking, pressure, speed, and positions best turn you on. When you've had your first climax, untie him and allow him to join in the fun of bringing you to another.

216. Occasionally remove your wet finger from your glistening, musky depths and put it in his mouth to suck.

217. A bank teller I know says, "My lover gets wildly excited when I kneel over his chest, pinning down his arms with my legs, and then rub my clit and vagina. He says he loves to see my aroused sex and the ecstasy on my face, feel my tensed muscles, hear my panting, and inhale my scent. He usually has just enough arm movement to stroke his penis and time his orgasm with mine."

218. When you are on top during intercourse, give him an additional show and yourself greater pleasure by sitting up straight and massaging your flushed breasts. You may want to occasionally wet your finger in your mouth or vagina and moisten your stiffened nipple with it. Or lean back and stroke your clitoris as you keep thrusting on him.

219. When you feel especially bold, try kneeling over his face as you stroke your vaginal lips. He'll love the view; and you can occasionally allow him to lick you.

220. One bawdy friend of mine shares the following: "Nothing makes my boyfriend hotter than when I stroke his shaft to get him hard and start his pre-ejaculate fluids going. I take some on my fingers and put it in my mouth or massage my nipples or clit with it. Another thing I love to do is rub myself all over with his come juice. It's a great lubricant for self-massage, and it drives him crazy to watch me do this."

221. Self-pleasuring is a lovely accompaniment to oral sex as well. When he has his tongue buried in your dewy depths, you can get so carried away that you abandon restraint to massage your clitoris or caress your thighs and breasts. Or you can get the urge as you're kissing him too. As one very ladylike matron told me, "I feel so primal when I lick my husband's penis that a different me comes out. I don't feel shy at all about rubbing myself at the same time and even imitating with my fingers what I'd like him to be doing inside me. I always give him a good view of this, too, because it makes him really excited."

222. When you have both become more comfortable with this type of love-play, you should encourage your man to pleasure himself for you as well. It's highly erotic to watch each other simultaneously and to respond, even from a small distance, to the other's building arousal and orgasm. You can lie next to or opposite each other, legs perhaps entwined, and feast your eyes and senses for hours—or you can get a little more aggressive about it. One new bride, who was obviously getting her marriage

off to a flaming start, told me, "I'll never forget the excitement of watching my lover, kneeling between my outspread legs as I masturbated for him, stroking his engorged penis to orgasm right above me. Neither one of us could take our eyes off the spectacle of the other's sex in full, pulsing bloom. It was magnificent!" When you do this, try to retain some shred of your rational mind to observe how he is specially treating his love organ—that way, you'll know just how to make it your own later.

223. Self-pleasuring with your lover by phone can also be quite titillating. My friend Sara, who carried on a long-distance romance for over a year, says, "I used to talk to Jeff with one hand on the receiver and the other between my legs. I'd give him a blow-by-blow description of what I was doing, panting and moaning into the phone, or even putting the mouthpiece down below so he could hear the wet sounds I was making. Sometimes I'd start masturbating first and then call his answering machine as I got excited enough to come—and there'd just be these long drawn-out 'Ooooooo's' for a sexy message. He never looked at another woman the whole time he was gone."

224. The best way to overcome any jealousy your man might feel about your vibrator or dildo is to bring it to bed with you and let him play too. Share with him the lusty creature you become when a vibrator is throbbing you to

orgasm, and be sure to pet him a little at the same time. Then use your toy gently on him. Let him see how delicious it looks when you tease yourself with a dildo, telling him you always imagine it's his lovely thick limb, and invite him to thrust the dildo powerfully inside you while his own equipment is free to cradle elsewhere — like in your cleavage, the cleft of your bottom, or between your buttery love lips. Or put on sexy lingerie and give him his own personal X-rated show, with you as the female lead gyrating in flagrant abandon with the male star — your vibrating dildo. If you always involve him and let him see more of your passion than he'd normally be privileged to view, your toys will become not a threat but favorite tools for joint self-pleasures.

225. My friend Catherine has a very clever suggestion for including your man in the vibrator action. She says that when her husband is making love to her from behind, she often presses a vibrator to her thighs, pelvic mound, or clitoris. Not only does this raise her passion to fever heat, but it also transmits tingling pulsations to her lucky fellow's erection right through the walls of her throbbing flesh. Or when they are face-to-face, she simply lodges a small battery-powered vibrating dildo between her genitals and his. That way, each time he thrusts, they both get a powerful quivering jolt.

$226.$ Remember all those suggestions in Chapter 9 for using a vibrator on the back of your hand while your fingers tantalize your clitoris, vaginal walls, or G-spot? Well, simply substitute your lover's hand for your own, slipping his fingers seductively between the vibrator and your trembling flesh. He'll love participating firsthand in your pulsing, swelling excitement.

$227.$ With or without a vibrator, you might drive your man wildest of all by bringing yourself to the frenzied peak just before orgasm while he watches in panting fascination, then stopping completely, looking at him with fever in your eyes, and moaning, "Come fuck me *now!*"

> *She learned to be at home*
>
> *in her body, to be her*
>
> *own best friend, her*
>
> *favourite lover.*
>
> —Tee Corrinne,
>
> *Dreams of the Woman*
>
> *Who Loved Sex*

11

daily

goddess-

izers

"I make time for self-pleasuring every day, even if I have to lock myself in the bathroom, skip lunch, or tell my mate to give me an hour by myself. If I didn't, I'd be stressed out at work, a boring lover, and a crabby witch to my friends and family. They deserve better than that, and so do I."

—Anne, executive secretary

"My sexuality makes me feel alive, important, and good about myself."

—Sandy, housewife and mother of six children

"It makes me feel great to know that we women can be many different kinds of people, professional as well as sexy."

—Jennifer, computer specialist

"The more time I spend getting in touch with my inner sensuality, the better my day seems to go. It gets my sex hormones flying, and then men are drawn to me like magnets."

—Lelia, retired attorney

Like riding a bicycle, the knack of unleashing your auto-erotic Sex Goddess is not lost if you don't do it all the time.

But I've found that the greatest benefits of keeping her active in your life—enhanced health, well-being, and energy; stress reduction; charismatic self-confidence; hot lovemaking expertise; and constant sexual radiance—are made fully available only if you keep your self-pleasuring thermostat on high with regular practice. Smart, sexy women, like the ones quoted above, pleasure themselves and their Inner Sex Goddess—even if only in some small, five-minute way—every single day. Besides innately understanding that self-pleasure is necessary for their physical, emotional, and mental well-being, they feel it's a precious and delightful gift they love to unwrap as often as possible.

Like them, you should bestow upon yourself the same love and attention you would naturally give any romantic relationship. That's what keeps love affairs (and lovers) healthy, hot, and juicy. A love affair with yourself is no different. So schedule time for sensuality; delegate household chores to children, mate, or cleaning person; give up an hour at the health club; skip part of a gossip session (giving up gossip completely is of course unthinkable); knock a half hour off your shopping; do whatever you have to do to establish your self-pleasuring as a priority. Never forget that you *deserve* to live in a perpetually fresh garden of ecstatic delights. And, as a reigning Sex Goddess, your glorious kingdom extends to those you love and care for.

daily goddessizers

Even if you are the busiest woman on the planet, I'm sure you can find time for at least one of these quick and easy goddessizers every day. They'll keep your sensual motor purring and your Inner Sex Goddess glowing.

- In your morning shower, let the water run over your beautiful genitals. As you wash, massage your clitoris and dip your soapy fingers into your vagina.
- As you towel off, rub the rough terry cloth against your soft vulva.
- When you apply body lotion, massage your nipples for an extra minute.
- Admire your naked body as you dress. Preen, pose, and play.
- Whenever you go to the bathroom, touch your vulva lovingly.
- Move through your whole day being turned on by sounds, smells, beautiful scenes, awareness of your sexual juices, the sight of someone's full mouth, provocative ads, a glimpse of the moon.
- Caress a tree on the way to work.
- Sensitize your clitoris by lightly stroking it for ten minutes every day.

- Roll in fur.
- Squeeze and rub your thighs together, especially when you're on the gym machines.
- Exercise naked.
- Flex your PC muscle whenever you think of it; no one at the meeting will know.
- Stand in the wind, close your eyes, open your palms, inhale its freshness.
- Flash yourself in the mirror.
- Invent a hot fantasy while riding the bus to work, standing in line at the bank, or under the hair dryer at the beauty salon.
- Choose your lunch menu based on color and fragrance. Admire, lick, and smell your food.
- Give your Inner Sex Goddess a mental hug at least once every day. Like you, she thrives on attention, love, and praise. Ask her advice on what to wear.
- Indulge in a chocolate-covered ice-cream bar. Rub it on your lips and anywhere else you can get away with.
- Whenever you look in a mirror, tell yourself, "I love you. You are intelligent, powerful, sexy, beautiful, and irresistible." Blow yourself a kiss if no one's looking.
- While talking on the phone, massage your face, neck, and breasts.
- Occasionally bring your attention to your *hara*

(located about two inches below your navel), considered by martial arts specialists to be the body's center of gravity and power. This snaps you immediately into the present moment and the world of the senses. Float there as you experience your own sensuality, remaining motionless or stroking yourself luxuriously.

• Dance the hula as you file or dust.

• Self-pleasure in the "exotic" locations you visit every day—the ladies' room at work, a telephone booth, a restaurant bathroom stall, someone else's backyard, or an empty meeting room.

• On the commuter train, feel the heavy vibrations come up through your feet and into your legs, thighs, and pelvis. Let your body hum.

• Punctuate your housecleaning with short vibrator sessions—ten minutes fully clothed on the couch with the vibrator, ten minutes vacuuming, ten minutes back on the couch, ten minutes dusting, and so on.

• Wash dishes in the nude.

• Doodle pictures of body parts and other sensuous things. Write in your journal about all of the erotic things you've seen, smelled, touched, heard, and done today.

• In the grocery store, fondle the cucumbers and zucchini.

• Treat your self-pleasuring as a brief meditation. Close your eyes and drift in the alpha brain waves produced by using a vibrator on your erogenous zones. Tune in to your sensual intuition, daydreams, and creative juices.

• Lying in bed at night, massage and love your body. Go to sleep thinking of yourself as a sensual wonderland, a famous temptress, or the answer to your man's erotic dreams.

for special, languorous occasions

When you do have time for a longer, more luxurious visit with your Inner Sex Goddess, treat yourself to:

• an hour-long hot scented bath with candles, music, and wine
• an extended version of any of the "Seeds of Sensuality" activities from Chapter 2
• the hottest and longest fantasy or role-play you can dream up, complete with toys, clothes, and props
• the ritual of the Mirror of Sensual Transformation, with or without a vibrator
• a two-hour teasing session in which you bring yourself to the peak at least fifteen times before

you finally allow yourself to explode into one earth-shattering orgasm

• a two-hour teasing session in which you give yourself fifteen orgasms

• an X-rated video accompanied by candles, incense, wine, and a vibrator

• a lazy afternoon with a fantasy or real life love slave

• a languorous self-massage with aromatherapy oils or in a hot bath

• two hours of reading or writing erotic literature, massaging your breasts and genitals the whole time

For an extra treat, try this lovely Tantric sensual meditation:

Stimulate yourself to a peak of excitement, then close your eyes and focus on your *relaxed* breathing. Imagine yourself to be *in* your perineum or clitoris. Feel a sensation, heat, tingle, shape, color, or sound there. As you continue pleasuring yourself, breathe energy into this area and let your special sensation expand as you exhale. After a few moments move your imagined location high up into your womb and feel a different sensation there. Repeat the breathing and expanding. Next, travel to your navel with the same process, and then to your heart. As you fully experience the warmth and love in your heart, finally let yourself have an orgasm that washes deliciously over your entire body. Bask for a while in your sensual Nirvana before reentering the everyday world.

Your Inner Sex Goddess brings pleasure, confidence, and joy not only to you but, through you, to all those in your life. A whole world of women in such full sensual flower would be a beautiful garden indeed. So, like all of the mythological and real-life sex goddesses you've read about in this book, don't be afraid to get really decadent and outrageous. On the contrary, be proud of your multifaceted, lusty creativity. Remind yourself every day that you are a luscious, highly erotic woman—a true Sex Goddess divinely designed for pleasure and loving.

Freely radiate your resplendent sensuality, and the whole world will be transformed into your divine kingdom of love.

the inner sex goddess scrolls

---

books, magazines, music, and videos to get you in the mood

Of the millions of erotic books, magazines, videos, and pieces of music out there, here are just a few that have been highly recommended by the Inner Sex Goddesses of many ultra-sensual women (including my own) especially for self-arousal. Try them out and see which ones resonate for you. If you find a particular work that really brings your Aphrodite self out to play, explore the other pieces that author, composer, or director has done too. Visit your local sex toy store or browse the pages of home pleasure toy catalog or adult magazines for further choices. Shop the erotica section of your favorite bookstore. Ask the clerk at the video or music store for recommendations. Share suggestions with your friends. Keep your eyes and ears open and your Inner Sex Goddess antennae alert; once you start looking, you'll find that all sorts of wonderful erotica shows up naturally within your Sensual Domain. Happy trolling!

Literature

Delta of Venus by Anaïs Nin (actually *anything* by Nin is fabulously erotic)

Fanny Hill by John Cleland

Lady Chatterley's Lover and *Women in Love* by D. H. Lawrence

Cheri by Colette

Emmanuelle by Emmanuelle Arsan

The Story of O by Pauline Reáge

The Pearl by a collection of Victorian authors

Plaisir d'Amour by Anne-Marie Villefranche

The Pleasures of Loving, compiled by Maren Sell

The Black Cat books, any of them, published by Grove Press

Tropic of Cancer by Henry Miller

The Naked Lunch by William Burroughs

The Claiming of Sleeping Beauty, Beauty's Punishment, and *Beauty's Release* by A. N. Roquelaure

Exit to Eden by Anne Rice

The Erotic Comedies, or anything else, by Marco Vassi

The Gates of Paradise, edited by Alberto Manguel

Lust, edited by John and Kirsten Miller

My Secret Garden and *Forbidden Flowers* by Nancy Friday

Pleasures: Women Write Erotica by Lonnie Barbach, Ph.D.

Endless Love by Scott Spencer

The Intimate Kiss by Gershon Legman

"Song of Solomon" from the Bible

Erotic Poems, edited by Peter Washington
The Book of Eros, edited by Lily Pond and Richard Russo

Art Books
The Art of Arousal by Dr. Ruth Westheimer
The Erotic Edge by Lonnie Barbach, Ph.D.
The Erotic Arts by Peter Webb
Erotic Art of the East and *Primitive Erotic Art* by Philip Rowson

Adult Magazines
Playgirl
Woman on Top
Playboy
Penthouse (great for the pictorials with people making love)
Penthouse Letters (*hot* letters from readers)
Yellow Silk (collections of erotic writing)
Tantra
For Women
Paramour

Classical Music
Hungarian Rhapsody #2 by Liszt
Bolero by Ravel
The 1812 Overture by Tchaikovsky
Scheherazade by Rimsky-Korsakov
Symphony No. 9 ("Ode to Joy") by Beethoven
Canon in D Major by Pachelbel
Romeo and Juliet by Prokofiev

Meditation by Mischa Maisky, cello

The Double Life of Veronique soundtrack by Krzysztof Kieslowsky

Carmina Burana by Orff

The Firebird by Stravinsky

Suite No. 3 in D Major by Bach

"Love Death" aria from *Tristan und Isolde* by Wagner

"Celeste Aida" from *Aida* by Verdi

"O soave fanciulla" from *La Bohème* by Puccini

"Tu, tu, amore tu?" from *Manon Lescaut* by Puccini

Carmen by Bizet

Modern Music

"Leila" (original or "unplugged" version) by Eric Clapton

"Brown Sugar," "Let's Spend the Night Together," or countless other hits by the Rolling Stones

"Fields of Gold" by Sting

"Lay, Lady, Lay" by Bob Dylan

"Knights in White Satin" by the Moody Blues

"Black Magic Woman" by Santana

"Baby, Baby" by Smokey Robinson

"Let Me Stand Next to Your Fire" by Jimi Hendrix

"Stir It Up" by Bob Marley

"Love Me Tender" by Elvis Presley

Inside the Taj Mahal (flute) by Paul Horn

"Dream Lover" by Mariah Carey

"Crazy for You" by Madonna

"Caribbean Queen" by Billy Ocean

Rhythm of the Saints by Paul Simon

"You Make Me Feel Like a Natural Woman" by Aretha
Franklin

"Fly Me to the Moon" by Frank Sinatra

"Unforgettable" by Natalie and Nat King Cole

"Sweetest Taboo" by Sade

CrazySexyCool by TLC

"Purple Rain" by Prince

"Sex" by Morphine

"Funky Blues" by Charlie Parker

"Fooled Around and Fell in Love" by Elvin Bishop

Taj Mahal by Taj Mahal

Compact Jazz by Antonio Carlos Jobim

Nouveau Flamenco by Ottmar Liebert

Dreams by Kitaro

Enigma by Enigma

Chariots of Fire soundtrack by Vangelis

Adult Videos

Behind the Green Door

Delta of Venus

The Seven Seductions

Pandora's Mirror

Taboo American Style

Night Trips, House of Dreams, Hidden Obsessions (and any other films directed by Andrew Blake—he's one of the best)

Three Daughters (and any other films put out by Candida Royale and her Femme Productions; they are specifically directed toward women)

The Licorice Quartet (and anything else directed by Harry Paris)

Boiling Point, Cat House, The Girl with the Heart-Shaped Tattoo (and any other films directed by Toni English, a woman)

Better Sex (an instructional series)

Red Shoe Diaries (the half-hour TV series from Showtime)

8.95
SOP

BOOKS BY THOMAS WOLFE

From Death to Morning

FROM DEATH

TO

MORNING

by

Thomas Wolfe

Vigil strange I kept on the field one night.

CHARLES SCRIBNER'S SONS

NEW YORK

9 11 13 15 17 19 Q/P 20 18 16 14 12 10

SBN 684-10676-0 (trade cloth)
SBN 684-71940-1 (trade paper, SL)

Printed in the United States of America

Contents

From Death to Morning

No Door

It is wonderful with what warm enthusiasm well-kept people who have never been alone in all their life can congratulate you on the joys of solitude. I know whereof I speak. I have been alone a great deal in my life—more than any one I know—and I also knew, for one short period, a few of these well-kept people. And their passionate longing for the life of loneliness is astonishing. In the evening they are driven out to their fine house in the country where their wives and children eagerly await them; or to their magnificent apartments in the city where their lovely wife or charming mistress is waiting for them with a tender smile, a perfumed, anointed, and seductive body, and the embrace of love. And all of this is as a handful of cold dust and ashes, and a little dross.

Sometimes one of them invites you out to dinner: your host is a pleasant gentleman of forty-six, a little bald, healthily plump, well-nourished-looking, and yet with nothing gross and sensual about him. Indeed he is a most æsthetic-looking millionaire, his features, although large and generous, are full of sensitive intelligence, his manners are gentle, quietly subdued, his smile a little sad, touched faintly with a whimsy of ironic humor, as of one who has passed through all the anguish, hope, and tortured fury youth can know, and now knows what to expect from life and whose "eye-lids are a little weary," patiently resigned, and not too bitter about it.

Yet life has not dealt over-harshly with our host: the

evidence of his interest in un-monied, precious things is quietly, expensively, all around him. He lives in a pent-house apartment near the East River: the place is furnished with all the discrimination of a quiet but distinguished taste, he has several of Jacob Epstein's heads and figures, including one of himself which the sculptor made "two years ago when I was over there," and he also has a choice collection of rare books and first editions, and after admiring these treasures appreciatively, you all step out upon the roof for a moment to admire the view you get there of the river.

Evening is coming fast, and the tall frosted glasses in your hands make a thin but pleasant tinkling, and the great city is blazing there in your vision in its terrific frontal sweep and curtain of star-flung towers, now sown with the diamond pollen of a million lights, and the sun has set behind them, and the red light of fading day is painted upon the river—and you see the boats, the tugs, the barges passing, and the winglike swoop of bridges with exultant joy—and night has come, and there are ships there—there are ships—and a wild intolerable longing in you that you cannot utter.

When you go back into the room again, you feel very far away from Brooklyn, where you live, and everything you felt about the city as a child, before you ever saw or knew it, now seems not only possible, but about to happen.

The great vision of the city is burning in your heart in all its enchanted colors just as it did when you were twelve years old and thought about it. You think that same glorious happiness of fortune, fame, and triumph will be yours at any minute, that you are about to take your place among great men and lovely women in a life more fortunate and happy than any you have ever known—that it is all here, somehow, waiting for you and only an inch away if you will touch it, only a word away if you will speak it, only a wall, a door, a stride from you if you only knew the place where you may enter.

And somehow the old wild wordless hope awakes again that you will find it—the door that you can enter —that this man is going to tell you. The very air you breathe now is filled with the thrilling menace of some impossible good fortune. Again you want to ask him what the magic secret is that has given his life such power, authority, and ease, and made all the brutal struggle, pain, and ugliness of life, the fury, hunger, and the wandering, seem so far away, and you think he is going to tell you—to give this magic secret to you —but he tells you nothing.

Then, for a moment the old unsearchable mystery of time and the city returns to overwhelm your spirit with the horrible sensations of defeat and drowning. You see this man, his mistress, and all the other city people you have known, in shapes of deathless brightness, and yet their life and time are stranger to you than a dream, and you think that you are doomed to walk among them always as a phantom who can never grasp their life or make their time your own. It seems to you now that you are living in a world of creatures who have learned to live without weariness or agony of the soul, in a life which you can never touch, approach or apprehend; a strange city-race who have never lived in a dimension of time that is like your own, and that can be measured in minutes, hours, days, and years, but in dimensions of fathomless and immemorable sensation; who can be remembered only at some moment in their lives nine thousand enthusiasms back, twenty thousand nights of drunkenness ago, eight hundred parties, four million cruelties, nine thousand treacheries or fidelities, two hundred love affairs gone by—and whose lives therefore take on a fabulous and horrible age of sensation, that has never known youth or remembered innocence and that induces in you the sensation of drowning in a sea of horror, a sea of blind, dateless, and immemorable time. There is no door.

But now your host, with his faintly bitter and ironic smile, has poured himself out another good stiff drink of honest rye into a tall thin glass that has some ice in it, and smacked his lips around it with an air of rumination, and, after two or three reflective swallows, begins to get a trifle sorrowful about the life harsh destiny has picked out for him.

While his mistress sits prettily upon the fat edge of an upholstered chair, stroking her cool and delicate fingers gently over his knit brows, and while his good man Ponsonby or Kato is quietly "laying out his things" for dinner, he stares gloomily ahead, and with a bitter smile congratulates you on the blessed luck that has permitted you to live alone in the Armenian section of South Brooklyn.

Well, you say, living alone in South Brooklyn has its drawbacks. The place you live in is shaped just like a pullman car, except that it is not so long and has only one window at each end. There are bars over the front window that your landlady has put there to keep the thugs in that sweet neighborhood from breaking in; in winter the place is cold and dark, and sweats with clammy water, in summer you do all the sweating yourself, but you do plenty of it, quite enough for any one; the place gets hot as hell.

Moreover—and here you really begin to warm up to

your work—when you get up in the morning the sweet
aroma of the old Gowanus Canal gets into your nostrils, into your mouth, into your lungs, into everything
you do, or think, or say! It is, you say, one huge gigantic Stink, a symphonic Smell, a vast organ-note of
stupefying odor, cunningly contrived, compacted, and
composted of eighty-seven separate several putrefactions;
and with a rich and mounting enthusiasm, you name
them all for him. There is in it, you say, the smell of
melted glue and of burned rubber. It has in it the fragrance of deceased, decaying cats, the odor of rotten
cabbage, prehistoric eggs, and old tomatoes; the smell
of burning rags and putrefying offal, mixed with the
fragrance of a boneyard horse, now dead, the hide of a
skunk, and the noisome stenches of a stagnant sewer;
it has as well the——

But at this moment your host throws his head back
and, with a look of rapture on his face, draws in upon
the air the long full respiration of ecstatic satisfaction,
as if, in this great panoply of smells, he really had
found the breath of life itself, and then cries:

"Wonderful! Wonderful! Oh, simply *swell! Marvellous!*" he cries and then throws back his head again, with
a shout of exultant laughter.

"Oh, John!" his lady says at this point with a troubled
look upon her lovely face, "I don't think you'd like a
place like that at *all*. It sounds simply *dreadful!* I don't
like to hear of it," she says, with a pretty little shudder of
distaste. "I think it's simply terrible that they let people
live in places like that!"

"Oh!" he says, "it's wonderful! The power, the richness, and the beauty of it all!" he cries.

Well, you agree, it's wonderful enough. And it's got
power and richness—sure enough! As to the beauty—

that's a different matter. You are not so sure of that—
but even as you say this you remember many things.
You remember a powerful big horse, slow-footed, shaggy
in the hoof, with big dappled spots of iron gray upon
it that stood one brutal day in August by the curb. Its
driver had unhitched it from the wagon and it stood
there with its great patient head bent down in an infinite and quiet sorrow, and a little boy with black eyes
and a dark face was standing by it holding some sugar
in his hand, and its driver, a man who had the tough
seamed face of the city, stepped in on the horse with a
bucket full of water which he threw against the horse's
side. For a second, the great flanks shuddered gratefully
and began to smoke, the man stepped back on to the
curb and began to look the animal over with a keen
deliberate glance, and the boy stood there, rubbing his
hand quietly into the horse's muzzle, and talking softly
to it all the time.

Then you remember how a tree that leaned over into
the narrow little alley where you lived had come to life
that year, and how you watched it day by day as it
came into its moment's glory of young magic green.
And you remember a raw, rusty street along the water-
front, with its naked and brutal life, its agglomeration
of shacks, tenements, and slums and huge grimy piers,
its unspeakable ugliness and beauty, and you remember how you came along this street one day at sunset, and saw all of the colors of the sun and harbor,
flashing, blazing, shifting in swarming motes, in an
iridescent web of light and color for an instant on the
blazing side of a proud white ship.

And you start to tell your host what it was like and
how the evening looked and felt—of the thrilling smell
and savor of the huge deserted pier, of the fading light

upon old rusty brick of shambling houses, and of the blazing beauty of that swarming web of light and color on the ship's great prow, but when you start to tell about it, you cannot, nor ever recapture the feeling of mystery, exultancy, and wild sorrow that you felt then.

Yes, there has been beauty enough—enough to burst the heart, madden the brain, and tear the sinews of your life asunder—but what is there to say? You remember all these things, and then ten thousand others, but when you start to tell the man about them, you cannot.

Instead you just tell him about the place you live in: of how dark and hot it is in summer, how clammy cold in winter, and of how hard it is to get anything good to eat. You tell him about your landlady who is a hard-bitten ex-reporter. You tell him what a good and liberal-hearted woman she is; how rough and ready, full of life and energy, how she likes drinking and the fellowship of drinking men, and knows all the rough and seamy side of life which a newspaper reporter gets to know.

You tell how she has been with murderers before their execution, got the story from them or their mothers, climbed over sides of ships to get a story, forced herself in at funerals, followed burials to the graveyard, trampled upon every painful, decent, sorrowful emotion of mankind—all to get that story; and still remains a decent woman, an immensely good, generous, and lusty-living person, and yet an old maid, and a puritan, somehow, to the roots of her soul.

You tell how she went mad several years before, and spent two years in an asylum; you tell how moments of this madness still come back to her, and of how you went home one night several months before, to find her stretched out on your bed, only to rise and greet you as the great lover of her dreams—Doctor Eustace McNamee, a name, a person, and a love she had invented for herself. Then you tell of her fantastic family, her three sisters and her father, all touched with the same madness, but without her energy, power, and high ability; and of how she has kept the whole crowd going since her eighteenth year.

You tell about the old man who is an inventor who does not invent; of how he invented a corkscrew with the cork attached that would not cork; an unlockable lock; an unbreakable looking-glass that wouldn't look. And you tell how the year before, he inherited $120,000—the first money he had ever had—and promptly took it down to Wall Street where he was as promptly shorn of it, meanwhile sending his wife and daughters to Europe in the nuptial suite of a palatial liner and cabling them when they wanted to come back: "Push on to Rome, my children! Push on, push on! Your father's making millions!"

Yes, all this, and a hundred other things about this incredible, mad, fantastic, and yet high-hearted family which I had found in a dingy alleyway in Brooklyn I could tell my host. And I could tell him a thousand other things about the people all about me—of the Armenians, Spaniards, Irishmen in the alley who came home on week days and turned on the radio, until the whole place was yelling with a hundred dissonances, and who came home on Saturday to get drunk and beat their wives—the whole intimate course and progress of their lives published nakedly from a hundred open windows with laugh, shout, scream, and curse.

I could tell him how they fought, got drunk, and murdered; how they robbed, held up, and blackjacked, how they whored and stole and killed—all of which was part of the orderly and decent course of life for them—and yet, how they could howl with outraged modesty, complain to the police, and send a delegation to us when the young nephew of my landlady lay for an hour upon our patch of backyard grass clad only in his bathing trunks.

"Yuh gotta nekkid man out deh!" they said, in tones of hushed accusatory horror.

Yes, we—good sir, who are so fond of irony—we, old Whittaker, the inventor, and Mad Maude, his oldest daughter, who would grumble at a broken saucer, and then stuff lavish breakfasts down your throat, who would patiently water twenty little feet of backyard earth from April until August, and until the grass grew beautifully, and then would turn twenty skinny, swarthy, and half-naked urchins loose into it to stamp it into muddy ruin in twenty minutes while she played the hose upon their grimy little bodies; we, this old man, his daughters, and his grandson, three bank clerks, a cartoonist, two young fellows who worked for Hearst, and myself; we, good sir, who sometimes brought a girl into our rooms, got drunk, wept, confessed sinful and unworthy lives, read Shakespeare, Milton, Whitman, Donne, the Bible—and the sporting columns—we, young, foolish, old, mad, and bewildered as we were, but who had never murdered, robbed, or knocked the teeth out of a woman; we, who were fairly decent, kind, and liberal-hearted people as the world goes, were the pariahs of Balcony Square—called so because there was neither square nor balconies, but just a little narrow alleyway.

Yes, we were suspect, enemies to order and the public morals, shameless partakers in an open and indecent infamy, and our neighbors looked at us with all the shuddering reprehension of their mistrustful eyes as they beat their wives like loving husbands, cut one another's throats with civic pride, and went about their honest toil of murder, robbery, and assault like the self-respecting citizens they were.

Meanwhile a man was murdered, with his head bashed in, upon the step of a house three doors below me; and a drunken woman got out of an automobile one night at two o'clock, screaming indictments of her escort to the whole neighborhood.

"Yuh gotta pay me, ya big bum!" she yelled. "Yuh gotta pay me now! Give me my t'ree dollehs, or I'll go home an' make my husband beat it out of yuh!"

"Staht actin' like a lady!" said the man in lower tones. "I won't pay yuh till yuh staht actin' like a lady! Yuh gotta staht actin' like a lady!" he insisted, with a touching devotion to the rules of gallantry.

And this had continued until he had started the engine of his car and driven off at furious speed, leaving her to wander up and down the alleyway for hours, screaming and sobbing, cursing foully and calling down the vengeance of her husband on this suitor who had thus misused her—an indictment that had continued unmolested until three young ambitious thugs had seized the opportunity to go out and rob her; they passed my window running, in the middle of the night, one fearful and withdrawing, saying, "Jeez! I'm sick! I don't feel good! Wait a minute! Youse guys go on an' do it by yourself! I want a cup of coffee!"—And the others snarling savagely:

"Come on! Come on, yuh yellah bastad! If yuh don't come on, I'll moiduh yuh!" And they had gone, their quick feet scampering nimbly in the dark, while the woman's drunken and demented howls came faintly from the other end, and then had ceased.

Your host has been enchanted by that savage chronicle. He smites himself upon the brow with rapture, crying "Oh, grand! *Grand!* What a lucky fellow you are! If I were in your place I'd be the happiest man alive!"

You take a look about you and say nothing.

"To be free! To go about and see these things!" he cries. "To live among real people! To see life as it is, in the raw—the *real* stuff, not like this!" he says with a weary look at all the suave furnishings of illusion that surround him. "And above all else to be *alone!*"

You ask him if he has ever been alone, if he knows what loneliness is like. You try to tell him, but he knows about this too. He smiles faintly, ironically, and dismisses it and you, with a wise man's weary tolerance of youth: "I know! I know!!" he sighs. "But all of us are lonely, and after all, my boy, the real loneliness for most of us is *here*"—and he taps himself a trifle to the left of the third shirt-stud, in the presumptive region of his heart. "But you! Free, young, and footloose, with the whole world to explore— You have a fine life! What more, in God's name, could a man desire?"

Well, what is there to say? For a moment, the blood is pounding at your temples, a hot retort springs sharp and bitter to your lips, and you feel that you could tell him many things. You could tell him, and not be very nice or dainty with it, that there's a hell of a lot more that a man desires: good food and wonderful companions, comfort, ease, security, a lovely woman like the one who sits beside him now, and an end to loneliness— but what is there to say?

For you are what you are, you know what you know, and there are no words for loneliness, black, bitter, aching loneliness, that gnaws the roots of silence in the night.

So what is there to say? There has been life enough, and power, grandeur, joy enough, and there has also been beauty enough, and God knows there has been squalor and filth and misery and madness and despair enough; murder and cruelty and hate enough, and loneliness enough to fill your bowels with the substance of gray horror, and to crust your lips with its hard and acrid taste of desolation.

And oh, there has been time enough, even in Brooklyn there is time enough, strange time, dark secret time enough, dark million-visaged time enough, forever flowing by you like a river, even in cellar-depths in Brooklyn there is time enough, but when you try to tell the man about it you cannot, for what is there to say?

For suddenly you remember how the tragic light of evening falls even on the huge and rusty jungle of the earth that is known as Brooklyn and on the faces of all the men with dead eyes and with flesh of tallow gray, and of how even in Brooklyn they lean upon the sills of evening in that sad hushed light. And you remember how you lay one evening on your couch in your cool cellar depth in Brooklyn, and listened to the sounds of evening and to the dying birdsong in your tree; and you remember how two windows were thrown up, and you heard two voices—a woman's and a man's—begin to speak in that soft tragic light. And the memory of their words came back to you, like the haunting refrain of some old song—as it was heard and lost in Brooklyn.

"Yuh musta been away," said one, in that sad light.

"Yeah, I been away. I just got back," the other said.

"Yeah? Dat's just what I was t'inkin'," said the

other. "I'd been t'inkin' dat yuh musta been away."

"Yeah, I been away on my vacation. I just got back."

"Oh, yeah? Dat's what I t'ought meself. I was t'inkin' just duh oddeh day dat I hadn't seen yuh f'r some time, 'I guess she's gone away,' I says."

And then for seconds there was silence—save for the dying birdsong, voices in the street, faint sounds and shouts and broken calls, and something hushed in evening, far, immense, and murmurous in the air.

"Well, wat's t' noos sinct I been gone?" the voice went out in quietness in soft soft tragic light. "Has anyt'ing happened sinct I was away?"

"Nah! Nuttin's happened," the other made reply. "About duh same as usual—*you* know?" it said with difficult constraint, inviting intuitions for the spare painfulness of barren tongues.

"Yeah, I know," the other answered with a tranquil resignation—and there was silence then in Brooklyn.

"I guess Fatheh Grogan died sinct you was gone," a voice began.

"Oh, yeah?" the other voice replied with tranquil interest.

"Yeah."

And for a waiting moment there was silence.

"Say, dat's too bad, isn't it?" the quiet voice then said with comfortless regret.

"Yeah. He died on Sattiday. When he went home on Friday night, he was O. K."

"Oh, yeah?"

"Yeah."

And for a moment they were balanced in strong silence.

"Gee, dat was tough, wasn't it?"

"Yeah. Dey didn't find him till duh next day at ten

o'clock. When dey went to look for him he was lyin' stretched out on duh bat' room floeh."

"Oh, yeah?"

"Yeah. Dey found him lyin' deh," it said.

And for a moment more the voices hung in balanced silence.

"Gee, dat's too bad. . . . I guess I was away when all dat happened."

"Yeah. Yuh musta been away."

"Yeah, dat was it, I guess. I musta been away. Oddehwise I woulda hoid. I was away."

"Well, so long, kid. . . . I'll be seein' yuh."

"Well, so long!"

A window closed, and there was silence; evening and far sounds and broken cries in Brooklyn, Brooklyn, in the formless, rusty, and unnumbered wilderness of life.

And now the red light fades swiftly from the old red brick of rusty houses, and there are voices in the air, and somewhere music, and we are lying there, blind atoms in our cellar-depths, gray voiceless atoms in the manswarm desolation of the earth, and our fame is lost, our names forgotten, our powers are wasting from us like mined earth, while we lie here at evening and the river flows . . . and dark time is feeding like a vulture on our entrails, and we know that we are lost, and cannot stir . . . and there are ships there! there are ships! . . . and Christ! we are all dying in the darkness! . . . and yuh musta been away . . . yuh musta been away. . . .

And that is a moment of dark time, that is one of strange million-visaged time's dark faces.

Death the Proud Brother

THE face of the night, the heart of the dark, the tongue of the flame—I had known all things that lived or stirred or worked below her destiny. I was the child of night, a son among her mighty family, and I knew all that moved within the hearts of men who loved the night. I had seen them in a thousand places and nothing that they ever did or said was strange to me. As a child, when I had been a route boy on a morning paper, I had seen them on the streets of a little town—that strange and lonely company of men who prowl the night. Sometimes they were alone, and sometimes they went together in a group of two or three, forever in mid-watches of the night in little towns prowling up and down the empty pavements of bleak streets, passing before the ghastly waxen models in the windows of the clothing stores, passing below hard bulbous clusters of white light, prowling before the façades of a hundred darkened stores, pausing at length in some little lunchroom to drawl and gossip quietly, to thrust snout, lip, and sallow jowl into the stained depths of a coffee mug, or dully to wear the slow gray ash of time away without a word.

The memory of their faces, and their restless prowling of the night, familiar and unquestioned at the time, returned now with the strangeness of a dream. What did they want? What had they hoped to find as they prowled past a thousand doors in those little, bleak, and wintry towns?

Their hope, their wild belief, the dark song that the night awoke in them, this thing that lived in darkness

15

while men slept and knew a secret and exultant triumph, and that was everywhere across the land, were written in my heart. Not in the purity and sweetness of dawn with all the brave and poignant glory of its revelation, nor in the practical and homely lights of morning, nor in the silent stature of the corn at noon, the drowsy hum and stitch of three o'clock across the fields, nor in the strange magic gold and green of its wild lyric wooded earth, nor even in the land that breathed quietly the last heat and violence of day away into the fathomless depth and brooding stillness of the dusk—as brave and glorious as these times and lights had been—had I felt and found the mystery, the grandeur, and the immortal beauty of America.

I had found the dark land at the heart of night, of dark, proud, secret night: the immense and lonely land lived for me in the brain of night. I saw its plains, its rivers, and its mountains spread out before me in all their dark immortal beauty, in all the space and joy of their huge sweep, in all their loneliness, savagery, and terror, and in all their immense and delicate fecundity. And my heart was one with the hearts of all men who had heard the strange wild music that they made, filled with unknown harmonies and a thousand wild and secret tongues crying to men the exultant and terrible music of wild earth, triumph and discovery, singing a strange and bitter prophecy of love and death.

For there was something living on the land at night. There was a dark tide moving in the hearts of men. Wild, strange and jubilant, sweeping on across the immense and sleeping earth, it had spoken to me in a thousand watches of the night, and the language of all its dark and secret tongues was written in my heart. It had passed above me with the rhythmical sustentions of its mighty wing, it had shot away with bullet cries of a demonic ecstasy on the swift howlings of the winter wind, it had come softly, numbly, with a dark impending prescience of wild joy in the dull soft skies of coming snow, and it had brooded, dark and wild and secret, in the night, across the land, and over the tremendous and dynamic silence of the city, stilled in its million cells of sleep, trembling forever in the night with the murmurous, remote and mighty sound of time.

And I was joined in knowledge and in life with an indubitable certitude to the great company of men who lived by night and had known and loved its mystery. I had known all joys and labors and designs that such men know. I had known all things living on the earth by night, and finally, I had known by night the immortal fellowship of those three with whom the best part of my life was passed—proud Death, and his stern brother, Loneliness, and their great sister, Sleep. I had lived and worked and wrought alone with Loneliness, my friend, and in the darkness, in the night, in all the sleeping silence of the earth, I had looked a thousand times into the visages of Sleep, and had heard the sound of her dark horses when they came. And I had watched my brother and my father die in the dark mid-watches of the night, and I had known and loved the figure of proud Death when he had come.

Three times already I had looked upon the visage of death in the city, and now that spring I was to see it once again. One night—on one of those kaleidoscopic nights of madness, drunkenness, and fury that I knew that year, when I prowled the great street of the dark from light to light, from midnight until morning—I saw a man die in the city subway.

He died so quietly that most of us would not admit

at first that he was dead, so quietly that his death was only an instant and tranquil cessation of life's movement, so peaceable and natural in its action, that we all stared at it with eyes of fascination and unbelief, recognizing the face of death at once with a terrible sense of recognition which told us we had always known him, and yet, frightened and bewildered as we were, unwilling to admit that he had come.

For although each of the three city deaths that I had seen had come terribly and by violence, there would remain finally in my memory of this one a quality of terror, majesty, and grandeur which the others did not have.

The first of these deaths had occurred four years before in the month of April of my first year in the city. It had happened upon the corner of one of the dingy, swarming streets of the upper East Side, and in the way it had happened there had been a merciless, accidental, and indifferent quality which was far more terrible than any calculated or deliberate cruelty could have been, which spoke terribly and at once through the shining air, the joy and magic of the season, obliterating all the hope and exultancy in the hearts of men who saw it.

I was coming along one of the dingy cross-streets in the upper east-side district—a street still filled with the harsh and angular fronts of old brown-stone houses, which once no doubt had been the homes of prosperous people but were now black with the rust and grime of many years. These streets were seething with the violent and disorderly life of dark-faced, dark-eyed, strange-tongued people, who surged back and forth, innumerably, namelessly, with the tidal, liquid, and swarming fluency that all dark bloods and races have, so that the lean precision, the isolation, and the severe design characteristic of the lives of northern peoples—like something lonely, small, pitifully yet grandly itself—are fractured instantly by this tidal darkness. The numberless and ageless man-swarm of the earth is instantly revealed in all its fathomless horror, and will haunt one later in dreams, even if one sees only a half-dozen of these dark faces in a street.

Upon the corner of this swarming street, where it joined one of the great grimy streets that go up and down the city, and that are darkened forever by the savage violence and noise of the elevated structure, so that not only the light which swarms through the rusty iron webbing, but all the life and movement underneath it seems harsh, driven, beaten, violent, bewildered, and confused—on such a corner the man was killed. He was a little middle-aged Italian who had a kind of flimsy cart which was stationed at the curb, and in which he had a shabby and miscellaneous stock of cigarettes, cheap candies, bottled drinks, a big greasy-looking bottle of orange juice turned neck downward into a battered cylinder of white enamelled tin, and a small oil stove on which several pots of food—sausages and spaghetti—were always cooking.

The accident occurred just as I reached the corner opposite the man's stand. The traffic was roaring north and south beneath the elevated structure. At this moment an enormous covered van—of the kind so powerful and cumbersome that it seems to be as big as a locomotive and to engulf the smaller machines around it, to fill up the street so completely that one wonders at the skill and precision of the driver who can manipulate it—came roaring through beneath the elevated structure. It curved over and around, in an attempt to get ahead of a much smaller truck, and as it did so, swiped the little truck a glancing blow that wrecked it instantly, and sent it crashing across the curb into the vendor's wagon with such terrific force that the cart was smashed to splinters, and the truck turned over it completely and lay beyond it in a stove-in wreckage of shattered glass and twisted steel.

The driver of the truck, by the miracle of chance, was uninjured, but the little Italian vendor was mangled beyond recognition. As the truck smashed over him the bright blood burst out of his head in an instant fountain so that it was incredible so small a man could have such fountains of bright blood in him; and he died there on the sidewalk within a few minutes, and before the ambulance could reach him. A great crowd of shouting, dark-faced people gathered around the dying man at once, police appeared instantly in astonishing numbers, and began to thrust and drive in brutally among the excited people, cursing and mauling them, menacing them with their clubs, and shouting savagely:

"Break it up, deh! Break it up! On your way, now!" . . . "Where yuh goin'?" one snarled suddenly, grabbing a man by the slack of his coat, lifting him and hurling him back into the crowd as if he were a piece of excrement. "Break it up, deh! Break it up! G'wan, youse guys—yuh gotta move!"

Meanwhile the police had carried the dying man across the curb, laid him down on the sidewalk, and made a circle around him from the thrusting mob. Then the ambulance arrived with its furious and dreadful clangor of bells, but by this time the man was dead. The body was taken away, the police drove and lashed the crowds before them, whipping and mauling them along, as if they were surly and stupid animals, until at length the whole space around the wreck was clear of people.

Then two policemen, clearing the street again for its unceasing traffic, half pushed, half carried the twisted wreckage of the vendor's cart to the curb, and began to pick up his strewn stock, boxes, broken cups and saucers, fragments of broken glass, cheap knives and forks, and finally his tin spaghetti pots, and to throw them into the heap of wreckage. The spaghetti, pieces of brain, and fragments of the skull were mixed together on the pavement in a horrible bloody welter. One of the policemen looked at it for a moment, pushed the thick toe of his boot tentatively into it, and then turned away with a grimace of his brutal red face, as he said, "Jesus!"

At this moment, a little gray-faced Jew, with a big nose, screwy and greasy-looking hair that roached backward from his painful and reptilian brow, rushed from the door of a dismal little tailor's shop across the sidewalk, breathing stertorously with excitement, and carrying a bucket full of water in his hand. The Jew ran swiftly out into the street, with a funny bandy-legged movement, dashed the water down upon the bloody welter and then ran back into the shop as fast as he had come. Then a man came out of another shop with a bucket full of sawdust in his hand which he began to strew upon the bloody street until the stain was covered over. Finally, nothing was left except the wreckage of the truck and the vendor's cart, two policemen who conferred quietly together with notebooks in their hands, some people staring with dull fascinated eyes upon the blood-stain on the pavement, and little groups of people on the corners talking to one another in low, excited tones, saying:

"Sure! I seen it! I seen it! Dat's what I'm tellin' yuh! I was talkin' to 'm myself not two minutes before it happened! I saw duh whole t'ing happen! I was standin' not ten feet away from 'im when it hit him!"—as they revived the bloody moment, going over it again and again with an insatiate and feeding hunger.

Such was the first death that I saw in the city. Later, the thing I would remember most vividly, after the horror of the blood and brains and the hideous mutilation of man's living flesh were almost forgotten, was the memory of the bloody and battered tins and pots in which the vendor had cooked his spaghetti, as they lay strewn on the pavement, and as the policeman picked them up to fling them back into the pile of wreckage. For later it seemed these dingy and lifeless objects were able to evoke, with a huge pathos, the whole story of the man's life, his kindly warmth and smiling friendliness—for I had seen him many times—and his pitiful small enterprise, to eke out shabbily, but with constant hope and as best he could, beneath an alien sky, in the heart of the huge indifferent city, some little reward for all his bitter toil and patient steadfastness—some modest but shining goal of security, freedom, escape, and repose, for which all men on this earth have worked and suffered.

And the huge indifference with which the vast and terrible city had in an instant blotted out this little life, soaking the shining air and all the glory of the day with blood, the huge and casual irony of its stroke—for the great van which had wrecked the truck and killed the man, had thundered ahead and vanished, perhaps without its driver even knowing what had happened—was evoked unforgettably, with all its pity, pathos, and immense indifference, by the memory of a few battered pots and pans. This, then, was the first time I saw death in the city.

The second time I saw death in the city, it had come by night, in winter, in a different way.

About mid-night of a night of still bitter cold in February, when the moon stood cold and blazing in the white-blue radiance of the frozen skies, a group of people were huddled together upon the sidewalk of one of those confusing and angular streets which join Seventh Avenue

near Sheridan Square. The people were standing before
a new building which was being put up there, whose front
stood raw and empty in the harsh brown-livid light a
few feet away. Upon the curb, the watchman of the
building had made a fire in a rusty ash-can, and this fire
now whipped and blazed in the frozen air with a crack-
ling flame to which some of the people in the group would
go from time to time to warm their hands.

Upon the icy pavement before the building, a man was
stretched out on his back and a hospital interne, with the
tubes of a stethoscope fastened to his ears, was kneeling
beside him moving the instrument from place to place on
the man's powerful chest, which was exposed. An ambulance, its motor throbbing with a quiet and reduced power
that was somehow ominous, was drawn up at the curb.

The man on the pavement was about forty years old
and had the heavy shambling figure, the brutal and
powerful visage, of the professional bum. On the scarred
and battered surface of that face it seemed that every
savage violence of weather, poverty, and physical degrada-
tion had left its mark of iron, during the years the vagabond had wandered back and forth across the nation, until
now the man's features had a kind of epic brutality in
which a legend of lonely skies and terrible distances, of
pounding wheel and shining rail, of rust and steel and
bloody brawl, and of the wild and savage earth, was
plainly written.

The man lay on his back, as still and solid as a rock,
eyes closed, his powerful, brutal features upthrust in the
rigid and stolid attitude of death. He was still living, but
one side of his head, at the temple, had been bashed in—
a terrible, gaping wound which he had got when he
wandered, drunk and almost blind with the cheap alcohol
or "smoke" which he had been drinking, into the build-

ing, and had fallen forward across a pile of iron beams, against one of which he had smashed his head. The great black stain of the wound had run down across one side of his face and on the ground, but it had almost ceased to bleed, and in the freezing air the blood was clotting rapidly.

The man's rag of dirty shirt had been torn open and his powerful breast also seemed to swell forward with the same rigid and stolid immobility. No movement of breath was visible: he lay there as if carved out of rock, but a dull, flushed, unwholesome looking red was still burning on his broad and heavy face, and his hands were clenched beside him. His old hat had fallen off and his bald head was exposed. This bald head, with its thin fringe of hair upon each side, gave a final touch of dignity and power to the man's strong and brutal face, that was somehow terrible. It was like the look of strength and stern decorum that one sees on the faces of those powerful men who do the heavy work in the trapeze act at the circus, and who are usually bald-headed men.

None of the people who had gathered there about the man showed any emotion whatever. Instead, they just stood looking at him quietly with an intent yet indifferent curiosity, as if there were in the death of this vagabond something casual and predictable which seemed so natural to them that they felt neither surprise, pity, nor regret. One man turned to the man next to him, and said quietly, but with assurance, and a faint grin:

"Well, dat's duh way it happens to dem in duh end. Dey all go like dat sooner or later. I've neveh known it to fail."

Meanwhile, the young interne quietly and carefully, yet indifferently, moved his stethoscope from place to place, and listened. A policeman with a dark, heavy face, pitted, seamed, and brutal-looking, stood over him, surveying the scene calmly as he gently swung his club, and ruminating slowly on a wad of gum. Several men, including the night watchman and a news-dealer on the corner, stood quietly, staring. Finally, a young man and a girl, both well dressed, and with something insolent, naked, and ugly in their speech and manner that distinguished them as being a cut above the others in education, wealth, position—as young college people, young city people, young Village, painting, writing, art-theatre people, young modern "post-war generation" people—were looking down at the man, observing him with the curiosity with 'which, and with less pity than, one would regard a dying animal, and laughing, talking, jesting with each other with a contemptible and nasty callousness that was horrible, and that made me want to smash them in the face.

They had been drinking, but they were not drunk: something hard and ugly was burning nakedly in them—yet, it was not anything forced or deliberate, it was just hard-eyed, schooled in arrogance, dry and false, and fictional, and carried like a style. They had an astonishing literary reality, as if they might have stepped out of the pages of a book, as if there really were a new and desolate race of youth upon the earth that men had never known before—a race hard, fruitless, and unwholesome, from which man's ancient bowels of mercy, grief, and wild exultant joy had been eviscerated as out of date and falsely sentimental to bright arid creatures who breathed from sullen preference an air of bitterness and hate, and hugged desolation to the bone with a hard fatality of arrogance and pride.

Their conversation had in it something secret, sweet, and precious. It was full of swift allusions, little twists

and quirks and subtleties of things about which they
themselves were in the know, and interspersed with all
the trade-marks of the rough-simple speech that at that
time was in such favor with this kind of people: the
"swell," the "grand," the "fine," the "simply marvellous."

"Where can we go?" the girl was asking him. "Will
Louie's still be open? I thought that he closed up at ten
o'clock."

The girl was pretty, and had a good figure, but both
face and body had no curve or fullness; body and heart
and soul, there was no ripeness in her, she was something
meager of breast, hard, sterile, and prognathous.

"If he's not," the young man said, "we'll go next door
to Steve's. He's open all night long." His face was dark
and insolent, the eyes liquid, the mouth soft, weak, pampered, arrogant, and corrupt. When he laughed, his voice
had a soft welling burble in it, loose, jeering, evilly assured.

"Oh, swell!" the girl was saying in her naked tone. "I'd
love to go there! Let's have another party! Who can we
get to go? Do you think Bob and Mary would be in?"

"Bob might be, but I don't think that you'll find Mary,"
said the young man, adroitly innocent.

"No!" the girl exclaimed incredulously. "You don't
mean that she's"—and here their voices became low,
eager, sly, filled with laughter, and the young man finally
could be heard saying with the burble of soft laughter in
his voice:

"Oh, I don't know! It's just another of those things!
It happens in the best of families, you know."

"No!" the girl cried with a little scream of incredulous
laughter. "You *know* she hasn't! After all she said about
him, too! . . . I think—that's—simply—priceless!" She
then said slowly: "Oh—I—think—that's—simply—*swell!*"

She cried: "I'd give anything to see Bob's face when he finds out about it!"—and for a moment they laughed and whispered knowingly together, after which the girl cried once more, with her little shout of incredulous laughter:

"Oh, this is too good to be true! Oh—I think that's *marvellous,* you know!"—then added quickly and impatiently:

"Well, who can we get to go, then? Who *else* can we get?"

"I don't know," the young man said, "it's getting late now. I don't know who we can get unless"—and here his soft dark mouth began to smile, and the burble of laughter appeared in his throat as he nodded towards the man upon the ground "—unless you ask our friend here if he'd like to come along."

"Oh, that would be *grand!*" she cried with a gleeful little laugh. Then for a moment she stared down seriously at the silent figure on the pavement. "I'd *love* it!" the girl said. "Wouldn't it be swell if we could get some one like that to go with us!"

"Well—" the young man said, indefinitely. Then, as he looked down at the man, his soft wet flow of laughter welled up and he spoke softly and slyly to the girl, "I hate to disappoint you, but I don't think we'll get our friend here to go. He looks as if he's going to have a bad head in the morning," and again his dark mouth began to smile, and the burble of soft laughter welled up in his throat.

"Stop!" the girl cried with a little shriek. "Aren't you mean!" she said reproachfully. "I think he's sweet. I think it would be simply marvellous to take some one like that on a party! He looks like a swell person," she continued, looking down at the man curiously. "He really does, you know."

"Well, you know how it is," the young man said. "He was a great guy when he had it!" The burble welled up richly in his soft throat. "Come on," he said. "We'd better go. I think you're trying to make him!"—and laughing and talking together in their naked and arrogant young voices, they went away.

Presently the interne got up, took the ends of the stethoscope from his ears, and spoke a few quiet and matter-of-fact words to the policeman, who scrawled something down in a small book. The interne walked over to the curb, climbed up into the back of the ambulance and sat down on one seat with his feet stretched out upon the other one, meanwhile saying to the driver: "All right, Mike, let's go!" The ambulance moved off smoothly, slid swiftly around the corner with a slow clangor of bells, and was gone.

Then the policeman folded his book, thrust it into his pocket, and, turning on us suddenly, with a weary expression on his heavy, dark, night-time face, stretched out his arms and began to push us all back gently, meanwhile saying in a patient and weary tone of voice: "All right, you guys! On your way, now. Yuh gotta move. It's all oveh."

And obedient to his weary and tolerant command, we moved on and departed. Meanwhile, the dead man lay, as solid as a rock, upon his back, with that great brutal face of power and fortitude, upthrust and rigid, bared with a terrible stillness, an awful dignity, into the face of the cold and blazing moon.

This was the second time that I saw death in the city.

The third time that I saw death in the city, it had come like this:

One morning in May the year before, I had been on

my way up-town, along Fifth Avenue. The day was glorious, bright and sparkling, the immense and delicate light of the vast blue-fragile sky, was firm and almost palpable. It seemed to breathe, to change, to come and go in a swarming web of iridescent and crystalline magic, and to play and flash upon the spires of the great shining towers, the frontal blaze and sweep of the tremendous buildings, and on the great crowd which swarmed and wove unceasingly on the street, with vivid and multifarious points of light and color, as if the light were shining on a lake of sapphires.

Up and down the great street as far as the eye could reach, the crowd was surging in the slow yet sinuous convolutions of an enormous brilliantly colored reptile. It seemed to slide, to move, to pause, to surge, to writhe here and to be motionless there in a gigantic and undulant rhythm that was infinitely complex and bewildering, but that yet seemed to move to some central and inexorable design and energy. So did the great surge of the man-swarm look from afar, but when one passed it by at close range it all broke up into a million rich, brilliant, and vivid little pictures and histories of life, all of which now seemed so natural and intimate to me that I felt I knew all the people, that I had the warm and palpable substance of their lives in my hands, and knew and owned the street itself as if I had created it.

At one place, a powerful motor with a liveried chauffeur would snake swiftly in toward the curb, and a uniformed door-man of some expensive shop would scramble with obsequious haste across the sidewalk and open the door for some rich beauty of the upper crust. The woman would get out swiftly with a brisk sharp movement of her well-shod little feet and slender ankles, speak a few incisive words of command to her attentive driver, and then walk swiftly across the sidewalk towards the shop with a driving movement of her shapely but rather tailored-looking hips and a cold impatient look on her lovely but hard little face. To her, this great affair of seduction, attraction, and adornment for which she lived —this constant affair of clothing her lovely legs to the best advantage, setting off her solid shapely little buttocks in the most persuasive fashion, getting varnished, plucked, curled, perfumed, and manicured until she smelled like an exotic flower and glittered like a rare and costly jewel —was really as stern a business as her husband's job of getting money, and not to be trifled with or smiled at for a moment.

Again, some lovely and more tender, simple, and good-natured girl would come by on the pavements, jaunty and rich with some glowing spot of color—a scarf of red or blue, or a gay hat—her hair fine-spun and blown by light airs, her clear eyes fathomless and luminous with a cat-like potency and health, her delicate loins undulant with a long full stride, and her firm breasts rhythmical with each step she took, her mouth touched by a vague and tender smile as she passed by.

Elsewhere, dark-eyed, dark-faced, gray-faced, driven, meager, harassed and feverish-looking men and women would be swarming along, but the shining light and magic of the day seemed to have touched them all with its sorcery, so that they, too, all seemed filled with hope, gayety, and good nature, and to drink in as from some source of central and exultant energy the glorious intoxication of the day.

Meanwhile in the street the glittering projectiles of machinery were drilling past incredibly in their beetle-bullet flight, the powerful red-faced police stood like towers in the middle of the street stopping, starting, driving them on or halting them with an imperious movement of their mast-like hands.

Finally, even the warm odors of the hot machinery, the smells of oil, gasoline, and worn rubber which rose up from the bluish surface of the furious street, seemed won-, derful, mixed as they were with the warm, earthy and delicious fragrance of the trees, grass, and flowers in the Park, which was near by. The whole street burst into life for me immediately as it would on such a day for every young man in the world. Instead of feeling crushed down and smothered beneath its cruel and arrogant blaze of power, wealth, and number, until I seemed to drown in it, a nameless atom, it now seemed to me to be a glorious pageantry and carnival of palpable life, the great and glamorous Fair of all the earth, in which I was moving with certitude as one of the most honored and triumphant figures.

At this moment, with the Park in view, with the sight of the trees, in their young magic green, and all the flash and play of movement, color, and machinery, in the square before the Park, I halted and began to look with a particular interest at the people working on a building which was being erected there across the street. The building was not large, and neither very tall nor wide: it rose up ten flights with its steel girders set against the crystal air with a graceful and almost fragile delicacy, as if already, in this raw skeleton, the future elegance and style of the building were legible.

For I knew that this building was to house the great business which was known as Stein and Rosen and, like the man who once had shaken the hand of John L. Sullivan, I had a feeling of joy, pride, and familiarity when I looked at it. For the sister of a woman that I loved was a director of this mighty shop, its second-in-command, its first in talent and in knowledge, and from that woman's merry lips I had often heard the fabulous stories of what took place daily there. She told of the glittering processions of rich women who came there for their finery; of actresses, dancers, millionaires' wives, moving-picture women, and of all the famous courtesans, who would pay as they bought, and would plank down the ransom of a king in thousand-dollar bills for a coat of chinchilla fur; and of the stupendous things these legendary creatures said.

Through the portals of this temple in the daytime would move the richest women and the greatest harlots in the country. And an exiled princess would be there to sell them underwear, an impoverished duchess would be there to sell perfumery, and Mr. Rosen himself would be there to greet them. He would bend before them from the waist, he would give his large firm hand to them, he would smile and smile with his large pearly teeth, as his eyes went back and forth about his place continually. He would wear striped trousers and he would walk up and down upon rich carpets, he would be splendid and full of power like a well-fed bull, and somehow he would be like that magnificent horse in Job who paweth in the valley and saith among the trumpets, "Ha! Ha!"

And all day long they would be calling all over the place for her sister, who seldom spoke and rarely smiled. They could not get along without her, they would be asking for her everywhere, the rich woman would demand her, and the famous courtesan would say she had to speak to her. And when she came to them, they would say: "I wanted to speak to you, because the rest of them know nothing. You are the only one who understands me. You are the only one I can talk to," and yet they could not talk to her, because she never spoke.

But they would want to be near her, to confess to her, to pour their words into her silence: her large still eyes would look at them and make them want to speak. Meanwhile the Rosens smiled.

Thus, while the countless man-swarm of the earth thronged all around me I stood there thinking of these things and people. I thought of Mr. Rosen, and of the woman and her sister, and of a thousand strange and secret moments of our lives. I thought how great Cæsar's dust could patch a wall, and how our lives touch every other life that ever lived, how every obscure moment, every obscure life, every lost voice and forgotten step upon these pavements had somewhere trembled in the air about us. "'Twere to consider too curiously, to consider so." "No! faith, not a jot!—" the step that passed there in the street rang echoes from the dust of Italy, and still the Rosens smiled.

And it seemed to me that all the crowded and various life of this great earth was like a Fair. Here were the buildings of the Fair, the shops, the booths, the taverns, and the pleasure-places. Here were the places where men bought and sold and traded, ate, drank, hated, loved, and died. Here were the million fashions that they thought eternal, here was the ancient, everlasting Fair, tonight bereft of people, empty and deserted, tomorrow swarming with new crowds and faces in all its million lanes and passages, the people who are born, grow old and weary, and who die here.

They never hear the great dark wing that beats in the air above them, they think their moment lasts forever, they are so intent that they scarcely see themselves falter and grow old. They never lift their eyes up to the deathless stars above the deathless Fair, they never hear the immutable voice of time that lives in the upper air, that never ceases, no matter what men live or die. The voice of time is distant and remote and yet it has all of the voice of million-noted life within its murmur, it feeds on life and yet it lives above it and apart from it, it broods forever like the flowing of a river round the Fair.

Therefore when I looked at the spare webbing of this building on that shining day, and knew that those ingots of lean steel, those flat blocks of fashionable limestone which already sheeted the building's basal front, and which in their slender elegance were somehow like the hips of the women that the building would adorn, had been spun marvellously from the gossamer substance of Parisian frocks, distilled out of the dearest perfumes in the world, shaped from the cunning in man's brain, and from the magic in a woman's hands—it all seemed good and wonderful to me.

For above, beyond, and through that web of steel, and over the whole pulse and surge of life in the great street, over all the sparkling surge and shift of the great Fair, I saw suddenly the blazing image of my mistress's jolly, delicate, and rosy face of noble beauty. And the image of that single face seemed to give a tongue to joy, a certitude to all the power and happiness I felt, to resume into its small circle, as into the petals of a flower, all of the glory, radiance, and variousness of life and of the street, until a feeling of such triumph and belief surged up in me that I thought I could eat and drink the city, and possess the earth.

Quite suddenly, as I stood there looking at the little figures of the men who were working on the building, walking along high up against the crystal air with a corky and scuttling movement as they swarmed back and forth across the girders, the thing happened with the murderous nonchalance of horror in a dream. Nine floors above the earth, a little figure was deftly catching in a bucket the nails or rivets of red-hot steel which a man with tongs was tossing to him from the forge. For a moment, the feeder had paused in his work, had turned, tongs in hand, for a breather, and had spoken to a man upon another girder. The catcher, meanwhile, grateful for this respite, had put his bucket down and stood erect, a cigarette between his lips, the small flame of a match held in the cave of his brown cupped hands. Then the feeder, his throat still loud with laughter from some scrap of bawdry irrelevant to steel, turned to his forge, gripped with his tongs a glowing rivet, and his throat still trembling with its laughter, tossed deftly, absently, casually, in its accustomed arc, that nail of fire. His scream broke in upon the echoes of his laughter, carrying to the glut of faultless and accurate machinery in the street below him its terrible message of human error.

His scream was "Christ!" and at that word so seldom used for love and mercy the startled eyes of the other man leaped from his match upon the death that whizzed toward him. Even in the six feet of life that still remained to him, his body had its time for several motions. It half turned, the knees bent as if for a spring out into space, the shoulder stooped, the big brown hands groping in a futile, incompleted gesture for the bucket. Then, half crouched and rigid with palms curved out in a kind of grotesque and terrible entreaty, and one foot groping horribly into thin air, he met his death squarely, fronting it. For a moment after the rivet struck him, his body paused, crouched, rigid, like a grotesque image, groping futilely and horribly into space with one clumsy foot, and with a wire of acrid smoke uncoiling at his waist. Then his shabby garments burst into a flame, the man pawed blindly out in sickening vacancy and fell, a blazing torch lit by a single scream.

So that rich cry fell blazing through the radiant and living air. It seemed to me that the cry had filled up life —for a moment I had the sense that all life was absolutely motionless and silent save for that one cry. Perhaps this was true. It is certain that all life in that building had ceased—where but a moment before there had been the slamming racket of the riveting machines, the rattling of the winches, and the hammering of the carpenters, there was now the silence of a cataleptic trance.

Above the street, delicate and spare in the blue weather, two girders swung gently in the clasp of the chain, but all machinery had stopped. The signal-man leaned over bent, staring, his hands still stretched in warning for his mate. The feeder sat astride a girder, gripping it in his curved hands, his face bent forward sightlessly in an oblivion of horror. The body had fallen, like a mass of blazing oil waste, upon the wooden structure that covered the side- walk, then bounced off into the street.

Then the illusion of frozen silence, which seemed to have touched all the world, was broken. That crowd, which in the city seems to be created on the spot, to spring up from the earth like Gorgon-seed for every calamity, had already grown dense at the spot where the man had fallen. Several policemen were there, mauling, cursing, thrusting back the thickening ring that terribly suggested flesh-flies that work on something dead or sweet. And all the gleaming machinery in the street—which had been halted by the traffic lights—was again in motion.

There had been threat of a longer halt, a disruption of that inevitable flow, because several of the human units in the foremost squadrons of motors, who had witnessed the accident, refused now, under the strong drug of hor- ror, to "click" as good machinery ought. But they were whipped into action after a moment's pause by a ponder-

ous traffic cop, who stood in the center of the street, swinging his mighty arm back and forth like a flail, sowing the
air with rich curses, his accents thickened in the long ape-
like upper lip. So, the lights burned green again, the
clamors in the street awoke, the hot squadrons of machinery crawled up and down: an army of great beetles
driven by an ape. Then the racket of the riveters began
anew, high up above the street in the blue air the long
arm of the derrick moved, a chain with its balanced
weight of steel swung in and down.

Already the body had been carried inside the building,
the police were charging like bulls into the persistent
crowd, dispersing them. In a closed car, a young woman,
bright with the hard enamel of city elegance, stared
through the window, her little gloved hand clenched upon
the glass, her face full of manicured distress. And as she
looked, she kept murmuring sharply and monotonously:
"Quick! quick! be quick!" Before her, her driver bent
stolidly over his work. He was upset, but he could not
show it. Perhaps he was thinking: "Jesus! I've got to get
her out of this quick. What'll *he* say if she tells him
about it? He can't blame me. I can't help what the *other*
guy does! That's *his* lookout. You never know what's
gonna happen. A guy's got to think of everything at
once."

He took a chance. Smoothly, swiftly, he skirted three
cars and slid into the first rank between cursing drivers,
just as the lights changed. The lady settled back in her
seat with a look of relief. Thank Heaven, that was over!
George was so smart. He got in ahead of every one: you
never knew how he did it! He had done *that* beautifully.

I leaned against a building. I felt empty and dizzy. It
seemed to me suddenly that I had only two dimensions—

that everything on earth was like something cut out of
stiff paper, with no thickness.

"Brightness falls from the air." Yes, brightness had
fallen suddenly from the air, and with it all the marrowy
substance of life. The vitality of life and air and people
was gone. What remained to me was only a painting of
warmth and color that my sick eyes viewed with weariness and disbelief. Everything in that street went up and
down. It seemed to me suddenly that everything was
thin, two-dimensioned, without body and fullness. The
street, the people, the tall thin buildings: these were all
plane lines and angles. There were no curves in the street
—the only thing that curved had been that one rich cry.

And just as the light of noon had gone out of the day
so had the image of that woman's face, struck by the
casual horror of this death with all its evocations of a life
she knew, now suffered a transforming and sorrowful
change.

For where that radiant, good, and lovely face had just
the moment before wrought for me its magic certitude
and unity of exultant joy, now all this magic world of
health and life was shattered by this nameless death, was
drowned out in the torrent of this man's nameless blood,
and I could see her face no longer as it had looked at noon.

Rather that man's blood and death had awakened the
whole black ruin in my heart, the hideous world of death-
in-life had instantly returned with all its thousand phantom shapes of madness and despair and, intolerably, un-
answerably, like the unsearchable mystery of love and
death, the bitter enigma of that face of radiant life was
now fixed among these shapes of death to drive me mad
with its unsearchable mystery.

For in the image of that face was held all the pity and
the wild regret of love that had to die and was undying,

of beauty that must molder into age and wither to a handful of dry dust and yet was high as a star, as timeless as a
river, undwarfed beneath the whole blind horror of the
universe, and taller than man's tallest towers, and more
enduring than steel and stone.

And then the shapes of death would wake and move
around her, and I could only see her now fixed and secure
in an infamous and arrogant power, which could not be
opposed or beaten by any man, and against which, like a
maddened animal, I could do nothing but batter my life
and brains out on the pavements, as this man had done,
or madden horribly into a furious death among the other
nameless, faceless, man-swarm atoms of the earth.

I saw her, impregnably secure in an immense, complex,
and corrupt city-life—a life poisonous, perverse, and sterile
that moved smoothly in great chambers of the night
ablaze with baleful suavities of vanity and hate, where the
word was always fair and courteous, and the eye forever
old and evil with the jubilation of a filthy consent. It was
a world of the infamous dead so powerful in the entrench-
ments of its obscene wealth, its corruption that was
amorous of death and faithlessness, its insolence of a jaded
satiety, and its appalling weight of number and amount
that it crushed man's little life beneath its ramified assault
and killed and mutilated every living thing it fed upon—
not only the heart and spirit of youth, with all the hope
and pride and anguish in him, but also the life and body
of some obscure worker whose name it did not know,
whose death, in its remote impregnability, it would never
hear or care about.

I tried to get the fingers of my hate upon that immense
and shifting world of shapes and phantoms, but I could
not. I could track nothing to its tangible source, trace
nothing to some fatal certitude. Words, whispers, laugh-

ter, even an ounce of traitorous flesh, all the immense and moving tapestry of that cruel and phantasmal world were all impalpable and hovered above me, the deathless and invincible legend of scorn and defeat.

Then, even as I stood there in the street, the blind horror left me with the magic instancy in which it always came and went; all around me people seemed to live and move, and it was noon, and I could see her face the way it was again, and thought that it was the best face in the world, and knew that there was no one like her.

Two men came rapidly back across the street from the dispersing crowd and one of them was talking in a low earnest tone to the other:

"Jeez!" he said. "Dat gul! Did yuh see her? Sure, sure, he almost fell on top of her! . . . Sure, dat's what I'm tellin' yuh! . . . She fainted! . . . Dey had to carry her into a stoeh! . . . Jeez!" he said. In a moment, and in a quietly confidential tone, he added: "Say—dat makes duh fourt' one on dat building—did yuh know dat?"

Then I saw a man beside me with a proud, shrinking, and sensitive face, set in a blind sightless stare that kept looking through people, feeding on something that could not be seen. As I looked, he moved, turned his head slowly, and presently in the dull voice of some one who has had an opiate he said "What? The fourth? The fourth?"— although no one had spoken to him. Then he moved his thin hand slowly, and with an almost meditative gesture over his forehead and eyes, sighed wearily and slowly like some one waking from a trance or some strong drug, and then began to walk ahead uncertainly.

This was the third time I saw death in the city.

Later, the thing I was to remember vividly about

these three deaths, in contrast to the fourth one, was this: That, where the first three deaths had come by violence, where almost every circumstance of horror, sudden shock, disgust and terror, was present to convulse the hearts and sicken and wither up the flesh of those who saw death come, the city people, when their first surprise was over, had responded instantly to death, accepting its violence, bloody mutilation, and horror calmly, as one of the natural consequences of daily life. But the fourth time that I saw death come, the city people were stunned, awed, bewildered, and frightened, as they had not been before; and yet the fourth death had come so quietly, easily, and naturally that it seemed as if even a child could have looked at it without terror or surprise.

This is the way it happened:

At the heart and core of the most furious center of the city's life—below Broadway at Times Square—a little after one o'clock in the morning, bewildered, aimless, having no goal or place to which I wished to go, with the old chaos and unrest inside me, I had thrust down the stairs out of the great thronging street, the tidal swarm of atoms who were pressing and hurrying forward in as fierce a haste to be hurled back into their cells again as they had shown when they had rushed out into the streets that evening.

Thus, we streamed down from free night into the tunnel's stale and fetid air again, we swarmed and hurried across the floors of gray cement, we thrust and pushed our way along as furiously as if we ran a race with time, as if some great reward were to be won if only we could save two minutes, or as if we were hastening onward, as fast as we could go, toward some glorious meeting, some happy and fortunate event, some goal of beauty, wealth, or love on whose shining mark our eyes were fastened.

Then, as I put my coin into the slot, and passed on through the wooden turnstile, I saw the man who was about to die. The place was a space of floor, a width of cement which was yet one flight above the level of the trains, and the man was sitting on a wooden bench which had been placed there to the left, as one went down the incline to the tunnel.

The man just sat there quietly at one end of the bench, leaned over slightly to his right with his elbow resting on the arm of the bench, his hat pulled down a little, and his face half lowered. At this moment, there was a slow, tranquil, hardly perceptible movement of his breath—a flutter, a faint sigh—and the man was dead. In a moment, a policeman who had watched him casually from a distance walked over to the bench, bent down, spoke to him, and then shook him by the shoulder. As he did so, the dead man's body slipped a little, his arm slid over the end of the bench and stayed so, one hand hanging over, his shabby hat jammed down, a little to one side, upon his head, his overcoat open, and his short right leg drawn stiffly back. Even as the policeman shook him by the shoulder, the man's face was turning gray. By this time a few people, out of the crowds that swarmed constantly across the floor, had stopped to look, stared curiously and uneasily, started to go on, and then had come back. Now, a few of them were standing here, just looking, saying nothing, casting uneasy and troubled looks at one another from time to time.

And yet I think that we all knew the man was dead. By this time another policeman had arrived, was talking quietly to the other one, and now he, too, began to look curiously at the dead man, went over and shook him by the shoulder as the other one had done, and then after a few quiet words with his comrade, walked off rapidly. In a minute or two he came back again and another policeman was with him. They talked together quietly for a moment. One of them bent over and searched the man's pockets, finding a dirty envelope, a wallet, and a grimy-looking card. After prying into the purse and taking notes upon their findings they just stood beside the dead man, waiting.

The dead man was a shabby-looking fellow of an age hard to determine, but he was scarcely under fifty, and hardly more than fifty-five. And, had one sought long and far for the true portrait of the pavement cipher, the composite photograph of the man-swarm atom, he could have found no better specimen than this man. His only distinction was that there was nothing to distinguish him from a million other men. He had the kind of face that one sees ten thousand times a day upon the city streets, and cannot remember later.

This face, which even when alive, it is true, was of a sallow, sagging, somewhat paunchy and unwholesome hue and texture, was dryly and unmistakably Irish—city-Irish—with the mouth thin, sunken, slightly bowed, and yet touched with something loose and sly, a furtive and corrupt humor. And the face was also surly, hang-dog, petulant, and servile—the face of one of those little men—a door-man at a theatre, a janitor in a shabby warehouse, office building, or cheap apartment house, the father-in-law of a policeman, the fifth cousin of a desk-sergeant, the uncle of a ward heeler's wife, a pensioned door-opener, office-guarder, messenger, or question-evader for some Irish politician, schooled to vote dutifully for "the boys" upon election day, and to be flung his little scrap of patronage

for service rendered and silence kept, apt at servility, fawning, cringing to those sealed with the mark of privilege
and favor, and apt at snarling, snapping, gratuitous and im-
pudent discourtesy to those who had no power, no privilege, no special mark of favor or advancement to enlarge
them in his sight. Such was indubitably the man who
now sat dead upon the subway bench.

And that man's name was legion, his number myriad.
On his gray face, on his dead sunken mouth, the ghost of
his still recent life and speech sat incredibly, until it
seemed we heard him speak, listened to the familiar tones
of his voice again, knew every act and quality of his life,
as certainly as if he were yet alive, as he snarled at one
man: "I can't help dat, I don't know nuttin' about dat,
misteh. All I know is dat I got my ordehs, an' my ordehs
is to keep every one out unless dey can prove dey've gotta
date wit' Misteh Grogan. How do *I* know who you are?
How can *I* tell what yoeh business is? What's dat got to
do wit' me? No, seh! Unless you can prove you gotta
date wit' Misteh Grogan, I can't let yuh in. . . . Dat may
be true . . . and den again it may not be. . . . Wat t'
hell am *I* supposed t' be? A mind-readeh, or somp'n?
. . . No, misteh! Yuh can't come in! . . . I got my
ordehs an' dat's all I know."

And yet, the next moment, this same voice could whine,
with a protesting servility, its aggrieved apology to the
same man, or to another one: "W'y didn't yuh say yuh
was a friend of Misteh Grogan's? . . . W'y didn't yuh
tell me befoeh you was his brudder-in-law? . . . If yuh'd
told me dat, I'd 'a' let yuh by in a minute. *You* know how
it is," here the voice would drop to cringing confidence,
"so many guys come in here every day an' try to bust dere
way right in to Misteh Grogan's office when dey got no
bizness dere. . . . Dat's duh reason dat I gotta be kehful.

. . . But now dat I know dat you're O. K. wit' Misteh Grogan," it would say fawningly, "you can go on in any time yuh like. Any one dat's O. K. wit' Misteh Grogan is *all right,*" that voice would say with crawling courtesy. *"You* know how it is," it whispered, rubbing sly, unwholesome fingers on one's sleeve, "I didn't mean nuttin'—but a guy in my position has gotta be kehful."

Yes, that was the voice, that was the man, as certainly as if that dead mouth had just moved, that dead tongue stirred and spoken to us its language. There he was, still with the sallow hue of all his life upon his face, as it faded visibly, terribly before us to the gray of death. Poor, shabby, servile, fawning, snarling, and corrupted cipher, poor, meager, cringing, contriving, cunning, drearily hopeful, and dutifully subservient little atom of the million-footed city. Poor, dismal, ugly, sterile, shabby little man —with your little scrabble of harsh oaths, and cries, and stale constricted words, your pitiful little designs and feeble purposes, with your ounce of brain, your thimbleful of courage, the huge cargo of your dull and ugly superstitions. Oh, you wretched little thing of dough and tallow, you eater of poor foods and drinker of vile liquors. Joy, glory, and magnificence were here for you upon this earth, but you scrabbled along the pavements rattling a few stale words like gravel in your throat, and would have none of them, because the smell of the boss, the word of the priest, the little spare approvals of Mike, Mary, Molly, Kate, and Pat were not upon them—and tonight the stars shine, great ships are blowing from the harbor's mouth, and a million more of your own proper kind and quality go stamping on above your head, while you sit here *dead* in your gray tunnel!

We look at your dead face with awe, with pity, and with terror, because we know that you are shaped from our own clay and quality. Something of us all, the high, the low, the base, and the heroic, the rare, the common, and the glorious lies dead here in the heart of the unceasing city, and the destiny of all men living, yes, of the kings of the earth, the princes of the mind, the mightiest lords of language, and the deathless imaginers of verse, all the hope, hunger, and the earth-consuming thirst that can incredibly be held in the small prison of a skull, and that can rack and rend the little tenement in which it is confined, is written here upon this shabby image of corrupted clay.

The dead man was wearing nondescript clothing, and here again, in these dingy garments, the whole quality, the whole station of his life was evident, as if the clothes he wore had had a tongue, a character, and a language of their own. They said that the man had known poverty and a shabby security all his life, that his life had been many degrees above the moment-by-moment desperation of the vagabond and pauper, and many degrees below any real security, substance, or repose. His garments said that he had lived from month to month rather than from day to day, always menaced by the fear of some catastrophe—sickness, the loss of his job, the coming on of age—that would have dealt a ruinous blow to the slender resources which he had built between him and the world, never free from the fear of these calamities, but always just escaping them.

He wore an unpressed baggy gray suit which he filled out pretty well, and which had taken on the whole sagging, paunchy, and unshapely character of his own body. He had a small pot belly, a middling fleshiness and fullness which showed he had known some abundance in his life, and had not suffered much from hunger. He was wearing a dingy old brown felt hat, a shabby gray over-coat, and a ragged red scarf—and in all these garments there was a quality of use and wear and shabbiness that was inimitable and that the greatest costume-artist in the world could never have duplicated by intent.

The lives of millions of people were written in these garments. In their sag and hang and worn dingy textures, the shabby lives of millions of pavement ciphers were revealed, and this character was so strong and legible that as the dead man sat there and his face took on the corpsen gray of death, his body seemed to shrink, to dwindle, to withdraw visibly before our eyes out of its last relation-ship with life, and the clothes themselves took on a qual-ity and character that were far more living than the shape they covered.

And now the dead man's face had grown ghastly with the strange real-unreality of death that has such terrible irony in it, for, as one looks, the face and fig-ure of the dead seem to have no more of the sub-stance of mortal flesh than a waxen figure in a museum, and to smile, to mock, to stare, to mimic life in the same ghastly and unreal manner that a waxen figure would.

The turnstiles kept clicking with their dull wooden note, the hurrying people kept swarming past over the gray cement floor, the trains kept roaring in and out of the station below with a savage grinding vibrance, and from time to time, out of these swarming throngs, some one would pause, stare curiously for a moment, and stay. By this time, a considerable number of people had gath-ered in a wide circle about the bench on which the dead man sat, and curiously, although they would not go away, they did not press in, or try to thrust their way up close, as people do when some violent, bloody, or fatal accident has occurred.

Instead, they just stood there in that wide semi-circle, never intruding farther, looking at one another in an uneasy and bewildered manner, asking each other questions in a low voice from time to time which, for the most part, went unanswered since the person asked would squirm, look at his questioner uneasily and with wavering eyes, and then, muttering "I don't know," with a slight gesture of his arms and shoulders, would sidle or shuffle away. And from time to time the policemen, whose number by this time had grown to four, and who just stood around the man's body with a waiting and passive vacancy, would suddenly start, curiously and almost comically, into violent activity, and would come thrusting and shoving at the ring of people, pushing them back and saying in angry and impatient voices: "All right, now! Break it up! Break it up! Break it up! Go on! Go on! Go on! Yuh're blockin' up duh passage-way! Go on! Go on! Break it up, now! Break it up!"

And the crowd obediently would give ground, withdraw, shuffle around, and then with the invincible resiliency of a rope of rubber or a ball of mercury would return, coming back once more into their staring, troubled, uneasily whispering circle.

Meanwhile, the wooden stiles kept clicking with their dull, dead, somewhat thunderous note, the people kept thronging past to get their trains, and in their glances, attitudes, and gestures when they saw the ring of staring people and the man upon the bench, there was evident all of the responses which it is possible for men to have when they see death.

Some people would come by, pause, stare at the man, and then begin to whisper to one another in low uneasy tones: "What's wrong with him? Is he sick? Did he faint? Is he drunk—or something?" to which a man

might answer, looking intently for a moment at the dead
man's face, and then crying out heartily, with a hard
derisive movement of his hand, and yet with something
troubled and uncertain in his voice: "Nah! He's not sick
Duh guy is drunk! Dat's all it is. Sure! He's just passed
out. . . . Look at dem all standin' dere, lookin' at duh
guy!" he jeered. "Yuh'd t'ink dey neveh saw a drunk
befoeh. Come on!" he cried. "Let's go!" And they
would hurry on, while the man mocked at the crowd
with hard derisive laughter.

And indeed, the dead man's posture and appearance
as he sat there on the bench with his shabby old hat
pushed forward over his head, one leg drawn stiffly back,
his right hand hanging over the edge of the bench, and
his thin, sunken Irish mouth touched by a faint, loose,
rather drunken smile, was so much like the appearance
of a man in a drunken stupor that many people, as soon
as they saw his gray ghastly face, would cry out with a
kind of desperate relief in their voices: "Oh! He's only
drunk. Come on! Come on! Let's go!"—and would
hurry on, knowing in their hearts the man was dead.

Others would come by, see the dead man, start angrily,
and then look at the crowd furiously, frowning, shaking
their head in a movement of strong deprecation and disgust, and muttering under their breath before they went
on, as if somehow the crowd were guilty of some indecent and disorderly act which their own decent and
orderly souls abhorred.

Three little Jewesses and a young Jewish boy had come
in together, and pressed up in a group into the circle of
the crowd. For a moment the girls stood there, staring,
frightened, huddled in a group, while the boy looked
in a rather stupid and bewildered manner at the dead
man, finally saying nervously in a high stunned tone of

voice: "What's wrong wit' him? Have dey called duh ambulance yet?"

No one in the ring of silent people answered him, but in a moment a taxi-driver, a man with a brutal heavy night-time face, a swarthy, sallow, pitted skin, black hair and eyes, a cap, a leather jacket, and a shirt of thick black wool—this man turned and, jerking his head contemptuously toward the boy without looking at him, began to address the people around him in a jeering and derisive tone:

"Duh *ambulance!*" he cried. "Duh *ambulance!* Wat t' hell's duh use of duh *ambulance!* Jesus! Duh guy's dead an' he wants t' know if any one has called duh ambulance!" he cried, jerking his head contemptuously toward the boy again, and evidently getting some kind of security and assurance from his own jeering and derisive words. "Jesus!" he snorted. "Duh guy's dead an' he wants to know w'y some one don't call duh ambulance!" And he went off snorting and sneering by himself, saying "Jesus!" and shaking his head, as if the stupidity and folly of people were past his powers of understanding or consent.

The boy kept staring at the dead man on the bench with a fascinated eye of horror and disbelief. Presently he moistened his dry lips with his tongue, and spoke nervously and dully in a bewildered tone:

"I don't see him breathe or nuttin'," he said. "He don't move or nuttin'."

Then the girl beside him, who had been holding to his arm all this time, and who was a little Jewess with red hair, thin meager features, and an enormous nose that seemed to overshadow her whole face, now plucked nervously and almost frantically at the boy's sleeve, as she whispered:

"Oh! Let's go! Let's get away from heah! . . . Gee! I'm shakin' all oveh! Gee! I'm tremblin'—look!" she whispered, holding up her hand which was trembling visibly. "Let's go!"

"I don't see him breathe or nuttin'," the boy muttered dully, staring.

"Gee! Let's go!" the girl whispered pleadingly again. "Gee! I'm so noivous I'm tremblin' like a leaf—I'm shakin' all oveh! Come on!" she whispered. "Come on! Let's go!" And all four of them, the three frightened girls and the stunned bewildered-looking boy, hurried away in a huddled group, and went down the incline into the tunnel.

And now the other people who up to this time had only stood, looked uneasily at one another, and asked perplexed and troubled questions which no one answered, began to talk quietly and whisper among themselves, and one caught the sound of the word "dead" several times. Having spoken and heard this word, all the people grew very quiet and still, and turned their heads slowly toward the figure of the dead man on the bench, and began to stare at him with a glance full of curiosity, fascination, and a terrible feeding hunger.

At this moment a man's voice was heard speaking quietly, and with an assurance and certainty which seemed to say for every one what they had been unable to say for themselves.

"Sure, he's dead. The man's dead." The quiet and certain voice continued. "I knew all the time that he was dead."

And at the same time a big soldier, who had the seamed

and weathered face of a man who has spent years of service in the army, turned and spoke with a quiet and familiar assurance to a little dish-faced Irishman who was standing at his side.

"No matter where they kick off," he said, "they always leave that little black mark behind them, don't they?" His voice was quiet, hard, and casual as he spoke these words, and at the same time he nodded toward a small wet stain upon the cement near the dead man's foot where it had been drawn stiffly back.

The little dish-faced Irishman nodded as soon as the soldier had spoken, and with an air of conviction and agreement, said vigorously:

"You said it!"

At this moment, there was a shuffling commotion, a disturbance in the crowd near the gate beside the turnstiles, the people pressed back respectfully on two sides, and the ambulance doctor entered followed by two attendants, one of whom was bearing a rolled stretcher.

The ambulance surgeon was a young Jew with full lips, a somewhat receding chin, a little silky moustache, and a rather bored, arrogant and indifferent look upon his face. He had on a blue jacket, a flat blue cap with a visor which was pushed back on his head, and even as he entered and came walking slowly and indifferently across the cement floor, he had the tubes of the stethoscope fastened in his ears and was holding the end part in his hand. The two attendants followed him.

About every movement which the ambulance doctor made there was an air of habit, boredom, even weariness, as if he had been summoned too many times on errands such as this to feel any emotion. As he approached the policemen, they separated and opened up a path for him.

Without speaking to them he walked over to the dead man, unbuttoned his shirt and pulled it open, bent, and then began to use the stethoscope, listening carefully and intently for some seconds, then moving it to another place upon the dead man's tallowy, hairless, and ghastly-looking breast, and listening carefully again.

During all this time his face showed no emotion whatever of surprise, regret, or discovery. Undoubtedly, the doctor had known the man was dead the moment that he looked at him, and his duties now were only a part of that formality which law and custom demanded. But the people during all this time surged forward a little, with their gaze riveted on the doctor's face with awe, respect, and fascinated interest as if they hoped to read there the confirmation of what they already knew themselves, or as if they expected to see there a look of developing horror, pity, or regret which would put the final stamp of conviction on their own knowledge. But they saw nothing in the doctor's face but deliberation, dutiful intentness, and a look almost of weariness and boredom.

When he had finished with the stethoscope, he got up, took it out of his ears, and then casually opened the half-shut eyelids of the dead man for a moment. The dead eyes stared with a ghastly bluish glitter. The doctor turned and spoke a few words quietly to the police who were standing around him with their note-books open, with the same air of patience, custom, and indifference, and for a moment they wrote dutifully in their little books. One of them asked him a question and wrote down what he said, and then the doctor was on his way out again, walking slowly and indifferently away, followed by his two attendants, neither of whom showed any curiosity or surprise. The dead man, in fact, seemed to be under the control of a régime which worked with a merciless precision, which could not be escaped or altered by a jot, and whose operations all of its servants—doctors, stretcher-bearers, policemen, and even the priests of the church—knew with a weary and unarguable finality.

The police, having written in their books and put the books away, turned and came striding toward the crowd again, thrusting and pushing them back, and shouting, as they had before: "Go on! Go on! Break it up, now! Break it up!"—but even in the way they did this, there was this same movement of régime and custom, a sense of weariness and indifference, and when the people surged back into their former positions with maddening mercurial resiliency, the police said nothing and showed no anger or impatience. They took up their station around the dead man again, and waited stolidly, until the next move in their unalterable program should occur.

And now the people, as if the barriers of silence, restraint, and timidity had been broken, and the confusion and doubt in their own spirits dispersed by a final acknowledgment, and the plain sound of the word "death," which had at last been spoken openly, began to talk to one another easily and naturally as if they had been friends or familiar associates for many years.

A little to one side, and behind the outer ring of the crowd, three sleek creatures of the night and of the great street which roared on above our heads—a young smooth Broadwayite wearing a jaunty gray hat and a light spring overcoat of gray, cut inward toward the waist, an assertive and knowing-looking Jew, with a large nose, an aggressive voice, and a vulturesque smile, and an Italian, smaller, with a vulpine face, a ghastly yellow night-time skin, glittering black eyes and hair—all three smartly dressed and overcoated in the flashy Broadway manner—

now gathered together as if they recognized in one another men of substance, worldliness, and knowledge. They began to philosophize in a superbly knowing manner, bestowing on life, death, the brevity of man's days, and the futility of man's hopes and aspirations, the ripe fruit of their experience. The Jew was dominantly the center of this little group, and did most of the talking. In fact, the other two served mainly as a chorus to his harangue, punctuating it whenever he paused to draw breath with vigorous nods of agreement, and such remarks as "You said it!" "And I don't mean maybe!" or "Like I was sayin' to a guy duh otheh day—" an observation which was never completed, as the philosopher would be wound up and on his way again:

"And they ask us, f'r Christ's sake, to save for the future!" he cried, at the same time laughing with jeering and derisive contempt. "For the future!" Here he paused to laugh scornfully again. "When you see a guy like that you ask what for? Am I right?"

"You said it!" said the Italian, nodding his head with energetic assent.

"Like I was sayin' to a guy duh otheh day"—the other younger man began.

"Christ!" cried the Jew. "Save for the *future!* W'y the hell should *I* save for the future?" he demanded in a dominant and aggressive tone, tapping himself on the breast belligerently, glancing around as if some one had just tried to ram this vile proposal down his throat. "What's it goin' to getcha? You may be dead tomorrow! What the hell's the use in saving, f'r Christ's sake! We're only here for a little while. Let's make the most of it, f'r Christ's sake!—Am I right?" he demanded pugnaciously, looking around, and the others dutifully agreed that he was.

"Like I was sayin' to a guy duh otheh day," the young man said, "it only goes to show dat yuh——"

"Insurance!" the Jew cried at this point, with a loud scornful laugh. "The insurance companies, f'r Christ's sake! W'y the hell should any one spend their dough on insurance?" he demanded.

"Nah, nah, nah," the Italian agreed gutturally, with a smile of vulpine scorn, "dat's all a lotta crap."

"A lotta boloney," the young man said, "like I was sayin' to a guy duh otheh——"

"Insurance!" said the Jew. "W'y to listen to *those* bastuds talk you'd think a guy was gonna live forever! Save for the future, f'r Christ's sake," he snarled. "Put something by f'r your old age—your *old* age, f'r Christ's sake," he jeered, "when you may get what this guy got at any minute! Am I right?"

"You said it!"

"Put something by for a rainy day! Leave something for your children when you kick off!" he sneered. "W'y the hell should *I* leave anything for *my* children, f'r Christ's sake?" he snarled, as if the whole pressure of organized society and the demands of fifteen of his progeny had been brought to bear on him at this point. "No, sir!" he said. "Let my children look out for themselves the way *I* done!" he said. "Nobody ever did anything f'r me!" he said. "W'y the hell should *I* spend *my* life puttin' away jack for a lot of bastuds to spend who wouldn't appreciate it, noway! Am I right?"

"You said it!" said the Italian nodding. "It's all a lotta crap!"

"Like I was sayin' to dis guy—" the young man said.

"No, sir," said the Jew in a hard positive tone, and with a smile of bitter cynicism. "No, sir, misteh! Not for me! When I kick off and they all gatheh around the big cawfin," he continued with a descriptive gesture, "I want them *all* to take a good long look," he said.   I want them all to take a good long look at me and say: 'Well, he didn't bring nothing with him when he came, and he's not taking anything with him when he goes—but *there* was a guy,'" the Jew said loudly, and in an impressive tone, "'there was a guy who spent it when he had it— and *who didn't miss a thing!*'" Here he paused a moment, grasped the lapels of his smart overcoat with both hands, and rocked gently back and forth from heel to toe, as he smiled a bitter and knowing smile.

"Yes, sir!" he said presently in a tone of hard assurance.

"Yes, sir! When I'm out there in that graveyahd pushin' daisies, I don't want no bokays! I want to get what's comin' to me here and now! Am I right?"

"You said it!" the Italian answered.

"Like I was sayin' to a guy duh otheh day," the young man now concluded with an air of triumph, "yuh neveh can tell. No, sir! Yuh neveh can tell what's goin' t' happen. You're here one day an' gone duh next—so wat t' hell!" he said. "Let's make duh most of it."

And they all agreed that he was right, and began to search the dead man's face again with their dark, rapt, fascinated stare.

Elsewhere now, people were gathering into little groups, beginning to talk, to discuss, debate, philosophize, even to smile and laugh, in an earnest and animated way. One man was describing his experience to a little group that pressed around him eagerly, telling again and again, with unwearied repetition, the story of what he had seen, felt, thought and done when he first saw the dead man.

"Sure! Sure!" he cried. "Dat's what I'm tellin' yuh. I

seen him when he passed out. I was standin' not ten feet away from 'im! Sure! I watched 'im when he stahted gaspin' t' get his bret'. I was standin' dere. Dat's what I'm sayin'. I tu'ns to duh cop an' says, 'Yuh'd betteh look afteh dat guy,' I says. 'Deh's somet'ing wrong wit' 'im,' I says. Sure! Dat's when it happened. Dat's what I'm tellin' yuh. I was standin' dere," he cried.

Meanwhile, two men and two women had come in and stopped. They all had the thick clumsy figures, the dull-red smouldering complexions, the thick taffy-colored hair, bleared eyes, and broad, blunted, smeared features of the Slavic races—of Lithuanians or Czechs—and for a while they stared stupidly and brutally at the figure of the dead man, and then began to talk rapidly among themselves in coarse thick tones, and a strange tongue.

And now, some of the people began to drift away, the throng of people swarming homeward across the cement floor had dwindled noticeably, and the circle of people around the dead man had thinned out, leaving only those who would stay like flesh-flies feeding on carrion, until the body was removed.

A young Negro prostitute came through the gate and walked across the floor, glancing about her quickly with every step she took, and smiling a hideous empty smile with her thin encarmined lips. When she saw the circle of men she walked over to it and after one vacant look toward the bench where the dead man sat, she began to glance swiftly about her from right to left, displaying white, shining, fragile-looking teeth.

The thin face of the young Negress, which was originally of a light coppery color, had been so smeared over with rouge and powder that it was now a horrible, dusky yellow-and-purplish hue, her black eyelashes were coated with some greasy substance which made them stick out around her large dark eyes in stiff oily spines, and her black hair had been waved and was also coated with this grease.

She was dressed in a purple dress, wore extremely high heels which were colored red, and had the wide hips and the long thin ugly legs of the Negress. There was something at once horrible and seductive in her figure, in her thin stringy lower legs, her wide hips, her mongrel color, her meager empty little whore's face, her thin encarmined lips, and her thin shining frontal teeth, as if the last atom of intelligence in her bird-twitter of brain had been fed into the ravenous maw of a diseased and insatiable sensuality, leaving her with nothing but this thin varnished shell of face, and the idiot and sensual horror of her smile which went brightly and impudently back and forth around the ring of waiting men.

The Italian with the vulpine face, whose former companions, the Jew and the sleek young Broadwayite, had now departed, sidled stealthily over toward the Negress until he stood behind her. Then he eased up on her gently, his glittering eye feeding on her all the time in a reptilian stare, until his body was pressed closely against her buttocks, and his breath was hot upon her neck. The Negress said nothing but looked swiftly around at him with her bright smile of idiot and sensual vacancy, and in a moment started off rapidly, stepping along on her high red heels and long stringy legs, and looking back swiftly toward the Italian, flashing her painted lips and shining teeth at him in a series of seductive invitations to pursuit. The man craned his neck stealthily at the edges of his collar, looked furtively around with glittering eyes and vulpine face, and then started off rapidly after the girl. He caught up with her in the corridor beyond the stiles and they went on together.

The stiles still turned with their blunt, dull, wooden note, belated travellers came by with a lean shuffle of steps upon the cement floors, in the news-stand the dealer sold his wares, giving only an occasional and wearily indifferent glance at the dead man and the people, and in the cleared space round the bench the police were standing, waiting, with a stolid and impassive calm. A man had come in, walked across the space and was now talking to one of the police. The policeman was a young man with a solid strong-necked face that was full of dark color. He talked quietly out of the side of his mouth to the man who questioned him, and who was taking notes in a small black book. The man had a flabby yellowish face, weary eyes, and a flabby roll of flesh beneath his chin.

The people who remained, having greedily sucked the last drop of nourishment from conversation, now stood silent, staring insatiably at the dead man with a quality of vision that had a dark, feeding, glutinous and almost physical property, and that seemed to be stuck upon the thing they watched.

By this time an astonishing thing had happened. Just as the dead man's figure had appeared to shrink and contract visibly within its garments, as if before our eyes the body were withdrawing out of a life with which it had no further relationships, so now did all the other properties of space and light, the dimensions of width, length, and distance that surrounded him undergo an incredible change.

And it seemed to me that this change in the dimensions of space was occurring visibly and momently under my eyes, and that just as the man's body seemed to dwindle and recede so did the gray cement space around him grow tremendously. The space that separated him from the place where the police stood, and the gray space which separated us from the police, together with the distance of the tiled subway wall behind, all grew taller, wider, longer, enlarged themselves terrifically while I looked. It was as if we were all looking at the man across an immense and lonely distance. The dead man looked like a lonely little figure upon an enormous stage, and by his very littleness and loneliness in that immense gray space, he seemed to gain an awful dignity and grandeur.

And now, as it seemed to me, just as the living livid gray-faced dead men of the night were feeding on him with their dark and insatiate stare, so did he return their glance with a deathless and impassive irony, with a terrible mockery and scorn, which were as living as their own dark look, and would endure forever.

Then, as suddenly as it had come, that distorted vision was gone, all shapes and things and distances swam back once more into their proper focus. I could see the dead man sitting there in the gray space, and the people as they looked and were. And the police were driving forward again and thrusting at the people all about me.

But they could not bear to leave that little lonely image of proud death, that sat there stiffly with its grotesque, drunken dignity, its thin smile—as men are loyal to a lifeless shape, and guard and watch and will not leave it till the blind earth takes and covers it again. And they would not leave it now because proud death, dark death, the lonely dignity of proud dark death sat grandly there upon man's shabby image, and because they saw that nothing common, mean, or shabby on earth, nor all the fury, size, and number of the million-footed city could alter for an instant the immortal dignities of death, proud death, even when it rested on the poorest cipher in the streets.

Therefore they would not leave it from a kind of love and loyalty they bore it now; and because proud death was sitting grandly there and had spoken to them, and had stripped them down into their nakedness; and because they had built great towers against proud death, and had hidden from him in gray tunnels, and had tried to still his voice with all the brutal stupefactions of the street, but proud death, dark death, proud brother death, was striding in their city now, and he was taller than their tallest towers, and triumphant even when he touched a shabby atom of base clay, and all their streets were silent when he spoke.

Therefore they looked at him with awe, with terror and humility, and with love, for death, proud death, had come into their common and familiar places, and his face had shone terribly in gray tainted air, and he had matched his tongue, his stride, his dignities against the weary and brutal custom of ten million men, and he had stripped them down at length, and stopped their strident and derisive tongues, and in the image of their poorest fellow had shown them all the way that they must go, the awe and terror that would clothe them—and because of this they stood before him lonely, silent, and afraid.

Then, the last rituals of the law and church were observed, and the dead man was taken from their sight. The dead-wagon of the police had come. Two men in uniform came swiftly down the stairs and entered carrying a rolled stretcher. The stretcher was rolled out upon the cement floor, swiftly the dead man was lifted from the bench and laid down on the stretcher, and at the same moment, a priest stepped from the crowd, and knelt there on the floor beside the body.

He was a young man, plump, well kept, and very white, save for his garments, pork-faced, worldly, and unpriestly, and on his full white jaws was the black shaved smudge of a heavy beard. He wore a fine black overcoat with a velvet collar, and had on a scarf of fine white silk, and a derby hat, which he removed carefully and put aside when he knelt down. His hair was very black, fine-spun as silk, and getting thin on top. He knelt swiftly beside the dead man on the stretcher, raised a white, hairy hand, and as he did so, the five policemen straightened suddenly, whipped off their visored hats with a military movement, and stood rigidly for a moment, with their hats upon their hearts as the priest spoke a few swift words above the body, which no one could hear. In a moment a few of the people in the crowd also took off their hats awkwardly, and presently the priest got up, put on his derby hat carefully, adjusted his coat and scarf, and stepped back into the crowd again. It was all over in a minute, done with the same inhuman and almost weary formality that the ambulance doctor had shown.

Then the two uniformed stretcher-men bent down, took the handles of the stretcher, and, speaking in low voices to each other, lifted it. They started off at a careful step, but as they did so, the dead man's gray-tallow hands flapped out across the edges of the stretcher, and began to jog and jiggle in a grotesque manner with every step the stretcher-bearers took.

One of the men spoke sharply to another, saying, "Wait a minute! Put it down! Some one get his hands!"

The stretcher was laid down upon the floor again, a policeman knelt down beside the body and quickly stripped the dead man's necktie from his collar, which had been opened by the doctor and now gaped wide, showing a brass collar-button in the neck-band of the shirt, and the round greenish discoloration of the brass collar-button in the dead yellowed tissues of the neck. The policeman took the dead man's necktie, which was a soiled, striped, and stringy thing of red and white, and quickly tied it in a knot around the dead man's wrists in order to keep his hands from jerking.

Then the stretcher-bearers lifted him again, and started off, the police striding before them toward the gate-way, thrusting the people back, and crying:

"Get back, there! Get back! Make way! Make way! Make way!"

The dead man's hands were silent now, tied together across his stomach, but his shabby old garments trembled, and his gray-yellow cheek-flanks quivered gently with every step the stretcher-bearers took. The gaping collar ends flapped stiffly as they walked and his soiled white shirt was partially unbuttoned revealing a dead, bony, tallowy-yellow patch of breast beneath, and his battered old brown hat was now pushed down so far over his face that it rested on his nose, and, together with the thin sunken smile of his mouth, intensified the grotesque and horrible appearance of drunkenness.

As for the rest of him—the decaying substance that had been his body—this seemed to have shrunk and dwindled away almost to nothing. One was no longer conscious of its existence. It seemed lost, subsided to nothing and indistinguishable in a pile of shabby old garments—an old gray overcoat, baggy old trousers, an old hat, a pair of scuffed and battered shoes. This in fact was all he now seemed to be: a hat, a thin grotesquely drunken smile, two trembling cheek flanks, two flapping collar-ends, two gray-grimy claws tied with a stringy necktie, and a shabby heap of worn, dingy, and non-descript garments that moved and oscillated gently with every step the stretcher-bearers took.

The stretcher men moved carefully yet swiftly through the gate and up the stairs of an obscure side-opening which was marked "Exit." As they started up the grimy iron steps, the body sloped back a little heavily and the old brown hat fell off, revealing the dead man's thin, disordered, and gray-grimy hair. One of the policemen picked up the hat, saying to one of the stretcher bearers, "O.K., John, I've got it!" then followed him up-stairs.

It was now early morning, about half-past three o'clock, with a sky full of blazing and delicate stars, an immense and lilac darkness, a night still cool, and full of chill, but with all the lonely and jubilant exultancy of spring in it. Far-off, half-heard, immensely mournful, wild with joy and sorrow, there was a ship lowing in the darkness, a great boat blowing at the harbor's mouth.

The street looked dark, tranquil, almost deserted—as quiet as it could ever be, and at that brief hour when all its furious noise and movement of the day seemed stilled for a moment's breathing space, and yet preparing for another day. The taxis drilled past emptily, sparely, and at intervals, like projectiles, the feet of people made a lean and picketing noise upon the pavements, the lights burned green and red and yellow with a small hard lonely radiance that somehow filled the heart with strong joy and victory, and belonged to the wild exultancy of the night, the ships, the springtime, and of April. A few blocks farther up the street where the great shine and glitter of the night had burned immensely like a huge censer steaming always with a dusty, pollenated, immensely brilliant light, that obscene wink had now gone dull, and shone brownly, still livid but subdued.

When the stretcher-men emerged from the subway exit, the green dead-wagon of the police was waiting at the curb, and a few taxi-drivers with dark dingy faces had gathered on the sidewalk near the door. As the stretcher-men moved across the pavement with their burden, one of the taxi-men stepped after them, lifted his cap obsequiously to the dead man, saying eagerly:

"Taxi, sir! Taxi!"

One of the policemen, who was carrying the dead man's hat, stopped suddenly, turned around laughing, and lifted his club with jocular menace, saying to the taxi-man:

"You son-of-a-bitch! Go on!"

Then, still laughing, saying "Jesus!" he tossed the dead man's hat into the green wagon, into which the stretcher-men had already shoved the body. One of the stretcher-men closed the doors, went around to the driver's seat where the other was already sitting, took out a cigarette and lit it between a hard cupped palm and a twisted mouth, climbed up beside the driver saying "O. K., John," and the wagon drove off swiftly. The police looked after it as it drove off. Then they all talked together for a moment more, laughed a little, spoke quietly of the plans, pleasures, and duties of the future, said good-night all around, and walked off, two up the street toward the dull brown-livid smoulder of the lights, and three down the street, where it was darker, quieter, more deserted, and where the lights would shift and burn green, yellow, red.

The jesting taxi-man who had offered his services to the dead man on the stretcher turned briskly to his fellows with an air of something ended, saying sharply and jocosely:

"Well, whattya say, boy! Whattya say!"—at the same time sparring sharply and swiftly at one of the other drivers with his open hands. Then the taxi-drivers walked away toward their lines of shining, silent machines, jesting, debating, denying, laughing in their strident and derisive voices.

And again, I looked and saw the deathless sky, the huge starred visage of the night, and heard the boats then on the river. And instantly an enormous sanity and hope of strong exultant joy surged up in me again; and like a man who knows he is mad with thirst, yet sees real rivers at the desert's edge, I knew I should not die and strangle like a mad dog in the tunnel's dark. I knew I should see light once more and know new coasts and come into strange harbors, and see again, as I had once, new lands and morning.

Therefore, immortal fellowship, proud Death, stern Loneliness, and Sleep, dear friends, in whose communion I shall live forever, out of the passion and the substance of my life, I have made this praise for you:

To you, proud Death, who sit so grandly on the brows of little men—first to you! Proud Death, proud Death, whom I have seen by darkness, at so many times, and always when you came to nameless men, what have you ever touched that you have not touched with love and pity, Death? Proud Death, wherever we have seen your face, you came with mercy, love, and pity, Death, and brought to all of us your compassionate sentences of pardon and release. For have you not retrieved from exile the desperate lives of men who never found their home? Have you not opened your dark door for us who never yet found doors to enter, and given us a room who, roomless, doorless, unassuaged, were driven on forever through the streets of life? Have you not offered us your stern provender, Death, with which to stay the hunger that grew to madness from the food it fed upon, and given all of us the goal for which we sought but never found, the certitude, the peace, for which our over-laden hearts contended, and made for us, in your dark house, an end of all the tortured wandering and unrest that lashed us on forever? Proud Death, proud Death, not for the glory that you added to the glory of the king, proud Death, nor for the honor you imposed upon the dignities of famous men, proud Death, nor for the final magic you have given to the lips of genius, Death, but because you come so gloriously to us who never yet knew glory, so proudly and sublimely to us whose lives were nameless and obscure, because you give to all of us—the nameless, faceless, voiceless atoms of the earth—the awful chrysm of your grandeur, Death, because I have seen and known you so well, and have lived alone so long with Loneliness, your brother, I do not fear you any longer, friend, and I have made this praise for you.

Now, Loneliness forever and the earth again! Dark brother and stern friend, immortal face of darkness and of night, with whom the half part of my life was spent, and with whom I shall abide now till my death forever, what is there for me to fear as long as you are with me? Heroic friend, blood-brother of proud Death, dark face, have we not gone together down a million streets, have we not coursed together the great and furious avenues of night, have we not crossed the stormy seas alone, and known strange lands, and come again to walk the continent of night, and listen to the silence of the earth? Have we not been brave and glorious when we were together, friend, have we not known triumph, joy, and glory on this earth—and will it not be again with me as it was then, if you come back to me? Come to me, brother, in the watches of the night, come to me in the secret and most silent heart of darkness, come to me as you always came, bringing to me once more the old invincible strength, the deathless hope, the triumphant joy and confidence that will storm the ramparts of the earth again.

Come to me through the fields of night, dear friend, come to me with the horses of your sister, Sleep, and we shall listen to the silence of the earth and darkness once again, we shall listen to the heartbeats of the sleeping men, as with soft and rushing thunder of their hooves the strange dark horses of great Sleep come on again.

They come! Ships call! The hooves of night, the horses of great Sleep, are coming on below their manes of darkness. And forever the rivers run. Deep as the tides of Sleep the rivers run. We call!

They come: My great dark horses come! With soft and rushing thunder of their hooves they come, and the horses of Sleep are galloping, galloping over the land.

Oh, softly, softly the great dark horses of Sleep are galloping over the land. The great black bats are flying over us. The tides of Sleep are moving through the nation; beneath the tides of Sleep and time strange fish are moving.

For Sleep has crossed the worn visages of day, and in the night-time, in the dark, in all the sleeping silence of the towns, the faces of ten million men are strange and dark as time. In Sleep we lie all naked and alone, in Sleep we are united at the heart of night and darkness, and we are strange and beautiful asleep; for we are dying in the darkness, and we know no death, there is no death, there is no life, no joy, no sorrow and no glory on the earth but Sleep.

Come, mild and magnificent Sleep, and let your tides flow through the nation. Oh, daughter of unmemoried desire, sister of Death, and my stern comrade, Loneliness,

bringer of peace and dark forgetfulness, healer and re-
deemer, dear enchantress, hear us: come to us through the
fields of night, over the plains and rivers of the everlasting
earth, bringing to the huge vexed substance of this world
and to all the fury, pain, and madness of our lives the
merciful anodyne of your redemption. Seal up the porches
of our memory, tenderly, gently, steal our lives away from
us, blot out the vision of lost love, lost days, and all our
ancient hungers; great Transformer, heal us!

Oh, softly, softly, the great dark horses of Sleep are galloping over the land. The tides of Sleep are moving in the
hearts of men, they flow like rivers in the night, they flow
with glut and fullness of their dark unfathomed strength
into a million pockets of the land and over the shores of the
whole earth. They flow with the full might of their advancing and inexorable flood across the continent of night,
across the breadth and sweep of the immortal earth, until
the hearts of all men living are relieved of their harsh
weight, the souls of all men who have ever drawn in the
breath of anguish and of labor are healed, assuaged, and
conquered by the vast enchantments of dark, silent, all-
engulfing Sleep.

Sleep falls like silence on the earth, it fills the hearts of
ninety million men, it moves like magic in the mountains,
and walks like night and darkness across the plains and
rivers of the earth, until low upon lowlands, and high
upon hills, flows gently sleep, smooth-sliding sleep—oh,
sleep—sleep—sleep!

The Face of the War

... HEAT-BRUTAL August the year the war ended: here are four moments from the face of the war. One—at Langley Field: a Negro retreating warily out of one of the rude shed-like offices of the contracting company on the flying field, the white teeth bared in a horrible grimace of fear and hatred, the powerful figure half-crouched, ape-like, ready to leap or run, the arms, the great black paws, held outward defensively as he retreats under the merciless glazed brutality of the August sun, over the barren, grassless horror of hard dry clay, the white eyeballs fixed with an expression of mute unfathomable hatred, fear and loathing upon the slouchy, shambling figure of a Southern white—a gang boss or an over-seer—who advances upon him brandishing a club in his meaty hand, screaming the high thick throat-scream of blood-lust and murder: "I'll stomp the guts out of you, you God-damned black bastard! I'll beat his God-damn brains out!"—and smashing brutally with his club, coming down across the Negro's skull with the sickening resilient thud, heard clear across the field, of wood on living bone. Behind the paunch-gut white, an office clerk, the little meager yes-man of the earth, a rat in shirt-sleeves, quick as a rat to scamper to its hiding, quick as a rat to come in to the kill when all is safe, with rat's teeth bared—advancing in the shambling wake of his protector, fear's servile seconder, murder's cringing aide, coming in behind with rat's teeth bared, the face white as a sheet, convulsed with fear and with the coward's lust to kill without mercy or reprisal, the merciless sun blazing hot upon the arm-band buckles on the crisp shirt sleeve, and with a dull metallic glint upon the barrel of the squat blue automatic that he clutches with a trembling hand, offering it to his blood-mad master, whispering frantically —"Here! . . . Here, Mister Bartlett! . . . Shoot the bastard if he tries to hit you!"

Meanwhile, the Negro retreating slowly all the time, his terrible white stare of fear and hatred no longer fixed upon his enemy, but on the evil glint of that cylinder of blue steel behind him, his arms thrust blindly, futilely before him as his hated foe comes on, his black face, rilled and channelled first with lacings of bright red, then beaten to a bloody pulp as the club keeps smashing down with its sickening and resilient crack:

"You . . . God-damn . . . black . . . son-of-a-bitch!" the voice, thick, high, phlegmy, choked with murder. "I'll teach ye—" Smash! the cartilage of the thick black nose crunches and is ground to powder by the blow "—if a God-damned Nigger can talk back to a white man!"— Smash. A flailing, horribly clumsy blow across the mouth which instantly melts into a bloody smear through which the Negro, eyes unmoving from the blue glint of the steel, mechanically spits the shattered fragments of his solid teeth—"I'll bash in his God-damned head—the damned black bastard—I'll show him if he can—" Smash! Across the wooly center of the skull and now, the scalp ripped open to the base of the low forehead, the powerful black figure staggering drunkenly, bending at the knees, the black head sagging, going down beneath the blows, the arms still blindly thrust before him, upon one knee now on the barren clay-baked earth, the head sunk down completely on the breast, blood over all, the kneeling figure blindly rocking, swaying with the blows, the arms still out until he crashes forward on the earth, his arms outspread, face to one side and then, the final nausea of horror—the murderous kick of the shoe into the blood-pulp of the unconscious face, and then silence, nothing to see or hear now but the heavy, choked and labored breathing of the paunch-gut man, the white rat-face behind him with the bared rat's fangs of terror, and the dull blue wink of the envenomed steel.

Again, the coward's heart of fear and hate, the coward's lust for one-way killing, murder without danger to himself, the rat's salvation from the shipwreck of his self-esteem—armed with a gun now, clothed in khaki, riding the horse of his authority, as here. Three boys, all employed by the contracting company, are walking after supper on the borders of the flying field in the waning light of evening, coming dark. They are walking down near the water's edge, across the flat marshy land, they are talking about their homes, the towns and cities they have known and come from, their colleges and schools, their plans for an excursion to the beach at the week-end, when they draw their pay. Without knowing it, they have approached a hangar where one of the new war-planes with which the government is experimenting has been housed. Suddenly, the soldier who is there on guard has seen them, advances on them now, one hand upon the revolver in his holster, his little furtive eyes narrowed into slits. Face of the city rat, dry, gray, furtive, pustulate, the tallowy lips, the rasping voice, the scrabble of a few harsh oaths, the stoney gravel of a sterile, lifeless, speech:

"What are ya doin' here ya f—— little bastards!—Who told ya t'come f—— round duh hangah?"

One of the boys, a chubby red-cheeked youngster from

the lower South, fair-haired, blue-eyed, friendly and slow
of speech, attempts to answer:

"Why, mister, we just thought——"

Quick as a flash, the rat has slapped the boy across the
mouth, the filthy finger-tips have left their mottled print
upon the boy's red cheek, have left their loathsome, foul
and ineradicable print upon the visage of his soul forever:

"I don't give a f—— what ya t'ought, ya little p——!
Anuddeh woid out a ya f—— trap an' I'll shoot the s——
outa ya!" He has the gun out of its holster now, ready in
his hand; the eyes of the three boys are riveted on the dull
wink of its blue barrel with a single focal intensity of
numb horror, fascinated disbelief.

"Now get t' f—— hell outa here!" the hero cries, giving
the boy he has just slapped a violent shove with his free
hand. "Get t' f—— hell away from heah, all t'ree of
youse! Don't f—— aroun' wit me, ya little p——," the
great man snarls now, eyes a-glitter, narrow as a snake's,
as he comes forward with deadly menace written in his
face. "Annuddeh woid outa ya f—— traps, an' I'll shoot t'
s—— outa youse! On yuh way, now, ya p——! Get t'
hell away from me befoeh I plug yah!"

And the three boys, stunned, bewildered, filled with
shame, and sickened out of all the joy and hope with
which they had been speaking of their projects just a
moment before, have turned, and are walking silently
away. with the dull shame, the brutal and corrosive
hatred which the war has caused, aching and rankling in
their hearts.

Again, an image of man's naked desire, brutal and
imperative, stripped down to his raw need, savage and
incurious as the harsh pang of a starved hunger which
takes and rends whatever food it finds—as here: Over the

bridge, across the railway track, down in the Negro settlement of Newport News—among the dives and stews and
rusty tenements of that grimy, dreary and abominable
section, a rude shack of unpainted pine boards, thrown
together with the savage haste which war engenders, to
pander to a need as savage and insatiate as hunger, as old as
life, the need of friendless, unhoused men the world over.

The front part of this rawly new, yet squalid place, has
been partitioned off by rude pine boards to form the
semblance of a lunch room and soft drink parlor. Within
are several tables, furnished with a few fly-specked menu
cards, on which half a dozen items are recorded, and at
which none of the patrons ever look, and a wooden counter, with its dreary stage property of luke-warm soda pop,
a few packages of cigarettes and a box of cheap cigars beneath a dingy little glass case; and beneath a greasy glass
humidor, a few stale ham and cheese sandwiches, which
have been there since the place was opened, which will
be there till the war is done.

Meanwhile, all through the room, the whores, in their
thin and meager mummers, act as waitresses, move patiently about among the crowded tables and ply their
trade. The men, who are seated at the tables, belong for
the most part to that great group of unclassed creatures
who drift and float, work, drift, and starve, are now in
jail, now out again, now foul, filthy, wretched, hungry,
out of luck, riding the rods, the rusty box cars of a freight,
snatching their food at night from the boiling slum of
hoboes' jungle, now swaggering with funds and brief
prosperity—the floaters, drifters, and half-bums, that huge
nameless, houseless, rootless and anomalous class that
swarm across the nation.

They are the human cinders of the earth. Hard, shabby,
scarred and lined of face, common, dull and meager of

visage as they are, they have the look of having crawled that morning from the box car in the train yard of another city or of having dropped off a day coach in the morning, looking casually and indifferently about them, carrying a cardboard suitcase with a shirt, two collars and a tie. Yet a legend of great distances is written on them— a kind of atomic desolation. Each is a human spot of moving rust naked before the desolation of the skies that bend above him, unsheltered on the huge and savage wilderness of the earth, across which he is hurled—a spot of grimy gray and dingy brown, clinging to the brake-rods of a loaded freight.

He is a kind of human cinder hurled through space, naked, rootless, nameless, with all that was personal and unique in its one life almost emptied out into that huge vacancy of rust and iron and waste, and lonely and incommunicable distances, in which it lives, through which it has so often been bombarded.

And this atom finds its end at length, perhaps, at some unknown place upon the savage visage of the continent, exploded, a smear of blood on the rock ballast, a scream lost in the roar of pounding wheels, a winding of entrails round the axle rods, a brief indecipherable bobbing of blood and bone and brains upon the wooden ties, or just a shapeless bundle of old soiled brown and gray slumped down at morning in a shabby doorway, on a city street, beneath the elevated structure, a bundle of rags and bone, now cold and lifeless, to be carted out of sight by the police, nameless and forgotten in its death as in its life.

Such, for the most part, were the men who now sat at the tables in this rude house of pleasure, looking about them furtively, warily, with an air of waiting calculation, or indecision, and sometimes · glancing at one another with sly, furtive, rather sheepish smiles.

As for the women who attended them, they were prostitutes recruited, for the most part, from the great cities of the North and Middle-West, brutally greedy, rapacious, weary of eye, hard of visage, over-driven, harried and exhausted in their mechanical performance of a profession from which their only hope was to grasp and clutch as much as they could in as short a time as possible. They had the harsh, rasping and strident voices, the almost deliberately exaggerated and inept extravagance of profanity and obscenity, the calculated and over-emphasized style of toughness which one often finds among poor people in the tenement sections of great cities—which one observes even in small children—the constant oath, curse, jeer, threat, menace, and truculent abuse, which really comes from the terrible fear in which they live, as if, in that world of savage aggression and brute rapacity, from which they have somehow to wrest their bitter living, they are afraid that any betrayal of themselves into a gentler, warmer and more tolerant kind of speech and gesture, will make them suspect to their fellows, and lay them open to the assaults, threats, tyrannies, and dominations they fear.

So was it with these women now: one could hear their rasping voices everywhere throughout the smoke-filled room, their harsh jeering laughter, and the extravagant exaggeration and profusion with which they constantly interlarded their strident speech with a few oaths and cries repeated with a brutal monotony—such phrases as "Christ!"—"Jesus!"—"What t' God-damn hell do I care?" —"Come on! Whatcha goin' t' do now! I got no time t' —— around wit' yuh! If ya want t' —— come on an' pay me—if ya don't, get t' God-damn hell outa here"— being among the expressions one heard most frequently.

Yet, even among these poor, brutally exhausted and

fear-ridden women, there was really left, like something pitiably living and indestructible out of life, a kind of buried tenderness, a fearful, almost timid desire to find some friendship, gentleness, even love among the rabble-rout of lost and ruined men to whom they ministered.

And this timid, yet inherent desire for some warmer and more tender relation even in the practice of their profession, was sometimes almost ludicrously apparent as they moved warily about among the tables soliciting patronage from the men they served. Thus, if a man addressed them harshly, brutally, savagely, with an oath—which was a customary form of greeting—they would answer him in kind. But if he spoke to them more quietly, or regarded them with a more kindly smiling look, they might respond to him with a pathetic and ridiculous attempt at coquetry, subduing their rasping voices to a kind of husky, tinny whisper, pressing against him intimately, bending their bedaubed and painted faces close to his, and cajoling him with a pitiable pretense at seductiveness, somewhat in this manner:

"Hello there, big boy! . . . Yuh look lonesome sittin' there all by yourself. . . . Whatcha doin' all alone? . . . Yuh want some company? Huh?"—whispered hoarsely, with a ghastly leer of the smeared lips, and pressing closer —"Wanta have some fun, darling? . . . Come on!"— coaxingly, imperatively, taking the patron by the hand— "I'll show yuh a big time."

It was in response to some such blandishment as this that the boy had got up from his table, left the smoke-filled room accompanied by the woman, and gone out through a door at one side into the corridor that led back to the little partitioned board compartments of the brothel.

Here, it was at once evident that there was nothing to do but wait. A long line of men and women that stretched from one end of the hallway to another stood waiting for their brief occupancies of the little compartments at the other end, all of which were now obviously and audibly occupied.

As they came out into the hall, the woman with the boy called out to another woman at the front end of the line: "Hello, May! . . . Have ya seen Grace?"

"Aah!" said the woman thus addressed, letting cigarette smoke coil from her nostrils as she spoke, and speaking with the rasping, exaggerated and brutal toughness that has been described: "I t'ink she's in number Seven here havin' a ——."

And having conveyed the information in this delicate manner, she then turned to her companion, a brawny, grinning seaman in the uniform of the United States Navy, and with a brisk, yet rather bantering humor, demanded:

"Well, whatcha say, big boy? . . . Gettin' tired of waitin'? . . . Well, it won't be long now . . . Dey'll be troo in dere in a minute an' we're next."

"Dey better had be!" the sailor replied with a kind of jocular savagery. "If dey ain't, I'll tear down duh —— joint! . . . Christ!" he cried in an astounded tone, after listening attentively for a moment. "Holy Jeez!" he said with a dumbfounded laugh. "What t' hell are dey doin' in deh all dis time? Who is dat guy, anyway?—A whole regiment of duh Marines, duh way it sounds t' me! Holy *Je-sus!*" he cried with an astounded laugh, listening again —"Christ!"

"Ah, c'mon, Jack!" the woman said with a kind of brutal, husky tenderness, snuggling close to his brawny arm meanwhile, and lewdly proposing her heavy body against his. "Yuh ain't gonna get impatient on me now, are yuh? . . . Just hold on a minute moeh an' I'll give ya somet'ing ya neveh had befoeh!——"

"If yuh do," the gallant tar said tenderly, drawing his mighty fist back now in a gesture of savage endearment that somehow seemed to please her, "I'll come back here and smack yuh right in duh puss, yuh son-of-a-bitch!" he amorously whispered, and pulled her to him.

Similar conversations and actions were to be observed all up and down the line: there were lewd jests, ribald laughter, and impatiently shouted demands on the noisy occupants of the little compartments to "come on out an' give some of duh rest of us a chanct, f'r Chris' sake!" and other expressions of a similar nature.

It was a brutally hot night in the middle of August: in the hallway the air was stifling, weary, greasily humid. The place was thick, dense, stale and foul with tobacco smoke, the stench of the men, the powder and cheap perfume of the women and over all, unforgettable, overpowering, pungent, resinous, rude and raw as savage nature and man's naked lust, was the odor of the new, unpainted, white-pine lumber of which the whole shambling and haphazard place had been constructed.

Finally, after a long and weary wait in that stifling place, during which time the door of the compartments had opened many times, and many men and women had come out, and many more gone in, the boy and the woman with him had advanced to the head of the line, and were next in the succession of that unending and vociferous column.

Presently, the door of the room for which they waited opened, a man came out, shut the door behind him, and then went quickly down the hall. Then for a moment there was silence, impatient mutters in the line behind them, and at length the woman with the boy, muttering:

"I wondeh what t' hell she's doin' all dis time!— Hey!"

she cried harshly, and hammered on the door, "Who's in dere? . . . Come on out, f'r Chris' sake! . . . Yuh're holding up duh line!"

In a moment, a woman's voice answered wearily:

"All right, Fay! . . . Just a moment, dear. . . . I'll be there."

"Oh," the woman with the boy said, in a suddenly quiet, strangely tender kind of voice. "It's Margaret. . . . I guess she's worn out, poor kid." And knocking at the door again, but this time gently, almost timidly, she said in a quiet voice:

"How are yuh, kid? . . . D'ya need any help?"

"No, it's all right, Fay," the girl inside said in the same tired and utterly exhausted tone. "I'll be out in a moment. . . . Come on in, honey."

The woman opened the door softly and entered the room. The only furnishings of the hot, raw, and hideous little place, besides a chair, an untidy and rumpled looking bed, and a table, was a cheap dresser on which was a doll girdled with a soiled ribbon of pink silk, tied in a big bow, a photograph of a young sailor inscribed with the words, "To Margaret, the best pal I ever had—Ed"—and a package of cigarettes. An electric fan, revolving slowly from left to right, droned incessantly, and fanned the close stale air with a kind of sporadic and sweltering breeze.

And from moment to moment, as it swung in its half-orbit, the fan would play full upon the face and head of the girl, who was lying on the bed in an attitude of utter pitiable weariness. When this happened, a single strand of her shining hair, which was straight, lank, fine-spun as silk, and of a lovely red-bronze texture, would be disturbed by the movement of the fan and would be blown gently back and forth across her temple.

The girl, who was tall, slender, and very lovely was,

save for her shoes and stockings, naked, and she lay extended at full length on the untidy bed, with one arm
thrust out in a gesture of complete exhaustion, the other
folded underneath her shining hair, and her face, which
had a fragile, transparent, almost starved delicacy, turned
to one side and resting on her arm, the eyelids closed.
And the eyelids also had this delicacy of texture, were violet
with weariness, and so transparent that the fine net-work
of the veins was plainly visible.

The other woman went softly over to the bed, sat down
beside her, and began to speak to her in a low and tender
tone. In a moment the girl turned her head towards the
woman, opened her eyes, and smiled, in a faint and distant way, as of some one who is just emerging from the
drugged spell of an opiate:

"What? . . . What did you say, darling? . . . No,
I'm all right," she said faintly, and sitting up, with the
other woman's help, she swiftly pulled on over her head
the cheap one-piece garment she was wearing, which had
been flung back over the chair beside the bed. Then
smiling, she stood up, took a cigarette out of the package
on the dresser, lighted it, and turning to the boy, who was
standing in the door, said ironically, with something of
the rasping accent which the other women used, beneath
which, however, her pleasant rather husky tone was plainly evident.

"All right, 'Georgia'! Come on in!"

He went in slowly, still looking at her with an astounded stare. He had known her the first moment he
had looked at her. She was a girl from the little town
where the state university, at which he was a student, was
situated, a member of a family of humble decent people,
well known in the town: she had disappeared almost two
years before, there had been rumor at the time that one of

the students had "got her in trouble," and since that time
he had neither seen nor heard of her.

"How are all the folks down home?" she said. "How's
every one in Hopewell?"

Her luminous smoke-gray eyes were hard and bright
as she spoke, her mouth, in her thin young face, was hard
and bitter as a blade, and her voice was almost deliberately
hard and mocking. And yet, beneath this defiant scorn-
fulness, the strange, husky tenderness of the girl's tone
persisted, and as she spoke, she put her slender hand lightly
on his arm, with the swift, unconscious tenderness of
people in a world of strangers who suddenly meet some
one they know from home.

"They're all right," he stammered in a confused and
bewildered tone, his face beginning to smoulder with embarrassment as he spoke.

"Well, if you see any one I know," she said in the same
ironic tone, "say hello for me. . . . Tell 'em that I sent
my love."

"All right," he blurted out stupidly. "I—I—certainly
will."

"And I'm mad at you, 'Georgia,' " she said with a kind
of mocking reproachfulness, "I'm mad at you for not
telling me you were here. . . . The next time you come
here you'd better ask for me—or I'll be mad! . . . We
homefolks have got to stick together. . . . So you ask for
Margaret—or I'll be mad at you—do you hear?"

"All right!" he stammered confusedly again, "I certainly will."

She looked at him a moment longer with her hard bright
stare, her bitter, strangely tender smile. Then thrusting
her fingers swiftly through his hair, she turned to the
other woman and said:

"Be nice to him, Fay. . . . He's one of the folks from

down my way. . . . Good-bye, 'Georgia.' . . . When you
come back again you ask for Margaret."

"Good-bye," he said, and she was gone, out the door and
down that stifling little hall of brutal, crowding, and imperative desire, into the market-place again, where for
the thousandth time she would offer the sale of her young
slender body to whoever would be there to buy; to solicit,
take, accept the patronage of any of the thousand nameless and unknown men that the huge cylinder of chance
and of the night might bring to her.

He never saw her after that. She was engulfed into the
great vortex of the war, the huge dark abyss and thronging chaos of America, the immense, the cruel, the indifferent and the magic land, where all of us have lived and
walked as strangers, where all of us have been so small,
so lonely, and forsaken, which has engulfed us all at length,
and in whose dark and lonely breast so many lost and
nameless men are buried and forgotten.

This, then, was the third visage of calamity, the image
of desire, the face of war.

Again, the speed, haste, violence, savage humor and the
instant decisiveness of war:—A sweltering noon on one
of the great munition piers at Newport News where now
the boy is working as material checker. Inside the great
shed of the pier, a silent, suffocating heat of one hundred
ten degrees, a grimy, mote-filled air, pollenated with the
golden dust of oats which feed through a gigantic chute
into the pier in an unending river, and which are sacked
and piled in tremendous barricades all up and down the
length of that enormous shed.

Elsewhere upon the pier, the towering geometries of
war munitions: the white hard cleanliness of crated woods
containing food and shot provender of every sort—canned

goods, meat, beans, dried fruits, and small arms amunitions—the enormous victualling of life and death fed ceaselessly into the insatiate and receiving maw of distant war.

The sweltering air is impregnated with the smells of all these things—with smell of oats and coarse brown sacking, with the clean fresh pungency of crated boxes, and with the huge, drowsy and nostalgic compact of a pier—the single blend of a thousand multiform and mixed aromas, the compacted fragrance of the past, sharp, musty, thrilling, unforgettable, as if the savor of the whole huge earth's abundance had slowly stained, and worn through, and soaked its mellow saturation into the massive and encrusted timbers.

But now all work has ceased: all of the usual sounds of work—the unceasing rumble of the trucks, the rattling of winches and the hard, sudden labor of the donkey engines on the decks of ships, the great nets swinging up and over with their freight of boxes, the sudden rattling fall, and rise again, the shouts and cries of the black sweating stevedores, the sharp commands of the gang bosses, overseers, and loading men—all this has stopped, has for the moment given over to the measured stamp of marching men, the endless streams of men in khaki uniforms who have all morning long, since early light, been tramping through the pier and filing up a gangplank into the side of a great transport which waits there to engulf them.

The Negro stevedores sprawl lazily on loaded oat sacks round the grain chute, the checkers doze upon the great walled pile of grain or, kneeling in a circle down behind some oaty barricade, they gamble feverishly with dice.

Meanwhile, the troops come through. The sweltering brown columns tramp in, pause, are given rest, wearily shift the brutal impediment of the loaded knapsacks on their shoulders, /take off their caps, wipe their sleeves across their red sweating faces, curse quietly among themselves, and then wait patiently for the lines to move again.

Down by the ship-side, at the gangplank's end, a group of officers are seated at a table as the troops file by them, examining each man's papers as he comes to them, passing them on from hand to hand, scrawling signatures, filing, recording, putting the stamp of their approval finally on the documents that will release each little khaki figure to its long-awaited triumph of the ship, the voyage, the new land, to all the joy and glory it is panting for, and to the unconsidered perils of battle, war, and death, disease or mutilation, and the unknown terror, horror, and disgust.

But now a column of black troops is coming by. They are a portion of a Negro regiment from Texas, powerful big men, naïve and wondering as children, incorrigibly unsuited to the military discipline. Something, in fact, is missing, wrong, forgotten, out of place, with every one's equipment: one has lost his cap, another is without a belt, another is shy two buttons on his jacket, still another has mislaid his canteen, one is shy a good part of his knapack equipment, and dumbly, ignorantly bewildered at his loss —every one has lost something, left something behind, done something wrong, now misses something which he has to have.

And now, in one of the pauses of their march along the pier, each one of them pours out the burden of his complaint; into the sweltering misery of the heated air, the babel of black voices mounts. And the target of their bewilderment, the object on whom this whole burden of mischance and error is now heaped, the over-burdened and exhausted ruler to whom each now turns in his distress, and, with the naïve and confident faith of a child, asks for an instant solution of the tangled web of error in which he is enmeshed—is an infuriated little bullock of a white man, a first lieutenant, their commander, who during the mountainous accumulations of that catastrophic morning has been driven completely out of his head.

Now he stamps up and down the pier like a maddened animal, the white eyeballs, and the black, sweat-rilled faces follow him back and forth on his stamping and infuriated lunges with the patient, dutiful, and all-confiding trustfulness of children.

His red solid little face is swollen with choked fury and exasperation: as the unending chronicle of their woes mounts up he laughs insanely, clutches violently at the neck-band of his coat as if he is strangling, and stamps drunkenly and blindly about like a man maddened with the toothache.

And still they petition him, with the confident hope and certitude of trusting children that one word from their infallible governor will settle everything:—one tells about his missing belt, another of his forgotten canteen, another of his lost cap, his depleted and half-furnished knapsack—affectionately, incorrigibly, they address him as "Boss!" in spite of his curses, threats, entreaties, his final maddened screams that they must address him in a military manner, and the man stamps up and down, out of his wits with choking and unutterable exasperation, cursing vilely:

"You God-damned black bone-headed gang of sausage-brained gorillas!" he yells chokingly, and clutches at his throat—"Oh, you damned thick-skulled solid-ivory idiot brothers of a one-eyed mule! You sweet stinking set of ape-faced sons of bitches, you! If your brains were made of dynamite you wouldn't have enough to blow your

nose, you poor dumb suffering second cousins of an owl!
... Oh, you just wait, you ink-complected bastards, you!"
he now shouts with a kind of fiendish and anticipatory
pleasure. "Just wait until I get you in the front line
trenches—I'll line you up there till those German bastards
shoot you full of daylight if it's the last thing I ever live
to do, you ... damned ... ignorant ... misbegotten
... cross ... between a ... a ... a ... wall-eyed
possum and a camel's hump—why, you low-down, ignorant bunch of ... of——"

"Boss?"

"Don't call me Boss!" in a high, choking, almost
strangled gurgle. "You dumb son-of-a-bitch, how often
have I got to tell you not to call me BOSS!" he yells.

"I know, Boss—" in a plaintive tone—"but my belt-
buckle's busted. Is you got a piece of string?"

"A piece of string!" he chokes. "Why you damned—
you—you—a piece of string!" he squeaks, and finally defeated, he takes off his cap, throws it on the floor and,
sobbing, stamps upon it.

But an even greater affliction is in store for this unhappy
man. Down at the ship-side now, where the examining
officers are sitting at the table, there has come a sudden
pause, a disturbing interruption in the swift and mechanical dispatch with which the troops have been filing in
before them. Six of the big black soldiers in a group have
been stopped, sharply questioned, and then brusquely
motioned out of line.

The officer picks up his cap, yells, "What in Christ's
name is the matter now?" and rushes down to where they
stand, in an attitude of crushed dejection, with tears rolling down their ebony cheeks. A moment's excited inter-
rogation of the officers seated at the table informs him of
the trouble: the six Negroes, all of whom are members

of his command, have been under treatment for venereal diseases, but have somehow managed to sneak away from camp without a clean bill of health. Now their delinquency and stratagem of escape has been discovered, they have been denied their embarkation papers and weeping and begging, with the pitiable confidence which all these blacks put in their commanding officer, they are fairly grovelling before him, pleading with him that they be allowed to take ship with the rest of their companions.

"We ain't done nothin', Boss!" their leader, a huge ape of a man, black as ebony, is sniffling, pawing at the officer's sleeve. "Dey ain't nothin' wrong with us!"—"We don't want to stay heah in dis Gawd-damn hole, Boss!" another sniffles. "We want to go to France wheah you is! . . . Don't leave us behind, Boss! . . . We'll do anyt'ing you say if you'll jest take us along wid you!——"

"Why, you black clappy bastards!" he snarls—"I wish you were in hell, the lot of you! . . . How the hell do you expect *me* to do anything now at the last moment?" he yells, and filled with a frenzy that can find no stay or answer he goes stamping back and forth like a man gone mad with the very anguish of exasperation and despair. He charges into the midst of that small group of tainted and dejected blacks like a maddened little bull. He raves at them, he reviles them and curses them most foully, for a moment it seems that he is going to assault them physically. And they gather around him, weeping, entreating, crying, begging him for rescue and release, until at length, as if driven frantic by their clamor, he claps both hands to his ears and screaming, "All right, all right, all right! —I'll try—but if they let you go I hope they kill every clappy son-of-a-bitch in the first attack"—he rushes away to the table where the examining officers are seated at their work, engages them long and earnestly in a passionate and persuasive debate and finally wins them over to his argument.

It is decided that the infected Negroes shall be given a physical examination here and now upon the pier and a tall medical officer, delegated for this task, rises from the table, signs briefly to the rejected men, and accompanied by their red-faced little officer, marches them away behind the concealing barrier of the great wall of sacked oats.

They are gone perhaps ten minutes: when they return the Negroes are cavorting with glee, their black faces split by enormous ivory grins, and they are scraping around their little officer like frantic children. They fairly fawn upon him, they try to kiss his hands, they pat his shoulders with their great black paws—the story of their triumphant restoration to the fold is legible in every move they make, in everything they do.

The tall medical officer marches sternly ahead, but with a faint grin playing round the corners of his mouth, and the little red-faced officer is still cursing bitterly, but in his curses now there is a gentler note, the suggestion almost of a lewd tenderness.

And at length that brown, enormous, apparently interminable column has filed into the ship's great side, and there is nothing on the pier now but far lost sounds and silence, the breath of coolness, evening, the on-coming, undulant stride of all-enfolding and deep-breasted night.

Only the Dead Know Brooklyn

Dere's no guy livin' dat knows Brooklyn t'roo an' t'roo, because it'd take a guy a lifetime just to find his way aroun' duh f—— town.

So like I say, I'm waitin' for my train t' come when I sees dis big guy standin' deh—dis is duh foist I eveh see of him. Well, he's lookin' wild, y'know, an' I can see dat he's had plenty, but still he's holdin' it; he talks good an' is walkin' straight enough. So den, dis big guy steps up to a little guy dat's standin' deh, an' says, "How d'yuh get t' Eighteent' Avenoo an' Sixty-sevent' Street?" he says.

"Jesus! Yuh got me, chief," duh little guy says to him. "I ain't been heah long myself. Where is duh place?" he says. "Out in duh Flatbush section somewhere?"

"Nah," duh big guy says. "It's out in Bensonhoist. But I was neveh deh befoeh. How d'yuh get deh?"

"Jesus," duh little guy says, scratchin' his head, y'know —yuh could see duh little guy didn't know his way about —"yuh got me, chief. I neveh hoid of it. Do any of youse guys know where it is?" he says to me.

"Sure," I says. "It's out in Bensonhoist. Yuh take duh Fourt' Avenoo express, get off at Fifty-nint' Street, change to a Sea Beach local deh, get off at Eighteent' Avenoo an' Sixty-toid, an' den walk down foeh blocks. Dat's all yuh got to do," I says.

"G'wan!" some wise guy dat I neveh seen befoeh pipes up. "Whatcha talkin' about?" he says—oh, he was wise, y'know. "Duh guy is crazy! I tell yuh what yuh do," he says to duh big guy. "Yuh change to duh West End line at Toity-sixt'," he tells him. "Get off at Noo Utrecht

an' Sixteent' Avenoo," he says. "Walk two blocks oveh,
foeh blocks up," he says, "an' you'll be right deh." Oh, a
wise guy, y'know.

"Oh, yeah?" I says. "Who told *you* so much?" He got
me sore because he was so wise about it. "How long
you been livin' heah?" I says.

"All my life," he says. "I was bawn in Williamsboig,"
he says. "An' I can tell you t'ings about dis town you
neveh hoid of," he says.

"Yeah?" I says.

"Yeah," he says.

"Well, den, you can tell me t'ings about dis town dat
nobody else has eveh hoid of, either. Maybe you make it
all up yoehself at night," I says, "befoeh you go to sleep
—like cuttin' out papeh dolls, or somp'n."

"Oh, yeah?" he says. "You're pretty wise, ain't yuh?"

"Oh, I don't know," I says. "Duh boids ain't usin' my
head for Lincoln's statue yet," I says. "But I'm wise
enough to know a phony when I see one."

"Yeah?" he says. "A wise guy, huh? Well, you're so
wise dat some one's goin' t'bust yuh one right on duh
snoot some day," he says. "Dat's how wise *you* are."

Well, my train was comin', or I'da smacked him den
and dere, but when I seen duh train was comin', all I said
was, "All right, mugg! I'm sorry I can't stay to take keh
of you, but I'll be seein' yuh sometime, I hope, out in
duh cemetery." So den I says to duh big guy, who'd
been standin' deh all duh time, "You come wit me," I
says. So when we gets onto duh train I says to him,
"Where yuh goin' out in Bensonhoist?" I says. "What
numbeh are yuh lookin' for?" I says. *You* know—I
t'ought if he told me duh address I might be able to help
him out.

"Oh," he says, "I'm not lookin' for no one. I don't know no one out deh."

"Then whatcha goin' out deh for?" I says.

"Oh," duh guy says, "I'm just goin' out to see duh place," he says. "I like duh sound of duh name—Bensonhoist, y'know—so I t'ought I'd go out an' have a look at it."

"Whatcha tryin' t'hand me?" I says. "Whatcha tryin' t'do—kid me?" *You* know, I t'ought duh guy was bein' wise wit me.

"No," he says, "I'm tellin' yuh duh troot. I like to go out an' take a look at places wit nice names like dat. I like to go out an' look at all kinds of places," he says.

"How'd yuh know deh was such a place," I says, "if yuh neveh been deh befoeh?"

"Oh," he says, "I got a map."

"A *map?*" I says.

"Sure," he says, "I got a map dat tells me about all dese places. I take it wit me every time I come out heah," he says.

And Jesus! Wit dat, he pulls it out of his pocket, an' so help me, but he's *got* it—he's tellin' duh troot—a big map of duh whole f—— place with all duh different pahts mahked out. You know—Canarsie an' East Noo Yawk an' Flatbush, Bensonhoist, Sout' Brooklyn, duh Heights, Bay Ridge, Greenpernt—duh whole goddam layout, he's got it right deh on duh map.

"You been to any of dose places?" I says.

"Sure," he says, "I been to most of 'em. I was down in Red Hook just last night," he says.

"Jesus! Red Hook!" I says. "Whatcha do down deh?"

"Oh," he says, "nuttin' much. I just walked aroun'. I went into a coupla places an' had a drink," he says, "but most of the time I just walked aroun'."

"Just walked aroun'?" I says.

"Sure," he says, "just lookin' at t'ings, y'know."

"Where'd yuh go?" I asts him.

"Oh," he says, "I don't know duh name of duh place, but I could find it on my map," he says. "One time I was walkin' across some big fields where deh ain't no houses," he says, "but I could see ships oveh deh all lighted up. Dey was loadin'. So I walks across duh fields," he says, "to where duh ships are."

"Sure," I says, "I know where you was. You was down to duh Erie Basin."

"Yeah," he says, "I guess dat was it. Dey had some of dose big elevators an' cranes an' dey was loadin' ships, an' I could see some ships in drydock all lighted up, so I walks across duh fields to where dey are," he says.

"Den what did yuh do?" I says.

"Oh," he says, "nuttin' much. I came on back across duh fields after a while an' went into a coupla places an' had a drink."

"Didn't nuttin' happen while yuh was in dere?" I says.

"No," he says. "Nuttin' much. A coupla guys was drunk in one of duh places an' started a fight, but dey bounced 'em out," he says, "an' den one of duh guys stahted to come back again, but duh bartender gets his baseball bat out from under duh counteh, so duh guy goes on."

"Jesus!" I said. "Red Hook!"

"Sure," he says. "Dat's where it was, all right."

"Well, you keep outa deh," I says. "You stay away from deh."

"Why?" he says. "What's wrong wit it?"

"Oh," I says, "it's a good place to stay away from, dat's all. It's a good place to keep out of."

"Why?" he says. "Why is it?"

Jesus! Whatcha gonna do wit a guy as dumb as dat? I saw it wasn't no use to try to tell him nuttin', he wouldn't know what I was talkin' about, so I just says to him, "Oh, nuttin'. Yuh might get lost down deh, dat's all."

"Lost?" he says. "No, I wouldn't get lost. I got a map," he says.

A map! Red Hook! Jesus!

So den duh guy begins to ast me all kinds of nutty questions: how big was Brooklyn an' could I find my way aroun' in it, an' how long would it take a guy to know duh place.

"Listen!" I says. "You get dat idea outa yoeh head right now," I says. "You ain't neveh gonna get to know Brooklyn," I says. "Not in a hunderd yeahs. I been livin' heah all my life," I says, "an' I don't even know all deh is to know about it, so how do you expect to know duh town," I says, "when you don't even live heah?"

"Yes," he says, "but I got a map to help me find my way about."

"Map or no map," I says, "yuh ain't gonna get to know Brooklyn wit no map," I says.

"Can you swim?" he says, just like dat. Jesus! By dat time, y'know, I begun to see dat duh guy was some kind of nut. He'd had plenty to drink, of course, but he had dat crazy look in his eye I didn't like. "Can you swim?" he says.

"Sure," I says. "Can't you?"

"No," he says. "Not more'n a stroke or two. I neveh loined good."

"Well, it's easy," I says. "All yuh need is a little confidence. Duh way I loined, me older bruddeh pitched me off duh dock one day when I was eight yeahs old, cloes

an' all. 'You'll swim,' he says. 'You'll swim all right—
or drown.' An', believe me, I *swam!* When yuh know
yuh got to, you'll do it. Duh only t'ing yuh need is confidence. An' once you've loined," I says, "you've got nuttin' else to worry about. You'll neveh forget it. It's
somp'n dat stays wit yuh as long as yuh live."

"Can yuh swim good?" he says.

"Like a fish," I tells him. "I'm a regulah fish in duh
wateh," I says. "I loined to swim right off duh docks wit
all duh oddeh kids," I says.

"What would you do if yuh saw a man drownin'?" duh
guy says.

"Do? Why, I'd jump in an' pull him out," I says.
"Dat's what I'd do."

"Did yuh eveh see a man drown?" he says.

"Sure," I says. "I see two guys—bot' times at Coney
Island. Dey got out too far, an' neider one could swim.
Dey drowned befoeh any one could get to 'em."

"What becomes of people after dey've drowned out
heah?" he says.

"Drowned out where?" I says.

"Out heah in Brooklyn."

"I don't know whatcha mean," I says. "Neveh hoid of
no one drownin' heah in Brooklyn, unless you mean a
swimmin' pool. Yuh can't drown in Brooklyn," I says.
"Yuh gotta drown somewhere else—in duh ocean, where
dere's wateh."

"Drownin'," duh guy says, lookin' at his map. "Drownin'." Jesus! I could see by den he was some kind of
nut, he had dat crazy expression in his eyes when he
looked at you, an' I didn't know what he might do. So
we was comin' to a station, an' it wasn't my stop, but I
got off anyway, an' waited for duh next train.

"Well, so long, chief," I says. "Take it easy, now."

"Drownin'," duh guy says, lookin' at his map. "Drownin'."

Jesus! I've t'ought about dat guy a t'ousand times since den an' wondered what eveh happened to 'm goin' out to look at Bensonhoist because he liked duh name! Walkin' aroun' t'roo Red Hook by himself at night an' lookin' at his map! How many people did I see get drowned out heah in Brooklyn! How long would it take a guy wit a good map to know all deh was to know about Brooklyn!

Jesus! What a nut *he* was! I wondeh what eveh happened to 'im, anyway! I wondeh if some one knocked him on duh head, or if he's still wanderin' aroun' in duh subway in duh middle of duh night wit his little map! Duh poor guy! Say, I've got to laugh, at dat, when I t'ink about him! Maybe he's found out by now dat he'll neveh live long enough to know duh whole of Brooklyn. It'd take a guy a lifetime to know Brooklyn t'roo an' t'roo. An' even den, yuh wouldn't know it all.

Dark in the Forest, Strange as Time

SOME years ago, among the people standing on one of the platforms of the Munich railway station, beside the Swiss express, which was almost ready to depart, there were a woman and a man—a woman so lovely that the memory of her would forever haunt the mind of him who saw her, and a man on whose dark face the legend of a strange and fatal meeting was already visible.

The woman was at the flawless summit of a mature and radiant beauty, packed to the last red ripeness of her lip with life and health, a miracle of loveliness in whom all the elements of beauty had combined with such exquisite proportion and so rhythmical a balance that even as one looked at her he could scarcely believe the evidence of his eyes.

Thus, although not over tall, she seemed at times to command a superb and queenly height, then to be almost demurely small and cosy as she pressed close to her companion. Again, her lovely figure seemed never to have lost the lithe slenderness of girlhood, yet it was ripe, lavish, undulant with all the voluptuous maturity of womanhood, and every movement she made was full of seductive grace.

The woman was fashionably dressed; her little toque-like hat fitted snugly down over a crown of coppery reddish hair and shaded her eyes which had a smoke-blue and depthless quality that could darken almost into black, and change with every swiftest shade of feeling that passed across her face. She was talking to the man in low and tender tones, smiling a vague voluptuous smile as she looked at him. She spoke eagerly, earnestly, gleefully to him, and from time to time burst into a little laugh that came welling low, rich, sensual, and tender from her throat.

As they walked up and down the platform talking, the woman thrust her small gloved hand through the arm of his heavy overcoat and snuggled close to him, sometimes nestling her lovely head, which was as proud and graceful as a flower, against his arm. Again they would pause, and look steadfastly at each other for a moment. Now she spoke to him with playful reproof, chided him, shook him tenderly by the arms, pulled the heavy furred lapels of his overcoat together, and wagged a small gloved finger at him warningly.

And all the time the man looked at her, saying little, but devouring her with large dark eyes that were burning steadily with the fires of death, and that seemed to feed on her physically, with an insatiate and voracious tenderness of love. He was a Jew, his figure immensely tall, cadaverous, and so wasted by disease that it was lost, engulfed, forgotten in the heavy and expensive garments that he wore.

His thin white face, which was wasted almost to a fleshless integument of bone and skin, converged to an immense hooked nose, so that his face was not so much a face as a great beak of death, lit by two blazing and voracious eyes and colored on the flanks with two burning flags of red. Yet, with all its ugliness of disease and emaciation it was a curiously memorable and moving face, a visage somehow nobly tragic with the badge of death.

But now the time had come for parting. The guards were shouting warnings to the passengers, all up and down the platform there were swift serried movements, hurried eddyings among the groups of friends. One saw people embracing, kissing, clasping hands, crying, laughing, shouting, going back for one hard swift kiss, and then mounting hastily into their compartments. And one heard in a strange tongue the vows, oaths, promises, the jests and swift allusions, that were secret and precious to each group and that sent them off at once in roars of laughter, the words of farewell that are the same the whole world over:

"Otto! Otto! . . . Have you got what I gave you? . . . Feel! Is it still there?" He felt, it was still there: fits of laughter.

"Will you see Else?"

"How's that? Can't hear"—shouting, cupping hand to ear, and turning head sideways with a puzzled look.

"I—say—will—you—see—Else?" fairly roared out between cupped palms above the tumult of the crowd.

"Yes. I think so. We expect to meet them at St. Moritz."

"Tell her she's got to write."

"Hey? I can't hear you." Same pantomime as before.

"I—say—tell—her—she's got—to write"—another roar.

"Oh, yes! Yes!" Nodding quickly, smiling, "I'll tell her."

"—or I'll be mad at her!"

"What? Can't hear you for all this noise"—same business as before.

"I—say—tell—her—I'll—be—mad—if she—doesn't—write" roared out again deliberately at the top of his lungs.

Here, a man who had been whispering slyly to a woman, who was trembling with smothered laughter, now turned with grinning face to shout something at the departing friend, but was checked by the woman who seized him by the arm and with a face reddened by laughter, gasped hysterically.

"No! No!"

But the man, still grinning, cupped his hands around his mouth and roared:

"Tell Uncle Walter he has got to wear his——"

"How's that? Can't hear!"—cupping ear and turning head to one side as before.

"I—say," the man began to roar deliberately.

"No! No! No! Sh-h!" the woman gasped frantically, tugging at his arm.

"—to—tell—Uncle Walter—he—must—wear—his woolen——"

"No! No! No!—Heinrich! . . . Sh-h!" the woman shrieked.

"—The—heavy—ones—Aunt—Bertha embroidered with his—initials!" the man went on relentlessly.

Here the whole crowd roared, and the women screamed with laughter, shrieking protests, and saying:

"Sh-h! Sh-h!" loudly.

"Ja—I'll tell him!" the grinning passenger yelled back at him as soon as they had grown somewhat quieter. "Maybe—he hasn't—got—'em—any—more," he shouted as a happy afterthought. "Maybe—one—of—the—Fräuleins—down—there—" he gasped and choked with laughter.

"Otto!" the women shrieked. "Sh-h!"

"Maybe—one—of—the—Fräuleins—got them—away—from"—he began to gasp with laughter.

"O-o-o-t-to! . . . Shame on you—Sh-h!" the women screamed.

"Souvenir—from—old—München," roared back his fellow wit, and the whole group was convulsed again. When they had recovered somewhat, one of the men began in a wheezing and faltering tone, as he wiped at his streaming eyes:

"Tell—Else"—here his voice broke off in a feeble squeak, and he had to pause to wipe his eyes again.

"What?"—the grinning passenger yelled back at him.

"Tell—Else," he began again more strongly, "that Aunt —Bertha—oh! my God!" he groaned weakly again, faltered, wiped at his streaming eyes, and was reduced to palsied silence.

"What?—What?" shouted the grinning passenger sharply, clapping his hand to his attentive ear. "Tell Else what?"

"Tell—Else—Aunt—Bertha—is—sending—her—recipe —for—layer—cake," the man fairly screamed now as if he would get it out at any cost before his impending and total collapse. The effect of that apparently meaningless reference to Aunt Bertha's layer cake was astonishing: nothing that had gone before could approach the spasmodic effect it had upon this little group of friends. They were instantly reduced to a shuddering paralysis of laughter, they staggered drunkenly about, clasped one another feebly for support, tears streamed in torrents from their swollen eyes, and from their wide-open mouths there came occasionally feeble wisps of sound, strangled gasps, faint screams from the women, a panting palsied fit of mirth from which they finally emerged into a kind of hiccoughing recovery.

What it was—the total implication of that apparently banal reference which had thrown them all into such a convulsive fit of merriment—no stranger could ever know, but its effect upon the other people was infectious; they looked toward the group of friends, and grinned, laughed, and shook their heads at one another. And so it went all up and down the line. Here were people grave, gay, sad, serious, young, old, calm, casual, and excited; here were people bent on business and people bent on pleasure;

here people sharing by every act, word, and gesture the excitement, joy, and hope which the voyage wakened in them, and people who looked wearily and indifferently about them, settled themselves in their seats and took no further interest in the events of the departure—but everywhere it was the same.

People were speaking the universal language of departure, that varies not at all the whole world over—that language which is often banal, trivial, and even useless, but on this account curiously moving, since it serves to hide a deeper emotion in the hearts of men, to fill the vacancy that is in their hearts at the thought of parting, to act as a shield, a concealing mask to their true feeling.

And because of this there was for the youth, the stranger, and the alien who saw and heard these things, a thrilling and poignant quality in the ceremony of the train's departure. As he saw and heard these familiar words and actions—words and actions that beneath the guise of an alien tongue were identical to those he had seen and known all his life, among his own people—he felt suddenly, as he had never felt before, the overwhelming loneliness of familiarity, the sense of the human identity that so strangly unites all the people in the world, and that is rooted in the structure of man's life, far below the tongue he speaks, the race of which he is a member.

But now that the time had come for parting, the woman and the dying man said nothing. Clasped arm to arm they looked at each other with a stare of burning and voracious tenderness. They embraced, her arms clasped him, her living and voluptuous body drew toward him, her red lips clung to his mouth as if she could never let him go. Finally, she fairly tore herself away from him, gave him a desperate little push with her hands, and said, "Go, go! It's time!"

Then the scarecrow turned and swiftly climbed into the train, a guard came by and brutally slammed the door behind him, the train began to move slowly out of the station. And all the time the man was leaning from a window in the corridor looking at her, and the woman was walking along beside the train, trying to keep him in sight as long as she could. Now the train gathered motion, the woman's pace slowed, she stopped, her eyes wet, her lips murmuring words no one could hear, and as he vanished from her sight she cried, "Auf Wiedersehn!" and put her hand up to her lips and kissed it to him.

For a moment longer the younger man, who was to be this specter's brief companion of the journey, stood looking out the corridor window down the platform toward the great arched station sheds, seeming to look after the group of people departing up the platform, but really seeing nothing but the tall, lovely figure of the woman as she walked slowly away, head bent, with a long, deliberate stride of incomparable grace, voluptuous undulance. Once she paused to look back again, then turned and walked on slowly as before.

Suddenly she stopped. Some one out of the throng of people on the platform had approached her. It was a young man. The woman paused in a startled manner, lifted one gloved hand in protest, started to go on, and the next moment they were locked in a savage embrace, devouring each other with passionate kisses.

When the traveller returned to his seat, the dying man who had already come into the compartment from the corridor and had fallen back into the cushions of his seat, breathing hoarsely, was growing calmer, less exhausted. For a moment the younger man looked intently at the beak-like face, the closed weary eyes, wondering if this dying man had seen that meeting on the station platform, and what knowledge such as this could now mean to him. But that mask of death was enigmatic, unrevealing; the youth found nothing there that he could read. A faint and strangely luminous smile was playing at the edges of the man's thin mouth, and his burning eyes were now open, but far and sunken and seemed to be looking from an unspeakable depth at something that was far away. In a moment, in a profound and tender tone, he said:

"Zat vas my vife. Now in ze vinter I must go alone, for zat iss best. But in ze spring ven I am better she vill come to me."

All through the wintry afternoon the great train rushed down across Bavaria. Swiftly and powerfully it gathered motion, it left the last scattered outposts of the city behind it, and swift as dreams the train was rushing out across the level plain surrounding Munich.

The day was gray, the sky impenetrable and somewhat heavy, and yet filled with a strong, clean Alpine vigor, with that odorless and yet exultant energy of cold mountain air. Within an hour the train had entered Alpine country, now there were hills, valleys, the immediate sense of soaring ranges, and the dark enchantment of the forests of Germany, those forests which are something more than trees—which are a spell, a magic, and a sorcery, filling the hearts of men, and particularly those strangers who have some racial kinship with that land, with a dark music, a haunting memory, never wholly to be captured.

It is an overwhelming feeling of immediate and impending discovery, such as men might have who come for the first time to their father's country. It is like coming to that unknown land for which our spirits long so passionately in youth, which is the dark side of our soul, the strange brother and the complement of the land we have known in our childhood. And it is revealed to us instantly the moment that we see it with a powerful emotion of perfect recognition and disbelief, with that dream-like reality of strangeness and familiarity which dreams and all enchantment have.

What is it? What is this wild fierce joy and sorrow swelling in our hearts? What is this memory that we cannot phrase, this instant recognition for which we have no words? We cannot say. We have no way to give it utterance, no ordered evidence to give it proof, and scornful pride can mock us for a superstitious folly. Yet we will know the dark land at the very moment that we come to it, and though we have no tongue, no proof, no utterance for what we feel, we have what we have, we know what we know, we are what we are.

And what are we? We are the naked men, the lost Americans. Immense and lonely skies bend over us, ten thousand men are marching in our blood. Where does it come from—the sense of strangeness, instant recognition, the dream-haunted, almost captured, memory? Where does it come from, the constant hunger and the rending lust, and the music, dark and solemn, elfish, magic, sounding through the wood? How is it that this boy, who is American, has known this strange land from the first moment that he saw it?

How is it that from his first night in a German town he has understood the tongue he never heard before, has spoken instantly, saying all he wished to say, in a strange language which he could not speak, speaking a weird argot which was neither his nor theirs, of which he was not even conscious, so much did it seem to be the spirit of a language, not the words, he spoke, and instantly, in this fashion, understood by every one with whom he talked?

No. He could not prove it, yet he knew that it was

there, buried deep in the brain and blood of man, the utter knowledge of this land and of his father's people. He had felt it all, the tragic and insoluble admixture of the race. He knew the terrible fusion of the brute and of the spirit. He knew the nameless fear of the old barbaric forest, the circle of barbaric figures gathered round him in their somber and unearthly ring, the sense of drowning in the blind forest horrors of barbaric time. He carried all within himself, the slow gluttony and lust of the unsated swine, as well as the strange and powerful music of the soul.

He knew the hatred and revulsion from the never-sated beast—the beast with the swine-face and the quenchless thirst, the never-ending hunger, the thick, slow, rending hand that fumbled with a smouldering and unsated lust. And he hated the great beast with the hate of hell and murder because he felt and knew it in himself and was himself the prey of its rending, quenchless, and obscene desires. Rivers of wine to drink, whole roast oxen turning on the spit, and through the forest murk, the roaring wall of huge beast-bodies and barbaric sound about him, the lavish flesh of the great blonde women, in brutal orgy of the all-devouring, never-sated maw of the huge belly, without end or surfeit—all was mixed into his blood, his spirit, and his life.

It had been given to him somehow from the dark time-horror of the ancient forest together with all that was magical, glorious, strange and beautiful: the husky horn-notes sounding faint and elfin through the forests, the infinite strange weavings, dense mutations of the old Germanic soul of man. How cruel, baffling, strange, and sorrowful was the enigma of the race: the power and strength of the incorruptible and soaring spirit rising from the huge corrupted beast with such a radiant purity, and the powerful enchantments of grand music, noble poetry, so sorrowfully and unalterably woven and inwrought with all the blind brute hunger of the belly and the beast of man.

It was all his, and all contained in his one life. And it could, he knew, never be distilled out of him, no more than one can secrete from his flesh his father's blood, the ancient and immutable weavings of dark time. And for this reason, as he now looked out the window of the train at that lonely Alpine land of snow and dark enchanted forest he felt the sense of familiar recognition instantly, the feeling that he had always known this place, that it was home. And something dark, wild, jubilant, and strange was exulting, swelling in his spirit like a grand and haunting music heard in dreams.

And now, a friendly acquaintance having been established, the specter, with the insatiate, possessive curiosity of his race, began to ply his companion with innumerable questions concerning his life, his home, his profession, the journey he was making, the reason for that journey. The young man answered readily, and without annoyance. He knew that he was being pumped unmercifully, but the dying man's whispering voice was so persuasive, friendly, gentle, his manner so courteous, kind, and insinuating, his smile so luminous and winning, touched with a faint and yet agreeable expression of weariness, that the questions almost seemed to answer themselves.

The young man was an American, was he not? . . . Yes. And how long had he been abroad—two months? Three months? No? Almost a year! So long as that! Then he liked Europe, yes? It was his first trip? No? His fourth?—The specter lifted his eyebrows in expressive astonishment, and yet his sensitive thin mouth was touched all the time by his faint, wearily cynical smile.

Finally, the boy was pumped dry: the specter knew

all about him. Then for a moment he sat staring at the youth with his faint, luminous, subtly mocking, and yet kindly smile. At last, wearily, patiently, and with the calm finality of experience and death, he said:

"You are very young. Yes. Now you vant to see it all, to haf it all—but you haf nothing. Zat iss right—yes?" he said with his persuasive smile. "Zat vill all change. Some day you vill vant only a little—maybe, den, you *haf* a little—" and he flashed his luminous, winning smile again. "Und zat iss better—Yes?" He smiled again, and then said wearily, "I know. I know. Myself I haf gone eferyvere like you. I haf tried to see eferyt'ing—und I haf had nothing. Now I go no more. Eferyvere it iss ze same," he said wearily, looking out the window, with a dismissing gesture of his thin white hand. "Fields, hills, mountains, riffers, cities, peoples—you vish to know about zem all. Vun field, vun hill, vun riffer," the man whispered, "zat iss enough!"

He closed his eyes for a moment: when he spoke again his whisper was almost inaudible—"Vun life, vun place, vun time."

Darkness came, and the lights in the compartment were turned on. Again that whisper of waning life made its insistent, gentle, and implacable demand upon the youth. This time it asked that the light in the compartment be extinguished, while the specter stretched himself out upon the seat to rest. The younger man consented willingly and even gladly: his own journey was near its end and outside, the moon, which had risen early, was shining down upon the Alpine forests and snows with a strange, brilliant, and haunting magic which gave to the darkness in the compartment some of its own ghostly and mysterious light.

The specter lay quietly stretched out on the cushions

of the seat, his eyes closed, his wasted face, on which the two bright flags of burning red now shone with vermilion hue, strange and ghastly in the magic light as the beak of some great bird. The man scarcely seemed to breathe: no sound or movement of life was perceptible in the compartment except the pounding of the wheels, the leathery stretching and creaking sound of the car, and all that strange-familiar and evocative symphony of sounds a train makes—that huge symphonic monotone which is itself the sound of silence and forever.

For some time held in that spell of magic light and time, the youth sat staring out the window at the enchanted world of white and black that swept grandly and strangely past in the phantasmal radiance of the moon. Finally he got up, went out into the corridor, closing the door carefully behind him, and walked back down the narrow passageway through car after car of the rocketing train until he came to the dining car.

Here all was brilliance, movement, luxury, sensual warmth and gaiety. All the life of the train now seemed to be concentrated in this place. The waiters, surefooted and deft, were moving swiftly down the aisle of the rocketing car, pausing at each table to serve people from the great platters of well-cooked food which they carried on trays. Behind them the *sommelier* was pulling corks from tall frosty bottles of Rhine wine: he would hold the bottle between his knees as he pulled, the cork would come out with an exhilarating pop, and he would drop the cork then into a little basket.

At one table a seductive and beautiful woman was eating with a jaded-looking old man. At another a huge and powerful-looking German, with a wing collar, a shaven skull, a great swine face and a forehead of noble and lonely thought, was staring with a concentrated look of bestial gluttony at the tray of meat from which the waiter served him. He was speaking in a guttural and lustful tone, saying, "Ja! . . . Gut! . . . und etwas von diesem hier auch. . . ."

The scene was one of richness, power and luxury, evoking as it did the feeling of travel in a crack European express, which is different from the feeling one has when he rides on an American train. In America, the train gives one a feeling of wild and lonely joy, a sense of the savage, unfenced, and illimitable wilderness of the country through which the train is rushing, a wordless and unutterable hope as one thinks of the enchanted city toward which he is speeding; the unknown and fabulous promise of the life he is to find there.

In Europe, the feeling of joy and pleasure is more actual, ever present. The luxurious trains, the rich furnishings, the deep maroons, dark blues, the fresh, well-groomed vivid colors of the cars, the good food and the sparkling, heady wine, and the worldly, wealthy, cosmopolitan look of the travellers—all of this fills one with a powerful sensual joy, a sense of expectancy about to be realized. In a few hours' time one goes from country to country, through centuries of history, a world of crowded culture and whole nations swarming with people, from one famous pleasure-city to another.

And, instead of the wild joy and nameless hope one feels as he looks out the window of an American train, one feels here (in Europe) an incredible joy of realization, an immediate sensual gratification, a feeling that there is nothing on earth but wealth, power, luxury, and love, and that one can live and enjoy this life, in all the infinite varieties of pleasure, forever.

When the young man had finished eating, and paid his

bill, he began to walk back again through corridor after corridor along the length of the rocketing train. When he got back to his compartment, he saw the specter lying there as he had left him, stretched out upon the seat, with the brilliant moonlight still blazing on the great beak of his face.

The man had not changed his position by an inch, and yet at once the boy was conscious of some subtle, fatal change he could not define. What was it? He took his seat again and for some time stared fixedly at the silent ghostly figure opposite him. Did he not breathe? He thought, he was almost sure, he saw the motion of his breathing, the rise and fall of the emaciated breast, and yet he was not sure. But what he plainly saw now was that a line, vermilion in its moon-dark hue, had run out of the corner of the firm set mouth and that there was a large vermilion stain upon the floor.

What should he do? What could be done? The haunted light of the fatal moon seemed to have steeped his soul in its dark sorcery, in the enchantment of a measureless and inert calmness. Already, too, the train was slackening its speed, the first lights of the town appeared, it was his journey's end.

And now the train was slowing to a halt. There were the flare of rails, the switch-lights of the yard, small, bright, and hard, green, red, and yellow, poignant in the dark, and on other tracks he could see the little goods cars and the strings of darkened trains, all empty, dark, and waiting with their strange attentiveness of recent life. Then the long station quays began to slide slowly past the windows of the train, and the sturdy goat-like porters were coming on the run, eagerly saluting, speaking, calling to the people in the train who had already begun to pass their baggage through the window.

Softly the boy took his overcoat and suit-case from the rack above his head and stepped out into the narrow corridor. Quietly he slid the door of the compartment shut behind him. Then, for a moment, still unsure, he stood there looking back. In the semi-darkness of the compartment the spectral figure of the cadaver lay upon the cushions, did not move.

Was it not well to leave all things as he had found them, in silence, at the end? Might it not be that in this great dream of time in which we live and are the moving figures, there is no greater certitude than this: that, having met, spoken, known each other for a moment, as somewhere on this earth we were hurled onward through the darkness between two points of time, it is well to be content with this, to leave each other as we met, letting each one go alone to his appointed destination, sure of this only, needing only this—that there will be silence for us all and silence only, nothing but silence, at the end?

Already the train had come to a full stop. The boy went down the corridor to the end, and in a moment, feeling the bracing shock of the cold air upon his flesh, breathing the vital and snow-laden air into his lungs, he was going down the quay with a hundred other people, all moving in the same direction, some toward certitude and home, some toward a new land, hope, and hunger, the swelling prescience of joy, the promise of a shining city. He knew that he was going home again.

The Four Lost Men

SUDDENLY, at the green heart of June, I heard my father's voice again. That year I was sixteen; the week before I had come home from my first year at college, and the huge thrill and menace of the war, which we had entered just two months before, had filled our hearts. And war gives life to men as well as death. It fills the hearts of young men with wild song and jubilation. It wells up in their throats in great-starred night, the savage cry of all their pain and joy. And it fills them with a wild and wordless prophecy not of death, but life, for it speaks to them of new lands, triumph, and discovery, of heroic deeds, the fame and fellowship of heroes, and the love of glorious unknown women—of a shining triumph and a grand success in a heroic world, and of a life more fortunate and happy than they have ever known.

So was it with us all that year. Over the immense and waiting earth, the single pulse and promise of the war impended. One felt it in the little towns at dawn, with all their quiet, casual, utterly familiar acts of life beginning. One felt it in the route-boy deftly flinging the light folded block of paper on a porch, a man in shirt-sleeves coming out upon the porch and bending for the paper, the slow-clopping hoofs of the milk horse in a quiet street, the bottle-clinking wagon, and the sudden pause, the rapid footsteps of the milkman and the clinking bottles, then clopping hoof and wheel, and morning, stillness, the purity of light, and the dew-sweet bird-song rising in the street again.

In all these ancient, ever-new, unchanging, always

magic acts of life and light and morning one felt the huge impending presence of the war. And one felt it in the brooding hush of noon, in the ring of the ice-tongs in the street, the cool whine of the ice-saws droning through the smoking block, in leaf, and blade and flower, in smell of tar, and the sudden haunting green-gold summer absence of a street-car after it had gone.

The war had got in everything: it was in things that moved, and in things that were still, in the animate red silence of an old brick wall as well as in all the thronging life and traffic of the streets. It was in the faces of the people passing, and in ten thousand familiar moments of man's daily life and business.

And lonely, wild, and haunting, calling us on forever with the winding of its far lost horn, it had got into the time-enchanted loneliness of the magic hills around us, in all the sudden, wild and lonely lights that came and passed and vanished on the massed green of the wilderness.

The war was in far cries and broken sounds and cow-bells tinkling in the gusty wind, and in the far, wild, wailing joy and sorrow of a departing train, as it rushed eastward, seaward, war-ward through a valley of the South in the green spell and golden magic of full June, and in the houses where men lived, the brief flame and fire of sheeted window panes.

And it was in field and gulch and hollow, in the sweet green mountain valleys fading into dusk, and in the hill-flanks reddened with the ancient light, and slanting fast into steep cool shade and lilac silence. It was in the whole huge mystery of earth that, after all the dusty tumult of the day, could lapse with such immortal stillness to the hush, the joy, the sorrow of oncoming night.

The war had got into all sounds and secrecies, the sorrow, longing, and delight, the mystery, hunger and wild joy that came from the deep-breasted heart of fragrant, all-engulfing night. It was in the sweet and secret rustling of the leaves in summer streets, in footsteps coming quiet, slow, and lonely along the darkness of a leafy street, in screen doors slammed, and silence, the distant barking of a dog, far voices, laughter, faint pulsing music at a dance, and in all the casual voices of the night, far, strangely near, most intimate and familiar.

And suddenly, as I sat there under the proud and secret mystery of huge-starred, velvet-breasted night, hearing my father's great voice sounding from the porch again, the war, with a wild and intolerable loneliness of ecstasy and desire came to me in the sudden throbbing of a racing motor, far-away silence, an image of the cool sweet darkness of the mountainside, the white flesh and yielding tenderness of women. And even as I thought of this I heard the rich, sensual welling of a woman's voice, voluptuous, low, and tender, from the darkness of a summer porch across the street.

What had the war changed? What had it done to us? What miracle of transformation had it wrought upon our lives? It had changed nothing; it had heightened, intensified, and made glorious all the ancient and familiar things of life. It had added hope to hope, joy to joy, and life to life; and from that vital wizardry it had rescued all our lives from hopelessness and despair, and made us live again who thought that we were lost.

The war seemed to have collected in a single image of joy, and power, and proud compacted might all of the thousand images of joy and power and all-exulting life which we had always had, and for which we had never had a word before. Over the fields of silent and mysterious night it seemed that we could hear the nation marching, that we could hear, soft and thunderous in the night, the million-footed unison of marching men. And that single glorious image of all-collected joy and unity and might had given new life and new hope to all of us.

My father was old, he was sick with a cancer that flowered and fed forever at his entrails, eating from day to day the gaunt sinew of his life away beyond a hope or remedy, and we knew that he was dying. Yet, under the magic life and hope the war had brought to us, his life seemed to have revived again out of its grief of pain, its death of joy, its sorrow of irrevocable memory.

For a moment he seemed to live again in his full prime. And instantly we were all released from the black horror of death and time that hung above him, from the nightmare terror that had menaced us for years. Instantly we were freed from the evil spell of sorrowful time and memory that had made his living death more horrible than his real one could ever be.

And instantly the good life, the golden and jubilant life of childhood, in whose full magic we had been sustained by the power of his life, and which had seemed so lost and irrecoverable that it had a dreamlike strangeness when we thought of it, had, under this sudden flare of life and joy and war, returned in all its various and triumphant colors. And for a moment we believed that all would be again for us as it had been, that he never could grow old and die, but that he must live forever, and that the summertime, the orchard and bright morning, would be ours again, could never die.

I could hear him talking now about old wars and ancient troubles, hurling against the present and its lead-ers the full indictment of his soaring rhetoric that howled, rose, fell, and swept out into the night, piercing all quarters of the darkness with the naked penetration which his voice had in the old days when he sat talking on his porch in summer darkness, and the neighborhood attended and was still.

Now as my father talked, I could hear the boarders on the porch attending in the same way, the stealthy creak of a rocker now and then, a low word spoken, a question, protest or agreement, and then their hungry, feeding, and attentive silence as my father talked. He spoke of all the wars and troubles he had known, told how he had stood, "a bare-foot country boy," beside a dusty road twelve miles from Gettysburg, and had watched the ragged rebels march past upon the road that led to death and battle and the shipwreck of their hopes.

He spoke of the faint and ominous trembling of the guns across the hot brooding silence of the countryside, and how silence, wonder, and unspoken questions filled the hearts of all the people, and how they had gone about their work upon the farm as usual. He spoke of the years that had followed on the war when he was a stone-cutter's apprentice in Baltimore, and he spoke of ancient joys and labors, forgotten acts and histories, and he spoke then with familiar memory of the lost Americans—the strange, lost, time-far, dead Americans, the remote, voiceless, and bewhiskered faces of the great Americans, who were more lost to me than Egypt, more far from me than the Tartarian coasts, more haunting strange than Cipango or the lost faces of the first dynastic kings that built the Pyramids—and whom he had seen, heard, known, found familiar in the full pulse, and passion, and proud glory of his youth: the lost, time-far, voiceless faces of Buchanan, Johnson, Douglas, Blaine—the proud, vacant, time-strange and bewhiskered visages of Garfield, Arthur, Harrison, and Hayes.

"Ah, Lord!" he said—his voice rang out in darkness like a gong, "Ah, Lord!—I've known all of 'em since James Buchanan's time—for I was a boy of six when he took office!" Here he paused a moment, lunged forward violently in his rocking chair, and spat cleanly out a spurt of strong tobacco juice across the porchrail into the loamy earth, the night-sweet fragrance of the geranium beds. "Yes, sir," he said gravely, lunging back again, while the attentive, hungry boarders waited in the living darkness and were still, "I remember all of them since James Buchanan's time, and I've seen most of them that came since Lincoln!—Ah, Lord!" he paused briefly for another waiting moment, shaking his grave head sadly in the dark. "Well do I remember the day when I stood on a street in Baltimore—poor friendless orphan that I was!" my father went on sorrowfully, but somewhat illogically, since at this time his mother was alive and in good health, upon her little farm in Pennsylvania, and would continue so for almost fifty years—"a poor friendless country boy of sixteen years, alone in the great city where I had come to learn my trade as an apprentice—and heard Andrew Johnson, then the President of this *great* nation," said my father, "speak from the platform of a horse-car—and he was so drunk—so *drunk*—" he howled, "the President of this country was so *drunk* that they had to stand on each side of him, and hold him as he spoke—or he'd a-gone head over heels into the gutter!" Here he paused, wet his great thumb briefly, cleared his throat with considerable satisfaction, lunged forward violently again in his rocking chair and spat strongly a wad of bright tobacco juice into the loamy fragrance of the dark geranium bed.

"The first vote I ever cast for President," my father continued presently, as he lunged back again, "I cast in 1872, in Baltimore, for that *great* man—that brave and noble soldier—U. S. Grant! And I have voted for every Republican nominee for President ever since. I voted for Rutherford Hayes of Ohio in 1876—that was the year, as you well know, of the great Hayes-Tilden controversy, in 1880 for James Abram Garfield—that *great* good man," he said passionately, "who was so foully and brutally done to death by the cowardly assault of a murderous assassin." He paused, wet his thumb, breathing heavily, lunged forward in his rocking chair, and spat again. "In 1884, I cast my vote for James G. Blaine in the year that Grover Cleveland defeated him," he said shortly, "for Benjamin Harrison in 1888, and for Harrison again in 1892, the time that Cleveland got in for his second term—a time we will all remember to our dying days," my father said grimly, "for the Democrats were in and we had soup kitchens. And, you can mark my words," he howled, "you'll have them again, before these next four years are over— your guts will grease your backbone, as sure as there's a God in heaven, before that fearful, that awful, that cruel, inhuman and bloodthirsty Monster who kept us out of war," my father jeered derisively, "is done with you—for hell, ruin, misery, and damnation commence every time the Democrats get in. You can rest assured of that!" he said shortly, cleared his throat, wet his thumb, lunged forward violently and spat again. And for a moment there was silence and the boarders waited.

"Ah, Lord!" my father said at length sadly, gravely, in a low, almost inaudible tone. And suddenly, all the old life and howling fury of his rhetoric had gone from him: he was an old man again, sick, indifferent, dying, and his voice had grown old, worn, weary, sad.

"Ah, Lord!" he muttered, shaking his head sadly, thinly, wearily in the dark. "I've seen them all. . . . I've seen them come and go . . . Garfield, Arthur, Harrison, and Hayes . . . and all . . . all . . . all of them are dead. . . . I'm the only one that's left," he said illogically, "and soon I'll be gone, too." And for a moment he was silent. "It's pretty strange when you come to think of it," he muttered. "By God it is!" And he was silent, and darkness, mystery, and night were all about us.

Garfield, Arthur, Harrison, and Hayes—time of my father's time, blood of his blood, life of his life, had been living, real, and actual people in all the passion, power, and feeling of my father's youth. And for me they were the lost Americans: their gravely vacant and bewhiskered faces mixed, melted, swam together in the sea-depths of a past intangible, immeasurable, and unknowable as the buried city of Persepolis.

And they were lost.

For who was Garfield, martyred man, and who had seen him in the streets of life? Who could believe his footfalls ever sounded on a lonely pavement? Who had heard the casual and familiar tones of Chester Arthur? And where was Harrison? Where was Hayes? Which had the whiskers, which the burnsides: which was which?

Were they not lost?

Into their ears, as ours, the tumults of forgotten crowds, upon their brains the million printings of lost

time, and suddenly upon their dying sight the brief
bitter pain and joy of a few death-bright, fixed and
fading memories: the twisting of a leaf upon a bough,
the grinding felloe-rim against the curb, the long, distant and retreating thunder of a train upon the rails.

Garfield, Hayes, and Harrison were Ohio men; but
only the name of Garfield had been brightened by his
blood. But at night had they not heard the howlings
of demented wind, the sharp, clean, windy raining to
the earth of acorns? Had all of them not walked down
lonely roads at night in winter and seen a light and
known it was theirs? Had all of them not known the
wilderness?

Had they not known the smell of old bound calf and
well-worn leathers, the Yankee lawyer's smell of strong
tobacco spit and courthouse urinals, the smell of horses,
harness, hay, and sweating country men, of jury rooms
and court rooms—the strong male smell of Justice at the
county seat, and heard a tap along dark corridors where
fell a drop in darkness with a punctual crescent monotone of time, dark time?

Had not Garfield, Hayes, and Harrison studied law
in offices with a dark brown smell? Had not the horses
trotted past below their windows in wreaths of dust along
a straggling street of shacks and buildings with false
fronts? Had they not heard below them the voices of
men talking, loitering up in drawling heat? Had they
not heard the casual, rich-fibered, faintly howling country
voices, and heard the rustling of a woman's skirt, and
waiting silence, slyly lowered tones of bawdry and then
huge guffaws, slapped meaty thighs, and high fat choking laughter? And in the dusty dozing heat, while time
buzzed slowly, like a fly, had not Garfield, Arthur, Harrison, and Hayes then smelled the river, the humid,

subtly fresh, half-rotten river, and thought of the white flesh of the women then beside the river, and felt a slow impending passion in their entrails, a heavy rending power in their hands?

Then Garfield, Arthur, Harrison, and Hayes had gone to war, and each became a brigadier or major-general. All were bearded men: they saw a spattering of bright blood upon the leaves, and they heard the soldiers talking in the dark of food and women. They held the bridge-head in bright dust at places with such names as Wilson's Mill and Spangler's Run, and their men smashed cautiously through dense undergrowth. And they had heard the surgeons cursing after battles, and the little rasp of saws. They had seen boys standing awkwardly holding their entrails in their hands, and pleading pitifully with fear-bright eyes: "Is it bad, General? Do you think it's bad?"

When the canister came through it made a ragged hole. It smashed through tangled leaves and boughs, sometimes it plunked solidly into the fiber of a tree. Sometimes when it struck a man it tore away the roof of his brain, the wall of his skull, raggedly, so that his brains seethed out upon a foot of wilderness, and the blood blackened and congealed, and he lay there in his thick clumsy uniform, with a smell of urine in the wool, in the casual, awkward, and incompleted attitude of sudden death. And when Garfield, Arthur, Harrison, and Hayes saw these things they saw that it was not like the picture they had had, as children, it was not like the works of Walter Scott and William Gillmore Sims. They saw that the hole was not clean and small and in the central front, and the field was not green nor fenced, nor mown. Over the vast and immemorable earth the quivering heated light of afternoon was shining, a field swept rudely upward to a lift of rugged wood, and field by field, gulley by gulch by fold, the earth advanced in rude, sweet, limitless convolutions.

Then Garfield, Arthur, Harrison, and Hayes had paused by the bridge-head for a moment and were still, seeing the bright blood at noon upon the trampled wheat, feeling the brooding hush of six o'clock across the fields where all the storming feet had passed at dawn, seeing the way the rough field hedge leaned out across the dusty road, the casual intrusions of the coarse field grasses and the hot dry daisies to the edges of the road, seeing the rock-bright shallows of the creek, the sweet cool shade and lean of river trees across the water.

They paused then by the bridge-head looking at the water. They saw the stark blank flatness of the old red mill that somehow was like sunset, coolness, sorrow, and delight, and looking at the faces of dead boys among the wheat, the most-oh-most familiar-plain, the death-strange faces of the dead Americans, they stood there for a moment, thinking, feeling, thinking, with strong, wordless wonder in their hearts:

"As we leaned on the sills of evening, as we stood in the frames of the marvellous doors, as we were received into silence, the flanks of the slope and the slanted light, as we saw the strange hushed shapes upon the land, the muted distances, knowing all things then —what could we say except that all our comrades were spread quietly around us and that noon was far?

"What can we say now of the lonely land—what can we say now of the deathless shapes and substances— what can we say who have lived here with our lives, bone, blood, and brain, and all our tongueless languages, hearing on many a casual road the plain-familiar voices of Americans, and who to-morrow will be buried in the earth,

knowing the fields will steep to silence after us, the slant
light deepen on the slopes, and peace and evening will
come back again—at one now with the million shapes
and single substance of our land, at one with evening,
peace, the huge stride of the undulant oncoming night,
at one, also, with morning?

"Silence receive us, and the field of peace, hush of the
measureless land, the unabated distances; shape of the
one and single substance and the million forms, replen-
ish us, restore us, and unite us with your vast images of
quietness and joy. Stride of the undulant night, come
swiftly now; engulf us, silence, in your great-starred
secrecy; speak to our hearts of stillness, for we have,
save this, no speech.

"There is the bridge we crossed, the mill we slept in,
and the creek. There is a field of wheat, a hedge, a
dusty road, an apple orchard, and the sweet wild tangle
of a wood upon that hill. And there is six o'clock across
the fields again, now and always, as it was and will
be to world's end forever. And some of us have died
this morning coming through the field—and that was
time—time—time. We shall not come again, we never
shall come back again, we never shall come back along
this road again as we did once at morning—so, brothers,
let us look again before we go. . . . There is the mill,
and there the hedge, and there the shallows of the rock-
bright waters of the creek, and there the sweet and most
familiar coolness of the trees—and surely we have been
this way before!" they cried.

"Oh, surely, brothers, we have sat upon the bridge,
before the mill, and sung together by the rock-bright
waters of the creek at evening, and come across the
wheatfield in the morning and heard the dew-sweet
bird-song rising from the hedge before! You plain, oh-

most-familiar and most homely earth, proud earth of this huge land unutterable, proud nobly swelling earth, in all your delicacy, wildness, savagery, and terror—grand earth in all your loneliness, beauty and wild joy, terrific earth in all your limitless fecundities, swelling with infinite fold and convolution into the reaches of the West forever—American earth!—bridge, hedge, and creek and dusty road—you plain tremendous poetry of Wilson's Mill, where boys died in the wheat this morning—you unutterable far-near, strange-familiar, homely earth of magic, for which a word would do if we could find it, for which a word would do if we could call it by its name, for which a word would do that never can be spoken, that can never be forgotten, and that will never be revealed—oh, proud, familiar, nobly swelling earth, it seems we must have known you before! It seems we must have known you forever, but all we know for certain is that we came along this road one time at morning, and now our blood is painted on the wheat, and you are ours now, we are yours forever—and there is something here we never shall remember—there is something here we never shall forget!"

Had Garfield, Arthur, Harrison, and Hayes been young? Or had they all been born with flowing whiskers, sideburns, and wing collars, speaking gravely from the cradle of their mother's arms the noble vacant sonorities of far-seeing statesmanship? It could not be. Had they not all been young men in the 'Thirties, the 'Forties, and the 'Fifties? Did they not, as we, cry out at night along deserted roads into demented winds? Did they not, as we, cry out in ecstasy and exultancy, as the full measure of their hunger, their potent and inchoate hope, went out into that single wordless cry?

Did they not, as we, when young, prowl softly up and down in the dark hours of the night, seeing the gas-lamps flare and flutter on the corner, falling with livid light upon the corners of old cobbled streets of brown-stone houses? Had they not heard the lonely rhythmic clopping of a horse, the jounting wheels of a hansom cab, upon those barren cobbles? And had they not waited, trembling in the darkness till the horse and cab had passed, had vanished with the lonely recession of shod hoofs, and then were heard no more?

And then had Garfield, Arthur, Harrison, and Hayes not waited, waited in the silence of the night, prowling up and down the lonely cobbled street, with trembling lips, numb entrails, pounding hearts? Had they not set their jaws, made sudden indecisive movements, felt ter-ror, joy, a numb impending ecstasy, and waited, waited then—for what? Had they not waited, hearing sounds of shifting engines in the yards at night, hearing the hoarse, gaseous breaths of little engines through the grimy fan-flare of their funnels? Had they not waited there in that dark street with the fierce lone hunger of a boy, feel-ing around them the immense and moving quietness of sleep, the heartbeats of ten thousand sleeping men, as they waited, waited in the night?

Had they not, as we, then turned their eyes up and seen the huge starred visage of the night, the immense and lilac darkness of America in April? Had they not heard the sudden, shrill, and piping whistle of a de-parting engine? Had they not waited, thinking, feel-ing, seeing then the immense mysterious continent of night, the wild and lyric earth, so casual, sweet, and strange-familiar, in all its space and savagery and ter-ror, its mystery and joy, its limitless sweep and rude-ness, its delicate and savage fecundity? Had they not had a vision of the plains, the mountains, and the rivers flowing in the darkness, the huge pattern of the everlasting earth and the all-engulfing wilderness of America?

Had they not felt, as we have felt, as they waited in the night, the huge, lonely earth of night-time and America, on which ten thousand lonely sleeping little towns were strewn? Had they not seen the fragile network of light, racketing, ill-joined little rails across the land, over which the lonely little trains rushed on in darkness, flinging a handful of lost echoes at the river's edge, leaving an echo in the cut's resounding cliff, and being engulfed then in huge lonely night, in all-brooding, all-engulfing night? Had they not known, as we have known, the wild secret joy and mystery of the everlasting earth, the lilac dark, the savage, silent, all-possessing wilderness that gathered in around ten thousand lonely little towns, ten million lost and lonely sleepers, and waited, and abode forever, and was still?

Had not Garfield, Arthur, Harrison, and Hayes then waited, feeling wild joy and sorrow in their hearts, and a savage hunger and desire—a flame, a fire, a fury—burning fierce and lean and lonely in the night, burning forever while the sleepers slept? Were they not burning, burning, burning, even as the rest of us have burned? Were Garfield, Arthur, Harrison, and Hayes not burning in the night? Were they not burning forever in the silence of the little towns, with all the fierce hunger, savage passion, limitless desire that young men in this land have known in the darkness?

Had Garfield, Arthur, Harrison, and Hayes not waited then, as we have waited, with numb lips and pounding hearts and fear, delight, strong joy and terror stirring in their entrails as they stood in the silent

street before a house, proud, evil, lavish, lighted—certain,
secret, and alone? And as they heard the hoof, the
wheel, the sudden whistle and the immense and sleeping silence of the town, did they not wait there in the darkness, thinking:

"Oh, there are new lands, morning, and a shining
city. Soon, soon, soon!"

Did not Garfield, Arthur, Harrison, and Hayes, those
fierce and jubilant young men, who waited there, as we
have waited, in the silent barren street, with trembling
lips, numb hands, with terror, savage joy, fierce rapture
alive and stirring in their entrails—did they not feel, as
we have felt, when they heard the shrill departing warning of the whistle in the dark, the sound of great wheels
pounding at the river's edge? Did they not feel, as we
have felt, as they waited there in the intolerable sweetness, wildness, mystery, and terror of the great earth in
the month of April, and knew themselves alone, alive and
young and mad and secret with desire and hunger in the
great sleep-silence of the night, the impending, cruel, all-
promise of this land? Were they not torn, as we have
been, by sharp pain and wordless lust, the asp of time, the
thorn of spring, the sharp, the tongueless cry? Did they
not say:

"Oh, there are women in the East—and new lands,
morning, and a shining city! There are forgotten fume-
flaws of bright smoke above Manhattan, the forest of
masts about the crowded isle, the proud cleavages of
departing ships, the soaring web, the wing-like swoop
and joy of the great bridge, and men with derby hats
who come across the Bridge to greet us—come, brothers, let us go to find them all! For the huge murmur of
the city's million-footed life, far, bee-like, drowsy, strange
as time, has come to haunt our ears with all its golden

prophecy of joy and triumph, fortune, happiness and love such as no men before have ever known. Oh, brothers, in the city, in the far-shining, glorious, time-enchanted spell of that enfabled city we shall find great men and lovely women, and unceasingly ten thousand new delights, a thousand magical adventures! We shall wake at morning in our rooms of lavish brown to hear the hoof and wheel upon the city street again, and smell the harbor, fresh, half-rotten, with its bracelet of bright tides, its traffic of proud sea-borne ships, its purity and joy of dancing morning-gold.

"Street of the day, with the unceasing promise of your million-footed life, we come to you!" they cried. "Street of the thunderous wheels at noon, street of the great parades of marching men, the band's bright oncoming blare, the brave stick-candy whippings of a flag, street of the cries and shouts, the swarming feet, —street of the jounting cabs, the ringing hooves, the horse-cars and the jingling bells, the in-horse ever bending its sad nodding head toward its lean and patient comrade on the right—great street of furious life and movement, noon, and joyful labors, your image blazes in our hearts forever, and we come!

"Street of the morning, street of hope!" they cried. "Street of coolness, slanted light, the frontal cliff and gulch of steep blue shade, street of the dancing morning-gold of waters on the flashing tides, street of the rusty weathered slips, the blunt-nosed ferry foaming in with its packed wall of small white staring faces, all silent and intent, all turned toward *you*—proud street! Street of the pungent sultry smells of new-ground coffee, the good green smell of money, the fresh half-rotten harbor smells with all its evocation of your mast-bound harbor and its tide of ships, great street!—Street of the old buildings grimed richly with the warm and mellow dinginess of trade—street of the million morning feet forever hurrying onward in the same direction—proud street of hope and joy and morning, in your steep canyon we shall win the wealth, the fame, the power and the esteem which our lives and talents merit!

"Street of the night!" they cried, "great street of mystery and suspense, terror and delight, eagerness and hope, street edged forever with the dark menace of impending joy, an unknown happiness and fulfilment, street of gaiety, warmth, and evil, street of the great hotels, the lavish bars and restaurants, and the softly golden glow, the fading lights and empetalled whiteness of a thousand hushed white thirsty faces in the crowded theatres, street of the tidal flood of faces, lighted with your million lights and all thronging, tireless and unquenched in their insatiate searching after pleasure, street of the lovers coming along with slow steps, their faces turned toward each other, lost in the oblivion of love among the everlasting web and weaving of the crowd, street of the white face, the painted mouth, the shining and inviting eye—oh, street of night, with all your mystery, joy, and terror—we have thought of you, proud street.

"And we shall move at evening in the noiseless depths of sumptuous carpets through all the gaiety, warmth, and brilliant happiness of great lighted chambers of the night, filled with the mellow thrum and languor of the violins, and where the loveliest and most desirable women in the world—the beloved daughters of great merchants, bankers, millionaires, or rich young widows, beautiful, loving, and alone—are moving with a slow proud undulance, a look of depthless tenderness in their fragile, lovely faces. And the loveliest of them all," they cried, "is ours, is ours forever, if we want her! For, brothers, in the city, in the far-shining, magic, golden city, we shall move among great men and glorious women and know nothing but strong joy and happiness forever, winning by our courage, talent, and deserving the highest and most honored place in the most fortunate and happy life that men have known, if only we will go and make it ours!"

So thinking, feeling, waiting as we have waited in the sleeping silence of the night in silent streets, hearing, as we have heard, the sharp blast of the warning whistle, the thunder of great wheels upon the river's edge, feeling, as we have felt, the mystery of night-time and of April, the huge impending presence, the wild and secret promise, of the savage, lonely, everlasting earth, finding, as we have found, no doors to enter, and being torn, as we were torn, by the thorn of spring, the sharp, the wordless cry, did they not carry—these young men of the past, Garfield, Arthur, Harrison, and Hayes —even as we have carried, within their little tenements of bone, blood, sinew, sweat, and agony, the intolerable burden of all the pain, joy, hope and savage hunger that a man can suffer, that the world can know?

Were they not lost? Were they not lost, as all of us have been who have known youth and hunger in this land, and who have waited lean and mad and lonely in the night, and who have found no goal, no wall, no dwelling, and no door?

The years flow by like water, and one day it is spring again. Shall we ever ride out of the gates of the East again, as we did once at morning, and seek again, as we did then, new lands, the promise of the war, and glory, joy, and triumph, and a shining city?

O youth, still wounded, living, feeling with a woe unutterable, still grieving with a grief intolerable, still thirsting with a thirst unquenchable—where are we to seek? For the wild tempest breaks above us, the wild fury beats about us, the wild hunger feeds upon us—and we are houseless, doorless, unassuaged, and driven on forever; and our brains are mad, our hearts are wild and wordless, and we cannot speak.

Gulliver

SOME day some one will write a book about a man who was too tall—who lived forever in a dimension that he did not fit, and for whom the proportions of everything—chairs, beds, doors, rooms, shoes, clothes, shirts and socks, the berths of Pullman cars, and the bunks of transatlantic liners, together with the rations of food, drink, love, and women which most men on this earth have found sufficient to their measure—were too small.

He should write the story of that man's journey through this world with the conviction of incontrovertible authority, and with such passion, power, and knowledge that every word will have the golden ring of truth; and he will be able to do this because that man's life has been his own, because he has lived it, breathed it, moved in it, and made it his with every sinew of his life since he was fifteen years of age, and because there is no one on earth who understands that world, in all the joy and pain and strangeness of its incommunicable loneliness, as well as such a man.

The world this man would live in is the world of six feet six, and that is the strangest and most lonely world there is. For the great distances of this world are the fractional ones, the terrific differences are those which we can measure by a hand, a step, a few short inches, and that shut us as completely from the world we see, the life we love, the room, the door we want to enter, as if we saw them from the star-flung planetary distances of bridgeless and unmeasured vacancy. Yes, that world we see and want is even more remote from us than Mars, for it is almost ours at every instant, intolerably near and warm and palpable, and intolerably far because it is so very near—only a foot away if we could span it, only a word, a wall, a door away if we could utter, find, and enter it—and we are lashed on by our fury and devoured by our own hunger, captives in the iron and impregnable walls of our own loneliness.

To be a giant, to be one of those legendary creatures two miles high in the old stories—that is another thing. For a giant lives in his own world and needs and wants no other: he takes a mountain at a stride, drinks off a river in one gulp of thirst, wanders over half a continent in a day, and then comes home at night to dine in friendship with his fellow Titans, using a shelf of mountain as a table, a foothill as a stool, and the carcasses of whole roast oxen as the dainty morsels of his feast.

And to be a giant in a world of pygmy men—to be a mile-high creature in a world of foot-high men—that also is another thing. For sometimes his huge single eye is blinded by their cunning, he will make the mountains echo with his wounded cries, tear up a forest in his pain and fury, and will lash about him with an oak tree, and hurl ten-ton boulders torn from granite hills after the little ships of terror-stricken men.

He awakes at morning in a foreign land, his ship is wrecked, his comrades drowned, and he forsaken: a regiment of tiny creatures are swarming up across his body, they shoot their tiny arrows at his face and bind him down with countless weavings of a threadlike cord, and the terrific legend of his life among the pygmies becomes the instrument by which another giant whipped the folly, baseness, and corruption in the lives of men with the scorpion lash of the most savage allegory ever written.

And to be a pygmy in a world of pygmy men, that also is another thing. For where we all are inches tall, our size is only measured by proportion. We live elf-close and midget-near the earth, and desperately explore the tropic jungle of the daisy fields while monstrous birds —huge buzzing flies and booming bees and tottering butterflies unfurl the enormous velvet sails of their slashed wings as they soar over us. We think we are as tall, as big, as strong as any men that ever lived, and in our three-inch world our corn and wheat is good but is no higher than the grass. We wander through great gloomy forests no taller than scrub pine, there are no Atlantic depths and Himalayan heights, our grandest mountain ranges are just molehill high, and if the stars seem far, most far, to us, they are no farther than they seem to other men.

Finally, to be one of those poor giants and midgets of the time in which we live—one of these paltry eight- and nine-foot Titans, two-foot dwarfs of circuses—that also is a different thing. For now they live the life, and love the lights of carnival, and the world beyond those lights is phantom and obscure. Each day the world throngs in to sit beneath the canvas top and feed its fascinated eye on their deformities, and they display themselves before that world and are not moved by in- terest, touched by desire, from what they see of it. In- stead they live together in the world of freaks, and this world seems to them to have been framed inevitably by nature. They love, hate, plot, contrive, betray, and hope, are happy, sorrowful, and ambitious like all other men. The eight-foot giant and the two-foot dwarf are bosom friends. And three times a day they sit down and eat at table in an interesting and congenial society given charm and romance by The Fat Girl and The Bearded

Lady and piquant zest by the witty repartee of Jo-Jo-What-Is-It, The Living Skeleton, and The Tattooed Man. But that, as well, is not a tall man's world: it is another door he cannot enter.

For he is earthy, of the earth, like every man. Shaped from the same clay, breathing the same air, fearing the same fears, and hoping the same hopes as all men in the world, he walks the thronging streets of life alone— those streets that swarm forever with their tidal floods of five feet eight. He walks those streets forever a stranger, and alone, having no other earth, no other life, no other door than this, and feeding upon it with an eye of fire, a heart of intolerable hunger and desire, yet walled away from all the dimensional security of that great room of life by the length of an arm, the height of a head, the bitter small denial of a foot—seeing, feeling, knowing, and desiring the life that blazes there before his eyes, which is as near as his heart, and as far as heaven, which he could put his hand upon at every moment, and which he can never enter, fit, or make his own again, no more than if he were phantasmal substances of smoke.

It is a strange adventure—the adventure of being very tall—and in its essence it comes to have a singular and instinctive humanity. In an extraordinary way, a tall man comes to know things about the world as other people do not, cannot, know them. And the reason for this lies mainly in the purely fortuitous quality of a tall man's difference from average humanity. In no respect, save in respect to his unusual height, is a tall man different from other men. In no way is he less his brother's brother, or his father's son. In fact—astonishing as that fact may seem—the overwhelming probability is that a tall man never thinks of being tall, never realizes indeed, that he *is* tall until other people remind him of his height.

Thus, there was a tall man once and when he was alone he never thought of his great height; it never occurred to him that his dimensions were in any way different from those of most of the people that he saw around him every day upon the streets. In fact, he was the victim of an extraordinary delusion: for some reason which he could not define, he had a secret and unspoken conviction—an image of himself that was certainly not the product of his conscious reasoning, but rather the unconscious painting of his desire—that he was really a person of average height and size—a man of five feet eight or nine, no more. A moment's reflection would, of course, instantly tell him that this picture of himself was wrong, but his natural and instinctive tendency was to think— or rather *feel*—himself in this perspective. It was, therefore, only natural, that when his attention was rudely and forcibly brought to a realization of his unusual height—as it was a hundred times a day now by people on the street—he should receive the news with a sense of shocked surprise, bewilderment, and finally with quick flaring anger and resentment.

He would be going along a street at five o'clock when the city was pouring homeward from its work, and suddenly he would become conscious that people were watching him: would see them stare at him and nudge each other, would see their surprised looks travelling curiously up his frame, would hear them whisper to each other in astonished voices, and see them pass him, laughing, and hear their oaths and words of astounded disbelief, hilarious surprise. When this happened, he could have strangled them. As he heard their scoffs and jokes and exclamations—those dreary husks of a stale and lifeless humor which are the same the world over, which never change, and which have worn their weary rut into a tall man's heart and brain until he knows them as no one else can ever know them—he felt almost that he could *choke* them into wisdom, seize them, knock their heads together, snarl at them:

"God-damn you, but I'll show you that I am the same as you if I have to shake you into owning it!"

Thus he was the butt, a hundred times a day, of those clumsy, tiresome but well-intentioned jocularities to which, in course of time, a tall man becomes so patiently accustomed, so wearily resigned. And his own response to them was probably the same as that of every other tall man who ever lived and had to weather the full measure of man's abysmal foolishness. At first, he felt only the fierce and quick resentment of youth, the truculent sensitivity of youth's wounded pride, its fear of ridicule, its swift readiness to take offense, to feel that it was being flouted, mocked, insulted, its desire to fight and to avenge its wounded honor.

And then he felt a kind of terrible shame and self-abasement: a feeling of personal inferiority that made him envy the lot of average men, that made him bitterly regret the accident of birth and nature that had imprisoned a spirit fierce and proud and swift as flight, and burning as a flame, in such a grotesque tenement. And this feeling of shame and self-abasement and hatred of his flesh is the worst thing that a tall man knows, the greatest iniquity that his spirit suffers. For it is during this period that he comes to hate the body that has been given him by birth and nature, and by this act of hatred, he degrades himself and dishonors man. For this loathing for his body is like the ignoble hatred that a man may have for a loyal and ugly friend whose destiny is coherent with his own, and who must endure. And endure he does—this loyal ugly friend that is man's grotesque tenement—and goes with him everywhere in all his mad and furious marchings, and serves man faithfully like no other friend on earth, and suffers the insults and injuries that man heaps upon him, the frenzy, passion, and brute exhaustion, the scars, the sickness, and the pain, the surfeits of his master's intolerable hunger, and at the end, all battered, scarred, debased, befouled, and coarsened by his master's excess, is still with him, inseparable as nis shadow, loyal to the end—a friend homely, true, devoted, good as no one else can ever be, who sticks with us through every trouble, stays by us through every brawl, bears the brunt of all our drinking, eating, and our brutal battery, reels in and out of every door with us, and falls with us down every flight of stairs, and whom we one day find again before us—as a madman may discover light and sanity again and see the comrade, the protector and the victim of his madness steady there before him, grinning at him wryly through his puffed and battered lips, and saying with a rueful but an all-forgiving humor:

"Well—here we are again."

It is a strange adventure, a hard but precious education, that a tall man knows. For finally he comes to learn, through sweat and toil and bitter anguish, a stern but not a desolate humanity. He gets a kind of lonely wisdom that no one else on earth can get. And by the strange and passionate enigma of his destiny, he is drawn close to man by the very circumstance that shuts him out. He enters life through the very door that once he thought was shut against him, is of the earth, more earthy, by the fact of his exclusion. A tall man could not escape from life, or flee the world, even if he desired it: he is at once life's exile and life's prisoner; wherever he goes life reaches out and pulls him to it, will not let him go. And at the end, he learns the truth of Ernest Renan's bitter observation—that the only thing that can give one a conception of the infinite is the extent of human stupidity. And in the jibes, the jests, the drolleries that are shouted after him a dozen times a day in the streets because of his great height, in the questions that are asked concerning it, and in the innumerable conversations that it provokes, he acquires a huge and damning accumulation of evidence concerning man's fatal unity, the barren paucity of his invention, the desolate consonance of his wit.

For one such man, at least, it never changed, it was always the same: it went on day by day and month by month in the narrow crowded streets around him, and it would go on year after year in a hundred cities, a dozen countries, amid a thousand scattered places in all quarters of the world, and it would always be the same—a barren formula endlessly renewed with the unwearied pertinacity of an idiot monotony—it would always be the same.

He never found the slightest deviation in that barren formula. No one ever made an interesting or amusing observation about his height—and ten thousand people talked to him about it. No one ever said a funny or a witty thing about his height, and ten thousand people had their fling about it. No one ever showed the slightest understanding of the nature of a tall man's life, or asked a single shrewd and penetrating question about it —and yet the curiosity that his tallness caused was almost incredible, the conversations that he had, the questions that he had to answer were innumerable.

The barren formula was so endlessly repeated that at length it had worn its dull grooves into his brain, and he answered without thinking, replied without listening, giving mechanically the answers that they wished to hear, the tried and trusted formula that had served its purpose so many thousand times before, knowing in advance what every one would say.

Was it wit? Then let the diligent historian of the nation's wit give ear and pay attention to these drolleries which were shouted after one man's tall receding figure as he trod the pavements of ten thousand streets:

"Hey-y!"

"Hey-y! Youse guy!"

"Hey-y-y! . . . Holy Jeez! . . . Chizzus! . . . Look ut duh guy!"

"Hey-y, Mis-teh! . . . Is it rainin' up deh? . . . Cheezus! . . . Ho-lee Chee! . . . Will yuh lookut duh guy?"

"Hey-y—Mis-teh! . . . How's duh weatheh up deh? . . . Ho-lee Chee! . . . Take a lookut duh size of 'm, will yah?"

Such, then, were the evidences of the popular humor upon this subject—by a high authority it can solemnly be affirmed that these evidences were all there were.

Or was it conversation of a more polite and genteel sort—well-bred consolation, soothing affirmations, suave flatteries meant to hearten and give cheer? The formula in this kind of conversation ran as follows:

"You're ver-ee tall, aren't you?"

"Yes—hah! hah!—yes—hah! hah!—I suppose I am—hah! hah!—I suppose you noticed it!"

"Yes, I did—when you got up, it did seem ra-ther overwhelming the first time—(with hasty correction)—only of course, one doesn't notice it at *all* later . . . I

mean one forgets all about it . . . I *ree-lee* think you'd
be *awf-lee* glad you *are* that way . . . I *mean,* that's the
way most people would like to be . . . it does give you
such an advantage, doesn't it? . . . I *mean,* after *all,*
every one would be that way if they could—no one wants
to be *short,* do they? . . . Every one would much rather
be *tall.* . . . I *mean,* it makes every one look *up* to you,
doesn't it, wherever you go. . . . *Ree-lee,* I shouldn't
think you'd *mind* at all . . . I should think you'd be
glad you *are* that way . . . I *mean,* after *all,* it does give
you a great advantage, *doesn't* it? . . . Do you see what
I *mean?*"

"Yes . . . ah-hah-hah! . . . I certainly do! . . . ah-
hah-hah! . . . Yes, I certainly do see what you mean
. . . ah-hah-hah! . . . You're right about it . . . ah-hah-
hah! . . . I certainly do!"

Or was it friendly banter, now, a kindly curiosity of a
rougher sort, among a simple yet good-natured kind of
men? Suppose a scene, then: such a scene as one has
found ten thousand times within the labyrinth of night
upon the seaboard of the continent. It is an airless groove
in an old wall behind blind windows set in rotting brick:
within, a slab of bar, its wet shine puddled here and there
with rings of glasses; a battered rail of brass, not polished
recently; and a radiance of hard dead light; Leo, the bar-
man, with his jowled, swart face of night, professionally
attentive; and at the end, the dead stamped visages of
night, the rasping snarl of drunken voices, the elbows of
the barflies puddled in beer slop.

The buzzer rings, good Leo peers with hard mistrust
through opened slot, the door is opened, and the tall man
enters, to whom at once Pat Grogan—wit by nature, Kelt
by birth, and now the antic of good Leo's bar—approaches, with the small red eyes of rheum and murder

comically astare, ape-shoulders stooped, ape-knees bowed
and tucked under, and jowled ape-visage comically turned
upwards in a stare of ape-like stupefaction—all most
comical to see—while good Leo looks and chuckles heavily
and all the barflies grin. So, now, as follows:

Grogan (still crouching): *"Je-zus . . . Christ! . . . Ho-
lee Jeez!* . . . What's dat guy *standin'* on, anyway? . . .
(Leo and all the grinning barflies chortle with appreciative delight, and thus encouraged, Jolly Grogan carries
on) . . . Jee-zus! (with a slow bewildered lifting of his
red jowled face, he calculates the visitor from foot to head
—a delicate stroke, not lost by any means on grinning
Leo and his appreciative clientele) . . . Say-y! . . . When
I first saw dat guy I t'ought he was standin' on a box or
somep'n . . . (turning to Leo with an air of fine bewilderment). . . . Take a look ut 'im, will yuh? *Ho-lee*
Chee! . . . Who *is* dis guy, anyway? . . . (turning to all
the grinning others) . . . When I foist sees duh guy, I
says t' myself . . . What *is* dis, anyway? . . . Is duh
coicus in town or somep'n? (Turns again, gesturing to tall
visitor with air of frank bewilderment) . . . Take a look
at 'm, will yah? . . . (Satisfied with his success, he rejoins
his grinning and appreciative comrades, and for some
time further regales them by taking astounded glances at
the tall visitor, shaking his head in a bewildered way, and
saying in an unbelieving tone) . . . But *Je-sus!* . . . Take
a look at 'm, will yah?" etc.

And now Leo, shaking his head slowly to himself with
appreciative admiration of his client's wit, approaches
the tall visitor and still chuckling heartily at the recollection, leans over the bar and whispers confidingly:

"Dat's Mistuh Grogan. . . . (A trifle apologetically)
He's been drinkin' a little so don't pay no attention to
anyt'ing he says. . . . He didn't mean nuttin' by it—

(with ponderous assurance) Nah-h! . . . He's one of duh nicest guys yuh eveh saw when he's not drinkin' . . . he's only kiddin' anyway . . . he don't mean nuttin' by it . . . but *Je-sus!* (suddenly laughs heartily at the recollection, a heavy, swarthy, and deliberate hah-hah-hah that sets all of his night-time jowls a-quiver) . . . I had t' laff when he pulled dat one about yuh standin' on a box or somep'n . . . hah! hah! hah! hah! hah! . . . But he don't mean nuttin' by it! . . . Nah-h! . . . One of duh nicest guys yuh eveh saw when he's not drinkin'! . . . When he pulled dat one aboutcha standin' on a box or somep'n, I had t' laugh . . . duh way he said it! . . . Standin' on a box or somep'n—dat's a good one! . . . Hah! Hah! Hah! Hah! Hah!" . . . (and goes heavily away, heaving with slow nocturnal laughter, shaking his head slowly to himself).

Now, as the visitor stands drinking by himself, the barflies cluster at the other end in excited controversy, from which disputatious murmurs may be heard from time to time—such vehement scraps of affirmation or denial as the following:

"Nah-h! . . . Guh-*wan!* . . . Watcha givin' me? . . . He's more'n dat . . . I'll betcha on it! . . . Nah-h! . . . Guh-*wan!* . . . He's oveh *seven* if he's an inch! . . . Guh-*wan!* . . . I'll betcha on it! . . . *All* right! All right! . . . Guh-wan and *ast* him den! . . . But he's more'n dat! I'll betcha on it!" . . .

One of the debaters now detaches himself from his disputatious group, and beer glass in hand, approaches the lone visitor. . . . A face not bad, not vicious, not unfriendly: face of a city-man in the late forties—the face of the cartoonist-drawing—lean, furrowed, large-nosed, deeply seamed, a little sunken around the mouth, almost metallically stamped, and wisely knowing, cynically assured—the nerve-ends stunned, the language strident, utterly, unmistakably, the city's child.

The City's Child (grinning amiably, a trifle apologetically, lowering his voice, and speaking with a natural tension of his lips, out of the corners of his mouth): . . . "Podden me, Mac . . . I hope yuh don't mind my astin' yuh a question . . . but my frien's an' me has been havin' a leetle oggument aboutcha . . . an' I gotta little question dat I'd like t' ast yuh. . . . Yuh don't mind, do yuh?"

The Tall Stranger (grinning mechanically and laughing an agreeable and complaisant laugh of utter falseness): "Why, no! . . . ah-hah-hah! . . . Not at all! . . . ah-hah-hah! . . . Go right ahead, it's perfectly all right. . . . Ah-hah-hah."

The City's Child: "Because if yuh do I wantcha t' say so . . . I guess a lotta guys ast yuh duh same question an' I t'ought mebbe yuh might get tired hearin' it—you know what I mean? . . . A lotta guys might get tired of bein' ast duh same question so many times . . . (with an expression of difficulty on his face, shrugs his shoulders expressively and says hopefully) *You* know?"

The Tall Stranger: "Why . . . ah-hah-hah! . . . Yes . . . I think I do. . . . That is to say, go right ahead . . . ah-hah-hah . . . it's quite all right."

The City's Child: "I guess so many guys have ast yuh dis same question dat yuh can guess already what it is —can't yuh?"

The Tall Stranger: "Why, yes—no—ah-hah-hah! . . . That is to say—*Yes!* . . . I think I can!"

The City's Child: "Well, den, Mac . . . if yuh *don't* mind . . . if it's all right . . . I was just goin' t' ast yuh . . . (whispering persuasively) . . . just t' settle a little oggument I been havin' wit' my frien's—*How tall are yuh?* . . . (hastily). Now if yuh don't want t' tell me, it's O.K. . . . Yuh know how it is, *some* guys . . ."

The Tall Stranger: "Not at all—ah-hah-hah—that is to say, *yes*—ah-hah-hah . . . it's quite all right . . . I don't mind at all. . . . I'm between six feet five and six feet six . . . that is, I haven't measured for some time . . . but I was between six feet five and six feet six the last time that I measured. . . . (Apologetically) That's been some time ago . . . several years ago since I last measured . . . but . . . ah-hah-hah . . . it was between six feet five and six feet six and I don't think I've grown much since then . . . ah-hah-hah. . . . Between six feet five and six feet six."

The City's Child (with an astonished but somewhat disappointed air): "Is *dat* a fact? . . . I t'ought you was more'n dat! . . . I t'ought you was aroun' seven foot . . . but anotheh guy oveh heah said you wasn't more'n six foot seven or eight . . . (reflectively). Six foot five or six, eh? . . . Is dat a fact? . . . I t'ought you was more'n dat!"

The Tall Stranger: "No . . . ah-hah-hah . . . a lot of people think so . . . but I guess that's right . . . about six feet five or six."

The City's Child (jocularly): "Say! . . . Yuh know watta guy like *you* oughta do! . . . Yuh know what *I'd* do if I was big as you——"

The Tall Stranger: "Why, no . . . ah-hah-hah— What's that?"

The City's Child: "I'd go in duh ring an' fight Dempsey . . . I'd fight *all* dose guys. . . . Dat's what I'd do. . . . A guy as big as you could hit an awful wallop. . . . and wit' your reach dey couldn't touch yuh. . . . Dat's what I'd do if I had yoeh size! I'd go in duh ring—yes, sir!—Dat's just duh t'ing I'd do if I was big as *you*."

The Tall Stranger (rising glibly and mechanically to the occasion): "Well, you'd better be glad you're not. . . . You don't know how lucky you are."

The City's Child (in a slow, interested voice): "Oh yeah?"

The Tall Stranger (getting off his little speech rapidly and glibly): "Sure. A guy like me has nothing but trouble everywhere he turns."

The City's Child (with awakened interest): "Oh yeah?"

The Tall Stranger: "Sure. They don't make anything big enough to fit you."

The City's Child (with an air of slow, surprised revelation): "Say! I guess dat's right, at dat!"

The Tall Stranger: "Sure it is! You can't get a bed long enough to sleep in——"

The City's Child (curiously): "I guess yuh got to sleep all doubled up, heh?"

The Tall Stranger: "Sure I have. Like this, see!" (Here he makes a zigzag movement with his hand and the City's Child laughs hoarsely.)

The City's Child: "Wat d' yuh do about clo'es? I guess yuh gotta have everyt'ing made to ordeh, huh?"

The Tall Stranger: "Sure." (And according to the formula, now tells his fascinated listener that the cot he sleeps on is a foot too short for him, that he cannot stretch out straight in a berth or a steamer bunk, that he cracks his head against the rafters as he descends a steep flight of stairs, that he cannot find room for his knees in theatres or buses—and all the rest of it. When he has finished, the City's Child strokes his head with a movement of slow and almost disbelieving revelation, and then saying slowly, "Well, what d'yuh t'ink of dat?" returns to impart the fascinating information he has gathered to the waiting group of his expectant and interested friends.)

So, in ten thousand streets and towns and places of the earth, ran the undeviating formula:—a formula that never changed, that was the same forever—and that showed the tall and lonely man the barren unity of life, and that finally, curiously, in a poignant and inexplicable fashion, gave him a faith in man, a belief in man's fundamental goodness, kindliness, and humanity, as nothing else on earth could do.

The Bums at Sunset

SLOWLY, singly, with the ambling gait of men who have just fed, and who are faced with no pressure of time and business, the hoboes came from the jungle, descended the few feet of clay embankment that sloped to the road bed, and in an unhurried manner walked down the tracks toward the water tower. The time was the exact moment of sunset, the sun indeed had disappeared from sight, but its last shafts fell remotely, without violence or heat, upon the treetops of the already darkening woods and on the top of the water tower. That light lay there briefly with a strange unearthly detachment, like a delicate and ancient bronze, it was no part of that cool, that delicious darkening of the earth which was already steeping the woods—it was like sorrow and like ecstasy and it faded briefly like a ghost.

Of the five men who had emerged from the "jungle" above the tracks and were now advancing, in a straggling procession, toward the water tower, the oldest was perhaps fifty, but such a ruin of a man, such a shapeless agglomerate of sodden rags, matted hair, and human tissues, that his age was indeterminable. He was like something that has been melted and beaten into the earth by a heavy rain. The youngest was a fresh-skinned country lad with bright wondering eyes: he was perhaps not more than sixteen years old. Of the remaining three, one was a young man not over thirty with a ferret face and very few upper teeth. He walked along gingerly on tender feet that were obviously unaccustomed to the work he was now putting them to: he was a triumph of dirty elegance—he wore a pin-striped suit heavily spattered with grease stains and very shiny on the seat: he kept his coat collar turned up and his hands thrust deeply into his trouser pockets—he walked thus with his bony shoulders thrust forward as if, in spite of the day's heat, he was cold. He had a limp cigarette thrust out of the corner of his mouth, and he talked with a bare movement of his lips, and a curious and ugly convulsion of his mouth to the side: everything about him suggested unclean secrecy.

Of the five men, only the remaining two carried on them the authority of genuine vagabondage. One was a small man with a hard seamed face, his eyes were hard and cold as agate, and his thin mouth was twisted slantwise in his face, and was like a scar.

The other man, who might have been in his mid-fifties, had the powerful shambling figure, the seamed face of the professional vagabond. It was a face and figure that had a curious brutal nobility; the battered and pitted face was hewn like a block of granite and on the man was legible the tremendous story of his wanderings—a legend of pounding wheel and thrumming rod, of bloody brawl and brutal shambles, of the savage wilderness, the wild, cruel and lonely distances of America.

This man, somehow obviously the leader of the group, walked silently, indifferently, at a powerful shambling step, not looking at the others. Once he paused, thrust a powerful hand into the baggy pocket of his coat, and drew out a cigarette, which he lit with a single motion of his cupped hand. Then his face luxuriously contorted as he drew upon the cigarette, he inhaled deeply, letting the smoke trickle slowly out through his nostrils after he had drawn it into the depths of his mighty lungs. It was a powerful gesture of sensual pleasure that suddenly gave to the act of smoking and to the fragrance of tobacco all of their primitive and pungent relish. And it was evident that the man could impart this rare quality to the simplest physical acts of life—to everything he touched— because he had in him somehow the thrilling qualities of exultancy and joy.

All the time, the boy had been keeping step behind this man, his eyes fixed steadily upon the broad back. Now, as the man stopped, the boy came abreast of him, and also stopped, and for a moment continued to look at the man, a little uncertainly, but with the same expression of steadfast confidence.

The bum, letting the smoke coil slowly from luxurious nostrils, resumed his powerful swinging stride, and for a moment said nothing to the boy. Presently, however, he spoke, roughly, casually, but with a kind of coarse friendliness:

"Where yuh goin', kid?" he said. "To duh Big Town?"

The boy nodded dumbly, seemed about to speak, but said nothing.

"Been there before?" the man asked.

"No," said the boy.

"First time yuh ever rode the rods, huh?"

"Yes," said the boy.

"What's the matter?" the bum said, grinning. "Too many cows to milk down on the farm, huh? Is that it?"

The boy grinned uncertainly for a moment, and then said, "Yes."

"I t'ought so," the bum said, chuckling coarsely, "Jesus! I can tell one of youse fresh country kids a mile off by duh way yuh walk. . . . Well," he said with a rough blunt friendliness, in a moment, "stick wit me if you're goin' to duh Big Town. I'm goin' dat way, too."

"Yeah," the little man with the mouth like a scar now broke in, in a rasping voice, and with an ugly jeering laugh:

"Yeah. You stick to Bull, kid. He'll see yuh t'roo. He'll show yuh de —— woild, I ain't kiddin' yuh! He'll take yuh up to Lemonade Lake an' all t'roo Breadloaf Valley—won't yuh, Bull? He'll show yuh where de ham trees are and where de toikeys grow on bushes—won't yuh, Bull?" he said with ugly yet fawning insinuations. "You stick to Bull, kid, an' you'll be wearin' poils. . . . A-a-a-ah! yuh punk kid!" he now said, with a sudden turn to snarling viciousness.

"Wat t'hell use do yuh t'ink we got for a punk kid like you—Dat's duh trouble wit dis racket now! . . . We was all right until all dese kids begin to come along! . . . Wy t'hell should we be boddered wit him!" he snarled viciously. "Wat t'hell am I supposed to be—a noice-maid or sump'n? . . . G'wan, yuh little punk," he snarled once more, and lifted his fist in a sudden backhand movement, as if to strike the boy. "Scram! We got no use fer yuh! . . . G'wan, now. . . . Get t'hell away from here before I smash yuh one."

The man named Bull turned for a moment and looked silently at the smaller bum.

"Listen, Mug!" he said quietly, in a moment. "You leave duh kid alone. Duh kid stays, see?"

"A-a-a-ah!" the other man snarled sullenly. "What is dis anyway?—A —— noic'ry, or sump'n?"

"Listen," the other man said, "yuh hoid me, didn't yuh?"

"A-a-ah, t'hell wit it!" the little man muttered. "I'm not goin' t' rock duh —— cradle f'r no punk kid."

"Yuh hoid what I said, didn't yuh?" the man named Bull replied in a heavy menacing tone.

"I hoid yuh. Yeah!" the other muttered.

"Well, I don't want to hear no more outa your trap. I said duh kid stays—and he stays."

The little man muttered sullenly under his breath, but said no more. Bull continued to scowl heavily at him a moment longer, then turned away and went over and sat down on a handcar which had been pushed up against a tool-house on the siding.

"Come over here, kid," he said roughly, as he fumbled in his pocket for another cigarette. The boy walked over to the handcar.

"Got any smokes?" the man said, still fumbling in his pocket. The boy produced a package of cigarettes and offered them to the man. Bull took a cigarette from the package, lighted it with a single movement, between his tough seamed face and his cupped paw, and then dropped the package of cigarettes in his pocket, with the same spacious and powerful gesture.

"T'anks," he said as the acrid smoke began to coil luxuriously from his nostrils. "Sit down, kid."

The boy sat down on the handcar beside the man. For a moment, as Bull smoked, two of the bums looked quietly at each other with sly smiles, and then the young one in the soiled pin-stripe suit shook his head rapidly to himself, and, grinning toothlessly with his thin sunken mouth, mumbled derisively:

"Cheezus!"

Bull said nothing, but sat there smoking, bent forward a little on his knees, as solid as a rock.

It was almost dark; there was still a faint evening light, but already great stars were beginning to flash and blaze in cloudless skies. Somewhere in the wood there was a sound of water. Far off, half heard, and half suspected, there was a faint dynamic throbbing on the rails. The boy sat there quietly, listening, and said nothing.

One of the Girls in Our Party

The mid-day meal was ended and "the tour"—a group of thirty women, all of them teachers from the public schools of the American Middle West—had got up from their tables and left the dining-room of the sedate little Swiss hotel where they were quartered. Now they were gathered in the hall beyond: their voices, shrill, rasping and metallic, were united in a clamor of strident eagerness. In a moment one of the older women, who wore an air of authority, returned to the dining-room, and looking through the door at two young women who were still seated at one of the tables hastily bolting a belated luncheon, called imperatively:

"Miss Turner! Miss Blake! Aren't you coming? The bus is here."

"All right!" Miss Turner, the smaller of the two women, was the one who answered. "In a moment."

"Well, you hurry then," the woman said in an admonishing tone as she turned to go. "Every one else is ready: we're waiting on you."

"Come on," Miss Turner said quickly, in a lowered tone, as she turned to Miss Blake, "I guess we'd better go. You know how cranky they get if you keep them waiting."

"Well, you go on then," said Miss Blake calmly. "I'm not coming." Miss Turner looked at her with some surprise. "I've decided to pass this one up. I've got some letters to answer, and if I don't do it now, they just won't get answered."

155

"I know," said Miss Turner. "I haven't written a word to any one in two weeks. The way they keep you on the go there's no time to write." The two women got up from the table, moved toward the door, and there faced each other in a gesture of instinctive farewell. Then for a moment each stood in a constrained and awkward silence, as if waiting for the other one to speak. It was Miss Turner who first broke the pause:

"Well," she said, "I guess that means I won't see you again, will I?"

"Why?" Miss Blake said. "You'll come back here before you get your train, won't you?"

"No," said Miss Turner, "I don't think so. They've taken our baggage to the station and I think we're going to get out there on the way back—I mean, all the girls in *my* party."

"Well," Miss Blake said, in her curiously flat and toneless way, "I guess I won't see you, then—not until we get to Vienna, anyway. I'll see you there."

"Yes," Miss Turner agreed, "and I want to hear all about it, too. I almost wish I were going along with you —I've always wanted to see Italy—I'd almost rather go there than where we're going, but then you can't take in everything at one time, can you?"

"No," Miss Blake agreed, "you certainly can't."

"But I think it's just wonderful how much you do see!" Miss Turner went on with considerable enthusiasm. "I mean, when you consider that the whole tour only lasts six weeks from the time you leave home, it's wonderful how much you do take in, isn't it?"

"Yes," Miss Blake said, "it certainly is."

"Well, good-bye. I guess I'd better go."

"Yes, you'd better," Miss Blake answered. "I wouldn't want you to miss the bus. Good-bye."

"Good-bye," Miss Turner answered, "I'll see you in Vienna. Have a good time, and take care of yourself, now."

"All right," Miss Blake said flatly. "You do the same."

Miss Blake watched the bus go, then turned and went quickly upstairs to her room and set to work on her unfinished letters. She wrote:

England was the first place we went to when we left the ship. We were in England a whole week, but it rained all the time we were in London. The coffee that they drink is awful. All the traffic goes to the left in London, and none of the girls could get used to this. Miss Cramer, who is one of the girls in our party, came within an inch of being run over one day because she was looking in the wrong direction; I know they have a lot of accidents. London was also the place where Miss Jordan slipped and fell and sprained her ankle when getting out of the bus. She is one of the girls in our party. She didn't get to see anything of London because she was in bed all the time we were there and has been walking on a cane with her ankle taped ever since. But we took two bus-tours while we were in London that covered the whole city. In the morning we saw the Bank of England and the Tower of London and the Crown Jewels and came back for lunch to an old inn where Doctor Johnson, who was a good friend of Shakespeare's, used to eat. Miss Barrett was especially interested in this as she teaches English literature in the Senior High at Moline. She is one of the girls in our party. After lunch we saw Trafalgar Square with Nelson's Monument and the National Gallery. We didn't stay long at the National Gallery, we just stopped long enough to say we'd seen it. Then we visited the Houses of Parliament, Westminster Abbey with the Poets' Corner, and Buckingham Palace with the sentinels on duty walking up and down. We got there just as the King and Queen were driving out; we got a good look at her but you could hardly see the King because of that big hat she was wearing. You couldn't help feeling sorry for the poor man.

As Miss Webster said, he did look so small and henpecked peeking out from behind the edges of that big hat. Miss Webster is one of the girls in our party.

We also spent a day at Oxford. We had good weather there, it didn't rain at all the day we were there. Then we spent a day at Stratford-on-Avon where Shakespeare was born. But as Miss Webster said, they've fixed that house up a lot since he lived in it. It didn't rain the morning of the day we went to Stratford-on-Avon but it started in again as we were coming back. It rained most of the time we were in England. No wonder everything is so green.

The next country that we visited was Holland. Of all the countries we have been to I like Holland best. Everything was so clean in Holland. We spent three days in Holland, and it didn't rain the whole time we were there. We were in Amsterdam for a day, and we went out to the Island of Marken where all the people were dressed up in their quaint costumes and even the children wore wooden shoes just the same as they have done for hundreds of years. Miss Turner took some pictures of some children. She is making a collection to show to her classes when she gets back home. It is a very interesting collection, and most of the pictures came out very well. Miss Turner is one of the girls in our party.

We spent another whole day at Haarlem and The Hague. We saw the Palace of Peace and some pictures by Rembrandt, including "The Anatomy Lesson," which of course was interesting to me and some more "grist for the mill" as I will be able to make use of all this material in my drawing class when school takes up again.

In Holland we had the nicest guide we met on the whole trip. Every one was crazy about him, we have thought so often of him, and laughed so much about him, since. He was an old man named Singvogel, and when Miss Watson, who is one of the girls in our party asked him what that name meant, he said the name meant Song-Bird, so after that we called him our Song-Bird. You couldn't get the best of Mr. Singvogel, no matter what you said. He always had an answer ready for you. We have laughed so much about it since whenever we thought of Mr. Singvogel.

Singvogel iss my name unt dat means Sonk-birt. Sonk-birt by name, sonk-birt by nature; if you are nice to me perhaps I sink for you. Now ve are comink to de olt shot-tower. It vas conshtructed in de year uff sixteen hundert unt t'venty-nine mit contribushions mait by all de burghers uff de town. De roof is uff golt unt silfer conshtructed vich vas gifen by de laities from deir chewells, ornaments unt odder brecious bossessions. De two fickures dat you see on top uff de olt glock iss subbosed to represent de burgermeister uff dat beriod, Pieter Van Hondercoetter, unt his vife Matilda. Upon de shtroke uff t'ree o'glock you vill see dem come out on de blatform, turn unt shtrike mit golten mallets on de bell—so! it comes now, vatch it!—so! *vun!* de burgermeister shtrikes upon his seit vun time—you see?—so! now! *two!*—de laity shtrikes upon her seit vun time—so! now! *t'ree*—de burgermeister shtrikes upon his seit—now it iss t'ree o'glock—all iss ofer for anodder hour—unt laities, dat's de only time dat a man has effer been known to haf de last vort mit a vooman.

Oh, you couldn't get the best of Mr. Singvogel, we used to tease him but he always had an answer ready for you.

Now, laities, dis tower vas erected at a cost of t'welluf million guilders vich iss fife million dollars in real money. It took ofer sixteen years to built it, de golt, chewells unt odder brecious metals in de roof alone is vort ofer vun million two hundert unt fifty t'ousand dollars. De tower is two hundert unt sixty-t'ree feet tall from top to bottom unt dere iss tree hundert sixty-fife shtone steps in de shtair-case, vun for effery day in de year, engrafed mit de name uff a citizen who gafe money for de tower. If you vould like to gount de shteps yourself you gan now glimb to de top but ass for me I t'ink I shtay here. For ald'ough my name iss Sonk-birt, I am now too olt to fly.

Mr. Singvogel always had a joke for everything. Well, we all climbed up to the top of the tower then and when we got back down Miss Powers said that Mr. Singvogel was wrong because she had counted three hundred and sixty-seven steps both ways, and Miss Turner swore that he was right, that she had made it three hundred and sixty-five both up and down. And then Mr. Singvogel said: "Vell, laities, I tell you how it iss. You are both wronk because I liet to you. I forgot to tell you dis iss leap year, unt ven leap year gomes dere is alvays vun shtep more. Dis year you find dat dere is t'ree hundert sixty-six if you gount again."

Well, we had to laugh then because you couldn't get the best of Mr. Singvogel. But Miss Powers was awfully mad and swore that she was right, that she had counted three hundred and sixty-seven both ways. She and Miss Turner had an argument about it and that's why they've hardly spoken to each other since. But we all liked Holland, it didn't rain there, and every one was crazy about Mr. Singvogel.

We were in Paris for four days, and it only rained once. We were really only there three days, we got there late at night, and we were all so tired that we went to bed as soon as we got to the hotel. But we didn't get much sleep, it was the noisiest place you ever saw, and those little taxi horns they have kept tooting all night long right under your window until it almost drove you crazy. Some of the girls thought they'd lost their baggage, it failed to arrive when we did, they almost had a fit. It didn't get there until the day we left for Switzerland and Miss Bradley said her whole stay in Paris was ruined by worrying about it. Miss Bradley is one of the girls in our party.

We took a bus tour the first day and saw Notre Dame and the Latin Quarter, the Eiffel Tower and the Arch de Triumph, and came back and had lunch at the hotel. After lunch some of the girls went shopping, but the rest of us went to the Louvre. We didn't stay long, just long enough to see what it was like, and to see the Mona Lisa. One night we all had tickets for the Opera, where we saw Faust. The next night we went to the Folies Bergères and the last night we went up to Montmartre in busses to see the night life there.

Today we are in Montreux: this is the place where the tour splits up, some of the party leaving us to take the trip along the Rhine, and then to Munich, Salzburg, and the Bavarian Alps, while the rest of us are seeing Switzerland and Italy. After visiting Milan, Venice, Florence, Rome, and the Austrian Tyrol, we will join up with the other group in Vienna two weeks from now.

All of us were sorry to say good-bye to most of the girls, but we know it will only be for two weeks' time, and we are all looking forward eagerly to our meeting in Vienna and relating our experiences to one another. But, frankly, there are one or two of the girls we wouldn't miss if we never saw them again. There are always one or two on a party like this who can't adjust themselves to the group, and do their best to spoil the trip for every one. That Miss Powers was one of them. She was always losing her baggage, or forgetting something, and leaving it behind; we got so tired of having her yapping all the time that there were three hundred and sixty-seven steps in that old shot tower, that she was right and Miss Turner wrong, until Miss Turner finally said: "All right, have it your own way—there were three hundred and sixty-seven—who cares abou·· it? Only, for heaven's sake, forget about it, and give the rest of us some peace."

Of course, that only made Miss Powers madder than ever, she was furious about it. She was certainly a pest, if I ever saw one. She was forever coming up to one of the girls and asking her to write something in her memory book. She carried that memory book with her wherever she went; I believe she slept with it under her pillow.

Now when one of the girls wants to be funny, she says, "Won't you please write something in my memory book?"—

It's become a regular joke with us. But Miss Powers was certainly a nuisance, and none of the girls are sorry to say good-bye to her.

We have been spending the day in Switzerland. We all visited the League of Nations in Geneva and the famous castle of Chillon this morning. This afternoon, while I am writing this letter, every one has gone for a bus tour through the Alps. We are leaving for Rome to-night.

Well, it has been a wonderful trip and a wonderful experience, as well as being very educational. I can hardly wait now until I get home and have time to think over the many beautiful things I have seen.

The tour has been well run and well conducted from start to finish. And on the whole the girls are enthusiastic about the way the trips have been managed. Of course when you have to cover so many countries—we will have covered nine countries—England, Holland, Belgium, France, Switzerland, Italy, Austria, Czechoslovakia, and Germany—by the time we set sail for home again, just thirty-one days after we disembarked—it is wonderful to think of all you do take in in such a short space of time.

I get a little confused sometimes when I try to remember all the places we have been to and all the wonderful things we've seen, and if I come back again I think I will take it a little more slowly and travel in a smaller party, with just a friend or two. But I'm certainly glad I took this tour, it gives you a chance to look around and pick out the high spots, so you will know what you want to see when you come back a second time. And it has certainly been very educational. Still, I won't be sorry to see home again. I am looking forward to it already.

I'm dying to see you and have a good long talk with you as soon as I get back. I'm starved for news. What has happened? Is Ted still going with the Trumbull girl, or has he found himself a new "inamorata"? ("Ain't love grand?" Especially when you are seventeen—hah! hah!) Have you been out to the lodge this summer, and were Bill and Lola there? Couldn't we get them to take us out the first week-end after I get back? It will be good to get a cup of real coffee for a change. Summer has come and gone before I knew it, and soon autumn will be here again.

. . . and the smell of the woodsmoke in Ohio and the flaming maples, the nights of the frosty stars, the blazing moons that hang the same way in a thousand streets, slanting to silence on the steeple's slope; nights of the wheel, the rail, the bell, the wailing cry along the river's edge, and of the summer's ending, nights of the frost and silence and the barking of a dog, of people listening, and of words unspoken and the quiet heart, and nights of the old October that must come again, must come again, while we are waiting, waiting, waiting in the darkness for all of our friends and brothers who will not return.

I'll see you in September.

The Far and the Near

On the outskirts of a little town upon a rise of land that swept back from the railway there was a tidy little cottage of white boards, trimmed vividly with green blinds. To one side of the house there was a garden neatly patterned with plots of growing vegetables, and an arbor for the grapes which ripened late in August. Before the house there were three mighty oaks which sheltered it in their clean and massive shade in summer, and to the other side there was a border of gay flowers. The whole place had an air of tidiness, thrift, and modest comfort.

Every day, a few minutes after two o'clock in the afternoon, the limited express between two cities passed this spot. At that moment the great train, having halted for a breathing-space at the town near by, was beginning to lengthen evenly into its stroke, but it had not yet reached the full drive of its terrific speed. It swung into view deliberately, swept past with a powerful swaying motion of the engine, a low smooth rumble of its heavy cars upon pressed steel, and then it vanished in the cut. For a moment the progress of the engine could be marked by heavy bellowing puffs of smoke that burst at spaced intervals above the edges of the meadow grass, and finally nothing could be heard but the solid clacking tempo of the wheels receding into the drowsy stillness of the afternoon.

Every day for more than twenty years, as the train had approached this house, the engineer had blown on the whistle, and every day, as soon as she heard this signal, a woman had appeared on the back porch of the little house and waved to him. At first she had a small child clinging to her skirts, and now this child had grown to full womanhood, and every day she, too, came with her mother to the porch and waved.

The engineer had grown old and gray in service. He had driven his great train, loaded with its weight of lives, across the land ten thousand times. His own children had grown up and married, and four times he had seen before him on the tracks the ghastly dot of tragedy converging like a cannon ball to its eclipse of horror at the boiler head —a light spring wagon filled with children, with its clustered row of small stunned faces; a cheap automobile stalled upon the tracks, set with the wooden figures of people paralyzed with fear; a battered hobo walking by the rail, too deaf and old to hear the whistle's warning; and a form flung past his window with a scream—all this the man had seen and known. He had known all the grief, the joy, the peril and the labor such a man could know; he had grown seamed and weathered in his loyal service, and now, schooled by the qualities of faith and courage and humbleness that attended his labor, he had grown old, and had the grandeur and the wisdom these men have.

But no matter what peril or tragedy he had known, the vision of the little house and the women waving to him with a brave free motion of the arm had become fixed in the mind of the engineer as something beautiful and enduring, something beyond all change and ruin, and something that would always be the same, no matter what mishap, grief or error might break the iron schedule of his days.

The sight of the little house and of these two women gave him the most extraordinary happiness he had ever known. He had seen them in a thousand lights, a hundred weathers. He had seen them through the harsh bare light of wintry gray across the brown and frosted stubble of the earth, and he had seen them again in the green luring sorcery of April.

He felt for them and for the little house in which they lived such tenderness as a man might feel for his own children, and at length the picture of their lives was carved so sharply in his heart that he felt that he knew their lives completely, to every hour and moment of the day, and he resolved that one day, when his years of service should be ended, he would go and find these people and speak at last with them whose lives had been so wrought into his own.

That day came. At last the engineer stepped from a train onto the station platform of the town where these two women lived. His years upon the rail had ended. He was a pensioned servant of his company, with no more work to do. The engineer walked slowly through the station and out into the streets of the town. Everything was as strange to him as if he had never seen this town before. As he walked on, his sense of bewilderment and confusion grew. Could this be the town he had passed ten thousand times? Were these the same houses he had seen so often from the high windows of his cab? It was all as unfamiliar, as disquieting as a city in a dream, and the perplexity of his spirit increased as he went on.

Presently the houses thinned into the straggling outposts of the town, and the street faded into a country road—the one on which the women lived. And the man plodded on slowly in the heat and dust. At length he stood before the house he sought. He knew at once that he had found the proper place. He saw the lordly oaks before the house, the flower beds, the garden and the arbor, and farther off, the glint of rails.

Yes, this was the house he sought, the place he had passed so many times, the destination he had longed for with such happiness. But now that he had found it, now that he was here, why did his hand falter on the gate; why had the town, the road, the earth, the very entrance to this place he loved turned unfamiliar as the landscape of some ugly dream? Why did he now feel this sense of confusion, doubt and hopelessness?

At length he entered by the gate, walked slowly up the path and in a moment more had mounted three short steps that led up to the porch, and was knocking at the door. Presently he heard steps in the hall, the door was opened, and a woman stood facing him.

And instantly, with a sense of bitter loss and grief, he was sorry he had come. He knew at once that the woman who stood there looking at him with a mistrustful eye was the same woman who had waved to him so many thousand times. But her face was harsh and pinched and meager; the flesh sagged wearily in sallow folds, and the small eyes peered at him with timid suspicion and uneasy doubt. All the brave freedom, the warmth and the affection that he had read into her gesture, vanished in the moment that he saw her and heard her unfriendly tongue.

And now his own voice sounded unreal and ghastly to him as he tried to explain his presence, to tell her who he was and the reason he had come. But he faltered on, fighting stubbornly against the horror of regret, confusion, disbelief that surged up in his spirit, drowning all his former joy and making his act of hope and tenderness seem shameful to him.

At length the woman invited him almost unwillingly into the house, and called her daughter in a harsh shrill voice. Then, for a brief agony of time, the man sat in an ugly little parlor, and he tried to talk while the two women stared at him with a dull, bewildered hostility, a sullen, timorous restraint.

And finally, stammering a crude farewell, he departed. He walked away down the path and then along the road toward town, and suddenly he knew that he was an old man. His heart, which had been brave and confident when it looked along the familiar vista of the rails, was now sick with doubt and horror as it saw the strange and unsuspected visage of an earth which had always been within a stone's throw of him, and which he had never seen or known. And he knew that all the magic of that bright lost way, the vista of that shining line, the imagined corner of that small good universe of hope's desire, was gone forever, could never be got back again.

In the Park

THAT year I think we were living with Bella; no, we weren't, I guess we were living with Auntie Kate—well, maybe we were staying with Bella: I don't know, we moved around so much, and it's so long ago. It gets all confused in my mind now; when Daddy was acting he was always on the go, he couldn't be still a minute; sometimes he was playing in New York, and sometimes he went off on a tour with Mr. Mansfield and was gone for months.

Anyway, that night when the show was over we went out onto the street and turned up Broadway. We were both so happy and excited that we fairly bounded along, and that was the way it was that night. It was one of the first fine days in spring, the air was cool and delicate and yet soft, and the sky was of a velvety lilac texture, and it was glittering with great stars. The streets outside the theatre were swarming with hansoms, four-wheelers, private carriages and victorias; they kept driving up in front of the theatre all the time and people kept getting into them.

All of the men looked handsome, and all of the women were beautiful: every one seemed to be as happy and elated as we were, it seemed as if a new world and new people had burst out of the earth with the coming of spring—everything ugly, dull, sour, and harsh had vanished—the streets were flashing with life and sparkle. I saw all of it, I felt myself a part of it all, I wanted to possess it all, and there was something I wanted to say so much it made my throat ache, and yet I could not say it because I could not find the words I wanted. I could not think of anything else to say—it sounded foolish, but suddenly I seized my father's arm and cried: "Oh, to be in April, now that England's there."

"Yes!" he shouted, "Also in Paris, Naples, Rome, and Dresden! Oh, to be in Budapest!" cried Daddy, "now that April's here and the frost is on the pumpkin, and the dawn comes up like thunder out of the night that covers me."

He seemed to have grown young again; he was the way he used to be when I was a little girl and I would knock at his study door and he would call out in a wonderful actor's voice, "Enter, Daughter of Des-o-la-tion, into this abode of mis-er-ee."

His eyes sparkled, and he threw back his head and laughed his wild and happy laugh.

I think that must have been the year before he died; I was about eighteen: I was a beauty—I was like peaches and cream——

In those days when he was acting I used to meet him after the theatre and we would go somewhere to eat. *There* was a fellow after your heart: the very best was *just* about good enough for him. New York was awfully nice in those days. They had such nice places to go to—I don't know, they didn't have all this noise and confusion; it seems like another world sometimes. You could go to White's or Martin's or Delmonico's—there were a lot of nice places. There was also a place called Mock's; I never went there, but one of the first things I remember as a child was hearing Daddy come home late at night and say he'd been to Mock's. When he came home, I would listen at the grating of the heater in my room and

I could hear him and the other actors talking to my mother: it was fascinating; and sometimes it was all about Mock's. "Oh, have you been to Mock's?" I thought I heard my mother say. "Oh, yes! I have been to Mock's," my father said. "And what did you have at Mock's?" my mother said. "Oh, I had some oysters and a glass of beer and some mock-turtle soup at Mock's," my father said.

We used to go to White's almost every night after the show, with two priests who were friends of Daddy's: Father Dolan and Father Chris O'Rourke. Father Dolan was a big man with the bluest eyes I ever saw, and Father Chris O'Rourke was a little man with a swarthy and greasy face: it was all full of black marks, it was one of the strangest faces I ever saw; but there was something very powerful and sweet about it. Father Dolan was a very fine, high sort of man: he was very kind and jolly, but he also had a fine mind and he was very outspoken and honest. He loved the theatre, he knew a great many actors, a great many of them went to his Church, and he loved my father. He was a great scholar, he knew the plays of Shakespeare almost by heart—he and Daddy used to tag each other's lines, to see who knew the most. I never knew my father to catch him up but once and that was on a line from "King Lear," "The prince of darkness is a gentleman"—Father Dolan said it came from "As You Like It."

How those fellows loved to eat and drink: if one of them had to say Mass the next day we had to hurry, because you can't eat or drink after midnight if you are saying Mass the next day. Because of this, both these priests would immediately take out their watches and lay them on the table before them when they sat down. Father Chris O'Rourke drank nothing but beer and as soon as he sat down a waiter would bring him a half-dozen glasses which he would drink at once. But if these two priests had a glass of beer on the table before them when midnight came, they left it: no matter what it was, no matter whether they'd finished eating or drinking or not, when the stroke of midnight came these fellows quit, if they were going to say Mass the morning after.

Father Chris O'Rourke would eat and drink for almost an hour as if his life depended on it: he was very near-sighted, he wore thick glasses, and from time to time he would seize his watch and bring it right under his nose while he peered and squinted at it. Because of his own hurry to get through before twelve o'clock, he thought every one else must be the same way: he was afraid some one would not get fed, and he was always urging and belaboring people to hurry up and eat. Father Dolan loved to eat, too, but he was a great talker: sometimes he would get to talking to Daddy and forget to eat: when he did this Father Chris O'Rourke would almost go out of his head, he would keep nudging and poking at Father Dolan and pointing at his watch with a look of agony on his face, leaning over and muttering at him in an ominous sort of way, "You're going to be *late!* It's almost *twelve!*"

"Bedad, then!" said Father Dolan, "I'll be late!" He was a big man, but he had a funny little Irish voice; it was very crisp and jolly and had a little chuckling lilt in it, and it seemed to come from a long way off. "I never saw a man like ye, Chris, to be always thinkin' of his belly! Did the great Saints of the Church spend their time guzzlin' and crammin', or did they spend it in meditatin' and prayin' an' mortifyin' their flesh? Did ye never hear of the sin of gluttony?"

"Yis," said Father Chris O'Rourke, "that I have, an'

I've also heard of the wicked sin of wanton waste. Shame on ye, Dan Dolan, wit yer talk about the great Saints of the Church: there was niver a great Saint yit that would praise a man fer wastin' what the Lord had set before him. Do ye think I'll sit here an' see good food go to waste whin there's poor people all over the world tonight that's goin' witout?"

"Well," said Father Dolan, "I've read most of the argyments of the learned reasoners of the Church, as well as the damnable heresies of the infidels, all the way from St. Thomas Aquinas to Spinozey, an' in me young days I could split a hair meself wit the best of them, but in all me life I niver heard the beat of that one: it makes Aristotle look like Wordsworth's Idiot Boy. Bedad, if ye can prove that what ye're doin' wit yer gorgin' is feedin' the poor all over the earth, I won't put anything past yer powers of reasonin', Chris—ye could show the Pope that Darwin was a Jesuit, an' he'd believe ye!"

Well, as I say, when we got to the restaurant the first thing Father Chris O'Rourke would do was to lay his watch upon the table, and the first thing Daddy would do was to order two or three bottles of champagne: they used to know we were coming and it would be waiting for us in great silver buckets full of ice. Then Daddy would pick up the menu—it was a great big card simply covered with the most delicious things to eat, and he would frown and look serious and clear his throat, and say to Father Dolan, "What does the pontificial palate crave, Dan?"

After the play, that night, we went to White's and these two priests were waiting for us when we got there. A little later Mr. Gates came in—he's still alive, I saw him on the street the other day, he's getting quite old.

He was married to one of the most beautiful women you ever saw, and she was burned to death in an automobile accident. He saw the thing happen right under his eyes: isn't that the most horrible thing you ever heard of? Well, you could tell by the way Mr. Gates walked that he was awfully excited about something: he was another of these great fat fellows, and you could see his old jowls quivering as he came.

"Good God!" said Daddy, "here comes Bunny with a full head of steam on!"

Mr. Gates began to speak to Daddy half across the room, all of the people stopped and stared at him.

"Joe! Joe!" he said—he had a funny hoarse kind of voice, one of those foggy whiskey voices; I think he drank a good deal. "Joe, do you know what I've done? I've just bought a horseless carriage. Come on! You're going for a ride with me!"

"Now, wait! Wait! Wait!" said Daddy, holding up his hand just like an actor. "Not so fast, Bunny! Sit down and have a bite to eat first, and tell us about it. When did you do this desperate deed?"

"Today," Mr. Gates said in a sort of hoarse whisper. "Do you suppose I've done right?"

He looked around at us with his old eyes simply bulging out of his head and with a sort of scared look on his face. Oh! We laughed so much about it: Father Dolan began to laugh, and Daddy had to pound him on the back, he got to coughing so!

Mr. Gates was an awfully nice man: he was a great fat fellow, but he was so handsome; there was something so delicate about him, his mouth kept trembling and twitching so when he was excited and wanted to say something. I think that was why they called him Bunny.

So Daddy said, "Sit down and have something to eat and then we'll see."

Mr. Gates said, "Say, Joe, I've got the mechanic outside here, and I don't know what to do with him."

"You mean you hired him for keeps?" Daddy said.

"Yes," Mr. Gates said, "and I'm damned if I'm not embarrassed! I don't know what to do with him. I mean, what is his social standing?"

"Does he wash?" Daddy said.

"Well," said Mr. Gates, looking at Father Dolan, "I think he uses holy water."

"Oh, Mr. Gates!" I said. "How awful! Right before Father Dolan, too!"

But Father Dolan laughed just as I knew he would: he was another great fat fellow, he was an awfully nice man. Father Chris O'Rourke laughed, too, but I don't think he liked it so much.

"I mean," Mr. Gates said, "I don't know how to treat the man. Is he above me, or below me, or what?"

"It looks to me," Daddy said, "as if he were on top of you. I think you've gone and got yourself saddled with a black elephant."

Daddy was so wonderful like that, everybody loved him. Mr. Gates was so worried about the driver: it all seems so funny now to think back on it—he didn't know whether the man was to eat at the table with his family, and be treated like one of them, or what. There was something so delicate about Mr. Gates: he was big and fat, but a very sensitive, fine person.

"It looks like a neat little problem in social etiquette, Bunny," Daddy said. "Well, let's have him in here for a bite to eat. We'll see what he looks like."

So Mr. Gates went out and got him, and pretty soon he came back with him, and he was really an awfully nice young fellow: he had a little mustache, and he wore a Norfolk jacket and a flat cap, and everybody stared so, and nudged each other, he was awfully embarrassed. But Daddy was wonderful with people, he made him feel right at home. He said, "Sit down, young fellow. If we're going to run an engine we've got to feed the driver."

So he sat down, and we had a wonderful meal: you'd get great juicy chops in that place, cooked in butter, and steaks an inch thick, and the most marvellous oysters and sea food.

I know it was pretty late in the season, but we started off with oysters and champagne: I don't think the young fellow was used to drinking. Daddy kept filling up the young fellow's glass, and he got quite drunk. He was awfully funny, he kept talking about his responsibility.

"It's a terrible responsibility to know that all these lives are dependent on you," he said; then Daddy would fill up his glass again.

"A moment's hesitation in a crisis," he said, "and all is lost."

"A truer word was never spoken," said Daddy, and he filled his glass up again.

"A man must have a clear brain and a steady hand," he said.

"Right you are," said Daddy. "This will make you so steady, son, that you will get practically paralyzed."

Mr. Gates and Father Dolan laughed so much that the tears began to trickle down their cheeks. Oh, we had an awfully good time in those days, there was something so innocent about everything.

Then we all got up to go, and I was really quite nervous: the poor kid could hardly stand up, and I didn't know what was going to happen. Daddy was so

happy and excited, there was something so wild about
him, his eyes danced like devils, and he threw back his
head and laughed, and you could hear him all over the
place.

Father Chris O'Rourke had to hold Mass the next
morning, and he left us, but Father Dolan came along.
We all went outside, with the young man being helped
along by Daddy and Mr. Gates, and every one in the
restaurant followed us outside, and Mr. Gates told me to
sit up front beside the driver. God, I was proud! And
Daddy and Mr. Gates and Father Dolan got in behind;
how they ever did it I don't know, it must have been
awfully small—I think Daddy must have sat on Father
Dolan's lap. Oh, yes! I know he did.

And everybody cheered as we started off: the actors
followed us out of the restaurant and stood looking after
us as we drove off into the lilac and velvet darkness, and
I can still remember how I looked back and saw their
smiling and unnatural faces, their bright masks, their
lonely and haunted eyes. They kept shouting funny
things at Daddy and asking if he had any last messages,
and De Wolfe Hopper was there and he ran around pretending to be a horse and neighing, and trying to climb
up a lamp-post. Oh, it was thrilling!

So Mr. Gates said, "Whither away, Joe?"

And Daddy said, "To the Golden Gate and may she
never stop!"

Then Daddy said to the young fellow who was driving, "How fast can she go, son?" and the young fellow
said, "She can do twenty miles an hour without any
trouble."

"Downhill, you mean," said Daddy just to tease him,
so we started to go, and God! I was thrilled! It seemed to
me we were flying. I suppose he did go twenty miles an

hour, but it seemed like a hundred would now and we passed a policeman on a horse and the horse got frightened and tried to run away and God! the cop was so mad: he came galloping after us and shouted for us to stop, and Daddy laughed just like a crazy man and said, "Go on, son! Go on! There's not a horse in the world can catch you!"

But the young fellow was scared and he slowed down and then the cop came up and said what did we mean, and where did we think we were, and he'd a good mind to put us all under arrest for disturbing the peace at that hour of night, with "that thing"; he kept calling it "that thing" in such a scornful way, and I got so angry at him, I thought it was so beautiful, it was painted the richest kind of winey red, it looked good enough to eat, and I was so mad to think the man should talk that way.

I don't know why it made me mad, but I think the reason must have been that the car didn't seem to me like a thing at all. It's hard to tell you how it was, but it was almost as if the car were some strange and beautiful and living creature which we had never known before but which now gave to all our lives a kind of added joy and warmth and wonder. And I believe that was the way it was with those first motor cars. Somehow each one of them seemed different from all the others, each one seemed to have a different name, a separate life and personality; and although I know they would look crude and funny and old-fashioned now, it was all different then. We had never seen or known them in the world before, we had only dreamed or heard they could exist, and now that I was riding in one, it all seemed unbelievable and yet gloriously real and strange, as every beautiful thing is when it first happens to you. The car was as magical to me as if it had come out of some other world like Mars, and yet the very moment that I saw it I seemed to have known about it always, and it seemed to belong to that day, that hour, that year, somehow to be a part of all that happened that night; to belong to Daddy and the priests and Mr. Gates, the young mechanic and all the haunted faces of the actors, and to all the songs we sang that year, the things we did and said, and something strange and innocent and lost and long ago.

I can remember now the way the old car looked, so well that I could close my eyes and draw it for you. I can remember its rich wine color, its great polished lamps of brass, the door that opened in its round, fat back, and all its wonderful and exciting smells—the strong and comforting smell of its deep leather, and the smells of gasoline and oil and grease that were so strong and warm and pungent that they seemed to give a kind of thrilling life and ecstasy to everything in the whole world. They seemed to hold the unknown promise of something wonderful and strange that was about to happen and that belonged to the night, and to the mystery and joy of life, the ecstasy of the lilac dark, as all the smells of flowers and leaf and grass and earth belonged to them.

So I guess that was the reason that I got so mad when I heard the policeman call the car "that thing," although I did not know the reason then. It looked as if the cop were going to run us in, but then Daddy got up out of Father Dolan's lap, and when the cop saw Father Dolan of course he got very nice to us: and Mr. Gates talked to him and gave him some money, and Daddy joked with him and made him laugh, and then Daddy showed him his police badge and asked him if he knew Big Jake Dietz at police headquarters, and told him he was one of Jake's best friends, and then I was so proud to see the way the cop came round.

And the cop said for us all to go into Central Park and we could ride all we damn pleased for all he cared, but you wouldn't catch him in one of those things, they'd blow up on you at any moment and then where'd you all be? And Daddy said he hoped we'd all be in Heaven, and what's more we'd take our own priest with us, so there'd be no hitch in any of the formalities, and we all got so tickled and began to laugh and the cop did too, and then he began to brag about his horse, and God! it *was* a beautiful horse, and he said give him a horse always, that they'd never make one of those things that could go faster than a horse. The poor fellow! I wonder what he'd say now!

And Daddy teased him and said the time would come when you'd have to go to the zoo to see a horse, and the policeman said by that time you'd have to go to a junkshop to see a motor-car, and Daddy said, "The trouble with us is that we're anachronisms." And the policeman said, well, he didn't know about that, but he wished us luck and hoped we all got out of it alive.

So he rode off and we drove into Central Park and started off as hard as we could go and began to climb a hill, when sure enough, we broke down just as the policeman said we would. I guess the young fellow may have had too much to drink, he seemed wild and excited, but anyway we saw a hansom halfway up the hill in front of us and he cried out, "Watch me pass them," and did something to the car, and just as we got up even with them and were trying to go by, the car coughed and spluttered and stood still. Well, we could hear the people in the hansom laughing, and one of them shouted something back to us about the tortoise and the hare. And I

felt so mad at them and so humiliated and so sorry for
our driver, and Daddy said, "Never mind, son, the race
may not always be to the swift, but even the hare will
sometimes have his day."

But our young fellow felt so bad he couldn't say a
word. He got out of the car and walked round and round
it, and finally he began to explain to us the way it happened and how it could never happen again in a hundred
years. And well, you see it was this way, and well, you
see it was that. And we didn't understand a word of what
he was saying, but we felt so sorry for him that we told
him he was right. So he began to poke around inside of
it, and then he would turn something here and twist
something there, and grab the crank and whirl it round
and round until I was afraid he was going to wring his
arm off. Then he would get down on his back and
crawl in under it and bang and hammer at something
underneath. And nothing happened. Then he would get
up and walk round and round the car again and mutter
to himself. Finally, he gave up and said he was afraid
we'd have to get out of the car and take a hansom if we
wanted to get home without walking. So we started to
get out, and the mechanic was so mad and so embarrassed
at the way his car had acted that he grabbed it and shook
it as if it were a brat. And nothing happened.

He gave it one last try. He grabbed the crank like a
crazy man and began to whirl it round and round until
he was exhausted. And when nothing happened he suddenly shouted out, "Oh, damn that thing," kicked it in
the tire as hard as he could, and collapsed across the radia-
tor, sobbing as if his heart would break. And I don't
know what that did to it or how it happened, but suddenly the car began to chug and wheeze again, and there

we were ready to go, and the young fellow with a grin that stretched from ear to ear.

So we went on up that hill and coasted down the next, and now we really seemed to fly. It was like soaring through the air, or finding wings you never knew you had before. It was like something we had always known about and dreamed of finding, and now we had it like a dream come true. And I suppose we must have gone the whole way round the park from one end to another, but none of us really knew how far we went or where we were going. It was like that kind of flight you make in dreams, and sure enough, just like something you are waiting for in a dream, we came tearing around a curve in the road and there before us we could see the same hansom we had tried to pass upon the hill. And the minute that I saw it I knew that it was bound to happen, it seemed too good to be true, and yet I had felt sure all the time that it was going to turn out just this way. And that was the way it was with all of us, we threw back our heads and roared with laughter, we yelled and waved our hands at all the people in the cab, we went tearing by them as if they were rooted to the earth, and as we passed them Daddy turned and shouted back at them, "Cheer up, my friends, they also serve who only stand and wait."

So we passed them by and left them far behind us and they were lost; and now there was nothing all around us but the night, the blazing stars, the lilac darkness in the park, and God! but it was beautiful. It was just the beginning of May and all the leaves and buds were coming out, they had that tender feathery look, and there was just a little delicate shaving of moon in the sky, and it was so cool and lovely, with the smell of the leaves, and the new grass, and all the flowers bursting from the earth till you could hear them grow: it seemed to me the loveliest thing that I had ever known, and when I looked at·my father, his eyes were full of tears and he cried out, "Glory! Oh, glory! Glory!" and then he began in his magnificent voice, "What a piece of work is a man! how noble in reason! how infinite in faculty! in form and moving how express and admirable! in action how like an angel! in apprehension how like a god!"

And the words were so lovely, the music was so grand, that somehow it made me want to cry, and when he had finished he cried out, "Glory!" once again, and I saw his wild and beautiful brow there in the darkness, and I turned my eyes up toward the sky and there were the tragic and magnificent stars, and a kind of fate was on his head and in his eyes, and suddenly as I looked at him I knew that he was going to die.

And he cried, "Glory! Glory!" and we rode all through the night, and round and round the park, and then dawn came, and all of the birds began to sing. And now the bird-song broke in the first light, and suddenly I heard each sound the bird-song made. It came to me like music I had always heard, it came to me like music I had always known, the sounds of which I never yet had spoken, and now I heard the music of each sound as clear and bright as gold, and the music of each sound was this: at first it rose above me like a flight of shot, and then I heard the sharp, fast skaps of sound the bird-song made. And now they were smooth drops and nuggets of bright gold, and now with chittering bicker and fast-fluttering skirrs of sound the palmy, honied bird-cries came. And now the bird-tree sang, all filled with lutings in bright air; the thrum, the lark's wing, and tongue-trilling chirrs

arose. And now the little brainless cries arose, with liquor-
ous, liquefied lutings, with lirruping chirp, plumbellied
smoothness, sweet lucidity. And now I heard the rapid
kweet-kweet-kweet-kweet-kweet of homely birds, and
then their pwee-pwee-pwee: others had thin metallic
tongues, a sharp cricketing stitch, and high shrew's caws,
with eery rasp, with harsh, far calls—these were the
sounds the bird-cries made. All birds that are awoke in
the park's woodland tangles; and above them passed the
whirr of hidden wings, the strange lost cry of the unknown birds in full light now in the park, the sweet confusion of their cries was mingled. "Sweet is the breath of
morn, her rising sweet with charm of earliest birds," and
it was just like that, and the sun came up, and it was like
the first day of the world, and that was the year before he
died and I think we were staying at Bella's then, but
maybe we were staying at the old hotel, or perhaps we
had already moved to Auntie Kate's: we moved around
so much, we lived so many places, it seems so long ago,
that when I try to think about it now it gets confused
and I cannot remember.

The Men of Old Catawba

On the middle-Atlantic seaboard of the North American continent and at about a day's journey from New York, is situated the American State of Old Catawba. In area and population the State might almost strike a median among the States of the Union: its territory, which is slightly more than fifty thousand square miles, is somewhat larger than the territories of most of the Atlantic coastal States, and, of course, much smaller than the great areas of the immense but sparsely populated States of the Far West. Upon this area, which is a little smaller than the combined areas of England and Wales, there live three million people, of whom the third part are black. Catawba, therefore, is about as big as England, and has about as many people as Norway.

The State possesses, however, a racial type and character that is probably much more strongly marked and unified than those of any European country. In fact, although America is supposed by many of her cities to be a confusion of races, tongues, and peoples, as yet unwelded, there is perhaps nowhere in the world a more homogeneous population than that of Old Catawba. Certainly, there are far greater differences in stature, temperament, speech, and habit between a North German and a South German, a North Frenchman and a Southern Frenchman, a North of England man and a Devon man, a North Italian and a South Italian, than between a Catawban from the East and one from the West.

The name "Catawba" is, of course, an Indian name: it is the name of a tribe that is now almost extinct but which at one time flourished in considerable strength and numbers. The chief seat of the tribe was in South Carolina, and there is at the present time a reservation in York County of that State where the remnant is gathered together.

The way in which the State of Catawba got its name rests entirely upon misconception: the tribe that the early explorers encountered were not Catawbas, they belonged probably to a group that is now wholly extinct. Yet, so strong is the power of usage and association that any other name would now seem unthinkable to a native of that State. People outside the State have often said that the name has a somewhat tropical laziness in its sound, particularly when prefixed with the word "old," but there is very little that is tropical or exotic either in the appearance and character of Catawba itself, or of the people who inhabit it. To them, the name Catawba perfectly describes the State: it has the strong, rugged, and homely quality that the earth has.

In the state documents during the period of the royal proprietors, the territory is invariably referred to as "Catawba," or "His Majesty's Colony in the Catawbas": the name "Old Catawba" does not begin to appear in state papers until twenty or thirty years before the Revolution, and for what reason no one knows. The typical American method in naming places has been to prefix the word "new" to the name—*New* England, *New* York, *New* Mexico—to distinguish these places from their older namesakes. But if *New* York indicates the existence somewhere of an *old* York, *old* Catawba does not indicate the existence of a new one. The name undoubtedly grew out of the spirit of the people who had dwelt there over a century, and the name did not come from a sentimental affection, it grew imperatively from a conviction of the spirit. It is one of those names that all men begin to use at about the same time, a perfect and inevitable name that has flowered secretly within them, and that now must be spoken.

Any one who has ever lived in the State for any length of time is bound to feel this: the word "old" is not a term of maudlin affection, it describes exactly the feeling that the earth of that State inspires—the land has a brooding presence that is immensely old and masculine, its spirit is rugged and rather desolate, yet it broods over its people with stern benevolence. The earth is a woman, but Old Catawba is a man. The earth is our mother and our nurse, and we can know her, but Old Catawba is our father, and although we know that he is there, we shall never find him. He is there in the wilderness, and his brows are bowed with granite: he sees our lives and deaths and his stern compassion broods above us. Women love him, but only men can know him: only men who have cried out in their agony and their loneliness to their father, only men who have sought throughout the world to find him, can know Catawba: but this includes all the men who ever lived.

Catawba got discovered in this way: a one-eyed Spaniard, one of the early voyagers, was beating up the Amercian coasts out of the tropics, perhaps on his way back home, perhaps only to see what could be seen. He does not tell us in the record he has left of the voyage how he happened to be there, but it seems likely that he was on his way home and had been driven off his course. Subsequent events show that he was in a very dilapidated condition, and in need of overhauling: the sails were rent, the ship was leaking, the food and water stores

were almost exhausted. During the night in a storm off
one of the cruelest and most evilly celebrated of the Atlantic capes, the one-eyed Spaniard was driven in and
almost wrecked. By some miracle of good fortune he
got through one of the inlets in the dark, and when light
broke he found himself becalmed in an enormous inlet
of pearl-gray water.

As the light grew he made out seawards a long almost
unbroken line of sandy shoals and islands that formed
a desolate barrier between the sea and the mainland, and
made this bay or sound in which he found himself. Away
to the west he descried now the line of the shore: it was
also low, sandy, and desolate-looking. The cool gray
water of morning slapped gently at the sides of his ship:
he had come from the howling immensity of the sea into
the desert monotony of this coast. It was as bleak and
barren a coast as the one-eyed Spaniard had ever seen.
And indeed, for a man who had come up so many times
under the headlands of Europe, and had seen the worn
escarpments of chalk, the lush greenery of the hills, and
the minute striped cultivation of the earth that greet the
sailor returning from a long and dangerous voyage—
and awaken in him the unspeakable emotion of earth
which has been tilled and used for so many centuries,
with its almost personal bond for the men who have lived
there on it, and whose dust is buried in it—there must
have been something particularly desolate about this
coast which stretched away with the immense indifference of nature into silence and wilderness. The Spaniard
felt this, and the barren and desert quality of the place
is duly recorded in his log, which, for the most part, is
pretty dry reading.

But here a strange kind of exhilaration seizes the
Spaniard: it gets into his writing, it begins to color and

pulse through the gray stuff of his record. The light of the young rising sun reddened delicately upon the waters; immense and golden it came up from the sea behind the line of the sea-dunes, and suddenly he heard the fast drumming of the wild ducks as they crossed his ship high up, flying swift and straight as projectiles. Great heavy gulls of a size and kind he had never seen before swung over his ship in vast circles, making their eerie creaking noises. The powerful birds soared on their strong even wings, with their feet tucked neatly in below their bodies; or they dove and tumbled through the air, settling to the water with great flutterings and their haunted creaking clamor: they seemed to orchestrate this desolation, they gave a tongue to loneliness and they filled the hearts of the men who had come there with a strange exultancy. For, as if some subtle and radical changes had been effected in the chemistry of their flesh and blood by the air they breathed, a kind of wild glee now possessed the one-eyed Spaniard's men. They began to laugh and sing, and to be, as he says, "marvellous merry."

During the morning the wind freshened a little; the Spaniard set his sails and stood in toward the land. By noon he was going up the coast quite near the shore, and by night he had put into the mouth of one of the coastal rivers. He took in his sails and anchored there. There was nearby on shore a settlement of "the race that inhabits these regions," and it was evident that his arrival had caused a great commotion among the inhabitants, for some who had fled away into the woods were now returning, and others were running up and down the shore, pointing and gesticulating and making a great deal of noise. But the one-eyed Spaniard had seen Indians before: that was an old story to him now, and he was not disturbed. As for his men, the strange exuber-

ance that had seized them in the morning does not seem
to have worn off, they shouted ribald jokes at the Indians,
and "did laugh and caper as if they had been madde."

Nevertheless, they did not go ashore that day. The one-
eyed Spaniard was worn out, and the crew was exhausted:
they ate such food as they had, some raisins, cheese, and
wine, and after posting a watch they went to sleep,
unmindful of the fires that flickered in the Indian village,
of sounds and chants and rumors, or of the forms that
padded softly up and down the shore.

Then the marvellous moon moved up into the skies,
and blank and full, blazed down upon the quiet waters of
the sound, and upon the Indian village. It blazed upon
the one-eyed Spaniard and his lonely little ship and crew,
on their rich dull lamps, and on their swarthy sleeping
faces; it blazed upon all the dirty richness of their ragged
costumes, and on their greedy little minds, obsessed then
as now by the European's greedy myth about America,
to which he remains forever faithful with an unwearied
and idiot pertinacity: "Where is the gold in the streets?
Lead us to the emerald plantations, the diamond bushes,
the platinum mountains, and the cliffs of pearl. Brother,
let us gather in the shade of the ham and mutton trees,
by the shores of ambrosial rivers: we will bathe in the
fountains of milk, and pluck hot buttered rolls from the
bread vines."

Early the next morning the Spaniard went ashore with
several of his men. "When we reached land," he writes,
"our first act was to fall down on our knees and render
thanks to God and the Blessed Virgin without Whose
intervention we had all been dead men." Their next
act was to "take possession" of this land in the name
of the King of Spain, and to ground the flag. As we read
to-day of this solemn ceremony, its pathos and puny

arrogance touch us with pity. For what else can we feel for this handful of greedy adventurers "taking possession" of the immortal wilderness in the name of another puny fellow four thousand miles away, who had never seen or heard of the place and could never have understood it any better than these men? For the earth is never "taken possession of": it possesses.

At any rate, having accomplished these acts of piety and devotion, the Spaniards rose from their prayers, faced the crowd of Indians who had by this time ventured quite close to all this unctuous rigamarole, and discharged a volley from their muskets at them ("lest they become too forward and threatening"). Two or three fell sprawling on the ground, and the others ran away, yelling, into the woods. Thus, at one blast, Christianity and government were established.

The Spaniards now turned their attention to the Indian village—they began to pill and sack it with the deftness of long experience; but, as they entered one hut after another and found no coffers of nuggets or chests of emeralds, and found indeed that not even the jugs and pots and cooking utensils were of gold or silver, but had been crudely fashioned from baked earth, their rage grew; they felt tricked and cheated, and began to smash and destroy all that came within their reach. This sense of injury, this virtuous indignation has crept into the Spaniard's record—indeed, we are edified with a lot of early American criticism which, save for a few archaisms of phrasing, has a strangely familiar ring, and might almost have been written yesterday: "This is a wild and barbarous kind of race, full of bloudie ways, it exists in such a base and vile sort of living that is worthier of wild beestes than men: they live in darkness and of the artes of living as we know them they are ignorant, one could think that God Himself has forgot them, they are so farre remote from any lighte."

He comments with disgust on the dried "stinkeing fysshe" and the dried meat that hung in all the huts, and on the almost total lack of metals, but he saves his finest disdain for a "kinde of weede or plante," which they also found in abundant quantity in all the dwellings. He then goes on to describe this "weede or plante" in considerable detail: its leaves are broad and coarse and when dried it is yellow and has a strong odor. The barbarous natives, he says, are so fond of the plant that he has seen them put it in their mouths and chew it; when his own men tried the experience, however, they quickly had enough of it and some were seized with retchings and a puking sickness. The final use to which the plant is put seems to him so extraordinary that he evidently fears his story will be disbelieved, for he goes on, with many assurances and oaths of his veracity, to describe how the plant may be lighted and burned and how "it giveth a fowle stinkeing smoak," and most wonderful of all, how these natives have a way of setting it afire and drawing in its fumes through long tubes so that "the smoak cometh out again by their mouth and nostryls in such wyse that you mighte thinke them devils out of helle instead of mortyl men."

Before we leave this one-eyed fellow, it is ironic to note with what contempt he passes over "the gold in the streets" for which his bowels yearn. As an example of one-eyed blindness it is hard to beat. For here was gold, the inexhaustible vein of gold which the marvellous clay of the region could endlessly produce, and which mankind would endlessly consume and pay for; and the

Spaniard, devoured by his lust for gold, ignores it with a grimace of disgust and a scornful dilation of his nostrils. That act was at once a history and a prophecy, and in it is all the story of Europe's blundering with America.

For it must be said of all these explorers and adventurers, the early ones and the late ones, who came back from their voyages to the Americas embittered because they did not find gold strewn on the earth, that they failed not because there was no gold, but because they did not know where and how to look for it, and because they did not recognize it when they had it under their noses—because, in short, they were one-eyed men. That gold, real gold, the actual honest ore, existed in great quantities, and often upon the very surface of the earth as these men supposed, has since been abundantly shown: it is only one of the minor and less interesting episodes of American history—a casual confirmation of one of Europe's fairy tales. They tried to think of the most wonderful fable in the world, these money-haters, and they evolved the story of gold on the ground.

It was a story as naïve and not as beautiful as a child's vision of the lemonade spring, the ice cream mountains, the cake and candy forests but, at any rate, America confirmed this little fable about gold in one short year of her history, and then proceeded to unpocket and unearth vast stores of wealth that made the visions of these old explorers look absurd. For she unearthed rivers of rich oil and flung them skywards, she dug mountains of coal and iron and copper out of the soil, she harvested each year two thousand miles of golden wheat, she flung great rails across the desert, she bridged the continent with the thunder of great wheels, she hewed down forests of enormous trees and floated them down rivers, she grew cotton for the world, her soil was full of sugars, citric pungencies, of a thousand homely and exotic things, but still the mystery of her earth was unrevealed, her greatest wealth and potencies unknown.

The one-eyed Spaniard, however, saw none of these things. He looted the village, murdered a few of the Indians, and advanced eighty or one hundred miles inland, squinting about for treasure. He found a desolate region, quite flat, with soil of a sandy marl, a coarse and undistinguished landscape, haunted by a lonely austerity, and thickly and ruggedly forested—for the most part with large areas of long-leaf pine. As he went inland the soil deepened somewhat in hue and texture: it had a clayey, glutinous composition, and when rain fell he cursed it. It grew coarse grasses and tough thick brush and undergrowth: it could also grow enough of the pungent weed whose fumes had so disgusted him to fill the nostrils of the earth with smoke forever. There was abundance of wild game and fowl, so that the one-eyed Spaniard did not go hungry; but he found no nuggets and not even a single emerald.

The one-eyed Spaniard cursed, and again turned eastward toward the sea. Swift and high and straight as bullets the ducks passed over him, flying toward the coastal marshes. That was all. The enormous earth resumed its silence. Westward, in great hills that he had never seen, cloud shadows passed above the timeless wilderness, the trees crashed down at night athwart the broken boil of clean steep waters, there was the flash and wink of a billion little eyes, the glide and thrumming stir, the brooding ululation of the dark; there was the thunder of the wings, the symphony of the wilderness, but there was never the tread of a booted foot.

The Spaniard took to his ship, and set sail gladly. He was one-eyed and he had found no gold.

The Catawba people are great people for all manner of debate and reasoned argument. Where the more fiery South Carolinian or Mississippian will fly into a rage and want to fight the man who doubts his word or questions his opinion, the eye of the Catawban begins to glow with a fire of another sort—the lust for debate, a Scotch love of argument. Nothing pleases a Catawban better than this kind of dispute. He will say persuasively, "Now let's see if we can't see through this thing. Let's see if we can't git to the bottom of this." A long, earnest, and even passionate discussion will ensue in which the parties on both sides usually maintain the utmost good temper, kindliness, and tolerance, but in which they nevertheless pursue their arguments with great warmth and stubbornness. In these discussions several interesting traits of the Catawban quickly become manifest: the man is naturally a philosopher—he loves nothing better than to discuss abstract and difficult questions such as the nature of truth, goodness, and beauty, the essence of property, the problem of God. Moreover, in the development of his arguments the man loves the use of homely phrases and illustration, he is full of pungent metaphors drawn from his experience and environment; and in discussing an ethical question—say, the "moral right" of a man to his property, and to what extent he may profit by it —the Catawban may express himself somewhat in this manner:

"Well, now, Joe, take a case of this sort: suppose I buy a mule from a feller over there on the place next to mine, an' suppose I pay a hundred and fifty dollars fer that mule."

"Is this a one-eyed mule or a two-eyed mule you're buy-in'?" Joe demands with a broad wink around at his listening audience.

"It's a two-eyed mule," the first man says good-humor-edly, "but if you've got any objections to a two-eyed mule, we'll make it a one-eyed mule."

"Why, hell, no! Jim," the other man now says, "I ain't got no objections, but it seems to me if you're goin' to have a two-eyed mule you ought to have something bet-ter than a one-eyed argyment."

There is a roar of immense male laughter at this retort, punctuated with hearty slappings of thigh and knee, and high whoops in the throat.

"*'Od-damn!*" one of the appreciative listeners cries, when he can get his breath, "I reckon that'll hold 'im fer a while."

The story of the "two-eyed mule and the one-eyed argyment" is indeed an immense success, it is the kind of phrase and yarn these people love, and it is destined for an immediate and wide circulation all over the com-munity. It may even be raised to the dignity of proverbial usage, so that one will hear men saying, "Well, that's a two-eyed mule an' a one-eyed argyment if I ever saw one," and certainly the unfortunate Jim may expect to be greeted for some time to come in this way:

"Howdy, Jim. I hear you've gone into the mule busi-ness," or, "Hey, Jim, you ain't bought no two-eyed mules lately, have you?" or, "Say, Jim: you ain't seen a feller with a one-eyed argyment lookin' fer a two-eyed mule, have you?"

Jim knows very well that he is "in" for this kind of treatment, but he joins in the laughter good-humoredly, although his clay-red face burns with a deeper hue and he awaits the resumption of debate with a more dogged and determined air.

"Well, that's all right about that," he says, when he can make himself heard. "Whether he's a one-eyed mule or a two-eyed mule is neither here nor there."

"Maybe one eye is here, an' t'other there," some one suggests, and this sets them off again at Jim's expense. But Jim has the determination of the debater and the philosopher, and although his face is pretty red by now, he sticks to his job.

"All right," he says at length, "say I got a mule, anyway, an' he's a good mule, an' I paid one hundred and fifty dollars fer him. Now!" he says, pausing and lifting one finger impressively. "I take that mule an' work him on my farm fer *four* years. He's a *good* mule an' a *good* worker an' durin' that time he pays fer himself *twice* over! Now!" he declares again, pausing and looking triumphantly at his opponent, Joe, before resuming his argument.

"All right! All right!" Joe says patiently with an air of resignation. "I heard you. I'm still waitin'. You ain't *said* nothin' yet. You ain't *proved* nothin' yet."

"Now!" Jim continues slowly and triumphantly. "I gave one hundred and fifty dollars fer him but he's earned his keep an' paid fer himself *twice* over."

"I heard you! I heard you!" says Joe patiently.

"In other words," some one says, "you got back what you paid fer that mule with one hundred and fifty dollars to boot."

"Egs-actly!" Jim says with decision, to the group that is now listening intently. "I got back what I put into him an' I got one hundred fifty dollars to boot. Now here comes another feller," he continues, pointing indefinitely

towards the western horizon, who *needs* a good mule,
an' he sees *my* mule, an' he *offers to buy it!*" Here Jim
pauses again, and he turns and surveys his audience with
triumph written on his face.

"*I* heard you. *I'm* listenin'," says Joe in a patient and
monotonous voice.

"How much does *he* offer you?" some one asks.

"Now, wait a minute! I'm comin' to that," says Jim
with a silencing gesture. "This here feller says, 'That's a
perty good mule you got there!' 'I reckon he'll do!' I say.
'I ain't got no complaint to make!' 'I'm thinkin' of buyin'
a mule myse'f,' he says. 'That so?' I say. 'Yes,' he savs,
'I could use another mule on my farm. You ain't thinkin'
of sellin' that mule there, are you?' 'No,' I say, 'I ain't
thinkin' of it.' 'Well,' he says, 'would you consider an
offer fer him?' 'Well,' I say, 'I might an' I might not.
It all depends.' 'How much will you take fer him?' he
says. 'Well,' I say, 'I ain't never thought of sellin' him
before. I'd rather you'd make an offer. How much will
you give?' 'Well,' he says, 'how about three hundred
dollars?'"

There is a pause of living silence now while Jim turns
finally and triumphantly upon his audience.

"*Now!*" he cries again, powerfully, and decisively, leaning forward with one big hand gripped upon his knee
and his great index finger pointed toward them.

"I'm *listenin'*," Joe says in a calm but foreboding tone.

"I *got* my money back out o' that mule," Jim says, beginning a final recapitulation.

"Yes, an' you got another hundred an' fifty to boot,"
some one helpfully suggests.

"That makes *one* hundred per cent clear profit on my
'riginal investment," Jim says. "Now here comes a feller

who's willin' to pay me three hundred dollars on top of that. That makes *three* hundred per cent."

He pauses now with a conclusive air.

"Well?" says Joe heavily. "Go on. I'm still waitin'. What's the argyment?"

"Why," says Jim, "the argyment is this: I *got* my money back——"

"We all *know* that," says Joe. "You got your money back and a hundred per cent to boot."

"Well," says Jim, "the argyment is this: Have I any *right* to take the three hundred dollars that feller offers me?"

"Right?" says Joe, staring at him. "Why, what are you talkin' about? Of course, you got the right. The mule's yours, ain't he?"

"Ah!" says Jim with a knowing look, "that's just the point. *Is* he?"

"You *said* you bought an' *paid* fer him, didn't you?" some one said.

"Yes," said Jim, "I did that, all right."

"Why hell, Jim," some one else says, "you just ain't talkin' sense. A man's got the right to sell his own property."

"The *legal* right," Jim says, "the *legal* right! Yes! But I ain't talkin' about the *legal* right. I'm talkin' about the *mawral* right."

They gaze at Jim for a moment with an expression of slack-jawed stupefaction mixed with awe. Then he continues:

"A man's got a right to buy a piece of property an' to sell it an' to git a fair profit on his investment. I ain't denyin' that. But has *any* man," he continues, "a right— a mawral right—to a profit of three hundred per cent?"

Now Jim has made his point, he is content to rest for a moment and await the attack that comes, and comes immediately: after a moment's silence there is a tumult of protest, derisive laughter, strong cries of denial, a confusion of many voices all shouting disagreement, above which Joe's heavy baritone finally makes itself heard.

"Why, Jim!" he roars. "That's the damndest logic I ever did hear. I did give you credit fer havin' at least a *one*-eyed argyment, but I'm damned if this argyment you're givin' us has any eyes a-tall!"

Laughter here, and shouts of agreement.

"Why, Jim!" another one says with solemn humor, with an air of deep concern, "you want to go to see a doctor, son: you've begun to talk funny. Don't you know that?"

"*All* right. *All* right!" says Jim doggedly. "You can laugh all you please, but there's two sides to this here question, no matter what you think."

"Why, Jim!" yet another says, with a loose grin playing around his mouth. "What you goin' to do with that two-eyed mule? You goin' to *give* him away to that feller simply because you got your money out of him?"

"I ain't sayin'!" says Jim stubbornly, looking very red in the face at their laughter. "I ain't sayin' what I'd do. Mebbe I would and mebbe I wouldn't."

There is a roar of laughter this time, and the chorus of derisive voices is more emphatic than ever. But for some moments now, while this clamor has been going on, one of the company has fallen silent, he has fallen into a deep study, into an attitude of earnest meditation. But now he rouses himself and looks around with an expression of commanding seriousness.

"Hold on a moment there, boys," he says. "I'm not so sure about all this. I don't know that Jim's such a fool as you think he is. 'Pears to me there may be something in what he says."

"Now!" says Joe, with an air of finality. "What did I tell you! The woods are full of 'em. Here's another 'un that ain't all there."

But the contest is now just beginning in earnest: it goes on furiously, but very seriously, from now on, with these two Horatiuses holding their bridge valiantly and gaining in strength and conviction at each assault. It is a remarkable circumstance that at almost every gathering of Catawbans there are one or more of these minority warriors, who become more thoughtful and dubious as their companions grow more vociferous in their agreement and derision, and who, finally, from a first mild expression of doubt, become hotly embattled on the weaker side, and grow in courage and conviction at every breath, every word they utter, every attack they make or repel.

And it has always been the same with the Catawba people. Their character has strong Scotch markings: they are cautious and deliberate, slow to make a radical decision. They are great talkers, and believe in prayer and argument. They want to "reason a thing out," they want to "git to the bottom of a thing" through discussion, they want to settle a thing peaceably by the use of diplomacy and compromise. They are perhaps the most immensely conservative people on earth, they reverence authority, tradition, and leadership, but when committed to any decision, they stick to it implacably, and if the decision is war, they will fight to the end with the fury of maniacs.

Until very recent years these people were touched scarcely at all by "foreign" migration, whether from any of the other States, or from Europe: even today the number of "foreign-born" citizens is almost negligible, the

State has the largest percentage of native-born inhabitants in the country. This stock proceeds directly from the stock of the early settlers, who were English, German, and Scotch, particularly Scotch: the frequency with which Scotch names occur—the Grahams, the Alexanders, the McRaes, the Ramsays, the Morrisons, the Pettigrews, the Pentlands, etc.—is remarkable, as is also a marked Scottishness of physique, a lean, angular, big-boned and loose-jointed structure, a long-loping stride, an immense vitality and endurance, especially among the mountaineers in the western part of the State. In fact, during the recent war, it was found by the Army examiners that Catawba furnished easily the tallest troops in the service, and that their average height was a good inch and a half above the average for the country. From this it must not be supposed, as some philological pedagogues have supposed, with the mincing and accurate inaccuracy which is usual in this kind of people, that Old Catawba is today a magnificent anachronism populated with roistering and swashbuckling Elizabethans, "singing" (the pedagogues gloatingly remark of the mountaineers) "the *very* songs their ancestors sang in England four centuries ago, in a form that is practically intact," or with warlike and mad-eyed Kelts, chanting the same ballads as when they stormed across the border behind the Bruces.

No. The Catawban of today is not like this, nor would he want to be. He is not a colonist, a settler, a transplanted European; during his three centuries there in the wilderness, he has become native to the immense and lonely land that he inhabits, during those three centuries he has taken on the sinew and color of that earth, he has acquired a character, a tradition, and a history of his own: it is an obscure history, unknown to the world and not to be found in the pages of books, but it is a magnificent history, full of heroism, endurance, and the immortal silence of the earth. It lives in his heart, it lives in his brain, it lives in his unrecorded actions; and with this knowledge he is content, nor does he feel the need of ballads or Armadas to trick him into glory.

He does not need to speak, he does not need to affirm or deny, he does not need to assert his power or his achievement, for his heart is a lonely and secret heart, his spirit is immensely brave and humble, he has lived alone in the wilderness, he has heard the silence of the earth, he knows what he knows, and he has not spoken yet. We see him, silent and unheralded, in the brief glare of recorded event—he is there in the ranks of the American Revolution, and eighty years later he is there, gloriously but silently, in the ranks of the Civil War. But his real history is much longer and much more extraordinary than could be indicated by these flares of war: it is a history that runs back three centuries into primitive America, a strange and unfathomable history that is touched by something dark and supernatural, and that goes back through poverty, and hardship, through solitude and loneliness and death and unspeakable courage, into the wilderness. For it is the wilderness that is the mother of that nation, it was in the wilderness that the strange and lonely people who have not yet spoken, but who inhabit that immense and terrible land from East to West, first knew themselves, it was in the living wilderness that they faced one another at ten paces and shot one another down, and it is in the wilderness that they still live.

The real history of Old Catawba is not essentially a history of wars or rebellions; it is not a history of politics or corrupt officials; it is not a history of democracy or plutocracy or any form of government; it is not a history of business men, puritans, knaves, fools, saints, or heroes; it is not a history of culture or barbarism.

The real history of Old Catawba is a history of solitude, of the wilderness, and of the eternal earth, it is the history of millions of men living and dying alone in the wilderness, it is the history of the billion unrecorded and forgotten acts and moments of their lives; it is a history of the sun and the moon and the earth, of the sea that feathers eternally against the desolate coasts, and of great trees that smash down in lone solitudes of the wilderness.

The history of Old Catawba is the history of millions of men living alone in the wilderness, it is the history of millions of men who have lived their brief lives in silence upon the everlasting earth, who have listened to the earth and known her million tongues, whose lives were given to the earth, whose bones and flesh are recompacted with the earth, the immense and terrible earth that makes no answer.

Circus at Dawn

THERE were times in early autumn—in September—when the greater circuses would come to town—the Ringling Brothers, Robinson's, and Barnum and Bailey shows, and when I was a route-boy on the morning paper, on those mornings when the circus would be coming in I would rush madly through my route in the cool and thrilling darkness that comes just before break of day, and then I would go back home and get my brother out of bed.

Talking in low excited voices we would walk rapidly back toward town under the rustle of September leaves, in cool streets just grayed now with that still, that unearthly and magical first light of day which seems suddenly to re-discover the great earth out of darkness, so that the earth emerges with an awful, a glorious sculptural stillness, and one looks out with a feeling of joy and disbelief, as the first men on this earth must have done, for to see this happen is one of the things that men will remember out of life forever and think of as they die.

At the sculptural still square where at one corner, just emerging into light, my father's shabby little marble shop stood with a ghostly strangeness and familiarity, my brother and I would "catch" the first street-car of the day bound for the "depot" where the circus was—or sometimes we would meet some one we knew, who would give us a lift in his automobile.

Then, having reached the dingy, grimy, and rickety depot section, we would get out, and walk rapidly across the

205

tracks of the station yard, where we could see great flares
and steamings from the engines, and hear the crash and
bump of shifting freight cars, the swift sporadic thunders of
a shifting engine, the tolling of bells, the sounds of great
trains on the rails.

And to all these familiar sounds, filled with their exultant prophecies of flight, the voyage, morning, and the
shining cities—to all the sharp and thrilling odors of the
trains—the smell of cinders, acrid smoke, of musty, rusty
freight cars, the clean pine-board of crated produce, and
the smells of fresh stored food—oranges, coffee, tange-
rines and bacon, ham and flour and beef—there would
be added now, with an unforgettable magic and familiarity, all the strange sounds and smells of the coming
circus.

The gay yellow sumptuous-looking cars in which the
star performers lived and slept, still dark and silent, heavily and powerfully still, would be drawn up in long
strings upon the tracks. And all around them the sounds
of the unloading circus would go on furiously in the
darkness. The receding gulf of lilac and departing night
would be filled with the savage roar of the lions, the mur-
derously sudden snarling of great jungle cats, the trum-
peting of the elephants, the stamp of the horses, and with
the musty, pungent, unfamiliar odor of the jungle animals: the tawny camel smells, and the smells of panthers,
zebras, tigers, elephants, and bears.

Then, along the tracks, beside the circus trains, there
would be the sharp cries and oaths of the circus men, the
magical swinging dance of lanterns in the darkness, the
sudden heavy rumble of the loaded vans and wagons as
they were pulled along the flats and gondolas, and down
the runways to the ground. And everywhere, in the thrilling mystery of darkness and awakening light, there would

be the tremendous conflict of a confused, hurried, and yet orderly movement.

The great iron-gray horses, four and six to a team, would be plodding along the road of thick white dust to a rattling of chains and traces and the harsh cries of their drivers. The men would drive the animals to the river which flowed by beyond the tracks, and water them; and as first light came one could see the elephants wallowing in the familiar river and the big horses going slowly and carefully down to drink.

Then, on the circus grounds, the tents were going up already with the magic speed of dreams. All over the place (which was near the tracks and the only space of flat land in the town that was big enough to hold a circus) there would be this fierce, savagely hurried, and yet orderly confusion. Great flares of gaseous circus light would blaze down on the seared and battered faces of the circus toughs as, with the rhythmic precision of a single animal—a human riveting machine—they swung their sledges at the stakes, driving a stake into the earth with the incredible instancy of accelerated figures in a motion picture. And everywhere, as light came, and the sun appeared, there would be a scene of magic, order, and of violence. The drivers would curse and talk their special language to their teams, there would be the loud, gasping and uneven labor of a gasoline engine, the shouts and curses of the bosses, the wooden riveting of driven stakes, and the rattle of heavy chains.

Already in an immense cleared space of dusty beaten earth, the stakes were being driven for the main exhibition tent. And an elephant would lurch ponderously to the field, slowly lower his great swinging head at the command of a man who sat perched upon his skull, flourish his gray wrinkled snout a time or two, and then solemnly wrap it around a tent pole big as the mast of a racing schooner. Then the elephant would back slowly away, dragging the great pole with him as if it were a stick of match-wood.

And when this happened, my brother would break into his great "whah-whah" of exuberant laughter, and prod me in the ribs with his clumsy fingers. And further on, two town darkeys, who had watched the elephant's performance with bulging eyes, would turn to each other with ape-like grins, bend double as they slapped their knees and howled with swart rich nigger-laughter, saying to each other in a kind of rhythmical chorus of question and reply:

"He don't play with it, do he?"

"No, *suh!* He don't send no boy!"

"He don't say 'Wait a minute,' do he?"

"No, suh! He say 'Come with me!' That's what he say!"

"He go boogety—boogety!" said one, suiting the words with a prowling movement of his black face toward the earth.

"He go rootin' faw it!" said the other, making a rooting movement with his head.

"He say 'Ar-rumpf'!" said one.

"He say 'Big boy, we is on ouah way'!" the other answered.

"Har! Har! Har! Har! Har!"—and they choked and screamed with their rich laughter, slapping their thighs with a solid smack as they described to each other the elephant's prowess.

Meanwhile, the circus food-tent—a huge canvas top without concealing sides—had already been put up, and now we could see the performers seated at long trestled tables underneath the tent, as they ate breakfast. And the savor of the food they ate—mixed as it was with our strong excitement, with the powerful but wholesome smells of the animals, and with all the joy, sweetness, mystery, jubilant magic and glory of the morning and the coming of the circus—seemed to us to be of the most maddening and appetizing succulence of any food that we had ever known or eaten.

We could see the circus performers eating tremendous breakfasts, with all the savage relish of their power and strength: they ate big fried steaks, pork chops, rashers of bacon, a half dozen eggs, great slabs of fried ham and great stacks of wheat-cakes which a cook kept flipping in the air with the skill of a juggler, and which a husky-looking waitress kept rushing to their tables on loaded trays held high and balanced marvellously on the fingers of a brawny hand. And above all the maddening odors of the wholesome and succulent food, there brooded forever the sultry and delicious fragrance—that somehow seemed to add a zest and sharpness to all the powerful and thrilling life of morning—of strong boiling coffee, which we could see sending off clouds of steam from an enormous polished urn, and which the circus performers gulped down, cup after cup.

And the circus men and women themselves—these star performers—were such fine-looking people, strong and handsome, yet speaking and moving with an almost stern dignity and decorum, that their lives seemed to us to be as splendid and wonderful as any lives on earth could be. There was never anything loose, rowdy, or tough in their comportment, nor did the circus women look like painted whores, or behave indecently with the men.

Rather, these people in an astonishing way seemed to have created an established community which lived an ordered existence on wheels, and to observe with a stern fidelity unknown in towns and cities the decencies of family life. There would be a powerful young man, a handsome and magnificent young woman with blonde hair and the figure of an Amazon, and a powerfully-built, thick-set man of middle age, who had a stern, lined, responsible-looking face and a bald head. They were probably the members of a trapeze team—the young man and woman would leap through space like projectiles, meeting the grip of the older man and hurling back again upon their narrow perches, catching the swing of their trapeze in mid-air, and whirling thrice before they caught it, in a perilous and beautiful exhibition of human balance and precision.

But when they came into the breakfast tent, they would speak gravely yet courteously to other performers, and seat themselves in a family group at one of the long tables, eating their tremendous breakfasts with an earnest concentration, seldom speaking to one another, and then gravely, seriously and briefly.

And my brother and I would look at them with fascinated eyes: my brother would watch the man with the bald head for a while and then turn toward me, whispering:

"D-d-do you see that f-f-fellow there with the bald head? W-w-well he's the heavy man," he whispered knowingly. "He's the one that c-c-c-catches them! That f-f-fellow's got to know his business! You know what happens if he m-m-misses, don't you?" said my brother.

"What?" I would say in a fascinated tone.

My brother snapped his fingers in the air.

"Over!" he said. "D-d-done for! W-w-why, they'd be d-d-d-dead before they knew what happened. Sure!" he said, nodding vigorously. "It's a f-f-f-fact! If he ever m-m-m-misses it's all over! That boy has g-g-g-got to know his s-s-s-stuff!" my brother said. "W-w-w-why," he went on in a low tone of solemn conviction, "it w-w-w-wouldn't surprise me at all if they p-p-p-pay him s-s-seventy-five or a hundred dollars a week! It's a fact!" my brother cried vigorously.

And we would turn our fascinated stares again upon these splendid and romantic creatures, whose lives were so different from our own, and whom we seemed to know with such familiar and affectionate intimacy. And at length, reluctantly, with full light come and the sun up, we would leave the circus grounds and start for home.

And somehow the memory of all we had seen and heard that glorious morning, and the memory of the food-tent with its wonderful smells, would waken in us the pangs of such a ravenous hunger that we could not wait until we got home to eat. We would stop off in town at lunch-rooms and, seated on tall stools before the counter, we would devour ham-and-egg sandwiches, hot hamburgers red and pungent at their cores with coarse spicy sanguinary beef, coffee, glasses of foaming milk and doughnuts, and then go home to eat up everything in sight upon the breakfast table.

The Web of Earth

... In the year that the locusts came, something that happened in the year the locusts came, two voices that I heard there in that year. . . . Child! Child! It seems so long ago since the year the locusts came, and all of the trees were eaten bare: so much has happened and it seems so long ago. . . .

"What say?" I said.

Says, "Two . . . Two," says, "Twenty . . . Twenty."

"Hah? What say?"

"Two . . . Two," the first voice said; and "Twenty . . . Twenty," said the other.

"Oh, Two!" I cried out to your papa, and "Twenty . . . Twenty—can't you hear them?"

"Two . . . Two," it said again, the first voice over by the window, and "Twenty . . . Twenty" said the second, at my ear.

"Oh, don't you hear it, Mr. Gant?" I cried.

"Why, Lord, woman!" your papa said. "What on earth are you talking about? There's no one there," he said.

"Oh, yes, there is!" I said, and then I heard them once again, "Two . . . Two" and "Twenty . . . Twenty."

"There they are!" I said.

"Pshaw, Mrs. Gant," your papa said. "It's something you imagined. You fell asleep, you must have dreamed it."

"Oh, no, I didn't," I said. "It's there! It's there all right!"—because I *knew,* I *knew*: because I heard it just as plain!

"It's the condition you're in," he said. "You're tired and overwrought and you've imagined it."

Then all of the bells began to ring and he got up to go.

"Oh, don't go!" I said. "I wish you wouldn't go"—you know I had a premonition, and it worried me to see him go.

And then I heard it once again—"Two . . . Two," the first voice said, and "Twenty . . . Twenty," said the other . . . and I *know*, I *know*—why, yes! Lord God! don't I remember, boy!—the hour, the time, the very year it happened, to the day . . . because that was the year the locusts came at home and all of the trees were eaten bare.

But, say, then!—Ben—Steve—Luke—pshaw! Boy! *Gene!* I mean—I reckon Luke is thinking of me at this moment, that's why I keep calling you his name. Well, now—hah? What say?

"You started to tell me about two voices that you heard one time."

Oh, yes! That's so! Well, now, as I was—say! What was that? Hah?

"Those were the ships out on the harbor, Mama."

What say? Harbor? Ships? Oh, yes, I reckon now that's so. The harbor is yon way?

"No, Mama, it's the other way. You're turned around. It's just the other way: it's there."

Hah? *That* way? Why, no, child, surely not. . . . Are you telling me the truth? . . . Well, then, I'll vow! I *am* mixed up. I reckon comin' in that tunnel did it. But you couldn't lose me in the country; give me a landmark of some sort to go by and I'll be all right. . . . Why, boy, I'll vow! . . . There goes that thing again! Why, Lord! It sounds like some old cow! And here you are right on the edge of it! How did you ever come to such a place? Lord! Listen—do you hear it? I reckon that's a big one gettin' ready to pull out. . . . Lord, God! You're all alike: your daddy was the same—forever wantin' to be up and

gone. If I'd let him he'd have been nothing but a wanderer across the face of the earth. . . . Child, child, you
musn't be a wanderer all your days. . . . It worries me to
think of you away off somewheres with strange people.
. . . You mustn't spend your life alone with strangers.
. . . You ought to come back where your people came
from. . . . Child, child, it worries me. . . . Come back
again.

Well now, as I was goin' on to say, that night I heard
it, the first voice—pshaw! there goes that whistle once
again. Say, boy! I tell you what—it makes me want to
pick right up and light out with it! Why, yes, I'm not
so old! I could start out now—I tell you what, I've got
a good mind to do it—I'd like to start right out and just
see everything—why! all those countries: England, where
all our folks came from, and France, Germany, Italy—
say! I've always wanted to see Switzerland—that must
certainly be a beautiful spot—as the feller says, the Wonderland of Nature. . . .

Say . . . oh, now I hear it! . . . Now I know. . . .
Why, yes! It's out yon way. And where's the bridge, then,
that we walked across that night?

"It's here—right at the bottom of the street. Here!
Come to the window and look out. Don't you remember
how we came?"

Remember! Now, boy, you ask me if I can remember!
Lord, God! I reckon I remember things you never read
about—the way it was, the things they never wrote about
in books.

I reckon that they tried to put it down in books, all of
the wars and battles, child, I guess they got that part of
it all right, but Lord!—how could these fellers know the
way it was when they weren't born, when they weren't

there to see it: they made it seem so long ago and like it happened in some strange land—what could they know, child, of the way it was: the way the wind blew and the way the sun was shining, the smell of the smoke out in the yard, and Mother singin', and the scalded feathers, and the way the river swelled that spring when it had rained? The way the men looked as they marched back along the river road that day, as they were comin' from the war, and the things we said, and the sound of all the voices of the people who are dead, and the way the sunlight came and went, and how it made me sad to see it, and the way the women cried as we stood there in Bob Patton's yard, and the men marched by us, and the dust rose, and we knew the war was over. Lord, God! do I remember! Those are the things that I remember, child, and that's the way things were.

I can remember all the way back to the time when I was two years old, and let me tell you, boy, there's mighty little I've forgotten since.

Why, yes!—don't I remember how they took me by the hand that day and led me down into the holler—Bob Patton and your Uncle George—and here boy-like they had constructed an effigy of Willy and Lucindy Patton out of that old black mud they had there—you could mould it in your hands just like a piece of putty—and how I screamed and all—because I *knew*, I *knew*, I'd seen them both and I remembered them—why! Willy and Lucindy were two slaves that Cap'n Patton owned—oh, Lord! the blackest African niggers you ever saw, as Father said, charcoal would 'a' left a white mark on them, their parents had been taken right out of the jungle—and those white teeth, those gleaming white teeth when they grinned—but oh! the odor! that awful odor, that old black nigger-smell that nothin' could wash out, mother couldn't stand it, it made her deathly sick, when they passed through a room they left the smell behind them—and here these two devils of boys had made this effigy with pebbles they had taken from the creek for teeth, and to think of it!—that they should tell a child of two a thing like that—*why,* that it was Willy and Lucindy Patton I was lookin' at—"Look out!" says Bob, "they're going to eat you up," he says, and how I screamed—why, I remember it all the same as yesterday!

And don't I remember taking Brother Will up to the Indian Mound—of course the story went that there were Indians buried there, that's what it was, they said—and here this brook was filled up with this old black oily stuff that came out from the mound—of course, Father always gave it as his opinion there was oil there, that's what he said, you know, that some one would make a fortune some day if they dug a well there—and Will was only two and a half years old and George told him that the old black oil was squeezed out of the corpses of the Indians and how Will screamed and hollered when he told him—"Why," Mother said, "I could wring your neck for having no more sense than to frighten a child with such a story."

And yes, now! What about it? Don't I remember that winter when the deer come boundin' down the hill across the path and stopped and looked at me not ten feet away, and I screamed because I saw its antlers? Lord! I didn't know what to make of it, I'd never heard of such an animal, and how it bounded away into the woods again and how when I told Mother she said, "Yes, you saw a deer. That was a deer you saw all right. The hunters ran it down here off the mountain" and—why, yes! wasn't it only the next spring after that when I was a big girl four years old and remembered everything—that the Yankees began to

come through there, and didn't I hear them, didn't I see
them with my own eyes, the villains—those two fellers
tearing along the road on two horses they had stolen, as
hard as they could, as if all hell had cut loose after them—
why! it's as plain in my mind to-day as it was then, the way
they looked, two ragged-lookin' troopers bent down and
whippin' those horses for all that they were worth, with
bandanna handkerchiefs tied around their necks and the
ends of them whipping back as stiff and straight as if
they'd been starched and ironed—now *that* will give you
some idea of how fast they were goin'—and couldn't I hear
the people shoutin' and hollerin' all along the road that
they were comin', and how the women-folks took on and
made the men go out and hide themselves? "Oh, Lord,"
says Mother, wringin' her hands, "there they come!" and
didn't Addie Patton come running up the hill to tell
us, the poor child frightened out of her wits, you know
screaming, "Oh, they've come, they've come! And Grand-
father's down there all alone," she says. "They'll kill him,
they'll kill him!"

Of course we didn't know then that these two Yankee
stragglers were alone, we thought they were the advance
guard of a whole brigade of Sherman's troopers. But Law!
the rest of them never got there for a week, here these two
thieving devils had broken away, and I reckon were just
trying to see how much they could steal by themselves.
Why, yes! Didn't all the men begin to shoot at them then
as they went by and when they saw they didn't have the
army with them, and didn't they jump off their horses
and light out for the mountains on foot as hard as they
could, then, and leave the horses? And didn't some people
from way over in Bedford County come to claim the horses
when the war was over? They identified them, you
know, and said those same two fellers were the ones that

took 'em. And Lord! didn't they tell it how Amanda
Stevens set fire to the Bridge with her own hands on the
other side of Sevier so that those that were comin' in from
Tennessee were held up for a week before they got across
—yes! and stood there laughin' at them, you know; of
course they used to tell it on her that she said ("Lord!" I
said, "you know she wouldn't say a thing like that!") but
of course Amanda was an awful coarse talker, she didn't
care what she said, and they all claimed later that's just
the way she put it—"Why," she hollers to them, "you
don't need a bridge to get across a little stream like that,
do you? Well, you must be a pretty worthless lot, after
all," she said. "Why, down here," she says, "we'd call it
a pretty poor sort of man who couldn't —— across it,"
and, of course, the Yankees had to laugh then, that's the
story that they told.

And yes! Didn't they tell it at the time how the day
the Yankees marched into town they captured old man
Mackery? I reckon they wanted to have some fun with
him more than anything else, a great fat thing, you know,
with that swarthy yeller complexion and that kinky hair,
of course, the story went that he had nigger blood in him
and—what about it! he admitted it, sir, he claimed it then
and there in front of all the Yankees, I reckon hoping
they would let him off. "All right," the Yankees said,
"if you can prove that you're a nigger we'll let you go."
Well, he said that he could prove it, then. "Well, how're
you going to prove it?" they asked him. "I'll tell you
how," this Yankee captain says, calls to one of his troopers, you know, "Run him up and down the street a few
times, Jim," he says, and so they started, this soldier and
old man Mackery, running up and down in that hot sun
as hard as they could go. Well, when they got back, he
was wringin' wet with perspiration, Mackery, you know,

and the story goes the Yankee went over to him and took one good smell and then called out, "Yes, by God, he told the truth, boys. He's a nigger. Let him go!" Well, that's the way they told it, anyhow.

And yes! Don't I remember it all, yes! With the men comin' by and marchin' along that river road on their way into town to be mustered out and all of us ganged together there in the front yard of Uncle John's place to see them pass, Father and Mother and all the childern and all of the Patton and Alexander and Pentland tribes and these two black African niggers that I told you John Patton owned, Willy and Lucindy Patton, and your great-grandfather, boy, old Bill Pentland that they called Bill the Hatter because he could make them of the finest felt —learned how to treat the wool with chamber lye, oh! the finest hats you ever saw, why don't I remember an old farmer coming to our house in my childhood to give a hat to Uncle Sam to be reblocked, says, "Sam, old Bill Pentland made that hat for me just twenty years ago and it's as good," he says, "as it ever was, all it needs is to be blocked and cleaned," and let me tell you, every one that knew him said that Billy Pentland was certainly a man with a remarkable mind.

Now, boy, I want to tell you, I've always said whatever ability you had came from that side of the house, there's one thing sure, Bill Pentland was a man who'd 'a' gone far if he'd had the education. Of course he had no book-learnin' but they told it, you know, how he could argue and take sides on any question, hale and hearty, mind you, right up to the hour of his death, sent word down to Sam one day to come up there to see him, says, "Sam"—of course Sam told it how he found him building his fire and singin' a hymn, at peace with the world and without a thing

wrong with him—"Sam," he says, "I'm glad you've come.
There are matters I want to talk over with you. Lay down
on that bed," he says, "so we can talk." Well, that just
suited Sam, you know, oh! the *laziest* feller that ever lived,
he could spend his whole life just a-layin' round and talkin', "Why," he says, "what is it, Father? What's the matter?
Aren't you feelin' good?" he says. "Oh," says Bill, "I never
felt better, but I'm not goin' to be here with you much
longer," he says, "I've made up my mind it's time to die,
Sam, and I want to put my house in order before I go."
"Why, Father," Sam says, "what are you talkin' about,
what do you mean? There's nothing wrong with you."
"No, not a thing," says Bill. "Why, you'll be here for years
to come," says Sam. "No, Sam," the old man says, he
shook his head, you know. "I've just decided that it's my
time to go. I've had a Call. Now, I've lived out my full
three score years and ten," he says, "with some to spare
and I feel there's nothin' more I can do on earth, so I've
made up my mind." "Made up your mind?" says Sam,
"why, made up your mind to what?" "Why," he says,
"I've made up my mind to die, Sam." "Why, Father," says
Sam, "what are you talking about? You're not going to
die," he says. "Yes'" says Bill, "I've made up my mind
to die tomorrow," says, "I've made up my mind to die
at ten minutes after six tomorrow afternoon, and that's
the reason I sent for you." Well! they built up a roarin'
big fire and stayed up all night long talkin' together, and
oh! you know, Sam told it how the wind roared and
howled, and how they talked long, long into the night,
and they cooked breakfast, and lay around and talked
some more, and they cooked dinner and talked some
more and that old man was as well and strong as he'd
ever been, at peace with mankind, sir, and without a worry
in the world, but on the stroke of six, now, boy, I want

to tell you the kind of man *he* was, on the stroke of six, he turned to Sam and said, "Get ready, Sam," and at ten minutes after six to the dot, he looked at him again and said, "Good-bye, Sam: it's my time, I'm going, son," and he turned his face to the wall, sir, and *died*—now that's the kind of a man he was, that goes to show the kind of will-power and determination he had in *him*—and *let me tell you something:* we've all had it in us, that same thing, when it came our time to go, we *knew* it. Father went the same way, sir, kept wakin' up all day long to say, "Is it six o'clock, yet?"—couldn't seem to get it off his mind, you know— "Why, no, Father," I said, "it's only noon." Now, six, six, I kept a-thinkin', why does he keep asking if it's six? That *very day* sir, as the clock was striking the last stroke of six he breathed his last, I turned to Jim and whispered, "Six": he nodded, "Yes," he said. Of course we knew.

But here he was that day—don't I remember him? Old Bill Pentland standin' there with all the rest of us to watch the troops go by, a hale and hearty old man, sir, oh! married twice and had all those childern, eight by his first wife, Martha Patton, of course Father was one of *that* crowd and fourteen by that other woman—well, that's so, there *was* that other one, I reckon, that he'd had by that woman down in South Carolina, of course there was no record of the ceremony and I reckon what they said was true, but he brought that child home and sat her down at the table with all the rest of them and said to them all: "From this time on she is your sister and must be treated so," and that's the way it was all right. And here, to think of it! All these childern that he had went out and had big families of their own, those that didn't die early or get killed, until now there are hundreds of them living down there in Catawba in the mountains, and in

Georgia and Texas and out west in California and Oregon until now they are spread all over like a web—but that's where they came from, from that one old man, he was the only one there was to begin with, the son of that Englishman that came there back in Revolutionary days to sink those copper shafts out there in Yancey. Of course they say we've got great estates waitin' for us in England—I know Uncle Bob came to Father at the time Bill Pentland died and told him he ought to do something about it, but they decided against it, said the expense would be too great—but he was *there,* all right, Bill Pentland was there with all the rest of us the day they came back from the war. And here came all the troops, you know, and you could hear the men a-cheerin' and the women-folks a-crying, and every now and then you'd see one of the men drop out of line and then the women would start crying again, and here comes Uncle Bob—only sixteen, mind you, but he seemed like an old man to me—wearing a stovepipe hat I reckon he'd looted from some store and no shoes on, and here he comes and we all began to cry.

"Why, Lord!" says Bob, "this is a pretty homecomin' for a fact," he says, you know, trying to joke us along and cheer us up. "Why, I thought you'd be glad to see me," he says. "I didn't expect you all to bust out cryin'! Why, if that's the way you feel," he says, "I'm goin' back."

"Oh, Bob, Bob," his mother says, "you've got no shoes, poor child, you're barefooted," she says.

"No," says Bob, "I wore 'em out in my hurry to get home," he says, "I just walked them clean off my feet," he says, "but if I'd known it was going to be like this, I wouldn't have come so fast," he said, and of course that made 'em laugh.

But, child, that wasn't the reason that the women cried. So many had gone off that never would come home again and, of course, they knew it, they knew it, and then, didn't we all flock into the house, and hadn't they all been baking and cooking for a week and, let me tell you, poor as we were, that was a *meal,* no little dabs of stuff such as they give you nowadays: fried chickens—why we must have cooked two dozen of them—and boiled hams and pork and roasting ears and sweet pertaters and string beans and plates full of corn bread and hot biscuits and peach and apple dumplings and all kinds of jams and jellies and pies and cakes galore and all of the cider you could drink, and Lord! I wish you could have seen the way that Bob and Rufus Alexander and Fate Patton put that food away, why, as Mother said, you'd 'a' thought they hadn't had a square meal since they went to war and I reckon maybe she didn't miss it much either.

Why, wasn't I a big girl of five years old at the time, and saw it all, and remember it as well as I'm settin' here yes, and things that happened long before that—and things you never heard of, boy, with all your reading out of books: why, yes, didn't we learn to do everything ourselves and to grow everything we ate and to take the wool and dye it, yes, to go out in the woods and get the sumac and the walnut bark and all the walnut hulls and elderberries for the dyes and rinse the wool in copperas water until we had a hard fast black you couldn't take the shine off— why! it beat the stuff they have today all hollow—didn't I learn to do it with my own hands and couldn't I get the finest reds and greens and yellers that you ever saw, and didn't I learn to spin the flax and bleach it and make fine shirts and sheets and tablecloths myself, why, yes, don't I remember the day—oh! that strong rank smell, you know, of scalded feathers, with Mother plucking the chicken in the yard, and the smell of the smoke, and the fresh pine chips out by the chopping block, and all (that's where you got your sense of smell from, boy!) and the wind that howled and whistled through that old coarse grass, it made me sad to listen to it (that was the year just after Sally died) and I sat there at the wheel spinning away, and I can see it all, I remember just the way it was —when here they came along the river road, and you could hear them shout and holler out "Hurrah! hurrah!" I reckon they'd all been in to town to vote. "Hurrah!" they cried: "Hurrah for Hayes!" one crowd would cry and, "Hurrah for Tilden!" cried the other.

Lord God! do I remember! I reckon that I do! I remember things you never dreamed or heard of, boy.

"But what about those voices that you heard?"

Well, now, I say—that's what I'm telling you:

"Two-two," the first voice said, and "twenty-twenty," said the other. "What say?" I said. Says, "two-two," says, "twenty-twenty." "Hah? What say?" Says, "two-two," the first voice said, says "twenty-twenty," said the other.

Well, then—say! what about it!—I was thinking about it the other day. . . . I don't know . . . but it's pretty strange when you come to think about it, isn't it? Why, that very day, you know, the twenty-seventh of September, I remember because it was on the twenty-fifth, just two days before, that I had the talk with Ambrose Radiker, that's exactly when it was all right, about eleven o'clock in the morning, your papa was back there in his work-room lettering a tombstone he was getting ready to set up for a man out there in Beaverdam whose wife had died, when here he came, Mel Porter. Your papa said he marched right back into the work-room, sir, and stood there looking at him without sayin' a word: he just stood there shakin' his head and your papa said he certainly looked blue and depressed as if some awful calamity had befallen him,

so your papa said, "What's the matter, Mel? I never saw
you look so sad," he says.

"Oh, Will, Will," he says, and he just stood there shakin' his head at your papa, "if you only knew how I envy
you! Here you are with a good trade you can work at and
nothing to worry you: I'd give up everything I have in
the world if I could just change places with you!" "Why
what on earth are you talking about!" your papa said.
"You're a first-class lawyer with a good practice and here
you want to swap places with a stone-cutter who's got to
work with his hands and never knows where his next job's
comin' from," your papa said. "It's a curse and a care,"
your papa said, that's exactly the way he talked to him,
you know the way he had of talkin', he'd come right out
with a thing without mincin' words. "It's a curse and a
care," he said, "and it was a bitter day for me when I first
took it up: you've got to wait until they die to get a job
and then their families, ingrates that they are, will give
the work to one of your competitors: if I'd done the thing
I was cut out for, I'd 'a' studied law like you did and gone
into practice." Well, of course, they all said that, they said
that Mr. Gant would certainly have made a fine lawyer,
with his fluent command of language and all. "Oh, Will,
Will," he said, "you can just go down on your knees and
thank God that you didn't," he said. "At least you have
enough to eat," he said, "and when you go home at night
you can go to bed and sleep."

"Why, Mel," your papa said. "What on earth is wrong
with you? Something is worryin' you, that's one thing
sure." "Oh, Will," he said, shakin' his head, "it's those
men. I can't sleep at night for thinkin' about them!" Well,
he hadn't said *what* men, he hadn't mentioned their names,
but your papa knew right away who he was talkin' about,
it flashed over him all at once that he was referrin' to Ed

Mears and Lawrence Wayne and those other three murderers down there in the county jail he had defended. And
he had been down there to see them, he'd just come away
from there, your papa said he knew exactly where he'd
been the moment he looked at him, said his shoes and the
bottoms of his trousers were coated with that old red-clay
Niggertown dust, that's all in the world it was.

"Why, yes, Mel," your papa said, "I reckon it is pretty
hard, but you've got nothin' to blame yourself for," he
said. "You did all any one could expect you to do," he
said; says, "You did the best you could for them," he says;
says, "I don't see what you got to blame yourself about
now," he says.

"Oh, Will," he says, "it's the strain, the awful strain of
it," he says. "Here I've done all I could to save them," he
says, "and it looks as if there's nothing else I can do," he
says; says, "It looks to me as if they've got to hang," he says,
"and here are their wives and childern and all of their kinfolk beggin' me to save them and," he says, "Will, I just
don't know what else there is I can do," he says; says, "I've
racked my brain lookin' for a way out," he says, "and it
looks to me as if they've *got to swing*. I tell you what,"
he says, shakin' his head, and your papa said he looked
mighty blue, says, "it's an awful thing when you come to
think of it! What about it!" he says. "Here they've got
all those little childern dependent on them who have got
to grow up now with that awful stigma attached to their
name of knowin' they're the childern of men who were
hanged for murder. Why, it's awful, that's what it is,
Will," he says; says, "I can't sleep at night for thinkin'
about it."

Well, when your papa came home to dinner that day
he told me all about it, says, "I tell you what, it's pretty
hard on him, isn't it? I reckon he's done all he can but

he feels like he's in some way responsible for it, that maybe there's somethin' he failed to do that might have saved their lives," he says; says, "I couldn't help feelin' sorry for him," says "he was pale as a ghost: he looked as if he hadn't been able to sleep for a week." "Hm!" I says. "Now you listen to me: there's *something mighty funny* about this *somewheres.* I've never known a lawyer yet," I says, "who wasn't able to sleep because a client was goin' to be hanged, and you can just bet your bottom dollar," I says, "that Melvin Porter isn't losin' sleep on *that* account. The only reason they'll lose sleep," I says, "is because they're afraid they're not goin' to get paid or because they're stayin' awake figgerin' how they can get the best of some one, and if he told you *any such story* as that," I says, "you can depend upon it that he wasn't tellin' you the truth—there's a nigger in the woodpile somewheres: that story *just won't wash.*"

"No," your papa says, "I believe you're wrong," says, "I think you're doin' him an injustice."

"Why, pshaw, Mr. Gant!" I says. "I wouldn't be such a goose! There's not a word of truth in that story, all they've got to do is to appeal to your sympathies and you'll believe anything they tell you."

And of course that was just exactly how he was: he'd curse and rave and carry on, and then they'd tell him some big lie to get on his good side and he'd give them everything he had. Why! didn't Mel Porter's own brother, that miserable old rip, Rufus Porter—as the sayin' goes, if there's a just God in heaven he's getting today the punishment he deserves—with his old red face all stewed down like a persimmon with all the licker he'd drunk—why yes! when I was a girl didn't I see him myself march right down the aisle as big as you please, sir, that night at the meeting of the Sons of Temperance, arm in arm with Jeter

Alexander to sign the pledge and Lord! as I said later if you took all the rotten old licker they'd poured down their throats since then you'd have enough to float a battleship —come to your papa and got him to sign his note and stand security for him at the bank for fourteen hundred dollars. Pshaw! when I think of it! . . . I said to your papa, *"He's* the one who ought to be hanged! I could spring the trap myself!" I said; says to your papa, in that mealy voice he had, you know, says, "Oh, it will be all right, Will." Says, "You know I wouldn't let you lose a penny," when he didn't have a dollar to his name! "I'll vow, Mr. Gant!" I said at the time. "How on earth were you ever such a fool as to do such a thing!"

"Well," he said, "he swore it was all right—said he'd go down and dig ditches before he'd let me lose a penny."

"Yes," I said, "and you were *just* fool enough to believe him, weren't you!"

"Well," your papa said, "I've learned my lesson. There's one thing sure: I'll never get stung that way again," he said.

"All right," I said, "we'll wait and see."

Well, it wasn't two years before Rufe Porter tried the very same trick on him again; he had the gall to walk right into your papa's office, sir, as big as you please, and ask him to go his note for five hundred dollars. Your papa was so mad he took him by the collar and pitched him all the way out into the square and says, "If you ever come back here again, you God-damned mountain grill," that's just the way your papa talked to him, you know the way he talked, he didn't mince words when he was mad, "I'll kill you." Why yes! wasn't old Bill Smathers the chief of police at the time standin' right there on the steps of the City Hall and saw the whole thing? and he hollered right out to your papa, "Yes, and if I'm here when he does come back, Mr. Gant, I'll help you to do it," he says; says, "you did exactly the right thing," says, "the only pity is you didn't kill him now."

When your papa came home and told me about it, I said, "Yes, and he was *exactly right!* You should have finished the job then and there. That's exactly what you should have done. It would have been good riddance," I said, you know, I reckon I was pretty bitter, to think of it—here we were with six childern to support and to think that he would go flingin' his money away on that miserable old toper: I could 'a' wrung his neck for being such a fool. "Now, you look a-here," I said. "Let this be a lesson to you: don't you ever let him have a penny again, and don't you go lendin' money out to any one without consultin' me first. You're a married man with a family of little childern to support, and your first duty is to them." Well, he promised, of course—he said he'd never do such a thing again, and I suppose I believed him.

Well, sir, it wasn't three days before he went off on a big spree, he came home roaring drunk, I remember they sent word to us from Ambrose Radiker's saloon that he was up there and that we'd better come and get him: of course, they said they couldn't do anything with him and they thought they'd better let us know. So I went myself. *Oh!* Lord! . . . Why, child! you never knew him till later when he was getting old and tired—I reckon you thought he was bad enough then, but child! child! You don't know, you don't know. You never *saw* him! . . . that nigger of Radiker's told me. . . . **You know, that** big old pock-marked yellow nigger that they had—*told me* that he could drink more licker than any *four* men he ever saw. . . . He *told me,* mind you, that he'd seen him stand right up at **the bar and drink two quart bottles of that old rye licker** without stoppin'. "Yes," I said to Ambrose Radiker, "and *you let him! You,*" I said, you know I looked him right in the eye when I said it and he looked pretty sheepish, I tell you he did! "Here you are," I said, "a man with a wife and childern of your own, and you've got no more pride nor honor than to take money out of the pocket of a man who needs it to support his family. Why, they ought to tar and feather a man like you and ride him out of town on a rail," I said. I reckon I was pretty bitter but that's just exactly the way I talked to him.

Well. . . . I reckon it stung him. He didn't say anything for a minute, but, I tell you what, his face was a study. . . . Oh! that mortified look, you know, looked as if he'd 'a' been glad if the earth had opened and swallered him up at that moment. Then, of course, he said: "Why, Eliza! *We* don't want his money! We don't need it that bad. Why, your good will would be worth more to me than that," he says. "There are plenty of people who will come in here and drink and behave themselves," he said. "You know we don't try to lure him on to get him to come in here. Why," he said, "I'd be the happiest man alive if Mr. Gant took a solemn oath never to touch another drop of licker as long as he lived—yes and lived up to it, too. Because he's one man," he says, "that ought never to touch a drop! If he'd take one drink and then go on," he said, "why, he'd be all right, but one drink's no more use to him than a drop in the eye," he says, that's just the way he put it, "he's got to drink up half a bottle before he even feels it and then," he says, oh, shaking his head, "I tell you what, he is a caution. It's just a problem to know what to do with him. You never know what he's going to do next," he says; says, "we've had some terrible times with him.

"Ah, you don't know," he says. "He can get the queerest notions in his head of any man *I* ever saw," he said, "you never know what's comin' next. Why, one night," he said, "he began to holler and rave about Lydia. Why," Ambrose says, "he swore that she'd come back from the grave to haunt him because of the life he'd led. 'There she is,' he hollers, 'there! . . . there! . . . Don't you see her?'—he kept a-pointin' round the room and then he said she was looking at him over my shoulder. 'Why, no,' I says, 'there's no one there, Will, you're just imaginin' all that.' 'Yes, she is,' he says, 'and damn you you're trying to shield her. Get out of the way, or I'll kill you,' he says, and with that he ups and throws a quart bottle half full of licker right at my head—why, it's a wonder," he says, "that it didn't kill me: I saw it comin'," he says, "an ducked my head just in the nick of time but it smashed up a whole row of glasses we had settin' back behind the bar, and then," says Ambrose, "he got down on his knees and began prayin' to her and saying, 'Oh, Lydia, Lydia, say that you forgive me, baby,' and then he started talking about her eyes— 'There! . . . there!' he says, 'they're glarin' at me—don't you see them?—Oh, God have mercy on me!' he hollers, 'she's come back from the grave to curse me!' It was enough to curdle your blood to hear him," Ambrose says. "Why, that nigger Dan of mine," he says, "was so scared that he lit right out of here: I didn't see hide nor hair of him for two days," he says, "you know how superstitious a nigger is," he says, "a thing like that would frighten the life out of him." "Why, of course," I says, "and let me tell you something: I'm not so sure it's nothin' but superstition, after all."

Well, he gave me a mighty funny look, I tell you what, he did, and he says, "Why, Eliza! Surely you don't think there was anything in all that?" "I wouldn't be so sure," I says. "I could tell you some mighty strange things, I could tell you of things I've seen myself," I said, "and I don't know how you're goin' to account for them unless there is, sure enough, as the saying goes, a voice beyond the grave." Well, his face was a study, I can tell you. In a moment he looked me straight in the eyes and said: "*Who* was Lydia? Did he ever know any one by that name?" "Yes," I said, "he did. That was before you knew him," I said. "Was it his other wife—the one that died?" he said. "That's who," I said. "Yes, that's exactly who it was. And he's got a lot to remember and be sorry for, too," I said. Well, I didn't say any more, I didn't tell him your papa had had two other wives, I didn't tell him that he had been married and divorced from one woman way down in the eastern part of the state before he married Lydia, of course, Lydia was the only one the folks at home knew about. I reckon I was too proud to let any one know about Maggie Efird, it was considered a disgrace in those days to have anything to do with a divorced man and as for a divorced *woman,* why, of course, she wasn't considered much better than a chippy. If I'd known about it before I married him I don't reckon I'd 'a' had anything more to do with him: I'd 'a' been too mortified at the thought of lowerin' myself in that way. But, of course, he didn't tell me! Law, no! I'd been married to him almost a year before I knew anything about it.

Of course, he told it then, he had to admit it.

Why, yes! didn't old Mrs. Mason—child! I've often thought of her, that poor old woman, to think what she went through! Here she was, of course, livin' with us about a year after we got married, just to see that he got settled once again and tryin' to restore peace in her own family: tryin' to bring John and Eller Beals together again—of course John and Lydia were her childern by her first marriage, she married a man named Beals the first time, says: "Oh, Eliza, I'll help you any way I can. He'll be all right now if she just keeps away from him. If I can just keep them apart now, if I can just persuade her to go back to John and lead a decent life, I'll consider that my work in life is finished. I'll be able to die in peace," she said, oh, cryin', you know. "You don't know, you don't know," she says, "what I've lived through."

And then she told the whole story, you know, how they came to know him first, how they met him that first time down there in Sidney when he came to their house to live. Of course, he'd just come South to live: here he was workin' for John Arthur as a stonecutter, doin' all that work there on the State Penitentiary and I reckon at first he didn't have many friends; of course, he was a Yankee, and it was back in Reconstruction Days, and the feeling was still bitter.

Why, yes! Didn't he tell it himself about how bitter he was against us when he came South from Baltimore. "But my comin' was an accident," he said, "I firmly intended to go west. That was my boyhood ambition, and I'd have gone if John Arthur hadn't written me and told me to come on, that there was work to do," but, oh! he considered us nothing but a set of damned rebels and hangin' too good for us. Why! didn't they want to try Lee and Jefferson Davis as traitors—of course, his oldest brother George had been killed at Gettysburg and here he was all up in arms against us, sir—until he saw it all—and then he changed right over and cursed the government for allowin' it—why the black legislatures—there in Sidney and at that time he helped John Arthur build the penitentiary at Columbus, South Carolina—oh! some of the *blackest* niggers you ever laid your eye on, drinkin' and carousin' and squanderin' the taxpayers' money, dressed in the finest broadcloth, with big cigars in their mouth, if you please, and their feet stuck up on fine mahogany desks, the nasty stinking things—why didn't we see it all in that picture, "The Birth of the Nation" based upon Tom Dixon's book, "Yes," your papa says, "and every bit of it is true. I saw worse things than that myself." But that's the way he came, all right.

Well, he came there to their house, and they took him in, you know, as a boarder, Lydia and old Mrs. Mason. Of course, the old woman said, she admitted it, says, "Well, we were glad to have him. We were livin' there all alone," she said, "and we needed a man around the house. We felt safer havin' him," she said. "And I tell you what," she said, "Will was certainly a good man to have about the house. I've never known his equal," she said. Well, of course, I had to admit it: you've got to give the devil his due—with all his wanderin' and goin' away, he was as good a family man as ever lived. Now, boy, I want to tell you: he could do anything about a house, he could repair and fix anything, he could make anything with his hands, and let me tell you, sir; when you went downstairs in the morning you always found a good fire burning in the range; now, you didn't have to *wait,* you didn't have to go pokin' around to get a fire. Now he liked to *eat,* and he always had a hot stove waitin' for you. Why, Lord! as I said to him, "The way you make a fire, no wonder. Why any one could make a fire the way you do," I said, "pourin' half a can of kerosene oil on it every time. Why, mercy, man!" I cried, "you'll burn us all up some day, as sure as you're born!"—child! child! that awful waste! that awful extravagance! Oh, roaring up the chimney till the whole house shook with it, you know.

Now, boy, here's another thing: we've got to be fair,

we've got to be just, and he wasn't *all the way* to blame!
It wasn't *all* his fault: of course, the old woman admitted
it, I said to her: "But Mrs. Mason, see here! You *must* have
known something about him before he came to your house
to live. Now, he'd been livin' right there in the same town
with you, and surely you must have heard about him and
Maggie Efird before he came to your house. Now, livin'
in a little town like that, I don't see how it could have been
otherwise. *You must have known!"* Well, she had to admit it then, said: "Yes, we knew about it." Said, "Of
course, the story was he had to marry her, her father and
brothers made him, and I reckon he hated her for it ever
after. I guess that's why they got the divorce," she said.

I looked her straight in the eye: "Now," I said, "knowing that, you let me marry him, *a divorced man,* without
sayin' a word! Now, why didn't you tell me about it?" I
said—of course, she'd never said a word about it, if I'd
waited for *her* to tell me I would never have found out.
Here it was, you know, months after we got married, and
it all came to light by accident. I was cleanin' out the bottom drawer of that old walnut bureau, lookin' for a place
to put his shirts, and there it was—a stack of old letters
and papers, you know, that he'd put away there, I reckon
meaning to destroy them. Well, I picked them up, I did-
n't intend to look at them, I was goin' to put them in the
stove and burn them up. "Now, he's left them there," I
said, "intendin' to destroy them," but I had a premonition
—I don't know what else you'd call it—it flashed over me
all of a sudden, I reckon some providence left them there
for me to read, here it was, the final papers of his divorce
from Maggie Efird, and I could see it, I could read it!
There it was! a-starin' me in the face.

Well, I waited for him to come home you know, I had
them in my hand, said: "Here are some old letters I came

across cleanin' out your bureau drawer today. Do you want them?" I didn't let on, you know, I just looked at him as innocent as you please. Well, his face was a study, I tell you what, it was. "Give me those papers," he said, and made a snatch for them. "Did you read them?" he said. I didn't say a word, I just looked at him. "Well," he said, and his face had a mighty sheepish look, I tell you what, it did, "I intended to tell you about it, but I was afraid you might not understand."

"Understand," I said, "why what is there to understand? It's all written down there as plain as the nose on your face: you are *a divorced man* and you never told me a thing about it. You let me marry you believin' you were a widower, that Lydia was the only woman you were ever married to. I understand *that* much all right!"

"Well," he said, "that first marriage was a great mistake. I was led into it against my better judgment," he said. "I didn't want to worry you by tellin' you about it," he said. "Now," I said, "I'm going to ask you: I want to know. What was the trouble? Why were you divorced?" "Why," he said, "the decree was granted on grounds of incompatibility. She refused to live with me as my wife. She was in love with another man," he said, "and married me just to spite him. But from the moment we were married she never had anything to do with me. We never lived together for a moment as man and wife." "*Who* got the divorce," I said, "you or her?" He spoke right up quick as a flash, "I did," he said. "The decree was granted in my favor."

Well, I didn't let-on, I didn't say a word, but I knew, I *knew,* that he was lying. I had read that paper from beginning to end and the divorce had been given to *her.* Maggie Efird got the divorce, all right: I saw *that* much with my own eyes! But I didn't say anything, I just let him go on, "And you mean to say that she never lived with you as your wife?" I said.

"Not for a minute," he said, "I swear it."

Well, it was too much; that story was too fishy—here they told it on her, you know, old Mrs. Mason told me, that she was a good-lookin' girl, a high-stepper with lots of beaux before she married him, and, of course, they said that was the trouble—he *had* to marry her. I looked at him, you know, and shook my head: "No, sir," I said, "I don't believe you. There's something mighty queer about this somewhere. That story just won't wash. Now, you can't tell me that you lived with that woman eighteen months and never had anything to do with her. Now, I know *you,*" I said—you know I looked him straight in the eye—"I know *you,* and I know you couldn't have kept away from her. You'd 'a' got at her somehow," I said, "if you had to bore a hole through the wall!" Well, it was too much for him; he couldn't face me, he had to look away, you know, with a sort of sheepish grin.

"Well, now," I said, "what are you going to do with these old papers? Now, surely you don't want them any more," I said. "They're no use to you that I can see." "No," he said, "I hate the sight of them. They're a curse and a care and I never want to look at them again. I'm going to burn them up."

"Yes," I said, "that's what I think, all they do is bring up memories you ought to try to forget. You ought to destroy them."

"That's what I'll do," he said. "By God, I will!"

"But still" (I said)—as I was goin' on to say, you know, I said to the old woman, Mrs. Mason—"but still, you must have known all about him when he came there to your house to live. Now, Mrs. Mason, you must have known he'd been married to Maggie Efird and divorced from her. Surely, you must have known that," I said.

"Well, yes," she said, "I guess we did"—admitted it, you know.

"Well, now, I'm going to tell you how it was," she said —and then, of course, she told the story: it all came out. Now, boy, I want to tell you: I want to show you that it wasn't *all* your daddy's fault.

Now, I'm not sayin' a word against Lydia—of course, I knew *her* before I did *him,* when they first came there to live and she opened up a little millinery shop there on that corner of Academy street where the Greenwood Hotel now stands. I reckon the first real "store" hat I ever owned I bought from her out of my savin's as a school-teacher that time I taught all winter way back there in Yancey county. I got paid twenty dollars a month and my board and room and let me tell you something: I considered myself *rich.* Why, Lord, yes! didn't I save up enough out of it to make the first payment on the first piece of property I ever owned, that corner lot there on the south side of the square where your daddy built his shop after we got married, that's exactly where it was, sir, why, yes, wasn't I only twenty-two years old at that time I bought it, and Lord! I thought I'd done something *big,* you know! Here I was a property-owner and a taxpayer like Cap'n Bob Patton and old General Alexander, and all the rest of 'em (child, child! we were so poor, we'd gone through so much hardship since the war that I reckon that's what led me on, I reckon that's what got me into it: I was determined to own something of my own); why, yes: don't I remember how I ran all the way to town the day I got my first tax-statement, $1.83, that's all in the world it was then, and the money just a-burning a hole in my pocket! Lord! what a goose I must have been! afraid they'd try to take it away from me and sell me out under the sheriff's hammer before I got there.

Well, then, as I say, I got to know Lydia before I got to know your daddy. Here she was, you know, runnin' this little millinery store there on that northeast corner, and, as I say, the first "store" hat I ever owned I got from her. That's where it was, all right. Now, boy, I'm not saying a word against Lydia: for all I know she was a good, honest, hard-working woman and till she met your daddy she was all right. Of course, she was more than ten years older than he was, and that's exactly what the trouble was, that's where the shoe pinched, all right, that was the rub. Now your daddy was not *all the way* to blame: when he came there to their house to live he was only a young man in his early twenties and Lydia was thirty-six years old. Now, if it had been some young girl he led astray you could blame him more, but you can say what you please, Lydia was old enough to know better. Of course, he was a strong fine-lookin' man and all the women were right out after him, but she should have known, a woman that age should have had too much pride and self-respect—why I'd 'a' died before I did a thing like that!—to have follered and thrown herself at him the way *she* did! Why, of course! Didn't old Mrs. Mason admit it? Didn't she *tell* me? "Oh, Lydia!" she said, "Lydia!" shakin' her head, you know. "She went clean out of her head about him."

Here she'd been a decent respectable woman all her life, runnin' a little millinery shop down there, you know, and well thought of by every one in town—and, of course, I reckon, considered sort of an old maid, and to think she'd go and behave herself like that. "Oh, it was awful," the old woman said; says, "She never gave him a moment's peace, she kept after him all the time," and, of course, that's just what happened. You know your daddy; as the sayin' goes, he didn't stop to say his prayers when there was a woman around. It was the same old story: within a year's time he'd gone and got himelf all mixed up again, that woman was goin' to have a child and sayin' he'd ruined her and would have to marry her.

Well, he didn't know what to do. Told me himself, you know, admitted it, said: "I didn't want to marry her. I wasn't in love with her," he said. Well, he studied it all over and at last he decided to send her to Washington to see a doctor. So he wrote to Gil: of course Gil and your Aunt Mary were livin' there at the time—that was before Gil had follered him down South. Gil was workin' there in Washington as a plasterer, and they were brothers and he knew he could depend on him.

She went, he sent her, and I don't know just what happened, Gil never said and I didn't like to ask, but I guess it came before its time: they were riding in the day coach of a train comin' South again, some little town down there in the eastern part of the State, the conductor stopped the train and helped Gil carry her out into the station, and the next day she got up again and went on home. Now, give her her due, that woman had lots of grit: I reckon that's the way it was, all right.

Well, of course, the whole thing got found out. The story got known and your daddy had to marry her. And, I reckon, the feeling against him in the town was pretty bitter: here he was, you see, a Yankee, as the sayin' went, a damn Yankee, who'd come down there and ruined *two* of their women; of course, if there'd only been *one* it might have been different, but I reckon *two* of them was more than they could stomach. It got too hot for him; he had to leave. That was the time he decided to come to Altamont: of course Lydia had consumption and he thought the mountain air might do her good and I reckon he was afraid he had it, too—he'd been livin' with her and I guess he thought he had contracted it from her. When I first saw him he looked like a dead man, oh! as thin as a rail and that saller complexion, you know, from all the trouble and the worry he'd been through, I reckon. Well, then, Lydia sold out her stock—what little that she had—and closed her shop, and he sent her on ahead with old Mrs. Mason. Your daddy stayed behind down there a little bit, tryin' to close out what stock he had left in his marble yard, and to get what money he could, and then he came on, too, and that's how I came to know them first: when she was running that millinery shop on the corner there and he'd set up business in an old shack on the east side of the square. That's when it was, all right.

Now, boy, I was going on to tell you about that woman, Eller Beals. Up to this time, mind you, up to the time he moved up there from Sidney, she'd never had a thing to do with him. Of course, she had known him down there —she was the wife, you know, of Lydia's brother, John— but Law! they were too *fine,* you know, too *fine,* to have anything to do with your daddy, a common stone cutter who'd gone and disgraced the family like he had. Oh, they stormed and carried on about it, you know, when he got Lydia into this trouble. They wouldn't speak to him or have anything to do with him: he told me they hated the sight of him and that he hated them. And here within six months she had no more pride than to foller them all up there. Of course, she came because she had to come, I reckon: this John Beals was a shiftless good-for-nothin' sort of feller, and he couldn't support her, so she wrote Lydia and old Mrs. Mason and they told her to come on. Your daddy didn't know she was coming: they were afraid to tell him, and they thought they'd let her come and win him over afterwards. And that's just what happened: he came home one day to dinner and there she was—oh! the fine lady, if you please, all primped and powdered up and dressed to kill—that was the first he knew about it. Well, I guess it brought back bitter memories: he hated her so much he wouldn't speak to her, he picked up his hat and started to leave the house again, but she came up to him —oh, with her fine bonnet and the Langtry bang, and all: that was the way she fixed her hair, and put her arms around him, saying in that sugary voice: "Aren't you going to kiss me, Will?"— Oh! (as I said later) to think of it! the villain! he should have wrung her neck for her then and there, it'd been a good riddance! Says, "Can't we be friends, Will?"—after the way she'd acted, if you please— honeying up to him and takin' him in right there before his own wife and his wife's mother. "Can't we let bygones be bygones?" she says, getting him to kiss her, and all— "Why it served you right," I said, "for being such a fool! A man with no better sense than that deserves anything that happens to him!" And he agreed, admitted it, you know: "You're right," he said. So that's the way she came to be there with him.

This Eller Beals was a little dark black-and-white sort of a woman: she had this white skin, and hair as black as a raven's and coal-black eyes. She had this easy sugary sleepy way of talkin', all soft and drawly—like she'd just waked up out of a good long sleep. I could a-told him the first time I laid eyes on her that she was no good: she was a bad egg if ever I saw one, a charmer out to get the men and lead them on, you know, and bleed them out of everything they owned. Of course, she was a good-looking woman, there's no denying that, she had a good figger and this creamy-white complexion without a blemish on it. "Why, yes," I said to him later when he'd begin to brag about how pretty she was to look at. "Why, yes, I reckon so, that's true, but then," I said, "a whole lot of us could be pretty if we never lifted a finger to do a lick of work. Some of the rest of us could look real nice," I said, "if we didn't have to cook and wash and bring up childern." Well, he admitted it then, of course, said, "Yes, you're right."

And, here, to think of it! this villain misbehaving herself with him right under his wife's nose, sitting there primping herself and fixin' herself up pretty to entice him day after day, just livin' for him to come home and Lydia dying in that room upstairs, coughing her lungs out with every breath she took, and knowing about it all. Why, didn't he admit it! didn't he tell himself how Lydia said to him—of course, the poor thing knew that she was dying, says, "Will, I'm sick. I know I'm no good for you any more. I know I haven't got long to live and, Will," she said, "you can go where you like. You can do as you please," says, "I don't care, I'm dying, but Will," and then he told it how she looked him in the eye, "there's one thing I can't stand. In my *own* house! My *own* house!" Says, "Will, *you've got to leave my brother's wife alone!*" —Oh! he told it, admitted it, you know, says: "Ah, Lord! It's a crime upon my soul. I reckon if there's a just God in heaven I'll be punished for it."—And that poor old woman doing all the work, cooking and drudging for them all, with this little powdered-up trollop, that's all in the world she was, laying up waitin' for him and never liftin' a hand to help, why, they should have tarred and feathered her.

Well, as I say, when Lydia died, Eller kept right on livin' there: she wouldn't budge. And, of course, by that time he had lost his head about her, he was infatuated, you know, and he wanted her to stay. And that was the time John Beals came up to visit her, and I reckon he sized the situation up, he saw the way things were, and I suppose it went against the grain, it was a little more than he could stomach. Now, I always considered him a pretty poor sort of man: a man who would wink at a thing like that and let his wife run wild—but, give him his due, I reckon he had some spunk left in him, after all: he was out of work but he went down to Johnson City, Tennessee, and got him a job there as a hotel clerk. And then he wrote back for her, telling her to come on.

Well, she wouldn't go. She wrote him and told him she didn't love him and would never live with him again, said she was going to stay right where she was. Oh! she had it all fixed up in her mind, sir, she was going to get a divorce and marry your daddy—and him agreeing to it, if you please, like a moonstruck fool, just a-lavishin' gifts and money on her, with that poor old woman working like a nigger and weepin' and beggin' her to go on back to her husband where she belonged. But you couldn't reason with her, you couldn't budge her, oh! crazy in love with him, mind you, determined to have him.

Well, sir, John Beals wrote to her again, and this time he meant business, he'd reached the end of the rope. "Now you can make up your mind in a hurry what you're going to do," he said, "for I'm not going to put up with you any longer. You can decide now whether you're coming by yourself or whether I'm going to have to come and take you, but I want you to understand right now that if I have to come and take you from him, I'll come prepared, and I'm going to leave a damned dead Yankee behind me in the house when I do."

Well, she didn't answer him, and let me tell you, sir, he *came*: he got on a train and came to get her. And oh! old

Mrs. Mason said when she told me about it, shakin' and tremblin', you know. "Oh, I tell you, Eliza, it was awful. Here she'd locked herself in upstairs and wouldn't move, and here was John with a loaded pistol in his pocket, walkin' up and down the dining-room floor and saying, 'If she's not ready to go in half an hour I'll blow his brains out if it's the last thing I ever do,' and Will, pale as a ghost," the old woman said, "walkin' back and forth across the front porch, wringin' his hands, and her up there refusin' to go with John."

Well, they persuaded her somehow: I reckon she saw she'd have to go or there'd be bloodshed, and so she went along with him to Tennessee—but child! child! she hated it, she didn't want to go, she was bitter about it, she cursed them all. Well, that's the way it was, all right, before I married him.

And then, after we were married she kept on writing to him: the letters kept a-coming to him until finally I considered it my duty to write John Beals and inform him that his wife was misconductin' herself by writing letters to a married man, and that it was his business as her husband to stop her. Well, then, the letter came: she wrote him, you know, and I've never seen the like of it. She told him that I had written to her husband, she cursed him with every name she could think of, and she said: "If I had known you were going to marry her I'd have told her all I know about you, and you can be certain, no woman would have you if I told her all I know. Now she can have you and welcome to you; for no matter how much I may have hated her, her punishment will be greater than anything I ever wished for her."

Well, he brought it home and flung it in my face: "There you are, damn you," he said. "That's your work. Now, I want to tell you that you're setting in her place

here at my table because she left me, for you can rest assured if she had never gone, you would not be here—
and I want you always to remember it!"

Child! Child—I reckon I was young and proud, and it
made me bitter to hear him talk that way. I got up and
went out onto the porch and I wanted to go out and leave
him then and there, but I was carrying my first baby
around inside me, and it had rained and I could smell
the flowers, the roses, and the lilies, and the honeysuckle
vines, and all of the grapes a-gettin' ripe, and it was growing dark, and I could hear the people talking on their
porches, and I had nowhere to go, I could not leave him,
and "Lord God!" I said. "What shall I do? What shall
I do?"

Well, then, of course, as I was tellin' you, he'd go up
there to Ambrose Radiker's saloon, and he'd get to drinkin' and Ambrose told it on him how he'd imagine he was
seeing Lydia again, and how she'd come back from the
grave to haunt him. "Yes," I said, "and maybe he's not
far wrong about it."

"And then," says Ambrose, "that's not all, that's not the
only thing. He came in here one time and accused Dan
here of being a Chinaman,"—of course, you remember that
big yellow nigger Dan with all those small-pox splotches,
and, of course, I reckon your daddy in his drunken way
just took the notion into his head that Dan was a Chinaman. "Why, yes," says Ambrose, "he accused Dan of being a Chinaman and said he'd been sent here by somebody
or other to kill him, and all such stuff as that. 'Damn
you!' he says, 'I know what you're here for and I'll make
an end of us both right now: God damn you!' he says,
that's just the way he talked, you know, 'I'll cut your
heart out,' he says, oh, laughin'," says Ambrose, "in a crazy

blood-curdlin' manner, and then," he says, "he grabbed
up a carving knife off the lunch counter and started
round the bar to get the nigger. Why, it was awful!" he
says. "It almost scared the poor darkey to death," he says;
says, "Dan hadn't done anything to him," he says, "you
know, Dan never done no harm to any one. Well, we had
to do something, so we got the knife away from him, and
then," he says, "I tried to reason with him. 'Why, Will,'
I said, 'what have you got against Dan? Dan never did
no harm to you,' I said.

"So he says, 'He's a Chinaman and I hate the sight of
him'—oh, you know, he was crazy, you couldn't reason
with him at all. 'Why, no, he's not,' I said. 'Now, Will,
you know better than that,' I said. 'You've been comin''
in here for years,' I said, 'and you know Dan, and you
certainly know by now that he's no Chinaman,' I said.

" 'Why, no, sah, Mistah Gant,' says Dan, you know
nigger-like, he wanted to have *his* say, 'why you know
me,' he says, 'and you know I ain't no Chinaman.'

" 'Yes, he is,' he says, 'and by God I'm going to kill him.'

" 'Why, Will,' I says, 'he's not any Chinaman, and besides,' I said, 'even if he was, that wouldn't be any reason
for you wanting to kill him. Now, just use your reason
a little about this,' I said. 'A Chinaman's a man like any
one else,' I said. 'There's one thing sure, they were put
here for some purpose,' I said, 'like every one else, or they
wouldn't be here. Now it wouldn't be right to go and kill
a man that never did you any harm,' I said, 'just because
you think he's a Chinaman, would it?'

" 'Yes, by God,' he said, 'for they're a set of fiends out
of hell, they have drunk my heart's blood and now they
sit there gloatin' upon my death-rattle,' he said.

"And that's not the *only* time either," said Ambrose
Radiker, "that he's been that way." "What!" I said—of

course, you know, I didn't let on to Ambrose I knew anything about it at all—"do you mean he's carried on that
way before?" "Many's the time," he said, "I tell you what,
it's a mighty peculiar thing: there's something mighty
strange about it somewheres," he says. "He's got some
grievance against Chinamen, at some time or other he's
had trouble with them."

"No," I said, "you're wrong." I looked him straight in
the eye. "Not in *this* life," I said. "Why, what do you
mean?" he says, and, let me tell you, he gave me a mighty
queer look.

"I can't say no more," I said, "but there are things you
don't understand," I said. "Have *you* heard him talk like
that?" he said.

"Yes," I said. But I wouldn't tell him any more.

I could have told him, but I got to studying it all over
and "I thought I'd better not," I told your papa; says, "No,
I'm glad you didn't: you did right. I'm glad you said no
more." "But what is it, man? What's the reason for it?"
—I tried to reason with him about it—child, child, he always had it, that awful hatred, that bitterness—"now see
here, Mr. Gant, surely you must have some reason that
you should feel that way against them. People don't feel
that way without some cause: did one of them ever do you
an injury? Did you ever know one of them?" He shook
his head, says, "No. I never knew one in my life, but I've
always hated the sight of them since the first time I ever
saw one in my boyhood days in the streets of Baltimore.
The first thing that I saw when I came out of the ferry
house at San Francisco was a Chinaman—that awful yellow skin," he said, "and I hated the place from that time
on! But I don't know what the reason is—by God, I don't!
It's a pretty strange thing when you come to think of it—

unless," he said, and he looked at me, "I may have known them, as the saying goes, in some former life, some different reincarnation." I looked him straight in the eye: *"Yes,"* I said, "that's what I think it was, you've hit the nail on the head, all right. That's exactly what it was, it never came out of *this* world," and he looked at me, and let me tell you, sir, his face was a study.

And yes! why long years after that, you know, at the time of that Boxer Rebellion, didn't he come home one day all excited with the news! "It's come at last," he said, "as I predicted long ago: the pitcher went to the well once too often. They've declared war on China, and I'm going to enlist, by God, I will!" Oh! all up in arms against them, sir, and wantin' to leave everything, his family and business, to go out there and fight them. "No, sir, you will not!" I said. "You're a married man with a family of little childern to support and you're not going. If they need troops you let the others volunteer: your place is here. Besides," I said, "they wouldn't take you noway: they wouldn't have you, you're too old. They want the young men."

Well, I reckon it stung him, callin' him an old man like that: he flared right up, says, "I'm a better man than nine-tenths of them this minute, for we are livin' in a degenerate age, and if you think I'm not the equal of these nonentities an' nincompoops you see hangin' around the pool-rooms with a cigarette stuck out of the corner of their mouths, the miserable degenerates that they are, then God help you, woman, for the truth is not in you and you are like the bird that fouls its own nest!" Says, "I can do more work right now than any four of them!"

Well, when he put it that way I had to admit he was tellin' the truth: of course, your papa was an awful strong man. Why, Lord! haven't I heard them tell it on him how they'd go back there in his shop and find him liftin' up

one end of an eight hundred pound stone like it was nothin' with two big black niggers sweatin' and strainin' at the
other end of it that they could hardly budge, and "Yes,"
I said to Wade Eliot that first time that we took him up
to Hopkins, "I'll give you *my* theory now. I'll tell you what
my diagnosis is,"—and then, of course I told him, "now
my opinion is he helped to bring this trouble on by just
such things as that,"—("Why, what on earth do you mean,
Mr. Gant, by doin' such a thing! You're apt to strain
and rupture yourself first thing you know: let the niggers
do that kind of work, that's what you're paying them for."
"Why, Lord!" he said, "you know I couldn't do a thing
like that: if I depended on those niggers I'd never get anything done!") "But that was it, all right," I said to Doctor
Eliot. "He was hastenin' his own end by just such stuff as
that." "Yes," he said, "I agree with you, I think you're
right. That's it exactly," he said—"But *you*," I said, "you
have your family to consider, and *you're not goin'*." I put
my foot right down, you know, and then, of course, he
admitted I was right, he gave in, but *oh!*—child, child,
you don't know what it was like—California, China, anywheres! He'd have been up and gone if I'd a-let him: a
strange man.

Lord God! I never saw a man like that for wanderin'.
I'll vow! a rollin' stone, a wanderer—that's all he'd a-been,
oh! California, China, anywheres—forever wantin' to be
up and gone, who'd never have accumulated a stick of
property if I hadn't married him. Here Truman wrote to
him that time from California, this same Perfesser Truman, why, yes! the father-in-law of these two murderers
I'm telling you about (and how that night I got the warning, boy: "Two . . . Two—and Twenty . . . Twenty"),
Ed Mears and Lawrence Wayne, who married sisters, Tru-

man's daughters, why, yes!—but *oh!* the scholar and the gentleman, you know, no murderer to *him,* I can assure you—oh! too *fine,* too *fine,* oh! too *honorable,* you know: he wouldn't soil his hands with blood, always the finest broadcloth and the patent-leather shoes, wrote to him of course, to come on out there. Says, "The Lord has rained his blessings on this country with a prodigal hand,"—oh, the cultured gentleman with all that beautiful English and the flowery command of language, and all—says, "Come on out. This is the Wonderland of Nature, there's riches and abundance here beyond the dreams of avarice, and as yet," he says, "it's hardly been touched. If you come out now you'll be a rich man in fifteen years,"— he says—urgin' him to come, you know, says, "Sell out now. Sell everything you got and come on out." "Hm!" I says, "he's mighty anxious to get you out there, isn't he?" "Yes," says your daddy, "a new country and by God I'll do it." Then, worried-like, "What do you mean?" he says.

I didn't tell him: I just looked at him, I didn't speak. I just said, "Says come on out? And what about your wife and childern? What's to become of them?" I said. Says, "Oh, that part's all right," your papa said. "Says bring them with you, 'Sell out at once, bring Eliza and the childern with you,' your papa said. "That's what he said, all right." "I *thought* so! That's what I *thought,*" I said. "What do you mean?" he said. I looked at him. I didn't tell him.

I could have told him but I didn't want to worry him. Child! I didn't tell him but I *knew,* I *knew*—that man— now boy, I want to tell you—"I've come to say good-bye," he says—and let me tell you, boy, his face was a study— why! "Oh, we're sorry to see you go!" I said, "we'll miss you." "Yes," he said, and he looked me straight in the eye —oh! that *look,* you know, "and I'll miss *you!*" He looked straight at me when he said it. "Well, now," I said, you know I thought I'd turn it off, "we'll miss you too, both Mr. Gant and I—we'll both miss you. Now," I said, you know I thought I'd jolly him along to cheer him up, "when you get out there, I hope you won't forget us. I hope you'll write us. Why, yes," I said, "if it's the wonderful place they say it is, if you can pick gold up right off the streets *I'd* like to know about it, too," I said. "Why, yes, if that's the sort of place it is, I'd like to live there too—we might pack right up and come on out," I said. "Well, now," he said, "I wish you would, there's nothin' I'd like better," and I could see, child, I could tell—why, yes! now—long years after when your papa made that trip out there. (Now, boy, that was a wild goose chase—what did he do *that* for? Why did he go out there? Why did he waste that money?) "Oh," I said, "did you see Perfesser Truman?" the first question that I asked him, you know. "Yes," he says, "I saw him," and his face was a study, I can tell you. "Well, how is he? what's he doin'?" Of course I wanted to find out, you know. I wanted to hear the news. "Say," your papa says, "what about it?" and his face was a study. "You know he did nothin' but talk about you all the time I was there. Why," he says, "I believe the damned old fool was in love with you, by God I do." Well, I didn't say anything, I didn't want to worry him, but child, I had seen it in his eyes and I *knew, I knew!*

I'll vow! I never saw such a man for wantin' to wander around. Pshaw! I reckon maybe old Amanda Stevens was right about them. That's what she said, you know; of course, they told it on her when all her sons went off to the Civil War—she had eight, and every last one of them went to war, sir! And, of course, all of the people were comin' around to congratulate her for sendin' them, sayin' how proud she must be, and so on. "Send nothing!" she said. "They all lit out of here in the middle of the night without sayin' a word to me about it. If I had my way I'd bring every last one of them back here where they belong, helpin' me to run this place!" "Yes," they said, "but aren't you proud of them?" they said. "Proud?" she says, "why, Lord God"—of course, you know, Amanda had an awful rough way of talkin'—"what's there to be proud of? They're all alike! I never saw a man yet that could stay where he was five minutes. Why!" she says, "all of them act as if their tails were full of turpentine," she said. Of course she was bitter to think they should all light out that way to leave her alone to run the farm without tellin' her about it.

But, I tell you what, that was *certainly* a remarkable woman; lived to be eighty-seven and hale and hearty, sir, right up to the end. Yes! and would go anywheres, you know, in the dead of winter to help out any one that was sick, and all! Of course, they told it on her at the time—whew-w! what about it?—I remember sayin', "Oh, surely she didn't say a thing like that! you must be mistaken," I said—to think that a woman would talk that way to her own daughter—"if that don't beat all!" I said: why, they told it, you know, how her daughter Clarissy that married John Burgin, this same John Burgin I've been tellin' you about all along, boy, your own distant cousin on my mother's side of the house that Ed Mears killed, as I said to your papa at the time when he came home that day tellin' me what Melvin Porter had said, I said to him: "Let them hang! they killed that man in cold-blood," I said, "a good upright man with a family of little childern that never did any harm to any one," I said, "as wicked and cold-blooded a murder as I ever heard of, and hangin's too good for them," I said. Why, they told it of course how Clarissy's first baby came seven months after she was married. Well, it was all right, of course, nobody was blamin' the girl, it never entered their minds that she had done anything wrong, but she began to scream and holler like she'd lost her mind.

"Well," the doctor says, "the baby's all right, there's nothing wrong with the baby, but if something isn't done to stop that girl from cryin' this child won't have any mother before long."

"Well, I'll stop her," Amanda says, "or know the reason why," so she marches right into the bedroom and sits right down beside the girl: "Now you look a-here," she said, "there's nothing wrong with you and I'm not going to put up with your foolishness any longer." "Oh," the girl says, "I shall die of shame! I'll never be able to hold my head up again!"—weepin' and goin' on, you know. "Why, what's the matter?" Amanda says, "what have you done," she says, "that you should feel like that?" "Oh," the girl says, "I haven't done anything but my baby came before its time!" "Why, Lord God!" the old woman says—she came right out coarse with it, you know—"is that all that's troublin' you? I thought you had more sense than to let a thing like that bother you," she said. "Oh," the girl said, "they'll all be sayin' now that I misbehaved myself before I married John!" "Why, Lord God, let them say it, then," Amanda said, "what if they do? Tell 'em your ass is your own and you can do as you please with it!" That's exactly what she said, you know, and of course they told it on her. I know when I told your papa about it, he said, "Lord! you know she didn't say a thing like that!" But that's the story that they told.

Well, I said to him, "You're *not* going." I put my foot down, you know, and when he saw I meant it, he had to give in, of course. But as I say he always had it in him, that desire to go off somewheres, California, China—why, yes, say! what about it, as long as he lived he never got over that feeling he had against them. That time, you know, long after—why yes! you must remember, you were right there with us—no, I guess that's so. You must have been away at college. That was the year before the war ended, and we all went up there with him—Luke and Ben—I tell you what, I've often thought of it, that poor child: here we were all lookin' for Mr. Gant to die at any minute, when he had five more years to live, and *Ben* —*Ben* was the one! We never *thought,* we never *dreamed* that *he* would be the one, would be dead and buried in the grave within a year! And to think that your daddy would behave as he did—here he was, you know, eaten up with that awful cancer—Lord! how he ever did it! with that rotten old thing consumin' him, sending out its roots, you know, all through his blood.

Wade Eliot said to me, "I don't know what's holdin' him up," he says, "I never thought I'd see him again when he went away the last time," he says; says, "it is certainly a remarkable case," he says; says, "in all my life," he says, "I've never seen the beat of it." "Well," I says, "you must have some opinion," I says. "A great doctor like you who has operated on thousands of people must know all the signs and symptoms," I says—of course, you know, I wanted to draw him out and get him to tell me what *his* theory was. "Now," I said, "surely you've some sort of notion about it, Doctor Eliot, and if you have," I said, *"I want to know!* His family has a right to know," I said, "and I want to *know the worst.* How much longer has he got to live?" I said. I looked him square in the eye.

Well, sir, he just threw back his head and laughed.

"Live!" he says, "why, probably, till both you and I are
in our graves," he said—and, let me tell you, he didn't
miss it much! That man, here he was a fine-looking man
in the prime of life, why he'd be the last one any one
would expect to go, the doctor they called in for Wood-
row Wilson, and all. . . . Said he'd saved thousands of
lives, and here when his time comes he couldn't save his
own! They did everything on earth they could to save him
—as the sayin' goes, I reckon they exhausted all the resources of medical science but to no avail!—was dead and
in his grave, sir, within two years after your papa died.
I remember sayin' to McGuire when I read the news,
"Well, it only goes to show," I said, "that when your
time comes there is nothing that can save you. . . . I
don't know what you'd call it," I said, "but there is some
higher power, as sure as you're born, and when it calls
us," I said, "we've got to go, doctors and all." "Yes," he
said, "you are exactly right. There's something there,"
he said, "that we know nothing of"—and here he had
only a year longer to live himself, drinkin' himself to
death, you know, just grievin' over the way that woman
had acted. Of course, that nigger at the hospital told Luke
he'd come in there late at night so drunk he'd have to get
down on all-fours an' crawl upstairs like some big old
bear when he had to operate the first thing in the morning, said he'd get him to put him in a tub of cold water
with chunks of ice in it, said he'd seen him that way
many a time and put him to bed.

"Well," says Eliot, "I don't pretend to know anything
about it any more. I don't know what is keepin' him
alive," he says, "but there he is, and I don't want to make
any more predictions. He's not a man," he says, "he's four
men, and right now," he says, "he's got more real vitality
than the rest of us put together"—and of course, it was

true: right up to the end he could eat a meal that would put most people in the grave, two dozen raw oysters, a whole fried chicken, an apple pie, and two or three pots of coffee, sir. Why I've seen him do it time and again! with all sorts of vegetables, corn on the cob and sweet per-taters, string beans and spinach and all such as that. Of course, Eliot was honest about it: he came right out and admitted he couldn't say. "Now here," he said, "I want you to look after him until he enters the hospital. I want him to be ready for us when he comes in here," he said, "and you see to it that he behaves himself." "Well," I said, "I think he is going to be all right. He has promised, you know, and of course we are all going to do our best. Now," I said, "what can he eat? Do we have to put him on a diet? Can he have some oysters?" I said. Well, he laughed, you know, says, "Look here, I'd call that a pretty strange diet to put a sick man on." "Well," I said, "you know he's been lookin' forward to it. He's always loved oysters," I said, "he's always remembered how he could eat them by the dozen on the half shell in his boyhood here. He's looked forward to it so much," I said, "that I hate to disappoint him." "Oh, all right," Wade Eliot says, laughin', you know, "let him have them then. You couldn't kill him noway," he said, "but look a-here!" he said, and he looked me square in the eye, "I'm not worryin' about what he eats so much as what he drinks. Now," he says, "you keep him sober. I don't want to have to get him over a drunk when he gets in here," he says. "You put the fear of God into him," he says, "I know you, and you can do it. Now, you tell him," he said, "that if he goes off on another big spree he'll never live to get home. Tell him I said so."

Well, I told him what Wade Eliot had said. "You can have the oysters," I said, "he said that would be all right, but he says you're not to touch a drop of anything to drink,

or they may have to send you home in a box." "Why,
Lord! Mrs. Gant," your papa said, "you know I wouldn't
do a thing like that in my condition. If any one offered
me a drink I'd throw it out the window. Why, the very
sight of the stuff makes me sick at my stomach!" Well,
he promised, of course, and I reckon we all believed him.

Well, sir, it wasn't twenty-four hours before he went off
on a big spree and came home at two o'clock in the morning roaring drunk—I tell you what, I certainly felt sorry
for that woman. Why! here we were all stayin' there just
across from the hospital at Mrs. Barrett's, a good religious
woman, you know, a big churchgoer, and all, with her
livin' to make and that grown-up daughter to support
whose husband ran off with some other woman—and here
he comes in the dead of night howlin' and hollerin' that
it was nothing but a bawdy house that he was in and to
bring on the women. Why, of course, you might know he
waked the whole house up, they all got up to see what the
trouble was, and she knocked at the door tremblin', in her
night-gown and wringin' her hands. "Oh, Mrs. Gant,"
she says, "you'll have to get that man quiet or he'll ruin
me," she says; "get him out of here," she says, "I've never
had anything like that in *my* house before," she says, "and
if it gets out I'm disgraced"—and her childern, you know,
those two little boys she had, she sent them out on the roof
and there they were perchin' up there like monkeys, and
all of the people whisperin' together in the halls. Ben was
so mortified and bitter to think he would behave himself
like that. "By God," he said, "it'd serve him right if he
did die. After the way he's acted I wouldn't care."
Well, I got hold of the bottle, I found a bottle of licker
about a third full in one of his pockets, and pretty soon
he began beggin' for a drink: "No, sir," I said. "Not an-

other drop! Now you listen to me," I said. "You're a sick man: if you keep this up you'll never get home alive," I said. Well, he said he didn't care. "I'd as soon get it over with now," he says, "as go through all the torment and the agony." Well, he kept yelling for a drink, but we wouldn't let him have it—I took it and poured it out, any-way—and at last he got off to sleep. Then I took his clothes and locked them up in my trunk so he couldn't get out again.

We let him sleep it off. He slept right through until ten o'clock next morning and when he woke up he seemed to be all right, he wouldn't eat any breakfast, said it would make him sick, but I got him to drink some good hot coffee Mrs. Barrett brought up to him. She was certainly a kind, good-hearted Christian woman and your papa told her he was sorry for the way he had acted. Well, we tried to get him to get up and come with us then, none of us had had any breakfast, and we were going down the street to a lunchroom. "No," he said, "I don't feel like getting up, you go on: I want you to go on and get something to eat," he said.

Well, I knew he didn't have any more licker because I'd poured it out, and I knew he couldn't go out for any because his clothes were all locked up, so I thought it'd be all right if we left him alone for a little. Well, we went out and ate and we couldn't have been gone more than an hour, but when we came back he'd been drinkin' again, layin' up in the bed, you know, crazy-like, singin' a song to himself. "Why, Mama," Ben says, "I thought you told us you took his licker away from him and poured it out." "Why, I did," I said. "Well, he must have had another bottle that you didn't find," he said. "There's one thing sure, he's had plenty since we left him." "Well, now," I said, "if he's had anything to drink he's got it while we were away. It wasn't there in his room when we left," I said, "because I searched that place from top to bottom with a fine-tooth comb and you can just bet your bottom dollar there was no licker there." "Well, he's getting it from some one," Ben said, "and I'm going to find out who it is that's giving it to him. Let's ask Mrs. Barrett if any one has been here to see him." "Why, yes," I said, "that's the very thing.'"

So we all trooped downstairs and asked her if any one had been there for him. "No," she said, "no one has set foot in this house since you left it," she said, "I was on the look-out for just such a thing to happen," she said, "and if any one had been here I'd have known it." "Now there's something mighty strange about this somewheres," I said, "and I mean to get to the bottom of it. You childern come on," I said to Luke and Ben, "we're going to find out where this mystery is or know the reason why."

Well, when we got back upstairs to his room there he was, you know—and you could see it, you could tell it— he'd had something else to drink since we'd been downstairs. He was drunk as a lord. I marched right up to him: "Look a-here," I said, "you've been getting licker somewheres and I want to know who's been giving it to you." "Why, who-o? Me?" he says, in that drunken voice, "why, baby," he says, "you know me, I wouldn't touch a drop," he says—trying to hug and kiss me, you know, and all that. Well, we looked again, the childern and I, we searched that place high and low, but it was no use—there was certainly nothing there, or we'd 'a' found it.

Well, I got to studyin' about it, and it flashed over me all of a sudden—I don't know why I'd never thought of it before—"Come on, childern," I said to the boys, winkin' at them, you know; "come on, we'll go downtown and

see the sights. Mr. Gant, we'll be back in an hour or
so," I said, "you be ready when we come," I said. "We're
going to take you to the hospital at three o'clock."

Well, that just suited him, that was just what he wanted,
he said, "Yes, go on,"—of course he wanted to be left alone
so he could get more to drink. Well, we left him, we went
right down the hall to my room and I took the childern
in there and closed the door, easy-like, behind me. "Why,
Mama," Luke says, "what are you talking about? We can't
go off downtown and leave him alone like this while he's
drinking. No," he says, "he's been getting it somewhere
and I'm going to see to it that he gets no more if I have
to sit there and watch him," he says. "No," I said, "you
wait." "Why," he says, "what do you mean?" "Why,
don't you see?" I said—pshaw! I was so mad to think I
hadn't thought of it before, that miserable old toper Gus
Tolly from Seneca, South Carolina, that used to stop at
our house—here, he had the room right next to your papa
and was waitin' to be admitted over at Hopkins with the
same trouble your papa had, and here the two of them
were layin' up together a-swillin' it down as hard as they
could—"it's that rotten old Gus Tolly," I said, "who's been
lettin' him have it." "Why, damn him," says Luke, "I'll go
wring his neck for him," and he starts for the door. "No,
you don't," I said, "you wait a minute. I'll fix him."

Well, we waited, and sure enough, it wasn't five minutes before your papa's door opened easy-like and he came
creeping out into the hall, and then we heard him knock-
in' at Gus Tolly's door. Well, we heard Gus Tolly say,
"Have they gone yet?" and we waited a moment longer
until we heard the door shut again, and then we started.
I marched right up and knocked and in a moment Gus
Tolly says, "Who's there?" "You open the door," I said,
"and you'll find out." Well, he opened it, and his face had

a mighty sheepish look, I tell you. "Why, Mrs. Gant,"
he says, "is that you? Why, I thought you'd all gone to
town," he says. "Well now, didn't you get fooled that
time?" I said. "Mr. Gant is in here," he says in that
mealy voice, stickin' his old red nose out that was all covered with warts like a pickle, "we were just having a little
talk together," he says. "Yes," I said, "and it looks to me
you've been havin' something else besides. If it's only talk,"
I said, "I'd call it mighty strong talk that gets on people's
breath and smells up the place till you can't bear to come
near them." Oh! you know, awful, that old rank odor of
rye licker, you could 'a' cut it with a knife. "Now," I says,
"I've been talkin' all my life and it never had no such effect
as that on me." "Yes," says Luke, "and I see you've got a
whole bottle of that talk right there on the table before
you."

Well, we marched right in on him then, and there he
was, sir, sitting right up at the table, if you please, with a
whole quart bottle of licker before him fixin' to pour himself out a drink. Well, I reckon if looks could kill we'd
have all been dead, for he gave us one of the blackest and
bitterest looks you ever saw, and then he began to curse
and rave. Well, I got hold of the bottle and then he began to beg me to give him just one drink. "No, sir," I
said, "you're going into that hospital, and what's more
you're going *now*. We're not going to wait a minute longer." Of course, I knew that was the only way to handle
him; I'd seen him too many times before, and I knew if
we didn't take him he'd get licker somehow if he had to
drill a tunnel to get to it. "Yes," said Luke, "you're going
now if I have to drag you over there, and Ben will help me
do it." "No," said Ben, "I'll just be damned if I do! I don't
want to have anything more to do with him. He can do
as he likes." "Well," said Luke, "if we let him stay here

he'll drink himself to death." "Well, I don't give a damn if he does," said Ben, "if that's what he wants to do let him go right ahead. Maybe the rest of us would get some peace then if he did. He's always had his own way," he said, "he's never thought of any one but himself and I don't care what happens to him. I was lookin' forward to this trip," he said, "I thought we might all get a chance to enjoy ourselves a little and here he's gone and disgraced us all and ruined it for us. Now you can look after him if you like, but I'm done." Of course, the child was bitter: he'd been lookin' forward to comin', he'd saved up the money for the trip and had a nice new suit of clothes made before we left home, and here to think your papa would act this way, of course it was a bitter disappointment to us all. We *thought,* you know, we'd get him in the hospital and then have a little time to look around and see things for ourselves but *Law!* the way *he'd* been actin' it would have taken a whole regiment of men to look after him.

Well, he didn't want to go, of course, but he saw we meant business and he'd have to, so he went along back to his room with Luke and I got his clothes out, and we dressed him. Well, I began packin' away a few things I thought he'd need in the hospital, some nightshirts, and his bathrobe and slippers and so forth, and then I saw he had no clean shirts: the one he had on was filthy, I was ashamed to let him go in that, and I knew he'd need some clean ones after he'd begun to sit up again. "Why, where on earth are your shirts?" I said, "what have you done with them? I know that I put in six, you couldn't have lost 'em," I said, "where are they?" "Oh, they've got 'em, they've got 'em," he said in that maudlin tone, beginning to rave and carry on, you know, said, "Let 'em have them! Fiends that they are, they have impoverished and ruined me, they have drunk my heartsblood, now they can take what's left." "Why, what are you talking about?" I said, "who do you mean?" "Why, Mama," Luke said, "it's those Chinamen that run that laundry down there. They've got his shirts," he said, "why I took them there myself," he said, "but *that* was a week ago," he said; said, "I thought he'd gone and got them by this time." "Well, we'll march right down there and get them now," I said, "he can't go to the hospital wearing that thing he's got on. We'd all be disgraced!"

Of course, that just suited him: he said, yes, go on, he'd be all ready when we came back—of course, he wanted to get rid of us so he could drink some more. I said, "No, sir, when we leave this house you're coming with us."

So we started out. He went on ahead with Luke, and Ben stayed behind to go with me. Of course, Ben was proud and he refused to help him. "I'll carry his valise and come along with Mama," he said, "but I won't be seen with him." "What's the matter?" Luke said, "he's your father as much as mine," he said, "you're not ashamed to be seen with him, are you?" "Yes, by God, I am!" said Ben—that was just the way he put it. "I don't want any one to think I know him," he said. "Now you needn't expect me to help you," he said, "I'm no damned nursemaid," says, "I've done all I intend to do."

Well, then, we went on down the street to this laundry; it was down there a block or two below the hospital on the corner in a little old brick building and, of course, when we got there we could see them, these two Chinamen inside, just a-ironing away for all they were worth. "Well, this must be it," I said. "Yes, this is it, all right," said Luke, "this is the place." So, we all went in, and this

Chinaman asked him, says, "What do you want?" "Why, God damn it," your papa says, "I want my shirt." "Well," the Chinaman says, "Tickee, tickee"—kept sayin' "tickee," you know. Well, of course, Mr. Gant had been drinkin' and he didn't understand him. He got excited, you know, says, "Tickee hell! I don't want any tickee. I want my shirt!" "Well, now, you wait," I said to your papa, "now don't you worry," I says, "*I'll* talk to him. If your shirts are here, I'll get them for you." Of course, I knew I could talk to the Chinaman and reason with him about it. "Now," I said to him, winkin', you know easy-like, "you tell *me* about it. What is it you want?" I says, "Why," he says, "tickee, tickee." Now, I thought to myself, the man's all right—I could see it, you know—he's tryin' to say something, he's tryin' to explain something to us with this tickee. "Now," I says, "do you mean you're not finished with them yet?" I thought, of course, he might not have them done—but no, I thought, that can't be, he's had a whole *week's* time to do them in. Surely, I thought, he's had time enough. "No," he said, "tickee, tickee," and then, of course, he began jabberin' to the other feller and then they both came and they both began to shout and holler at us in that awful outlandish tongue. "Well," your papa says, "I'll make an end of it all now, by God I will! Little did I reck," he says, "that it would come to this." "Now, Mr. Gant," I said, "you be quiet and I'll get to the bottom of this. If your shirts are here I'll get them." Well, these two Chinamen had been arguin' about it together and I reckon the other one had told him that we didn't understand because he got one of those slips of paper then that they used—as I said to Luke later, it looked exactly like it was covered by old hen tracks—and he pointed to it, you know, and said, "Tickee, tickee."

"Oh!" I cried—of course, I caught on then, it flashed over me all of a sudden, I don't know why I'd never thought of it before! "Why, of course!" I said, "he means *ticket,* that's what he's trying to say," "Yes," he says, beginning to smile and grin, you know, *he* understood that much all right, "tickee, tickee." "Why, yes," I said winkin' at him, "that's just it—tickee." Of course, I suppose, with your papa hollerin' and goin' on I'd got confused, and that was the reason I hadn't understood before. "Why, Mr. Gant," I said, "he says he gave you a laundry ticket and he wants to see it." "No, I haven't got any ticket," he says, "I want my shirt." "Why, surely, you've got a ticket," I said, "what have you done with it? Surely you haven't gone and lost it." "I never had one," he said, you know—drunken-like. "Why, yes, he has," Luke said, "I remember giving it to him now. What did you do with the laundry ticket I gave you?" he said, "where is it? Speak, speak!" he says, shakin' him—the child was excited and upset, you know, to think he'd go and do a thing like that. "Don't stand there mumbling like an idiot! God damn it, where's the ticket?" Well, sir, we searched his pockets, we went through everything he had, and there was no ticket to be found, it wasn't *there!* "Well, now," I said to the Chinaman, "Mr. Gant has mislaid that ticket somewheres but I tell you what you do: you just let us have his shirts anyway and as soon as I find the ticket I'll bring it to you myself"—you know, tryin' to humor him along. "Oh, *no!*" he says, he couldn't do anything like that, and he began to jabber away, I reckon tryin' to tell us he didn't know where the shirts were and couldn't let us have them noway until we brought the ticket. Well, sir, the trouble started then and there: your papa grabbed him by the neck and says, "God damn you, I'm goin' to kill you," hittin' at him over the counter, you know, says, "fiend that you are, you have impoverished and ruined me, you have hounded me to the gates of death," he said, "but I'll make an end of you now before I go," says, "I'll take you with me."

Well, Ben and Luke got hold of him and pulled him off, but the damage was done: the other feller had gone screamin' and hollerin' out the door and he came back now with a policeman. "What's the meaning of all this?" the policeman says, "what's going on here?" he says, sizin' us all up, you know. "They have robbed me," your papa says, "and now, fearful, awful and blood-thirsty fiends that they are, they stand there plottin' my destruction." Why, he'd 'a' ruined us all, if he'd gone on: Luke shook him, you know, says, "Now you be quiet or you'll land in jail. You've made trouble enough." "No, now, officer," I said to the policeman—of course, I knew I had to be diplomatic—"there's been a little misunderstanding, but everything's all right." "Why," he says, "what happened?" "We're takin' my husband here to the hospital," I said—of course, I thought I'd let him know your papa was a sick man—"and we just came by to get some shirts we left here to be laundered." "Why, what's the matter?" he says, "won't they let you have them?" "Well," I said, "it seems they gave Mr. Gant a laundry ticket and I reckon he's mislaid it. At least, we haven't been able to find it yet. But the shirts are here," I said, "they're bound to have them: my son here brought them himself a week ago."

Well, he began to eye Luke then, and I tell you what! That child certainly made a good appearance. Of course, he was all dressed up nice in his sailor clothes—you know he'd got leave of absence to come up there from Norfolk and as Mrs. Barrett said, says, "That is certainly a fine-looking boy. I tell you," she says, "it does you good to look at him—makes you feel that no harm can come to a country as long as it's got boys like that to defend it," she says.

"Why, yes, Captain," Luke says—you know, callin' him that, I reckon, to make him feel good—"it's all right. The shirts are here all right," he says, "because I brought them myself but I guess my father accidentally mislaid the ticket." "Well," the policeman says to me, "would you *know* the shirts if you saw them?" "Why, Lord!" I said, "you know I would! I'd know them in the dark, I'd be able to pick them out by the size of them. Why, you *know,*" I said, lookin' him straight in the eye, "you can use your own reason," I said, "they wouldn't have another shirt in the house that would fit a man like that," I said. Well, he took one look at your papa, and then he began to laugh. "No," he said, "I reckon you're right. Well, I tell you what to do," he said, "you go around there yourself and pick 'em out," he said, "and I'll stay right here until you find them."

And that's exactly what he did. I marched right around behind the counter and that man stayed there until I found them. "Here they are!" I sang right out—way down at the bottom of a pile, you know, why I must have opened up fifty packages before I came to them and I tell you what! those two Chinamen didn't like it either, the looks that they gave us were oh! bitter, bitter. If that policeman hadn't been there to pertect us, I'll tell you what, I'd been alarmed, of course, there's no telling what 'people like that might do, especially with your papa ravin' and stormin' at them the way he did. I know I said to Luke later, after we'd taken him up and put him in the hospital, "I tell you what," I said, "I was glad to get out of that place. There was a look

in the eyes of those men I didn't like; it made my flesh
crawl!" "Yes," he said, "I felt the same way. Damned
if I don't believe papa was right about them: I wouldn't
trust one of them as far as I could throw an elephant,"
he said. "Well, child," I said, "he's had it a long time,
that feelin', you know, and you may rest assured there's
something there, something we can't understand," I said.

And, of course, that's just what I told Ambrose Radiker,
that day in his saloon long, long ago! "It's something,"
he said, "sure enough—and he's a terror when he has
it. I don't know what to do with him when he gets
that way." "Well, I tell you what to do," I said, "don't
sell him any licker when he asks for it. Now, the best
way to keep out of trouble," I said, "is to avoid it." "That's
right," he said. "Well, what do you want to put up with
it for?" I said. "Now, surely, you've got strength of
mind enough not to be forced into a thing against your
better judgment. You've got more sense than that," I
said. "Why, what can I do?" he said. "Why, you can
refuse him the next time he comes here after licker,"
I said, "that's exactly what you can do." "Why, Eliza,"
he said, "what good would that do? He'd only give that
old Rufe Porter the money and send him in here to buy
a bottle, and I'd rather see him spend his money on
himself," he says, "than squander it on that old toper."
"Why, you don't mean to tell me he ever did that," I
said. "Yes," says Ambrose, "that's exactly what he's done,
many a time. Rufe comes and buys the licker for him
and they drink it up together over at the shop." "Well,
that explains it then!" I said. "The cat's out of the bag
at last!" Of course, I knew then—I could see—just how
that villain had got him into his power, gettin' him to go
his note, and all: he'd get him drunk, of course, an'

then your daddy would do anything he told him to.

"*Yes!*" I said, that day he came home and told it how Mel Porter had been in to see him and was so upset because those men were going to hang. "Let them hang —and I wish that miserable old brother of his was going to be hanged with 'em." "Oh, you mustn't talk like that," he said, "I hate to hear you say such things." Of course, I was bitter against him. "Well," your papa says, "I couldn't help feeling sorry for Mel. I reckon he's been under a great strain and now he's all worried and grieved to think that all of them have got to hang." "Not a bit of it," I said, "if you swallered any such story as that you're more gullible than I am, you don't know Mel Porter as well as I do. Now you can mark my words," I said, "it's something else that's troublin' him." "No," he says, "I think you're wrong." "All right," I said, "you wait and see."

Well, he didn't have to wait long, either. That very night, sir, they made that break from jail. They got away scot-free, all five of them, and none of them was ever caught. "Ah-hah," I said to him, "what did I tell you? And you were just fool enough to think Mel Porter was worryin' about their bein' hanged, weren't you? You see, don't you?" "Well," he said, "I reckon you're right! I guess that's what was troublin' him. He knew about it!" "Knew about it! Why, of course!" I said. "That's just it!"—of course, we could see then that he'd known about it all along, he knew they were going to make the break that night, and in his heart he was dreadin' it—he was afraid something would go wrong and there'd be more bloodshed, for they were a set of desperate bloody men and they wouldn't have hesitated to kill any one who got in their way, and so, of course, the thought of it was weighin' on Mel Porter's conscience. "Well," your papa says, "it's an awful thing and I hate to think about it."

"What about it?" says Mr. Gant. "Dock Hensley came in to see me the other day and tried to give me two tickets for you and me to see it. To think of it!" he says, "here they were all boon companions six months ago, and now Dock is just waitin' for the moment when he springs the trap on them." "Why, yes," I said, "they were all thick as thieves together"—and, of course, that was true. Ed Mears and Lawrence Wayne and Dock Hensley had been bosom friends for twenty years—"and let me tell you something," I said, "I don't know that any of them are any worse than he is. Now," I said, "they're all tarred with the same brush: they are all violent men, and Dock Hensley has shed as much blood as any of them, and I reckon he knows it. The only difference," I said, "is that he has worn a badge and has always had the authority of the law to pertect him." Why, of course! didn't they tell it on him that time he was being tried for the murder of Reese McLendon—of course they freed him on grounds of self-defense and an officer in the performance of his duty, but I said at the time to your papa: "Now, you know as well as I do that that was nothing but a deliberate cold-blooded murder if ever there was one." Of course, Reese was an awfully strong man, and when he got drunk he was a holy terror—and, I guess, he'd killed plenty, too—but here he and Hensley were close friends, you know, had always got along fine together, and then they arrested him for bein' drunk and disturbin' the peace. Well, the story goes that he got to making so much noise that they had to take him out of the cell. Oh! they said you could hear him howlin' and hollerin' the whole way across the square, and they put him downstairs in what they called the dun-

geon; of course, it was nothing but an old cellar base-
ment with a dirt floor that the city had used one time
as a stable. Well, that was Hensley's defense: he said he
went down there to see if he couldn't reason with him
and do something to quiet him down, and of course, his
story was that McLendon had picked up an old horseshoe that he'd found laying around down there and
when he came in, he said, McLendon jumped on him
and tried to brain him with the horseshoe.

So his claim was that it was either his life or Mc-
Lendon's and he got the horseshoe out of his hand
and gave him a lick across the forehead with it that
killed him. Well, the rest of them told it when they
tried him that he came back upstairs all covered with
blood and said: "You'd better get a doctor for Reese.
I'm afraid I've killed him." Well, of course, when the
doctor got there he saw there was nothing he could do,
said McLendon was dead, you know. Why, the doctor
said it looked as if he'd hit him a hundred times with
the thing, said the whole side of his head was bashed
into jelly and he lay there welterin' in his blood. Oh,
they said it was awful.

Your papa went to that trial and he came home and
told about it: "I tell you what," he said, "in all my life
I've never heard anything to equal Zeb Pentland's address to the jury to-day"—of course, your cousin Zeb
was prosecutin' him— "It was a masterly effort," your
papa says, "I wish you could have heard it." "Well,"
I said, "what are they going to do? Will they convict
him?" "Why, Lord, no!" your papa said, "he'll go free.
He'll get off on grounds of self-defense, but I tell you
what," he said, "I wouldn't have been standing in his
shoes today for a million dollars. You can mark my

words," he said, "he'll never be able to forget what
Pentland said to him as long as he lives. His face
turned pale as he listened," he said, "and I reckon he'll
carry it with him to his grave." Of course, it came out
in the trial—Zeb Pentland proved it—how Dock Hensley had shot down and killed eighteen men since he
had been an officer of the law, and your papa said he
turned to the jury and told them, "You have given a
policeman's badge, you have armed with the full authority and pertection of the law a man without mercy and
without pity, to whom the shedding of human blood
means no more than the killing of a fly, you have given
him a loaded pistol and yet some of you," he said, "would
set this mad dog free again to ravin and destroy, and
take the lives of innocent and defenseless people. Look
at him as he sits there before you!" he said, "cowerin'
and tremblin' with the mark of Cain upon his brow and
with his hands red with the blood of all his victims! The
accusing fingers of dead men are pointed at him from
the grave," he said, "and their blood, could it have a
tongue, would cry aloud for his conviction as do the
tongues of all the widows and orphans he has made—"
Well, Mr. Gant said it was a powerful effort, said
Hensley turned pale and trembled as if the spirits of the
dead had come back to accuse him, sure enough. But
of course they acquitted him like every one predicted.

But, Lord! as I said to your papa, I could never stand
to go near the man after that time they had us to their
house for dinner and here he was, sir—he had it on the
table right where every one was going to eat!—to think
of it, I said!—why, the skull of a nigger he had shot and
killed—that he should have no more refinement, I said
to your papa, than to do a thing like that right there with
guests comin' to his house for dinner and before his own

childern, usin' it, mind you, as a sugar bowl! Oh, braggin' about it, you know, like he'd done something big,
with the top of the skull sawed off to make a lid and
a place in the forehead for the sugar to pour out where
the bullet hole was. Why it was enough to turn your
stomach, I couldn't touch a bite. When we got out, your
papa said, "Well that's the last time I'll ever go to *his*
house," he said, "I don't want to have anything to do
with a man who's got no more mercy in him than that.
It's enough to curdle your blood," he said, and from that
day on he never set foot in his house again. Oh! he
couldn't endure him, you know. But they say that's
exactly why he killed himself in the end—I know Gilmer
who was stayin' at the house brought me the news, came
right back to the kitchen, you know, says, "Well, it was
a terrible sight." Says, "I was the first one there. I heard
the explosion," he says, "right behind the new courthouse, and when I got there—there he was," he says, "all
sprawled out behind a pile of brick"; says, "they couldn't
tell who it was for a while, the whole top of his head
blown off so they couldn't identify him. Oh, *awful,* you
know."

"Well," I said, "I'm not surprised. Those who live by
the sword will perish by the sword," and, of course, that's
just what happened, I reckon his conscience got too much
for him, he couldn't face it any longer. Why, didn't
Amy tell Daisy way back there when they were both in
high school together, "Oh, daddy!" she says—the child
came right out with it, you know—"oh, we don't know
what to do with him. We're afraid he's goin' to lose
his mind," she says. "He wakes up in the middle of the
night screamin' and hollerin' and we think he's goin'
crazy," she said. "Ah-hah!" I said to your papa when I
heard it, "you see, don't you? The guilty fleeth when no

man pursueth." "Well," he said, "I reckon he's got a
lot to forget. He's got all those crimes upon his soul
and he can't forget them. It's the torment of a guilty
conscience as sure as you're born. It wouldn't surprise
me if he committed suicide some day," he said.

But, of course, for a long time there he seemed to get all
right. He quit the force and became a sort of religious
fanatic, a pillar of the Methodist Church, and all, right
down there among them in the amen corner every Sunday and yes! what about it! in the real estate business,
if you please, swellin' it around town in a big car, pro-
motin' *Hensley Heights,* and all such stuff as that, and
of course I reckon for a time there like all the rest of us
he made some money or *thought* he did.

I know when I bought those lots from W. J. Bryan
he told me Hensley had acted as agent in a couple of deals
for him, and I reckon Bryan was feelin' pretty good
about it, he began to brag about him, says: "I tell you
what: Hensley is certainly a fine upright sort of man,"
he says. "In all my dealin's with him," he says, "I don't
think I've ever heard him make use of a coarse expression, or utter a word that couldn't be spoken in the presence of a lady." Hm! I thought to myself, times have
certainly changed, I thought, but of course, I didn't say
anything, I just let him go on. "Yes," he says, "I've found
him honest and upright in all my dealin's with him and
what's more, you'll find him right in his seat in church
every Sunday morning. And for a man who says he
never had any schoolin'," he says, "his knowledge of the
Scriptures is profound," says, "I've tried him out myself
on texts from all parts of the Bible and I haven't managed to trip him up yet." Says, "It's a rare thing that you'll
find a business man in this day and time with so much
interest in spiritual matters," says, "he is certainly a

credit to the community." "Why, yes," I said, "I reckon you're right but then there are a whole lot of things about this community you don't know, Mr. Bryan. Of course," I said, "you're a recent comer and there may have been a time when Dock Hensley wasn't such a credit as he is now." "Why, when was that?" he said. "Well," I said, of course I wasn't going to tell him anything, winkin' at him, you know, "maybe we'd better let dead dogs lie. I reckon it was a long time ago, for a fact," I said, "about the time you first began to run for President."

Well, sir, he just threw back his head and hah-hahed. "Why, yes!" he said, "I reckon that was a long time ago, sure enough. Well, maybe you'd better say no more," he said; says, "but I'll bet you if there was anything I *did* want to know," he said, "you'd remember it." "Why, yes," I said, "of course, I don't believe in any one braggin' on themselves, but I've always been considered to have a pretty good memory," I said. "Well, I should say you have," he said, "I was tellin' my wife the other day," he says, "that it was remarkable to find a person who took as keen an interest in all that's goin' on as you do. Why," he says, "I said to her I believe you remember everything that ever happened to you." "Well, no," I said, "I wouldn't go so far as that. There may be a few things that I don't remember very well before I was two years old, but there hasn't been much I've missed out on since then." "Well, I just bet there's not," he said, laughin', you know, as big as you please. But, of course then I said to him—you know I didn't want to do the man an injury, I thought I would give him credit for his good points—said, "Well, Mr. Bryan, there are things we could say against any one," I said, "for there is no one alive that hasn't got his faults. Judge not lest ye be judged," I said. "That is certainly true," he said. "We

must all be charitable." "And I suppose if I wanted to,"
I said, "that I could tell you things about Dock Hensley
that might not be exactly to his credit, but," I said, "you
may rest assured on one score: he has certainly been a
home-lovin' man and he has stuck to his wife and childern: no matter what else he has done he has never been
guilty of no immorality or licentiousness, no one has
ever been able to say that about him," and of course,
that was true: they tried to prove *something* like that
on him in that trial, in order to discredit his character,
they tried to show that he'd gone running around after
other women besides his wife, but they couldn't do it,
sir—they had to give the devil his due—his morals were
pure.

"Why, Dock," your papa said, "you've been good friends
with those men for twenty years," says, "I don't see how
you've got the heart to do it." "Yes, I know," he says,
"it's an awful thing, but some one's got to do it. That's
part of my job, that's what the people elected me for,"
he says, "and besides I believe Ed and Lawrence would
rather have me do it anyway. I've talked it all over with
'em," he says—of course, they told it that he'd been goin' down there to the jail to see them, and that they were
all as thick as thieves, sir, laughin' and carryin' on together—says, "they'd rather have me do it than some
stranger." "Yes," Mr. Gant said, "but I should think
it would trouble your conscience. I don't see how you'd
be able to sleep at night after doin' such a thing." "Why,
pshaw! Mr. Gant," he said, "it wouldn't bother me at
all. I've done it many a time," he said, "all I've got to do
is spring the trap. Why, I think no more of it than I
would of wringin' a chicken's neck," he said. "What
about it!" your papa says to me, "did you ever hear of

such a man? Why it seems that all human feeling and mercy has been left out of him," he says.

Well, we never could find out if Dock Hensley was in on it or not—if he knew they were goin' to make that break—but if he did, it looked mighty funny that— "I tell you what," says Mr. Gant a day or two after it happened, "I believe we misjudged Dock Hensley," he says, "I believe he knew they were goin' to make that break all along and that's the reason," he says, "he was takin' it so easy." "Well, now," I said, "there's something mighty funny about it somewhere. If he knew about it why did he come to your office with those passes? Why was he so anxious to have us come and see it?" "Well," he says, "I reckon he did it in order to turn suspicion away from him." "No, sir," I said, "I don't believe a word of it. He was just waitin' his chance to hang 'em—yes, and gloatin' about it." Well, of course, Mr. Gant didn't want to believe it of him, said he didn't like to think that any man could be so callous.

Of course, they said later that the whole thing had been arranged for weeks: that was the story, you know, that John Rand, the jailer, had been fixed, as the sayin' goes, to let them make their getaway. Now they weren't able to prove anything on the man and he *may* have been an honest all-right sort of feller—but there was something mighty queer about it somewhere: here they found him, you know, in Ed's cell all trussed up as slick as a whistle and without a mark upon him, sir, to indicate he'd ever made the least resistance. Well, the story he told was that he'd gone in there to take Ed and Lawrence their supper and that they overpowered him and tied him up as soon as he came in, said they took his keys and unlocked the other three and skipped right out. Of course, those other three had nothing to do with Ed and Lawrence, they were just plain ordinary murderers, mountain grills, as your papa called them, down there waitin' to be hanged, and the story goes that Ed said to Lawrence, "well, we'll just turn them loose, too, while we're about it."

Well, there was something funny about John Rand's story. People didn't like the look of it. And then, within six months' time John Rand goes into business for himself, opens up a great big plumbing shop on South Main street with a stock that must have cost him thousands of dollars. "Look here," your papa said, "do you know what they're saying? They're saying that John Rand was bribed to let those men escape." "Well," I said, "they may be right. It's mighty funny," I said, "that a man who never earned over fifty dollars a month in his life gets money enough all of a sudden to start up a big business of his own. Now *where* did all that money come from: you've got to admit it looks fishy." "Yes," your daddy says, "but who bribed him? Where did the money come from?" he said. "Why," I said, "it came from Yancey County where all their kinfolk and relations live—that's exactly where it came from." "Why," he says, "are their people well-to-do?" "They've got *plenty,*" I said, "plenty—and they'd 'a' spent every last penny they had to see those men go free." Of course, I knew what I was talkin' about. "Look here," I said, "I've lived here all my life and I know those people better than you do. I grew up among them," I said, "and I want to tell you they'd 'a' stopped at nothing." Why, they said the money poured in there like water, said thousands of dollars were spent in their defense, why, yes! didn't they tell it that old Judge Truman alone—the brother of this same Perfesser Truman, of course, Ed Mears and Law-

rence Wayne married Perfesser Truman's daughters, they
both married sisters—didn't they tell it that Judge Truman alone, one of the biggest lawyers that they had in
Yancey, spent over ten thousand dollars in defendin'
them, "and you can rest assured," I told your papa, "that
that wasn't a drop in the bucket. Wherever they are
today, they're well provided for," I said, "and you need-
n't waste your pity on them." "Well," he said, "I'm glad
they got away. There's been enough bloodshed already.
I don't see any use in adding to it."

I shook my head. "No," I said, "you're wrong. They
should have been hanged and I'm sorry they didn't get
what was comin' to them, but," I said, "I'm glad *we* acted
as we did. I shouldn't have cared if they'd been caught,
but I don't want the blood of any man, guilty or innocent,
on my conscience." "No," he said, "nor do I." "But *you
know,*" I said, *"you know* as well as you're standin' there
that those men were guilty as hell"—that's just the way I
put it—why, *murder,* of course, as deliberate and cold-
blooded murder as any one was ever guilty of. Here they
told it at the trial that both of them walked in to that mica
mine on Saturday afternoon when they were payin' off,
and they were spoilin' for a fight—that's all in the world
it was. Why! I said to your papa at the time, if it had been
money they were after, if they'd wanted to hold up the
place, you might have seen some reason for it—but no!
they were out to start a row, and they'd come ready for it.
Of course, they'd both been drinkin' and when they drank
they were always up to devilment. And here, of course,
they began to abuse that paymaster—a decent law-abidin'
man, they said—and to hinder him from payin' off and, of
course, that was when John Burgin stepped into the office.
"Now, boys," he said, "I don't like to see you act like this.
Why don't you go on off now," he says, tryin' to reason

with them, you know, "before you get yourselves in trouble?" "Why, damn you," says Lawrence Wayne, "what business is it of yours what we do?" "Why, it's no business at all," John Burgin says, "only I don't like to see you act this way. I don't want to see you get into any trouble," he said, "and I know when you wake up tomorrow morning you're goin' to regret this thing." "Well, now," says Lawrence Wayne, "don't you worry how we're goin' to feel tomorrow morning. You worry about yourself. It's people like you," he says, "who don't wake up at all. Why, damn you," he says, "I never did like your face noway. Now you'd better go on," he says, "while you're still able to walk." "All right," John said, "I'll go. I don't want to have no trouble with you. I was just tryin' to reason with you to behave yourselves for the sake of your wives and childern, but if that's the way you feel about it, I'll go on." And they said he turned his back on them and was walkin' away when Ed Mears shot him, turned to Lawrence, they said, with a kind of a drunken grin, says, "Lawrence, do you reckon I can hit him?" and he shot that man down that never did him no harm, through the back of his head—and then, of course, they both cut loose on the paymaster and that man he had assistin' him—killed them all, and then skipped out. "But to think of it!" I said to your papa, "there was no excuse, no provocation as far as I can see—they were *simply out to kill*," I said, "and hangin's the only treatment they deserve." "Yes," he said, "but I'm glad we acted as we did."

Now, boy, I want to tell you:

"Two . . . Two," the first voice said, and "Twenty . . . Twenty," said the other.

I know exactly when it was—I'm goin' to tell you now: it was on the twenty-seventh day of September, sir, at twenty minutes to ten o'clock in the evening. The reason I know is—well, that's what I'm goin' to tell you—but it was just two days before that on the twenty-fifth day of the month, sir—that I'd had that talk with Ambrose Radiker in his saloon, that's exactly when it was. That was just after Mr. Gant had been off on that spree and they'd had to send for us to get him and bring him home. Now, I thought, I've had as much as I can stand, I won't put up with it any longer, and I marched right in there by myself to have it out with him.

Well, I could see that Ambrose was telling me the truth —that was the time of course he told me how your daddy raved and carried on in his delirium against the Chinese and how much trouble they'd had with him—give the devil his due, of course—saloon-keeper though he may have been, I believe he told the truth and was being honest with me. "Now," he said, "I've done everything I can but if there's anything more I can do to persuade him to stop drinkin' you tell me what it is and," he says, *"I'll* do it!" —and yes! didn't he stop in to see us that very evening on his way home, we were sitting there after supper, you know, your daddy reading the paper to me, and all, and says, "Will, I want you to promise me that you'll try to cut out drinkin'. I hate to see you do it," he said, "a man with your mind and your command of language and all—why there's nothing you couldn't accomplish if you set yourself to it!" "Why, yes," I said, "he's smart enough, all right. I don't believe there's a man in the community with half his natural ability," I said, "and he could go far if it wasn't for that accursed cravin' for licker. There's one thing sure," I said, "he never learned it from any of my people —you know, my father, Major Pentland," I said, "never touched a drop in his life and never allowed any one to come inside his house if he thought he drank." "Yes, I know," says Ambrose, "he is certainly a fine man and a credit to the community," he says, "and, Will," he says, "here you are with everything it takes to make a man happy—with a fine wife and a family of childern and a good business and, Will, for *their* sakes," he said, "you oughtn't to do it, you ought to cut out drinkin'." Well, your papa admitted he was right and he promised, you know, said he'd never touch another drop and Ambrose went on then—that was the very night it was, all right, the twenty-seventh of September.

Well, then, I heard it! "Two . . . Two," said one, and "Twenty . . . Twenty," said the other. "Why, Lord, woman!" says Mr. Gant, "there's no one there!"—went to the window and looked out, you know, says, "It's something you imagined. You don't hear anything," he said.

"Oh, yes, I do!" I said—of course, I was as sure of it as I was sitting there—"there it is again!" I said, and of course I heard it just as plain, "Two . . . Two," the first one over by the window said, and "Twenty . . . Twenty," the other one kept whispering in my ear.

And that was the time the bell began to ring—that courthouse bell, you know, banging it out as hard and fast as it could go. "Oh, Lord!" I said, "something's happened. What do you reckon it can be?" You could hear them the whole way to the square shoutin' and hollerin' and smashing in the windows of Curtis Black's hardware store to get the guns, that's what they did, all right, and then man-like, of course, your papa wanted to be up and gone, grabs his hat, you know, says, "I think I'll go and see!"

"Oh, don't go!" I said, "don't go! I wish you wouldn't go. You oughtn't to leave me while I'm in this condition," I said. "Why, Lord," he said, "I'll be back in half an hour. Why you're all right," he said, "there's nothing can happen to you." I shook my head—I had a premonition, I don't know what else you'd call it—but something *awful, awful,* some approachin' calamity. "I wish you wouldn't go," I said—but he was up and gone.

I looked at the clock as he went out the door and the minute hand stood just exactly at twenty minutes to ten o'clock.

So I waited. I felt it, you know, I didn't know what it was, but I knew that it was comin', and I listened to that old wooden clock there on the mantel—tock-tock, tock-tock, it said, ticking the minutes off, and let me tell you: that was the longest time I ever waited, each of those minutes seemed an hour. The clock struck ten.

And then I heard it—creepin' along the alley-way above our house, and then I heard the fence-wires creak outside the window, and then it dropped down on the flower-beds outside the house—and then it crept up soft and easy and began to crawl along the porch outside the sitting-room door. "Oh, Lord!" I said—it flashed over me all at once, the meaning of it—"they've come! they're here! What shall I do," I said, "left all alone here with the childern to face them, these bloody men?"

Of course, I saw it then—the meaning of that warning —"Two . . . Two," and "Twenty . . . Twenty"—they'd tried to warn me and your papa that they'd be there in twenty minutes. "He should have waited, he should have listened," I said, "that was what they were trying to tell him."

I went to the door—how on earth I ever mustered strength and courage in my condition, I don't know how I ever did it, but child! child! I must have been given strength and courage to face them by some higher power —and I flung it open. It was a pitch-black night along toward the beginning of autumn. It had been raining but the rain had stopped and Lord! it seemed that you could cut the darkness with an axe, everything still and heavy, frosty-like—that was the reason we could hear them all so plain up on the square, but not a sound, sir! not a word now!

"All right!" I sang right out into the dark, you know, like I wasn't afraid of anything. "I know you're there, Ed! You can come on in." He didn't speak. I listened. I could hear him breathing, heavy-like. "Now, surely," I said, "you're not going to be afraid of me. I'm all alone," I said, "I'm nothing but a defenseless woman, and you've got nothing to be afraid of"—of course, I knew that that would aggervate him.

Well, it stung his pride, he got right up and walked into the room: "I'm not afraid of any one," he said, "man nor woman." "Well, no," I said, "I reckon you're not. At least they all said you weren't afraid of John Burgin when you shot him in the back when he was walkin' away from you and surely," I said, "a man who's killed as many people as you have is not going to be afraid of one lone woman who's been left alone in the house without pertection. Now I know better than that," I said, "I know you're not afraid of *me*."

"No, Eliza," he said, "I'm not, and that's the reason that I'm here," he said. "You've got nothing to fear from me," he said, "I came here because I knew that I could trust you and you wouldn't give me away. I need your help," he said. Well, I reckon the look of the feller was too much for me, he looked like a hunted animal and *let me tell you,* I never want to see no such look in any one's eyes as I saw in his that night: if he'd been to hell and back it couldn't have been worse. It was too much for me, I couldn't have told on him then no matter what he'd done. "It's all right, Ed. You've nothing to fear from me, I won't give you away. And you can tell Lawrence," I said, "to come on in. I know he's out there."

Well, he gave me a mighty funny look. "Why, what do you mean?" he said, "Lawrence isn't here. He's not with me." "Yes, he is," I said. "I *know* he's there. I'm *sure* of it. And you can tell him so, and to come on in." "Why, how do you *know* he's there?" he said, worried, "What makes you so *sure* of it?" "Well, I tell you," I said, "I was *warned* about it, Ed. I knew that you were both coming." "Warned?" he said, beginning to get excited, you know, "Why, who warned you? Has any one been here? How did any one know?" he said. "No," I said, "you needn't get excited, Ed. Some one was here to warn me, all right, that you and Lawrence were coming, but it's no one you've got to be afraid of in *this* world. The next world is a different matter, of course," I said, "I can't tell you about that. You'll have to face that for yourself." Well, he looked at me and his eyes were sticking out of his head. *"Spirits?"* he said. "Yes," I said, "that's what they were, all right! Now I don't know *who* they were, but they came here to warn me, whisperin' in my ear, and they said you and Lawrence were on your way and would be here in twenty minutes."

Well, his face was a study, and at last he said: "No, Eliza, you're wrong. I don't want to alarm you," he said, "but if they were here they came here to warn you about something else. It wasn't me and Lawrence," he said, "I'll swear to that!" "Why, what do you mean?" I said. "I've told you," he said, "Lawrence isn't with me. We parted company outside the jail; we decided that was best and he lit out toward South Carolina. I'm going across the mountain," he said, "and if we get away we hope to meet again out West." "You look me in the eye," I said, "are you telling me the truth?" Well, he looked straight at me: "Yes," he said, "so help me God, it's true!"

Well, I looked at him and I saw, of course, that he was telling me the truth. "Well," I said, "it was something else, then, what it is I don't yet know, but I'll find out. Now," I said, "why did you come here to my house? What do you want?" I said. "Why," he said, "Eliza, I've got to get away across those mountains to-night, and I've got no shoes, I'm barefooted," he said. And then, of course, I saw, I reckon I'd been too excited to notice before, but there he was, ragged and bleeding, in his bare feet, and let me tell you he was a sight to behold and marvel at: here he was with no shoes and no coat and nothing to wear but an old ragged pair of pants that looked as if he'd been sleeping in them all the time he'd been in jail, and a dirty old flannel shirt that had been all ripped out beneath the shoulder, and here his hair was all matted and tangled up like a bird's nest, hanging down over his eyes and he must have had a six weeks' growth of beard upon his face —why it looked as if he hadn't had a shave or haircut since he went to jail, the very sight of him was enough to scare the life out of a grizzly bear. Why, as I told your papa later, they'd thought of everything to help him make his get-away except the things he needed most: here they'd given him a pistol and cartridges to kill people with—as if he hadn't killed enough already—but they didn't have sense enough to give him shoes to walk in or a coat to keep him warm. "If that don't beat all I ever heard of!" I told your papa.

"I've got to get them somehow," he said. "If I don't I'll cut my feet to pieces going across the mountains and

then," he said, "if I can't walk, I'm done for. They'll catch
me sure." "Why, of course," I said. "Well," he said, "that's
why I came here to see you, Eliza. I knew you wouldn't
give me up and I could depend on you to help me. Now,"
he says, "you can see for yourself I've got an awful big
foot and the only man I know," he says, "who wears a
shoe that would fit me is Mr. Gant. Now if you'll only
let me have a pair of his old shoes—anything you've got
—I'll pay you for them. I've got plenty of money," he said,
and he pulled out a big roll of bills, he had certainly come
well heeled, "and I'll pay you anything you say they're
worth." "No, Ed," I shook my head, "I don't want your
money"—of course, I couldn't have touched it, it'd been
like taking blood money—"but I'll give you the shoes."
So I went to the closet and got them out, a fine new pair,
sir, that your daddy had bought only a couple of months
before, in good condition, for he certainly took good care
of all his clothes. "Here they are," I said, "and I hope
you'll be able to use them." Well, he put them on then
and there, and they fitted him, sir, as if they'd been made
for him. Well, you know, murderer that he was, he showed
he still had feeling left in him, he took my hand and began
to cry, says: "I'll never forget what you've done as long
as I live. If there's ever anything I can do to pay you for it,"
he says, "I'll do it." "Well, you can do something," I said,
"and you can do it here and now." "What is it?" he said.
"I don't want your money," I said, "I wouldn't touch it.
You can have the shoes, Ed, and I hope they help you to
escape—you need the shoes," I said, "but you don't need
that pistol you're carryin' in your hip pocket." I could see
it, you know, making a big bulge when he walked. "Now
you've shed enough blood already," I said, "and come what
may, whether you escape or not, I never want to hear that

you've shed another drop of blood. You give that gun to me," I said, "and go on. If they catch you it won't do you any good."

Well, he looked at me a moment as if he couldn't make up his mind, and then he gave it to me. "All right," he said, "I reckon you're right. I don't suppose it'd do me much good noway and besides, if they do catch me I don't care. I've committed so many crimes in my life," he said, "that I don't care what happens to me now. I'd just as soon be out of it," he said. "No," I said, "I don't like to hear you talk like that. You've got a wife who's stuck by you through thick and thin and little childern, and now," I said, "you must begin to think of them. Go on off somewheres," I said, "where no one knows you and make a fresh start, and when you are ready, send for her and I *know* her," I said—I looked him in the eye—"I *know* her, and she'll come."

Well, it was too much for him. He couldn't speak, he turned his head away, said, "All right. I'll try!" "Now, you go on," I said. "I don't want them to find you here," I said, "and I hope that all goes well with you." "Goodbye," he said, "I'm going to try to lead a different life hereafter." "Yes, that's what you've got to do. You've got to try to atone for all the harm you've done. Go," I said, "and sin no more."

Well, he went. I heard the fence wires creak and I saw him going up the street, I reckon toward the mountain. He got away, all right. I never saw him again.

Well, he hadn't been gone ten minutes when here he came, you know, your daddy, all excited with the news he *thought* he had to tell.

"Well," he said, "they got away, all five of them. Hensley and a big mob have smashed the windows of Black's hardware store to get guns and he's out after them now with a posse."

"Yes," I said, "and you had to run all the way to town to find *that* out, didn't you? The next time you go chasing off like that bring me back something I don't know about." "Why," he said, "how did you hear? Do you know about it?" he said. "Know about it!" I said, "why I know more about it than you'll ever know," I said. "I got my information at first hand," I said, "and I didn't have to stir out of this house to get it, either." "Why," he says, "how was that? What do you mean?" "I've had a caller since you went away," I said. "Who was it?" he says. I looked at him. "Ed Mears was here," I said. "Good God!" your papa says, "do you mean to tell me that murderer was here—in my house? Have you given the alarm?" he says, "have you told the neighbors?" "No," I said. "Well, I'm going to," he says, "this very minute." And he started to go again. I stopped him. "No," I said, "you'll do no such thing. You'll stay here. Now, I gave him my promise not to give him away, and we're going to stick to it. You keep quiet." He studied about it for a moment. "Well," he said, "I reckon you're right. Maybe it's the best way, after all. But that's the strangest thing I ever heard about," he said. "By God it is!"

Well, they got away, all right. None of them were ever caught. Of course, years later when your daddy made that trip to California, Truman told him that both Ed and Lawrence had come to his house in Colorado when he was living there and, of course, the girls both follered them within six months or so. Lawrence's wife, who was Mary Truman, died out there in Colorado of consumption a year or two later, and I don't know for certain what ever

became of Lawrence. The story went that he settled down
in Kansas and got married again and had a big family of
childern and is living there right now, sir, a well-to-do
man and highly respected in his community.

Of course, we *know* what happened to Ed Mears. I got
the whole story from Dock Hensley. Truman told your
papa that Ed had come out there to Colorado and went
up into the mountains to some mining camp to work,
and, of course, when he was ready he sent for Addie, and
she follered him. Well, Truman said, she lived with him
up there a year or so and then she came down to her
father's house again. Oh! he told it, you know! Said it
was awful, she couldn't stand no more of it, said Ed was
going crazy and would go out of his mind sometimes
screaming and raving that the spirits of the dead men he
had killed had come back from the grave to haunt and
torment him. "You see, don't you," I said to your papa
when he told it, "you see what happens, don't you? I've
never known it to fail," I said. "The guilty fleeth when
no man pursueth." "Yes," he said, "that's it. A guilty conscience as sure as you're born," he said. "So I took her away
from him," said Truman. "I sent her back East where she
would never see him any more. Of course," he said, "he
threatened me—he threatened my life, but I could see that
the man was goin' crazy, and I wouldn't let her go back
to him," he said.

Well, Addie came home again and got a divorce: of
course, Cash Jeter took the case for her—that was long
before he got elected to the Senate, he was nothing but a
practising attorney at the time—and the story goes, in
the course of the proceedings he fell in love with her, and
marries her, if you please, within a month's time after she
got the final papers. "Well, they didn't wait long, did
they?" I said to your papa! "Now it does seem to me," I

said, "that they might have waited a decent length of time." "Ah, Lord!" your papa says, "the funeral baked meats did coldly furnish forth the marriage tables. 'Twas thrift Horatio with a vengeance," he says. "That's so," I said, "that's what it was, all right."

Well, then, they sent Dock Hensley West to get a man who'd killed some one, and, of course, when he came back he told it how he had run into Ed Mears in Mexico. Said he was on a boat somewheres going from Texas into Mexico follerin' on the trail of this murderer he'd been sent to get, I reckon, when here he saw him, face to face—Ed Mears. Dock said he'd grown a beard, but said he'd recognized him, "but I want to tell you," he says, "he's changed a lot. He's not the same man that you knew," he says. Dock said he looked like a dead man, said he was nothing but a shadder of his former self. "Why," he said, "he was only a bundle of skin and bone, he didn't have no more meat on him than a squirrel," he says. "Well," I said, "did he know you? Did he speak to you?"—of course, you know, I wanted to hear the story. "Why, Lord, yes!" Hensley said. "We roomed together for four days down there, hail-fellow-well-met and boon companions," he says. Then, he went on to say, you know, "Of course," he says, "when he first saw me on the boat he thought that I had come for him, he stepped right up," he said, "to surrender himself." "All right, Dock," he says, "I know you came down here to take me back and," he says, "I'm ready to go." "Why, no, Ed," I says, "you're wrong. I'm here for some one else. You're not the man I'm lookin' for," I said, "I don't want you—and besides," I said, "even if I did I've got no authority to arrest you, I've got no warrant for you." "Well," he said, "I'm comin' back anyway some day. I've one more killing to do yet before I die," he said, "and then they can take me and do what they like with me." "Why, who's that?" Dock says—asks him, "who do you want to kill?" he says. "Cash Jeter," he says. And then Dock told it how bitter he hated him for getting the divorce and marrying his wife.

So Dock said that before he left for home again Ed handed him a letter and asked him to deliver it to Jeter when he got back— and he said he *saw* that letter with his own eyes, mind you, and that in all *his* life he never read the like of it: "I may have been a murderer," Ed wrote, "and I've got many a crime upon my soul to atone for but in all my days I have never sunk so low as to steal a man's wife away from him. Now," he said, "you can set your house in order and get ready for me because I'm coming back. It may be a month, or it may be a year, or it may be ten years, but I'll *be* there," he said. "I've got a score to settle with you, and you get ready." Well, Dock said when he handed that letter to Jeter he opened it and read it and Dock said his face turned pale and you could see him tremble and I suppose, of course, his life was hell on earth from that day on until the news got back to them that Ed was dead—because, of course, Ed never lived to get there, the story went that he got killed in a saloon in Mexico. But you can rest assured that he'd 'a' come.

Well, that's the way it was, all right: that's just what happened.

But still and all—the thing was puzzlin' me, you know —"Two . . . Two," and "Twenty . . . Twenty"—what could it mean?

"Why, Lord," your papa said, "it didn't mean a thing! It never happened anyway," he said, "it's something you imagined."

"You wait," I said, "you wait and see."

It wasn't long. We didn't have long to wait.

It started in along some time before dinner, about one o'clock. Oh, Lord! it felt like something had tore loose inside me. And he was there, he'd come home early, here he was, you know, out in the backyard rendering the lard out of some hogs he'd bought. "Why, what on earth!" I cried. "What ever made you buy them?" Child, child! that awful waste, that awful extravagance! Why, as I told him, if it hadn't been for me he'd have spent every penny he earned featherin' the nests of the butchers and the farmers and the saloon-keepers—he couldn't resist 'em, you know. "Why, man alive!" I said, "what ever persuaded you to go and do a thing like that!" Here we were with hams and bacon in the pantry that he'd bought, six smoked hams, if you please, and here he comes with this whole hog. "Why, man, you'll kill us all with all this hog meat!" I said—yes! with lots of chickens of our own and a twelve-pound roast he'd sent down from the market—"Why, we'll get down sick," I said, "you'll have the childern all in bed! So much meat isn't good for people." To think of it! the waste, you know—child, child, many's the time I've sat down and cried about it, to think he'd go and squander away his money in that way. "Why, Lord!" I said, "I never saw such a glutton in my life!" I thought I'd appeal to his pride, you know. "Why, all you think of is your belly! Now stop here and consider for a moment: how do you ever expect to accumulate any property if everything you earn goes rolling down your gullet to feed your gut? Why, I'll vow! man! I believe all of your brains are in your belly!" Why, yes! he'd meet up with some old farmer who had a whole wagon load of stuff he wanted to get rid of so he could get out of town and hike for home again, and he'd buy him out, sir. Why, didn't I tell you! What about it! to think that he could be such a dunce—the time he sent this man home with forty dozen eggs—Lord!

I could have thrown them at him I was so aggervated!—
when here we had hens of our own layin' us fresh ones
every day as hard as they could. "Why, what ever
prompted you to do such a trick as that?" I said. "Well,"
he says, sheepish-like, "he let me have the lot at seven cents
a dozen. It was such a bargain," he says, "it seemed a pity
not to buy them." "Why I don't care," I said, "if he let
you have them for two cents a dozen, it was money thrown
away," I said, "we'll never use them." "Oh, we can use
them," he said. "We'll give 'em to the childern." "Why,
Lord, man, how you talk!" I said, "you'll get the childern
so sick of eggs they'll never look one in the face again.
They'll never eat 'em," I said, "they'll all go bad!" And he
looked pretty sheepish about it, I tell you what he did!
"Well," he says, "I thought I was actin' for the best. I guess
I was mistaken," he said.

   And yes! Didn't he come home one time with a whole
load of cantaloupes and watermelons—twenty-seven watermelons, if you please, and the Lord knows how many
cantaloupes, hundreds of 'em, I reckon. "To think you had
no better sense than that!" I said. "Oh, we'll eat 'em, we'll
eat 'em," he said. "The childern will eat 'em up," he says.
Yes, didn't Luke get down sick from eating them, "and
there's a doctor bill to pay," I told him . . . and all the
other times he'd come with wagon loads of roastin' ears
and termaters and string beans and sweet pertaters and
onions and radishes and beets and turnips and all kinds of
garden vegetables and all sorts of fruit, peaches and pears
and apples and plums, when here we had a big orchard
and garden right behind the house growin' everything we
needed. Why, it kept me busy thinkin' up ways to keep it
all from goin' to waste, said, "how do you ever expect me
to look after the childern if you keep dumping this stuff in
here on me?"—here I was in that condition, you know,

putting up preserves for all I was worth and him out there
rendering the lard out. Oh! the smell of it, that old strong
smell of fat, you know—right up to the very time, four
hundred and thirty-seven jars of preserved cherries,
peaches, apple, grape, and plum jelly, quince honey, preserved pears, termater ketchup, chow chow, pickled cucumbers, and all such stuff as that, why you couldn't get
into the pantry, it was stacked up to the ceiling, and *let me
tell you, now,* he could *eat:* now I've seen some good eaters
in my day and time but I've never seen any one who could
poke it away the way *he* could. I reckon he got it from
that crowd he came from up there, told it you know how
they'd come in from the fields in his boyhood and sit down
to a meal that would stall an ox. Why didn't I see the old
woman myself, when we were up there that time, eat a
whole chicken and three big hunks of pie—says to Au-
gusta, you know, "Daughter, fill my plate again," she says,
and she was in her seventies then—that's exactly how she
got her death, sir. "To think of it!" I said when I heard the
news—in her ninety-sixth year and fell out of her chair
and broke her leg while reachin' for an ear of corn: of
course it killed her, she was too old to recover from the
injury, her bones wouldn't knit together again, "but if that
don't beat all!" I said.

Why, I'll vow! It's a wonder his constitution stood it as
long as it did—brains and eggs and bacon and fried steak
and oatmeal and hot biscuits and sausage and two or three
cups of coffee for his breakfast, and two or three different
kinds of meat, liver and roast beef and pork and fish and
chicken, and a half dozen different vegetables, beans and
mashed pertaters and succotash and turnip greens and preserved peaches and pie, and all such as that, for dinner and
supper. "Why," I said to Wade Eliot, "I believe that's what
helped bring on this trouble. He's been diggin' his grave

with his teeth." "Well," he said, "he's been diggin' a long time, hasn't he?" and, of course, I had to admit it, but I'll vow! I sometimes think he might be alive today if he'd only used more judgment!

Well, then, I say, it hit me, those awful stabbing pains. I went to the window and called out to him, "Come! come quick!" And let me tell you, he didn't *wait:* he came a-running.

"Oh, it can't be!" I said. "There hasn't been time enough."

"That's what I think it is," he said. "I'm going for the doctor."

And he went.

That was the year the locusts came: it seems so long ago since the year that the locusts came, and all the earth was eaten bare, it seems so long ago. But no (I thought) the thing kept puzzlin' me, you know—it can't be that, there hasn't been time enough for that, it was only the year before in January—Lord! Lord! I often think of all that I've been through, and wonder that I'm here to tell it. I reckon for a fact I had the power of Nature in me; why! no more trouble than the earth takes bearing corn, all of the childern, the eight who lived, and all the others that you never heard about—all of the childern and less married life than any woman that I knew—and oh! to think of it, to think that he should say the things he did —cursin' and tauntin' me and runnin' wild with other women, when he had done it all, and like a devil when he saw what he had done. Lord! Lord! he was a strange man, a wild and savage man; sometimes it seemed I never got to know him: there was a devil in him somewhere, something wild and strange we never got to know about—the things he did and said were more than I could stand, they made me bitter and I prayed that God would punish him, but Lord! it was so long ago since the year that the locusts came, and I think of it all, the orange trees, the fig trees, and the singin' and all of the times we knew together. Oh! the good, the bad times, all of the happiness and bitter weepin', and there is something now that can't be said, I tried to hate him but now I have no words to say against him: he was a strange man but where he was no one was ever cold, no one was ever hungry, there was enough for all, and now when I remember him it seems so long ago since the year when the locusts came, and there's something that I want to say that can't be spoken.

That year—it was the year the childern had the typhoid and Steve and Daisy were just gettin' well again and I had taken them—Lord! how did I ever do it all alone—down to St. Augustine—and he came, he couldn't stay, of course, he follered us, and began to drink—I tried to find it but he got Steve to hide it in the sand up underneath the house—and to curse and rave when he had seen me, says, "Damn you! if you bring it back with you I'll kill you both!" And child, to think that he should talk like that, it made me bitter and I didn't stop to think: I walked the floor, I walked the floor and then I went out on the porch and leaned against a post—we were livin' in a cottage that I'd rented from some Northern people—and there was no rail—there was nothin' but that old loose sand there anyway, and I knew the childern wouldn't hurt themselves if they fell off—and Lord! What shall I do! What shall I do! I thought. . . .

The next day he had sobered up again and was all right and so toward sunset of that day we took the childern with us and set out for old Fort Marion, the Spanish Fort, down by the Ponce de Leon, and here were all the people

in their finery and the soldiers' band a-playin' and then
you heard the gun and the bugle blowin' as the flag came
down—yes—Toodle-oo! Toodle-oo!—that was the way the
bugle blew and all the little childern put their hands up
to their mouths to see if they could do it too, and the
birds flyin', the palm trees and the music and the smell of
water and the orange blossoms, and that old black fort
—why Lord! the walls were fourteen feet in places—with
the sun goin' down behind it like some big orange, and
the people listenin' to the music. In January of that year
the locusts came at home, and then I felt as if the whole
thing had torn loose inside me.

"Come on," I said. "We've got to go," and says, "What
is it?" "Oh, Lord!" I told him, "it's tearin me in two. Oh,
Lord! We'll never get there! Come!"—and we went, the
childern and all, and my feet slippin' and sinkin' in the
sand, until I thought I'd never get there, and that great
hunk of a thing tearing away at me, and he picked me up
and carried me the last part of the way into the house,
and I said, "You see, don't you? You see what you've done.
That's your work!" and he was frightened and his face
turned pale and he trembled as he looked and he said,
"My God! My God! What have I done!" and he walked
the floor, and it got dark, and I lay there, and all of the
childern were asleep around me, and he went out into the
yard, and we had a fig tree there, and I lay there in the
dark listenin' to people comin' by, and I could hear music
playin' somewheres and hear their voices laughin' and
singin', and smell all of the blossoms—oh! the magnolias
and the lilies and the roses, the poinsettias, and all the
other flowers they had there and the orange trees and all,
and the little childern sleepin' in the house, you know,
and see the sky all full of stars and Lord God! I thought,

what shall I do, what shall I do?—and that was the year the locusts came at home and now it seems so long ago.

But Lord! I reckon Nelson got it right that time, said, "You've got the power of nature in you for a fact. I've never seen the like of it," he said. Why, yes! didn't I have them all, and couldn't I make things grow by touchin' them, and wasn't it that way ever since I was a child— termaters and flowers and corn and vegetables—and all kinds of fruit. Why Lord! it seemed that all I had to do was stick my fingers in the earth and they'd come up for me. "Oh," says old man Shumaker, workin', you know to all hours in his garden till it looked like a checkerboard, everything standin' up straight and neat without a weed among it, like I reckon he'd been taught to do in Germany, says, "Oh! you mustn't let your garden go that way. You've got to weed it out or things will never grow." "You wait," I said, "you wait and see! They'll grow," I said, "they'll grow for me, and I'll have things as good as yours for all your work and grubbin'." And didn't I have onions and radishes and lettuce and termaters that beat him out of sight—why Lord! you could see them poppin' from the earth! and let me tell you, if the worst comes to the worst, I wouldn't starve, if I didn't have a penny I could live, I'd make the earth produce for me. I've done it and I could do it yet.

Why, yes! didn't I go in to the Catawba Coal Company here one day last winter to pay my bill and talk to him just two days before he dropped dead from that heart attack, and see him, you know, Miller Wright, not a day over seventy, pale as a ghost and trembling and shaking all over like a leaf? "Why, Miller," I said, "it worries me to see you in this condition. What is it? What's the matter?" "Oh," he says, trembling and shaking, "Eliza, it's the worry, the awful worry! I can't sleep no more for thinkin' of it." "Why, what is it?" I said; says, "Oh, Eliza, everything I ever had is gone! I'm penniless. Most of it went in real estate," he says, "and now that miserable bank has closed its doors. What am I going to do?" he said. "Do?" I said, "why you're going to do the same as me—profit by your mistakes and start all over." "Oh, but Eliza, Eliza," he said, shakin' his head at me, "it's too late —we're both past seventy and we're too old, too old," he said. "Old!" I said, "why, Lord God, I could start right out tomorrow and earn my living with the best of them." "Yes," he said, "but Eliza, what are you going to do?" "Do!" I said, "why, I tell you," I said, "I'm going to pitch right in and work hard till I'm eighty and then," I says, winkin' at him, you know, "I'm goin' to cut loose and *just raise hell,*" I said—that's exactly what I said, you know, I thought I'd jolly him up a bit and, of course, he had to laugh then, says, "Well, I reckon that's as good a plan as any." "Now, look here, Miller," I said, "you ought to know better than to give in like this. We've both been through the mill, and we've seen some mighty rough times—why, these people that they've got today don't know anything about it, they don't know what hardship is"—why, didn't we both grow old within five miles of each other and don't I remember it all, yes! every minute of it like it was today, the men marchin', and the women cryin', the way the dust rose, the times we went through and the way we had to work, the wool, the flax, the wheel, the things we grew and the things we had to make, and a thousand things you never dreamed or heard of, boy, the summertime, the river and the singin', the poverty, the sorrow, and the pain—we saw and had to do it all—"And *you!*" I said to Miller Wright. "You! You did it, too," I said, "and you remember!"

Well, he had to admit it then, you know, says, "Yes, you're right, I remember. But," he says—you know, he brightened up a bit, " could you do it *now*?" "Do it?" I said. "Why, I could do it like a flash. Now, Miller," I said, "suppose we did lose out. We're in the boat with lots of others. We all thought we were doing the right thing and I reckon we lost our heads," I said. "We allowed ourselves to be swept off our feet against our better judgment"—pshaw! when I think of it! I had my mind all made up . . . If I'd only known. . . . Why, I was just going to make another trade or two and then get out. Pshaw! I'll vow, I believe if it hadn't been for all these sharks and New York Jews and easy-money grafters that came in there over-night . . . *that* was the time I should have sold if I'd only had the sense to see it . . . and as for all that stuff we bought in Florida, I believe we'd have been all right today if that hurricane hadn't come along and hit us like it did, and then on top of it these lying villains out in California spread that story about the Mediterranean fruit-fly down in Florida. Why, Lord, there was no more fruit-fly there than at the North Pole—it was all part of a lying story they put out to ruin and injure Florida because they couldn't stand to see us get ahead of them, and Hoover and all his crowd playin' right along with them and abettin' them in their villainy because *he* came from California, if you please—that's all in the world it was, but Florida will come back in spite of all the lies they told about her, you can't down Florida!—"And Miller," I said, "the banks haven't got everything," I said. "They may think they have, but now," I said, winkin' at him, "I've got a secret that I'm goin' to tell you. I've still got a little patch of land out in the country that no one knows about and if the worst comes to the worst," I said, "I won't starve. I'll go out there and grow my food and I'll have plenty.

And if you go broke you can come on out," I said. "You won't go hungry, I can make things grow." "Oh, but Eliza," he said, "it's too late, too late. We're both too old to start again, and we've lost everything." "No," I said, "not everything. There's something left." "What is it?" he said. "We've got the earth," I said. "We've always got the earth. We'll stand upon it and it will save us. It's never gone back on nobody yet."

Well, here they came, you know, tearing along for all they were worth, your papa and Old Doctor Nelson. I lay there with those awful pains rending me as if they were going to tear me in two.

"But no," I said to Doctor Nelson. "It can't be that. I'm not ready for it yet. It's not been time, it's two weeks before my time," I said.

"No matter about that," he said. "*You're r*eady. It's *your* time," he said. "It's *your* time, sure enough."

And, sure enough, it was. Why! that was it, of course! —that's what I've been telling you, boy!—that explained it all.

"Two . . . Two," the first voice said, and "Twenty . . . Twenty" said the other:—

Twenty days later from that evening that Ed Mears came there to our house, to the minute, at twenty minutes to ten o'clock on the seventeenth day of October, *twins* were born—Ben and Grover were both born that night.

The next day as I lay there thinkin', it flashed over me, the meaning of it, of course I saw it all. The mystery was explained.

And that's the story, sir, that's just the way it happened.

"Two . . . Two," the first voice said, and "Twenty . . . Twenty," said the other.

I've told you now.

"What do you think of that?" I said to Mr. Gant. "You see, don't you?"

His face was a study. "It's pretty strange when you come to think of it," he said. "By God, it is!"

Lord, boy! What's that I hear now on the harbor? Hah? What say? A ship!—Now it will soon be April, and I must be going home again: out in my garden where I work, the early flowers and blossoms will be comin' out, the peach trees and the cherry trees, the dogwood and the laurel and the lilacs. I have an apple tree and it is full of all the birds there are in June: the flower-tree you planted as a child is blooming by the window where you planted it. (My dear child, eat good food and watch and guard your health: it worries me to think of you alone with strangers.) The hills are beautiful and soon it will be spring once more. (It worries me to think of you like this, alone and far away: child, child, come home again!)

O listen! . . .

Hah? What is it? . . .

Hah? What say? . . .

(Lord God! A race of wanderers!)

Child, child! . . . what is it?

Ships again!